The Design and Analysis of Experiments and Surveys

By
Dieter Rasch,
L. Rob Verdooren
and
Jim I. Gowers

Second Edition

R. Oldenbourg Verlag München Wien

This volume is the English version of the second edition of the bilingual textbook by Rasch, Verdooren and Gowers (1999): Fundamentals in the Design and Analysis of Experiments and Surveys - Grundlagen der Planung und Auswertung von Versuchen und Erhebungen. A parallel version in German is available from the same publisher.

Bibliografische Information der Deutschen Nationalbibliothek

Die Deutsche Nationalbibliothek verzeichnet diese Publikation in der Deutschen Nationalbibliografie; detaillierte bibliografische Daten sind im Internet über <http://dnb.d-nb.de> abrufbar.

© 2007 Oldenbourg Wissenschaftsverlag GmbH
Rosenheimer Straße 145, D-81671 München
Telefon: (089) 45051-0
oldenbourg.de

Lektorat: Wirtschafts- und Sozialwissenschaften, wiso@oldenbourg.de
Herstellung: Anna Grosser
Satz: DTP-Vorlagen der Autoren
Coverentwurf: Kochan & Partner, München
Gedruckt auf säure- und chlorfreiem Papier
Druck: MB Verlagsdruck, Schrobenhausen
Bindung: Thomas Buchbinderei GmbH, Augsburg

ISBN 978-3-486-58299-4

Aye, make yourself a plan
They need you at the top!
Then make yourself a second plan
Then let the whole thing drop.
For this bleak existence
Man is never bad enough
Though his sheer persistence
Can be lovely stuff.

From Bertolt Brecht Collected Plays, Song of the Inadequacy of Human Endeavour
Volume Two, Part Two.
The Threepenny Opera
Translated by Ralph Manheim and John Willet, London, Methuen Drama, 1979.

Contents

	Preface	1
1	Introduction	2
2	Planning Experiments and Surveys and the Description of Simple Designs	7
2.1	Basic Ideas	7
2.2	Introduction to the Principles of Planning Experiments	9
2.3	Multiple Measurements, the Principle of Replication	12
2.4	Using Strata or Blocks to Eliminate the Effects of Noise Factors	13
2.4.1	Basic Principles	13
2.4.2	Principles of Blocking and Stratification	15
2.5	Randomisation	18
2.5.1	Randomisation in Surveys - Random Sampling	19
2.5.2	Randomisation in Experimental Designs - Random Allocation	23
2.6	Block Designs	24
2.6.1	Basic Concepts	24
2.6.2	Completely Balanced Incomplete Block Designs	27
2.7	Factorial Designs	29
3	Design and Analysis of Completely Randomised Designs	31
3.1	Point Estimation of Parameters	33
3.1.1	Point Estimation of the Parameters of a Normal Distribution	37
3.1.2	Point Estimation of the Parameter p of a Binomial Distribution	39
3.1.3	Point Estimation in Surveys	40
3.2	Interval Estimation	45
3.2.1	Confidence Intervals for the Parameters of a Distribution	45
3.2.1.1	Confidence Intervals for the Expectation of the Normal Distribution	46
3.2.1.2	Confidence Intervals for the Expectation of the Normal Distribution in the Presence of a Noise Factor	52
3.2.1.3	Confidence Intervals for the Mean and Total from a Survey	54
3.2.1.4	Confidence Intervals for the Variance of the Normal Distribution	55
3.2.1.5	Confidence Intervals for Probabilities	57
3.2.2	Confidence Intervals for the Difference between the Means of Two Normal Distributions	60
3.2.2.1	The Difference between the Means of Normal Distributions – Paired Observations	61
3.2.2.2	The Difference between the Means of Normal Distributions - Two Independent Samples	63
3.3	Selection Procedures	66
3.4	Hypothesis Testing	71
3.4.1	Testing Hypotheses about the Mean of a Normal Distribution	75
3.4.2	Testing Hypotheses Concerning the Difference between the Means of Two Normal Distributions	79
3.4.2.1	Paired Observations	79
3.4.2.2	Independent Samples	80
3.4.3	Comparison of the Variances of Two Normal Distributions	87
3.4.4	Comparison between two Proportions using Independent Samples	90
3.4.5	Equivalence Tests	97

4	Analysis of Variance	99
4.1	One-way Analysis of Variance	99
4.1.1	One-way Analysis of Variance - Model I	100
4.1.2	One-way Analysis of Variance - Model II	106
4.2	Two-way Analysis of Variance	108
4.2.1	Two-way Analysis of Variance - Cross-classification	108
4.2.1.1	Two-way Analysis of Variance - Cross-classification - Model I	110
4.2.1.2	Two-way Analysis of Variance - Cross-classification - Model II	114
4.2.1.3	Two-way Analysis of Variance - Cross-classification - Mixed Model	118
4.2.1.4	Two-way Analysis of Variance - Cross-classification - Block Designs	122
4.2.2	Two-way Analysis of Variance - Nested Classification	126
4.2.2.1	Two-way Analysis of Variance - Nested Classification - Model I	128
4.2.2.2	Two-way Analysis of Variance - Nested Classification - Model II	131
4.2.2.3	Two-way Analysis of Variance - Nested Classification - Mixed Model, A Fixed and B Random	134
4.2.2.4	Two-way Analysis of Variance - Nested Classification - Mixed Model, B Fixed and A Random	135
4.2.3	Notes on the Procedure for Higher Classifications	136
4.3	Multiple Comparisons of Means	137
4.3.1	Pairwise Comparisons between the Means of k Populations	139
4.3.1.1	The Multiple t-Test	139
4.3.1.2	The Tukey Test	143
4.3.2	Multiple Comparisons with a Standard Population	144
4.3.2.1	The Multiple t-Test	144
4.3.2.2	The Dunnett Test	145
4.3.3	Overview of Minimal Sample Sizes	147
5	Regression Analysis	149
5.1	Scatter-plots	150
5.2	Model I and Model II in Regression Analysis	152
5.3	Parameter Estimation by the Method of Least Squares	155
5.4	Simple Linear Regression	160
5.4.1	Confidence Intervals	160
5.4.2	Optimal Designs in Model I	166
5.4.3	Hypothesis Testing	169
5.4.4	Special Problems in Model II	173
5.5	Multiple Linear Regression	176
5.5.1	Parameter Estimation	177
5.5.2	Confidence Intervals and Tests	182
5.5.3	Special Problems in Model II	183
5.5.4	Optimal Designs in Model I	186
5.6	Simple Polynomial Regression	186
5.7	Multiple Quadratic Regression	189
5.8	Intrinsically Non-linear Regression	197
6	Theoretical Assumptions and their Practical importance – the Robustness of Procedures	203

Appendix A Symbols   206

Appendix B Fundamentals in Statistics - Overview   209

B.1   Descriptive Statistics   209
B.1.1   Population   209
B.1.2   Population Mean and Variance   209
B.1.3   Graphical Description   211
B.1.4   A Rule of Thumb   213
B.2   Frequencies and Probabilities   213
B.2.1   Introduction   213
B.2.2   Combining Frequencies and Probabilities   214
B.2.2.1   Properties of Relative Frequencies   214
B.2.2.2   Probabilities   217
B.2.3   Probability Distributions   218
B.2.3.1   Definitions   218
B.2.3.2   Quantiles   224
B.2.4   Expectation   227
B.2.5   Variance   229
B.2.6   Covariance   231
B.3   Sampling Distributions   233
B.3.1   Sample Mean $\bar{x}$ 233
B.3.2   Sample Variance s^2 236

Appendix C Matrices   238

Tables   243

Table A1 P-Quantiles of the t-Distribution with f Degrees of Freedom (for   243
          $f = \infty$, P-Quantiles of the Standard Normal Distribution)
Table A2 P-Quantiles $\chi^2(f; p)$ of the χ^2-Distribution   244
Table A3 95%-Quantiles of the F-Distribution   246
Table A4 95%-Quantiles of the Studentised Range Distribution   248
Table A5 95%-Quantiles for the Two-sided Dunnett Test in an Optimal Design 250
Table A6 95%-Quantiles for the Two-sided Dunnett Test in a Balanced Design 252

References   254

Subject Index   257

Preface

This volume is the English version of the second edition of the bilingual textbook by Rasch, Verdooren and Gowers (1999). A parallel version in German is available from the same publisher.

This book is intended for students and experimental scientists in all disciplines and presumes only elementary statistical knowledge. This prerequisite knowledge is summarised briefly in appendix B. Knowledge of differential and integral calculus is not necessary for the understanding of the text. Matrix notation is explained in Appendix C.

As well as the correction of errors, the present edition differs from the first by the introduction of some new sections, such as that on testing the equality of two proportions (Section 3.4.4), and the inclusion of sequential tests. All new material is accompanied by descriptions of the relevant SPSS and CADEMO procedures.

Experimental design is treated partly using the computer package CADEMO. Any one wishing to understand the calculations or work through further investigations can do so in most cases by using a Demo-version of the CADEMO programs *light* or TRIQ, which can be downloaded from www.biomath.de. Since it is a demonstration version, its capability is limited, because only a limited set of parameters can be changed.

For data analysis, we use the statistical package SPSS version 12.

We often refer to the Verfahrensbibliothek (Procedures Library for Experimental Design and Analysis) (Rasch et al. 2007), which is abbreviated to VB in the text. This contains almost 2000 pages, giving very many more methods (the text is in German). Those who wish to use the SAS package will find the appropriate SAS subroutines in VB.

We thank Mr. Karsten Schlettwein from the FBN in Dummerstorf for preparing the camera-ready version of the text.
We shall be glad to receive any comments and suggestions for improvements, preferably by E-mail to one of us as follows:

dieter.rasch@boku.ac.at
rob.verdooren@numico-research.nl
jim@blaise.fsbusiness.co.uk

The authors, Rostock/Wien, Bennekom and Bristol, Spring, 2007.

1 Introduction

Empirical research: we understand this term to mean the acquisition of knowledge either through passive observations (as in surveys), or from experiments, where we actively influence or manipulate the research material and then make observations. Given the steadily increasing financial problems facing research institutions, how can empirical research be conducted as efficiently (cost-effectively) as possible? This book seeks to make a contribution to answering this question. The methods are in existence, but they are not widely used. The reasons for this stem on the one hand from the traditions of experimental research, and also from the behavioural patterns of the researchers themselves. Optimal research design implies that the objective of the investigation is determined in detail before the experiment or survey is carried out and that the precision requirements for the type of analysis planned for the data using the chosen statistical model are formulated, and that all possible things which could have a negative influence on the research work or could bias or disturb the results are considered. This all makes work, takes time, and is much more difficult than simply starting with the practical investigation and formulating the objective of the study after the data have been collected and then seeing what reliability the results have.

However, society, which in the end finances research, is becoming less and less tolerant of such ways of proceeding. Indeed in very sensitive areas, such as clinical and toxicological research, in experiments with animals or research into the cloning of organisms, it is a requirement to have the detailed research designs judged by regulatory committees before the study commences. Only after approval can the research begin. As well as the question of safeguards for mankind and nature, there is a related problem of saving costs.

Surveys and experiments are distinguished by the role which the investigators play. In surveys they hardly interfere with events, they merely observe. This is typical in economic and sociological research, but also occurs in parts of forestry science and in ecology and population biology. In other areas experiments take place, different feeds and fertilising agents are used, different therapies are compared. In industrial research one must frequently investigate the influence of various factors on the quality or quantity of an end product, or adjust production conditions to achieve an optimum. This can require the systematic variation of relevant factors.

In all these areas there are basic principles for selecting efficient (optimal) designs, which we will discuss in this volume. The most important factor here is that the design of the empirical investigation should be properly formulated. It is certainly true, and this will be clarified in examples, that this is often not a simple task, and can take up days or months. Since an experiment often lasts far longer than its analysis, one can quickly alter a false analysis of correctly obtained data, but often the most sophisticated analysis cannot save an insufficiently thought through experiment, which must therefore be repeated with consequent greatly increased costs.

Acquiring knowledge by empirical research starts with a deductive phase (pre-experimental). In addition to an outline description of the research problem, this phase includes a precise elaboration of the aim of the research, the exact definition of the precision demanded in connection with, for example, the probabilities of errors of the first and second kind in hypothesis tests, or the confidence coefficient and the expected width of confidence intervals, and will also include the selection or construction of an optimal design for the experiment.

After this the experiment or survey is performed. This is then followed by a post-experimental inductive phase consisting of the analysis of the experiment or the survey and the interpretation of the results. As a consequence of this, new hypotheses and new ideas or models may be derived.

All in all we can divide the process of empirical research into the following seven stages:

(i)   formulation of the problem,
(ii)   stipulation of the precision requirements,
(iii)   selecting the statistical model for the planning and analysis,
(iv)   the (optimal) design of the experiment or survey,
(v)   performing the experiment or the survey,
(vi)   statistical analysis of the observed results,
(vii)   interpretation of the results.

Although these seven stages should occur in the majority of empirical studies, there are occasions when this scheme does not fit. In sequential experiments, which are frequently used in medical experimentation or in statistical quality control, the size of the experiment is not fixed in advance and not all experimental units are treated or investigated at the same time. In such cases the size of the experiment is not fixed in advance in relation to the precision requirements. The size of a sequential experiment arises during the course of that experiment. The stages (iv), (v) and (vi) given above are carried out repeatedly until the desired precision is attained. We will illustrate this kind of experiment using the example of comparing two types of therapy, A and B. After each therapy has been given to at least two patients, the analysis can lead to one of the following decisions:

- A is better than B
- B is better than A
- A and B are equivalent
- the experiment goes on with A
- the experiment goes on with B.

In the first three of these cases the experiment terminates, otherwise it continues. Thus the sample size depends on the progress of the experiment and is therefore subject to chance.

In non-sequential investigations we first determine the size of the experiment, then the investigation is carried out and observations are analysed. In the above case of the comparison of therapies, when the previously determined numbers of patients have been treated with the two therapies, only the following three decisions are possible.

- A is better than B
- B is better than A
- A and B are equivalent.

Empirical research then has three separate phases, namely

1.   the planning of the investigation (stages (i) to (iv)),
2.   the performing of an experiment or of a survey (stage (v)),
3.   the analysis of the results (stages (vi) and (vii)).

It is absolutely necessary in the planning phase of an experiment or survey to choose the underlying model and also the method of analysis, because the precision requirements can only be determined in relation to these, and so the minimum sample size depends on them. In sequential experiments one cannot avoid setting out the precision requirements in advance, but unfortunately with fixed sample sizes it is all too easy to begin by collecting data and then decide on the sample size in an ad hoc fashion.

For example, suppose that we wish to estimate the mean μ of a distribution, and we want to determine the minimum sample size, so that the variance of the estimate is not greater than $0.5\sigma^2$. It is important to know whether we are going to estimate μ via the sample mean or the sample median since the variances of these estimators are different.

In this book we confine ourselves exclusively to so-called parametric methods for estimation, hypothesis testing and selection procedures. That is to say that we always assume a family of distributions, such as the normal or binomial distributions, and we use methods known to be optimal (and robust) for the evaluation of unknown parameters.

Methods which do not make such far reaching distributional assumptions, and for example only assume that the underlying distribution is continuous, are called non-parametric methods. One such procedure is the Wilcoxon (Mann-Whitney) test, which is often used in place of the Independent-samples t-test. It is often used when it is not known if normality can be assumed, and even more so when it is known that data does not follow the normal distribution. The corresponding t-test was derived using Normality assumptions, but robustness investigations (see RASCH and GUIARD (2004)) have shown, that it can always be used for the comparison of two means when the distributions are not normal. Since the experimental design problem has not been so well worked out for non-parametric procedures, these will not be dealt with in this book. For information on how to deal with variables measured on an ordinal scale, see for example RASCH und ŠIMEČKOVA (2007).

We now continue with some precise definitions of several basic terms used in this book, because the use of these terms vary in the literature. Our definitions are based on "Elsevier's Dictionary of Biometry" (RASCH, TIKU and SUMPF, 1994), which contains the description in English of 2700 concepts together with the translations of the terms into Dutch, French, German, Italian, Russian and Spanish.

Definition 1.1

The term *population* or *universe* will be taken to mean a set of objects or individuals having certain characteristics which we wish to make a statement about by means of empirical investigations of a subset (sample). Frequently it is not the objects possessing the characteristic, but rather the set of values of the characteristic which are considered as the population.

By Statistics we mean mathematical statistics, i.e. the science of drawing conclusions about a population by making inductive inferences from a sample drawn from it (this contrasts with Official Statistics, which are solely facts (often obtained from the whole population) which are listed in official publications.

In the following definition, we introduce the terms Investigation, Experiment and Survey.

Definition 1.2

By the umbrella term *Investigation* we mean
-    the active intervention (hereafter called "*Treatment*") by the researchers, in an existing situation, with the aim of observing the results of this intervention and analysing them. This is an *Experiment*.
-    the observation of one or more elements of a precisely defined population (without the above-mentioned "Treatment"). This is a *Sample Survey* or, more briefly, *Survey*.

From time to time Experiment is used as a synonym for Investigation. If an investigation consists of several stages which follow on from one another, and each depends on the results of the preceding stage, then we call it a *sequential* (mostly in experiments) or *multi-stage* (mostly in surveys) investigation. If the results of the experiment also depend on chance, i.e. the same conditions do not always give the same result, then we call the investigation a statistical (or stochastic) investigation.

Definition 1.3

By the term *experimental unit* we mean the individual or object which is treated in the experiment after randomisation, which concept will be introduced in chapter 2. By *sampling unit* we mean an element of the universe, which as the result of a sampling process is included in the sample. The experimental unit or sampling unit is the smallest unit which can be randomised.

The exact specification of the experimental units is extremely important for the design and analysis of experiments. Thus in animal experiments, an animal is not always an experimental unit. For example in a feeding experiment with group feeding, which means that only the quantity of food taken by the whole group and not by each individual is registered, it is the group which is the experimental unit, since only the group can be investigated, and it is the group, and not the individual animal, which constitutes the treated (i.e. provided with different food) unit. Conversely, a part of an animal can be the experimental unit (e.g. the eyes or half-carcasses). Observations (measurements) are made on the experimental units. The things that are observed or measured are called characteristics, which form the subject of the next definition. It is the measurements on the experimental units, which are analysed.

Definition 1.4

A quantity to be observed on the experimental units, or a quantity defining the experimental conditions is called a *character (trait)*. The values of a character which are measured or observed in the experimental units are called *experimental results*, or *measurements* or *observations*. In statistical models characters are modelled by random variables. The observations then correspond to the realisations of these random variables. If the character defines part of the experimental conditions it is called a *factor*. The possible values of this factor are then called *factor levels* (more shortly, *levels*). Factors can be modelled by either random or non-random variables. In the latter case the factors are called *fixed* factors.

Depending on the way a character (factor) is measured, we distinguish between *discrete* and *continuous, quantitative* and *qualitative* characters. Characters are qualitative if they are measured by a *nominal scale* (each possible realisation of the character being denoted by a name e.g. for colours: red, blue etc.) or by an *ordinal scale* (school grades: "very good" or 1; "good" or 2 etc.). Characters are *quantitative* if they are measured by scales higher than ordinal ones; they can be counted (events) or measured with instruments (length, weight). A character is called *discrete* if it can take only a finite or a countably infinite number of different possible values. If an uncountably infinite number of values may occur we call the character *continuous*. We should mention explicitly that the definition of a character includes not only its name but also its level of measurement. In the above example of school grades it is clear that they can be denoted by numbers or names but in both cases the measure is ordinal ("very good"' is better than "good"). Colours can be defined as nominal (and not ordinal since for instance red, green and blue have no natural order), but if we define them by their measured wavelength then they become continuous. The statements about the characteristics to be observed, and also on what scale they are to be measured, form part of the refinement of the formulation of the experiment (stage (i) of our seven stages).

Further definitions will be given in later chapters.

In chapter 2 we will introduce the basic principles of empirical research:

- randomisation
- replication
- elimination of noise (or nuisance) factors by blocking or stratification

and also the most important experimental designs and sampling schemes. In chapter 3 we describe the planning and analysis of so-called simple experimental designs and sampling schemes (with unrestricted randomisation). Included in these are the point and interval estimation of the mean and variance, the optimum choice of samples and the testing of hypotheses in one- and two-sample problems. For the two-sample problem, sequential experiments will also be dealt with.

Chapter 4 introduces the analysis of variance for one-way and two-way classifications and chapter 5 discusses regression analysis. In a short chapter 6 we discuss the practical importance of assumptions (such as normality), which are necessary for theoretical derivations. In accordance with the character of the book no proofs are given, but examples are worked through. What distinguishes this book from many others is the fact that first of all the planning is described (in the simplest case this is the determination of the sample size) and then the analysis. We hope thereby to encourage the wider use in the future of planning methods in experiments and surveys.

2 Planning Experiments and Surveys and the Description of simple Designs

2.1 Basic Ideas

In this introduction we consider various aspects of statistical experimental design. It was the late A. LINDER (1959) who stated that during the planning of an experiment the following questions (amongst others) have to be answered:
- what do I want to know?
- how accurately do I want to know it?
- why (for which population) do I want to know it?

Questions such as these are very useful in the refinement of the problem formulation (stage (i) in the schema of chapter 1), as the following simple examples will show. These questions should always be considered and answered very carefully.

Note!

A prerequisite for planning experiments effectively is to formulate the problem to be solved as precisely as possible.

We will illustrate this thesis by the following example, showing at the same time how stages (i) - (iii) of the seven stages mentioned in chapter 1 can be worked through.

Note!

We always distinguish between random variables and their realisations. Probability statements apply to random variables. Random variables are printed in bold, their realisations (observed values) are printed normally. In estimation problems we call a function of the random variables in a sample an estimator; its realisation is called an estimate.

Example 2.1.

For a certain type of lorry the average fuel consumption (in litres per 100 kilometres) when the lorries are used during the harvest at farms has to be determined. Is the research question adequately formulated? Clearly not (although at least the units of measurement of fuel consumption are given). It seems to be quite clear what we wish to know, but really we are far from a precise formulation of the problem (stage (i) in chapter 1) to be solved. But before we can make the formulation more precise we first have to choose a statistical model (stage (iii)). We answer Linder's question "why do I want to know it?" by defining the population from which the sample will be drawn. This is the total number of lorries of the type in question which have been or will be produced under the same conditions. This number is unknown but is very large so that it can be modelled by an infinite set (models are only ever approximate representations of reality), and we model, the fuel consumption y_i of the i-th lorry, as a random variable $\mathbf{y}_i$. What do we want to determine (or estimate, in statistical terminology)?

Certainly not $\mu_i = E(y_i)$. This expectation - the average fuel consumption of the i-th lorry only interests the owner of this particular lorry (whose journeys are indeed his population).

We require a general statement applicable to all farmers who use this type of lorry to bring in the harvest. We now continue modelling the situation described above. We assume that the average fuel consumption μ_i of the i-th car deviates by the random variable a_i from the overall mean fuel consumption. This deviation arises mainly from random variations of technical parameters of components of the car during production. Individual records y_{ij} of the i-th car in the j-th journey again vary randomly around μ_i by e_{ij} (a random error variable which depends for instance on the speed, temperature, wetness of the ground in the field, the experience of the driver etc.).

This leads us to the following model for the individual observations (measurements) y_{ij}:

$$y_{ij} = \mu + a_i + e_{ij} \qquad (i = 1, ..., a; j = 1, ..., n_i) \qquad (2.1)$$

In (2.1) it is assumed that a number a of the cars produced will be tested in such a way that from the i-th car n_i measurements of the petrol consumption are available. Further the conditions

$$E(a_i) = E(e_{ij}) = 0 \ , \operatorname{var}(a_i) = \sigma_a^2, \operatorname{var}(e_{ij}) = \sigma^2$$

have to be fulfilled and the different random variables on the right hand side of (2.1) are assumed to be stochastically independent.

After our first stage of a model choice, we can give a more precise description of the aim of our experiment.

Under special further assumptions like those about the distribution of the a_i and the e_{ij} a confidence interval (in the sense of chapter 3) for μ in model (2.1) will be constructed. Also the required precision of such an estimate has to be defined. This can be done in several ways. In our example we require that, given a confidence coefficient $1 - \alpha = 0.95$, the expected half-length of the confidence interval, is not larger than a value d given in advance. The aim of an optimal statistical design may now be the determination of positive integers a; $n_1, ..., n_a$ in such a way that the total costs of the experimentation are minimised but the precision required is guaranteed. For this we denote by c_1 the costs of the lorry to be used in the experiment and by c_2 the costs of a measurement (y_{ij}).

In this way stages (i) to (iii) of chapter 1 have been largely dealt with. Now we should go on to determinate the most cost effective experimental design, but for this we need techniques which are not dealt with until later chapters, and we will defer the determination of the optimal values of (a; $n_1, n_2, ..., n_a$) until chapter 4, where we will continue with this example.

To summarise:

Note!

The precise formulation of the research question requires:
-       *the choice of the statistical model*
-       *the formulation of the precision requirements for the results of the analysis*
-       *and, if we require an optimal design, the specification of the optimality criteria (in Example 2.1 these are the experimental costs).*

In this book when we speak about the planning of an experiment we only discuss the statistical aspects of this topic but not the equally important technical, financial, personal or material problems.

2.2   Introduction to the Principles of Planning Experiments

With the aid of an artificial example we will illustrate some errors that a naive researcher could make while doing experimental research. Experienced experimentalists may omit this section.

Example 2.2

An aspirant research worker (we will call him Rees Earcher) wants to know whether there is any difference between the daily milk production of Jersey and Holstein-Frisian cows. Therefore Rees has to conduct a survey (he will only observe and will not treat), and he rings up two farmers one of whom has only Jersey cows and the other only Holstein-Frisian. He asks each of them to tell him how much milk one of his animals yielded today. The result is:

1. milk yield of a Jersey cow: 41 kg
2. milk yield of a Holstein-Frisian cow: 29 kg.

Rees Earcher now concludes: "Jersey cows have a higher milk performance than Holstein-Frisians." This is clearly a ridiculously inadequate approach, but what is actually wrong? We will try to articulate this. One of Rees's friends, a statistician, explains the situation as follows: from the problem formulation it can be deduced that you really want to know whether the average daily milk production (in kg per day) of Jerseys and Holstein-Frisians can be considered as belonging to the same universe or to two different universes, and if the universes are different, which one has the greater mean. In statistics a universe (or population - but this term may be misleading in this example because animal breeders define a population from a genetic viewpoint) is a well-defined set of objects or individuals. Here for each breed of cattle we might choose all cows of that breed who were alive (and producing milk) at that time in a defined geographical region. We then take samples from these populations and measure their milk yields.

The statistician goes on to explain that it is not unusual for even two realisations (observations) of the same random variable to differ markedly from each other. About 99% of the values from a normally distributed random variable with a mean of 35 kg (the average of Rees's 41 and 29 kg) and a standard deviation of 3 kg (this could be a model for the characteristic under investigation) lie between 26 kg and 44 kg. Rees has therefore no grounds for drawing his conclusion quoted above. If however the 29 and 41 kg were not single measurements, but averages of a greater number of observations, then the observed difference between the numbers would have a greater significance, since averages of independent variables having the same standard deviation have a smaller standard deviation than individual values. To illustrate this more precisely we give the following definition.

9

Definition 2.1

We start with a random variable y which follows a distribution with expectation (mean) μ and variance σ^2 (and thus standard deviation σ). If the n components y_i of the vector $(y_1, y_2, ..., y_n)$ are mutually independent and all distributed exactly as y, then the vector is called an (abstract) *random sample* of size n.

Such an abstract random sample is a model for the random sampling process which is defined later.

Note!

If the components of an abstract random sample are distributed with mean μ and variance σ^2, then the arithmetic mean of those components is a random variable whose mean is also μ and whose variance is σ^2/n.

Thus the variability of a sample average is less than that of single values and becomes smaller as the sample size increases.
This is what we call "the principle of replication" or "the principle of multiple observations".

Example 2.2 - continued

As a result of this Rees tells the statistician that he is going to go back to the farmers and ask them to give him details of the further milk yields from these two cows on subsequent days. The statistician quickly points out that the assumption that the elements of a random sample are independent of each other will certainly not be satisfied if all the values come from the same (or related) cows.
Rees Earcher now asks each of his farmer friends for nine other milk records from unrelated cows in their herd and he is then able to calculate the averages of ten yields from each. Let us assume that he got the following results:
1. average daily milk yield of 10 Jersey cows: 38 kg
2. average daily milk yield of 10 Holstein-Frisian: 33 kg.
Again Rees Earcher concludes: "Jersey cows have a higher daily milk yield". He has now followed an important principle of sampling or of planning statistical experiments, namely that conclusions from statistical experiments never should be based on a single observation per universe.

Note!

In general the sample size will be denoted by n, but the number of replications in such designs as randomised blocks will be denoted in general by r (from replication).

Example 2.2 - continued

The new result is now a feather in Rees Earcher's cap and he presents it to a specialist for animal nutrition. The latter tells Rees that Holstein-Frisians usually have a higher daily milk yield than Jerseys. He asks Rees whether the levels of nutrition of the animals in the two herds are similar and comparable. Rees Earcher did not enquire about this but now asks the two farmers. He learns that at this time the Frisians are grazing all day in the field, but the Jerseys are in kept the cow shed and are fed very intensively with pellets. Rees Earcher is now aware that he should plan his investigation more seriously and he asks a specialist in animal husbandry whether there may be more factors influencing the milk production of cows besides the level of nutrition. He now learns that the milk production of cows, as well as being dependent on inheritable factors, depends very much on the day of lactation (the number of days since the birth of the calf) at which the milk yield was observed and further on the lactation period. The dependency of the milk production on the day of lactation can be described by a function, which has a steep ascent between the first and the 28th day of lactation (where there is a maximum) and then it decreases almost linearly until the 300th day. It is further known that the milk yield of a cow in the second lactation period is higher than in the first period but decreases again in subsequent lactation periods. Rees again asks the two farmers and learns that the production of the Jerseys was measured between the 25th and the 35th day of lactation, but the Frisians were between the 180th and the 220th day of lactation.

Now Rees Earcher feels lost, and again asks the statistician what to do. The statistician tells him that the results he got are not completely useless, provided he is able to find out the days of lactation corresponding to the 20 milk records and can get information about the function describing the dependency between the day of lactation and the milk yield, because he could then make the 20 milk yields comparable by standardising them. On the other hand it is difficult to see what he can do about the difference in nutrition levels. He suggests to Rees that he should plan the whole investigation more thoroughly, and gather data once again. At the same time it should be established whether 10 measurements for each breed will be sufficient.

This example shows how important it is to go carefully through stages (i) to (iv) of chapter 1 in the pre-experimental phase of an investigation. Otherwise it is likely that even after much wearisome data gathering a statistician will not be able to help the experimenter to answer the question being investigated. The example describes a situation where one or more factors can have an effect on the results of the experiment. Such factors are often of no interest to the experimenter and so do not form part of the experimental enquiry. Ignoring such a factor can lead to false conclusions as was the case in our example with the factors "day of lactation", "lactation period" and "level of nutrition" We call such factors nuisance factors or noise factors.

Note!

Important principles in the planning of experiments are :

1. *Replication*
2. *Randomisation*
3. *Reducing the possible effects of known noise factors.*

Further reading on experimental design can be found in, for example, the books by HINKELMANN and KEMPTHORNE (1994, 2005) or COCHRAN and COX (1957).

2.3 Multiple Measurements, the Principle of Replication

In the last section we saw that a scientific conclusion can hardly be based on an experiment with only one observation. One reason not mentioned there explicitly is that we usually have to estimate the variance of the trait under observation and for this we need at least two measurements (*replications*). Two replications are thus the absolute lower bound of the number of replications needed for a required precision. We explain what is meant by the following simple example.

Example 2.3

Assume that the expected yield of a certain wheat variety, measured in decitonnes per hectare (dt/ha), has to be estimated. The yield can be observed by cultivating this variety on small plots and expressing the yield in per hectare terms. The yield varies from plot to plot, even if the plots are very close to each other, and much higher variation can be expected between different locations or different years. Therefore it is important at an early stage in the precise formulation of the experimental question to define exactly the basic population for which the conclusions have to be relevant. Assume that we have to estimate the yield of the variety for the State of Iowa in 1995. In this case the universe or the underlying population contains all fields suitable and available for the cultivation of that crop in Iowa in 1995. Let us assume that the yields of this population can be modelled by a normally distributed random variable with expectation $\mu = 50$ and variance $\sigma^2 = 64$, i.e. the standard deviation $\sigma = 8$.

Independently of this assumption we will say that an estimate of the expectation is good if it deviates by not more than $1/8\ \sigma$ from the expectation (μ) to be estimated. This means, in our example, that the estimate $\hat{\mu}$ of μ must lie in the interval between 49 and 51 dt/ha.

Table 2.1 contains the probabilities (as a function of the number of plots), multiplied by 100, that the arithmetic mean $\bar{y}$ of the elements y_i of a random sample, used as an estimator for μ, lies no further than $\sigma/8$ from the expectation (μ) to be estimated. These probabilities are independent of the specific parameters of the example. In other words the table contains the probability $P(n)$ (expressed as a percentage) as a function of the sample size n. $\cdot P(n)$ is the probability that, if denotes y_i the i-th observation, the estimator $\bar{y}$ of μ lies in the interval ($\mu - \sigma/8$; $\mu + \sigma/8$).

From this table the effect of sample size on the attainable precision can be clearly seen. This topic will be taken further in chapter 3.

Table 2.1. *The probabilities P(n) (expressed as percentages) that the average of n observations from a normal distribution with expectation μ and variance σ^2 deviates not more than $\sigma/8$ from μ.*

n	$100\ P(n)$	n	$100\ P(n)$
1	9.95	20	42.38
2	14.03	25	46.80
3	17.14	30	50.64
4	19.74	40	57.08
5	22.01	50	62.32
6	24.05	100	78.87
7	25.91	200	92.29
8	27.63	500	99.48
9	29.23	1000	99.99
10	30.74	10000	100.00

2.4 Using Strata or Blocks to Eliminate the Effects of Noise Factors

2.4.1 Basic principles

If it turns out during the planning phase of an investigation that a factor (such as the day of lactation in example 2.2) could influence the outcome of an experiment or survey, then we should find ways of eliminating its effect as far as is possible.

In mathematical statistics there are standard procedures for at least partly eliminating the effect of a nuisance factor.

Firstly it can be done in a similar way as in the example of the lactation curve by standardising the measurements, provided that the nuisance factor is quantitative and the dependency of the measurement of interest on it is at least approximately known. By using the function describing this relation, all the measurements can be converted as though they were all obtained at the same value of the nuisance factor (in this case day of lactation).

In the case of a quantitative factor, one can also use analysis of covariance, although here we must know the form of the function describing the relation (for example linear or quadratic). The parameters are estimated from the observation of the pairs of values of the variable of interest and the nuisance factor. We shall not deal with this topic further in this book (see VB 3/42/3001, 3/42/3002). A general method, applicable also to qualitative noise factors, is that of forming blocks or strata according to the levels of the noise factor (see Section 2.4.2).

Even more generally applicable is randomisation. It is less effective, but does not require knowledge of what the noise factors might be.

Blocking (in experiments) and the analogous stratification in surveys are on the one hand similar to randomisation and on the other they are further principles of experimental design and will be treated in greater detail below.

Definition 2.2

Experimental results are dependent on the influence of the experimental conditions defined by the *factors*. In planning an experiment the non-random factors whose values can be determined by the research workers before or during the experiment are of special interest, because often the optimal choice of these values is a part of planning the experiment. The possible values of a factor are called *factor levels* or more shortly *levels*. If a factor is fixed during the experiment or if it has only one level, we call it a *constant factor*. It is then a part of the background or the basic conditions of the experiment. If it is the objective of an experiment to investigate the influence of a factor or factors and if the research worker varies the factor(s) systematically in the experimental design, then we call the factor(s) *design factor(s)*. If the evaluation of possible effects of some design factors is a part of the problem formulation of the experiment, then these are called *treatment factors*. The remaining design factors are called *block factors*. All the other factors that cannot systematically be varied but might have some influence on the experimental results are subsumed by the term *residual factors*. The residual and the block factors are the *noise factors*. Qualitative and quantitative factors are defined analogously to qualitative and quantitative characters.

Randomisation or random sampling
This procedure is appropriate when we do not know the noise factors. Randomisation can be regarded as the primary concept, with random sampling being subsumed within it. In a narrower sense we use randomisation in experiments for the random assignment of the experimental units (which strictly speaking should be chosen beforehand by random sampling from the population of all experimental units) to the treatments. We go into this in more detail in section 2.5.
When we take a random sample from a finite population whose elements are distributed over the levels of a nuisance factor, we expect that these levels will occur with frequencies approximating to their distribution in the population (this corresponds to a loose definition of a representative sample). In this way we try to keep the chance of a biased sample (i.e. a sample in which the distribution of the levels of the nuisance factor do not mirror even approximately their presence in the population) as small as possible. Methods of random sampling will be discussed in section 2.5.

Blocking and stratification
In experiments, the grouping together of experimental units which have the same level of a possible noise factor is called blocking; in sample surveys it is called stratification. The levels are called blocks or strata. If the factor has in reality little effect on the results, the loss of degrees of freedom in the analysis of variance of such designs may not be compensated by a decrease in the residual variance.

The decision between complete randomisation, covariance analysis (e.g. the standardisation of the day of lactation mentioned in section 2.2) and restricted randomisation after blocking or stratification, is an important step in the choice of model. In the next section we concentrate on blocking; stratification will be discussed together with sampling methods in section 2.5.

2.4.2 Principles of Blocking and Stratification

In this book we restrict ourselves to eliminating **one** noise factor by blocking or stratification. One method of eliminating two noise factors is to use so-called row-and-column designs, where the rows correspond to different levels of one factor and the columns to levels of the other (for details see VB 1/21/4200-1/21/4250).

Blocking is especially useful when the noise factor is qualitative, since analysis of covariance is not then available, but blocking is also possible when the noise factor is quantitative. In this case we can group its values into classes, and use these classes to define the levels of the noise factor.

We illustrate this using the day of lactation noise factor in example 2.2.

Example 2.2 - continued

The day of lactation when the milk yield was obtained is recorded together with the milk yield and the former is entered into a stratification scheme such as the following.

Stratum	Day	Stratum	Day
1	1-10	5	51-90
2	11-22	6	91-140
3	23-35	7	141-220
4	36-50	8	more than 220

Of course we need *a priori* information in order to choose the size and number of the blocks before the experiment begins (which should be the rule).

In field experiments such information can be obtained from so called blindfold experiments. These are experiments which are run using only one level of the factor being investigated (for example using only one variety of plant), in order to test whether the chosen levels of the noise factor lead to significant differences in the factor of interest. For details of field experiments, see THOMAS (2006).

Before we consider block designs in more detail, we would like to clarify their position in the planning of experiments. We will give a very general definition of experimental designs even though we have up till now only dealt with a few special cases.

Definition 2.3.

A *statistical experimental design* is a specification for the lay-out of a statistical experiment. It must ensure that no aspects which are important for the analysis or for the model choice and the attainable precision are neglected.

To explain the last statement in the definition let us consider a block design. As we will see below a block design defines which treatment occurs in which block and the distribution of the experimental units over the blocks and the random allocation of treatments to these units. Other important questions like who will do the experimental work on which day, when and where the experiment is performed and other problems do not belong to *statistical* experimental design, and will not be considered in this book.

Having said this, we will nevertheless use the term experimental design for short in place of statistical experimental design. Furthermore we would emphasise that this text deals exclusively with designs having a non-negligible stochastic component.

Definition 2.4

The *statistical planning of an experiment* includes the construction of a statistical experimental design and the determination of the *minimum sample size* which is necessary to achieve predetermined precision requirements in the context of a chosen statistical model for the analysis of the results.

Definition 2.5

A *statistical model y* for the result *y* of a statistical experiment is defined by a model equation (perhaps with side conditions) and by the distributional assumptions made about the random components of *y*.

Definition 2.6

We call an experimental design optimal if it is constructed to minimise the value of a given optimality criterion whilst keeping to the requirements of definition 2.2. For brevity we call such designs *optimal designs*.

Example 2.1 - continued
Example 2.1 can be used to illustrate these definitions. An experiment to estimate the average fuel consumption of a number of cars is certainly a *statistical* experiment. Any vector $(a; n_1, n_2, ..., n_a)$ with non-negative integers is a (statistical) experimental design, the equation (2.1) with its side conditions is a statistical model, and the *optimal design* for this problem is that vector

$(a; n_1, ..., n_a)$ minimising either $\sum_{i=1}^{a} n_i$ or the costs $a \cdot c_1 + (\sum_{i=1}^{a} n_i) \cdot c_2$ or another optimality criterion.

Definition 2.7

If an experiment involves only one treatment factor, its levels are called *treatments*. If there are several treatment factors, the combination of the levels of the treatment factors which are applied to a particular sampling unit is called a *treatment combination*. (Occasionally for brevity we refer to a treatment combination as simply a treatment).

Definition 2.8

In an experimental design N experimental units have to be assigned to the v treatments either completely randomly or in a restricted random manner.
An experimental design is *p-factorial* or *factorial* if each treatment is a factor level combination of $p > 1$ factors. An experimental design is called a *block design* if a noise factor is eliminated by blocking. The levels of the noise factor are then called *blocks*. The number k_i of experimental units in the *i*-th block is called the *block size*.

To construct a block design we proceed as follows. First we must specify the $b \geq 2$ levels of the noise factor which define the blocks. It must be possible to allocate each experimental unit unambiguously to a block. In the case of naturally occurring blocks, such as pairs of twins, the pairs of eyes of different patients, or litters of piglets there is no problem, but when blocks (or strata in surveys) are formed artificially, care must be taken to ensure that they do not overlap and that there are no experimental units which belong to none of the blocks. The number b of the blocks is determined as part of the experimental design process. In this book we assume that all b blocks have the same block size k.

Note!

In this book we assume that all b blocks have the same block size k.

Example 2.4

In an ophthalmic hospital the effects of two kinds of eye drops A and B have to be tested. It is expected that the effects of the eye drops vary more between the individual patients than between the left and the right eye of each patient. Ten patients are available for the experiment. The research worker defines the factor "patient" as a noise factor. Each patient is considered as a block with $k = 2$ experimental units, namely the two eyes. Further we assume that the position of the eye (left or right) does not have any influence on the experimental result. The block size is two (assuming that each patient can see with both eyes). It is important to realise that the 10 patients are not the experimental units - these are their $N = 20$ eyes. In the experimental design one of the eyes of each of the patients has to be treated with one of the medicines - say by A and the other eye with the medicine B. The reactions of the treatments are measured and in this way the difference in the effects of the eye drops can be estimated based on 10 individual comparisons. In this example $v = 2$ (A, B) treatments are allocated in $b = 10$ blocks (patients) with the block size $k = 2$ (eyes). Because each treatment occurs in each block, the design is called a *complete* block design. Unless stated otherwise we assume that a treatment occurs at most once in the same block.

Besides complete block designs we will often use *incomplete* block designs, in which not all treatments can occur in each block. The need for such designs stems from the fact that the number of treatments v can be larger than the block size k. Suppose for example that we have to compare the effects of 5 different eye drops A, B, C, D, E. Since only two treatments can be applied to any one patient, this experiment has to be laid out as an incomplete block design (the block size is limited to $k = 2$). Such a design can be found in Table 2.2.

Table 2.2   *Incomplete block design with v=5 treatments A, B, C, D, E in 10 blocks with size k=2.*

Patient No.	Treatments
1	A,B
2	A,C
3	A,D
4	A,E
5	B,C
6	B,D
7	B,E
8	C,D
9	C,E
10	D,E

An incomplete block design is called *balanced*, if each treatment is replicated the same number r times in the experiment (here $r = 4$) and if furthermore the number λ of the occurrences of each of the 10 possible treatment pairs is constant (here $\lambda = 1$). The fact that $\lambda = 1$ means that only one direct comparison between any two eye drops is possible. If we denote the results of the experiment i.e. the effects of treatment T (T equals $A, B, C, D,$ or E) for the i-th patient by $w_i(T)$ then the difference between, say A and B can be estimated directly by $w_1(A) - w_1(B)$. We can also further compare A and B via blocks containing A and B together with the same treatment, for example

$$\{w_2(A) - w_2(C)\} - \{w_5(B) - w_5(C)\}$$
$$\{w_3(A) - w_3(D)\} - \{w_6(B) - w_6(D)\}$$
$$\{w_4(A) - w_4(E)\} - \{w_7(B) - w_7(E)\}$$

The full analysis is described in section 4.2.1.4.
We gather together the terms used in the above example in the following definition.

Definition 2.9

Block designs are special experimental designs for reducing the influence of noise factors by blocking. A relatively homogeneous group of experimental units is called a *block*. Even though experimental designs with multiple blocking may also be called block designs, in the narrow sense block designs are experimental designs with blocking in just one direction. We say that a block is *complete* if each of the v treatments occurs at least once in this block, otherwise the block is called *incomplete*. A block design is called *complete* if all its blocks are complete and is called *incomplete* if at least one of its blocks is incomplete.

2.5   Randomisation

We use the term randomisation to describe a procedure by which the experimental units are randomly (by chance) selected from the population (random sampling), and it is also used in experiments for the process of randomly assigning the experimental units or blocks to the treatments or treatment combinations. As mentioned above, randomisation is used to try to minimise the distortion of the results of a survey or the confounding of the effects of known or unknown noise factors with the treatment effects being studied.

Randomisation is therefore generally essential, in order to ensure that the statistical model which forms the basis of the planning and analysis should reflect reality as adequately as possible.

2.5.1 Randomisation in Surveys - Random Sampling

In this section we shall briefly describe how the selection of a random sample of elements from a population is carried out in practice. This is accomplished by means of random sampling procedures. The method used depends on whether prior information on possible structurings in the population is available, and how this is to be used.

Let us suppose that the average income in a country is to be determined. It depends on the exact formulation, whether the structures in the society should be taken into consideration in the planning of the survey. Factors such as sex, age group, education could be related to the factors of interest, and the survey would then be planned and carried out in each level of the factor or factor combination. If we only want to find out the median income, and we want to use a sample survey rather than a full census, then care must be taken to ensure as far as possible that the sample does not consist exclusively or predominantly of people from one structure group. In this context *as far as possible* means with high probability. Random sampling procedures cannot eliminate misrepresentative samples which will give distorted results, but they can make the probability of their occurrence acceptably small.

Definition 2.10

We wish to draw a sample of size n (of different elements) from a population of size N ($n < N$). Any selection rule which ensures that all of the N elements of the population have the same chance of being chosen is called a *random sampling procedure*. A sample drawn using such a procedure is called a *random sample*.

If all the $\binom{N}{n}$ possible subsets have the same probability $\dfrac{1}{\binom{N}{n}}$, of being in the sample

then we speak of a pure or *unrestricted random sampling*.

You cannot tell from a sample whether it is random or not; you must find out how it was drawn. Nevertheless suspicions should be aroused when extreme samples appear. If a lottery issues 10,000 tickets, and somebody buys a single ticket and wins the top prize, then that would be unusual, but possible. In common parlance it would be called the luck of the draw, in our terminology we would say it was the result of a random sampling procedure. If the same person wins the top prize on three consecutive occasions and it then turns out that she is the sister of the lottery organiser, then one is entitled to entertain doubts. We refuse to accept results having such a small probability, and we assume that the underlying model is false. We presume that no random sampling procedure took place and that cheating is going on. Nevertheless there remains a small probability of getting this result by chance - it is 1/1 000 000 000 000.

In passing we note that this technique of rejecting models of reality which lead to the observed result having a very small probability, and accepting instead models under which it has a greater probability, is the basis of the statistical procedures in the following chapters.

There are several ways of carrying out a random sampling procedure in practice. If there exists a list of all the elements of the population (a so-called sampling frame), then we can obtain the sample using some form of random number generator. In many textbooks there are tables of random numbers with instructions on how to use them (for example what to do when a number is drawn which does not occur in the population).

A method which is sometimes simpler is called systematic sampling with a random starting point. It is applicable when the elements of the population are numbered consecutively from 1 to N and their order is unrelated to the characteristic being investigated. When N/n is an integer, we choose at random a number i between 1 and N/n and assign the elements numbered i, $N/n + i$, $2N/n + i$, ..., $(n-1)N/n + i$ to the sample. For more detail on this topic, and what to do when N/n is not an integer, see VB 1/31/1210.

Example 2.5
> A population contains $N = 100$ elements and a sample of size $n = 5$ is to be drawn. In unrestricted random sampling each element would be drawn with probability 0.05. Considering element 8 for example, it would be chosen as the first member of the sample with probability 1/100 and not chosen with probability 99/100. The probability that it is chosen in second position is thus 99/100×1/99 and that is also 0.01. Similarly we get 0.01 at each stage and the sum of these 5 probabilities gives us 0.05, the probability of this sample being chosen.
>
> If instead we choose at random a number between 1 and 100/5 = 20, e.g. 12, then using systematic sampling with random start point the elements 12, 32, 52, 72 and 92 will form our sample. Each element of the population has again a probability of 1/20 of being included in the sample.
> In both cases we are using a random sampling procedure, but only in the first is it unrestricted.
> Using this example we will now demonstrate how the PC-programme CADEMO-*light*, which we will call CL from now on, can be used to draw random samples. In the CL-Main-menu shown in Figure 2.1 we choose the item "Experimental Design" and then "Completely Randomised Design".

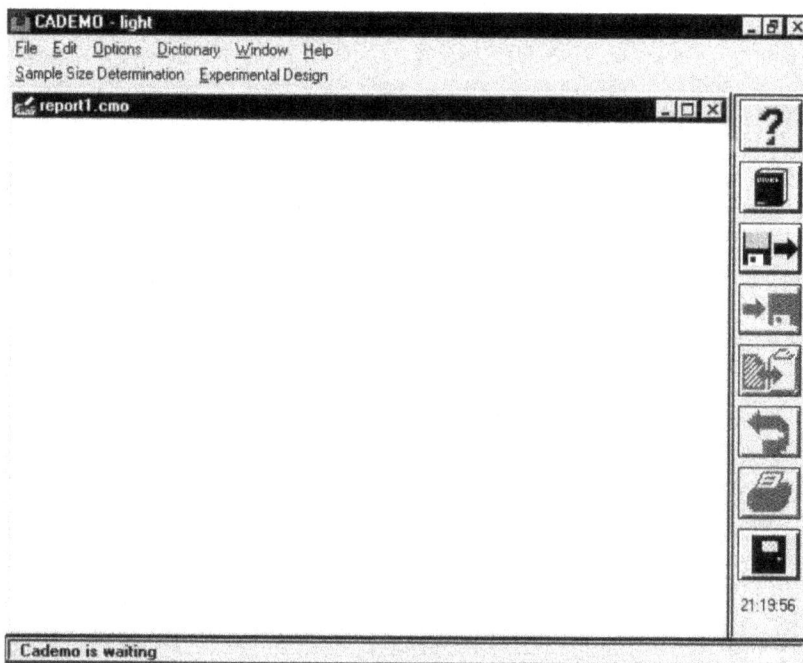

Figure 2.1 *The Initial Screen in CADEMO-light*

In the following dialogue box (Figure 2.2) we have specified that we wish to assign 100 experimental units to two treatments.

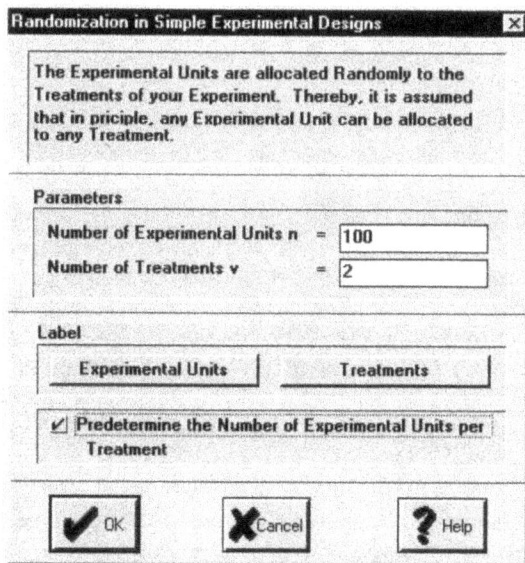

Figure 2.2 *The Dialogue Box for Randomisation*

We denote the two treatments by "Sample" and "Residual". After clicking the box "Predetermine the Number of Experimental Units per Treatment" we enter 5 for "Sample", and 95 for "Residual"). One result is shown in Figure 2.3; in another CL session the result would almost certainly be different.

1.Sample	26	33	55	90	96
2.Residual	1	2	3	4	5
	6	7	8	9	10
	11	12	13	14	15
	16	17	18	19	20
	21	22	23	24	25
	27	28	29	30	31
	32	34	35	36	37
	38	39	40	41	42
	43	44	45	46	47
	48	49	50	51	52
	53	54	56	57	58
	59	60	61	62	63
	64	65	66	67	68
	69	70	71	72	73
	74	75	76	77	78
	79	80	81	82	83
	84	85	86	87	88
	89	91	92	93	94

Figure 2.3 *Output Window showing a Random Sample of Size 5*

We now define a further type of restricted random sampling. Other procedures, such as for example transect sampling suitable for surveys of areas can be found in VB, Komplex 1/31.

Definition 2.11

If a given population of size N breaks down naturally into s subpopulations of size $N_1, N_2, ..., N_s$, or if it is divided into subpopulations according to the levels of a nuisance factor, we call these subpopulations *strata*. We use the term *stratified sampling* procedure when a survey is carried out with the total sample consisting of sub-samples of size n_i ($i = 1, ..., s$) drawn from the strata. The quantities n_i / N_i are called *stratum weights*. Stratified sampling procedures may be random or not (sometimes this is intended, for example if the survey costs differ among the strata, cost-optimising sample plans are often non-random, since elements in the cheaper strata may have a higher probability of being chosen than other elements). A *random stratified sampling* procedure is obtained when the sub-samples in the various strata are pure random samples with probabilities proportional to the stratum size, so that all the sample weights are equal.

Example 2.5 - continued

Let us assume that the population in Example 2.5 consists of 60 women and 40 men. Thus we have two natural strata with sizes in the ratio 3:2. In each pure random sample we would now take $n_1 = 3$ women and $n_2 = 2$ men. Each person in the population still has the same probability $3/60 = 2/40 = 0.05$ of being in the sample.

2.5.2   Randomisation in Experimental Designs - Random Allocation

Just as in sampling procedures we distinguish between pure and restricted forms of randomisation, we also do so in experimental designs. First of all we assume that our experimental material is not structured in any way, so that we do not have to consider blocks.

Definition 2.12

If in an experimental design we merely have to assign exactly n_i experimental units randomly to the i-th out of v treatments ($\Sigma n_i = N$), we call this a complete or *unrestricted randomisation* and we call the experimental design a simple or a *completely randomised design*.

In practice we can number the experimental units from 1 to N.

Then using a pure random sampling procedure we choose a random number between 1 and N and assign the corresponding unit to treatment number 1. If $n_1 \geq 2$ we choose another random number from the remaining N-1 numbers and allocate that unit again to treatment 1. We continue in this way until n_1 experimental units have been assigned to treatment 1. In the same way we choose n_2 experimental units for treatment 2 and so on until experimental units have been assigned to v-1 treatments.   The remaining experimental units then belong automatically to treatment v.

Example 2.6

From a population of male calves of a certain age, 16 were chosen. In a feeding experiment groups of four from these $N = 16$ animals are to be given one out of four different feeds. We denote the $v = 4$ feeds by 1, 2, 3 and 4. The outcome measure will be the average daily weight increase for each calf in g/day over a period of a week. We number the calves from 1 to 16, and call up the Experimental Design option in CL. If in Figure 2.2 we now enter $N = 16$ and $v = 4$ and leave the box for predetermined numbers unchecked, we will get a default assignment of equal numbers (4) of the calves to the four treatments. A possible allocation is shown in Figure 2.4.

```
Decision:
Type of Experimental Design is Known
Completely Randomized Experimental Design
Distribute Experimental Units as equally as
possible to the Treatments
```

Allocation Table

Treatments	Experimental Units			
1	2	9	10	13
2	4	7	11	16
3	1	3	6	15
4	5	8	12	14

Figure 2.4 *Random Allocation of 16 Experimental Units to 4 Treatments*

For all block designs the randomisation should be done as follows: the experimental units in each block have to be randomly assigned to the treatments which have been defined to occur in this block. The procedure described in 2.5.1 is therefore used for each block separately. We only have to replace N in 2.5.1 by the block size k and v by the number of treatments occurring in a block.

For complete block designs where each experimental unit in a block is uniquely assigned to one of the v treatments, the randomisation is finished.
If $k < v$ we proceed differently. In incomplete block designs, the abstract blocks obtained by a mathematical process (perhaps using the CL programme) are allocated at random to the real blocks: this applies also to the procedure described in section 2.5.1 in which $N = v = b$, where b denotes the number of blocks.

Example 2.4 - continued

The first case in example 2.4 with $v = 2$ types of eye-drops A and B merely requires the random allocation of A to one of the two eyes.
In the second case there were $v = 5$ treatments to be assigned to 10 blocks of size 2. The abstract blocks of the incomplete block design are listed in Table 2.2. The randomisation process has two steps. First the 10 treatment pairs (abstract blocks) are assigned randomly to the patients (real blocks). Secondly the two treatments are assigned randomly to the right and left eye.

2.6   Block Designs

2.6.1   Basic Concepts

To describe block designs the term *incidence matrix* is introduced.

Definition 2.13

An *incidence matrix* $N = (n_{ij})$ is a rectangular array with v rows and b columns with integer entries n_{ij}, where n_{ij} represents how many times the i-th treatment (represented by the i-th row) appears in the j-th block (represented by the j-th column). If all n_{ij} are either 0 or 1 then the incidence matrix and the corresponding block design are called *binary*.

The elements of incidence matrices of complete block designs are all positive ($n_{ij} \geq 1$). Incomplete block designs have incidence matrices with at least one element equal to zero in each column.

Mainly incomplete block designs are characterised in compact form in place of an incidence matrix. In compact writing a block is denoted by a bracket which includes the numbers of the treatments occuring in the block.

Example 2.7

A block design with 4 treatments and 6 blocks is defined by the incidence matrix:

$$
\begin{pmatrix}
1 & 0 & 1 & 0 & 0 & 0 \\
0 & 1 & 0 & 1 & 1 & 1 \\
1 & 0 & 1 & 0 & 0 & 0 \\
0 & 1 & 0 & 1 & 1 & 1
\end{pmatrix}
$$

Since this matrix contains zeros it represents an incomplete block design. In compact form it may be written in the form (1,3), (2,4), (1,3), (2,4), (2,4), (2,4). In this representation for example the first set of braces represents block 1 to which treatments 1 and 3 are assigned, and this corresponds to the first column of the matrix (representing block 1) having a 1 in rows 1 and 3 (representing the treatments).

Definition 2.14

A block design with a symmetrical incidence matrix is called a *symmetrical block design*. If in a block design all treatments occur equally often, i.e. the number of replications $r_i = r$, then we call this design *equi-replicated*. If in a block design the number of experimental units per block is the same for all blocks, we call this design *proper*. The number of experimental units in the j-th block will be denoted by k_j, thus for proper designs we have $k_j = k$.

It can easily be seen that both the sum of the replications r_i and the sum of the block sizes k_j have to be equal to the total number of experimental units of a block design. We therefore have for any block design:

$$\sum_{i=1}^{v} r_i = \sum_{j=1}^{b} k_j = N \qquad (2.4)$$

In the case of equi-replicated and proper block designs ($r_i = r$ and $k_j = k$) we get

$$vr = bk \qquad (2.5)$$

In symmetrical block designs we have $b = v$ and $r_i = k_i$ ($i = 1, ..., v$).

Definition 2.15

An incomplete block design is *connected* if for any pair (A_k, A_l) of the treatments $A_1, ..., A_v$ a chain of treatments starting with A_k and ending with A_l can be found in such a way that any consecutive treatments in the chain occur together at least once in a block. Otherwise the block design is called *disconnected*.

This definition may seem very abstract and its importance may not be clear. But the property of connectedness is extremely relevant to the analysis. Disconnected block designs can be considered and analysed as two (or perhaps more) independent experimental designs.

Example 2.7 - continued

In the design of Example 2.7 the first and the second treatment do not jointly occur in any of the 6 blocks. But also there is no chain in the sense of definition 2.15 to ensure that the design is connected. Hence it is a disconnected block design. What this means can be seen by "renumbering" the blocks and the treatments or, equivalently, by rearranging the columns and the rows of the incidence matrix.

We interchange blocks 2 and 3 (the second block becomes the third one and vice versa) and the treatments 1 and 4. In the incidence matrix the interchanges of columns 2 and 3, and rows 1 and 4, result in the following matrix:

$$
\begin{pmatrix}
0 & 0 & 1 & 1 & 1 & 1 \\
0 & 0 & 1 & 1 & 1 & 1 \\
1 & 1 & 0 & 0 & 0 & 0 \\
1 & 1 & 0 & 0 & 0 & 0
\end{pmatrix}
$$

It can now be seen that this experimental design is composed of two designs with two disjoint subsets of the treatments. In the first experiment 2 treatments (1 and 2) occur in 4 blocks. In the second experiment 2 further treatments (3 and 4) occur in 2 different blocks. Therefore, it is not possible to analyse the total experiment by one analysis of variance; this can only be done for the two parts separately, and by eventually pooling the residual sum of squares to increase the degrees of freedom, if the variances are assumed to be equal. Comparisons between treatments of the first group (1,2) and the second group (3,4) cannot be handled.

In this book we will only deal with complete block designs or with *connected* incomplete block designs, especially balanced incomplete block designs which we introduce in the next section.

2.6.2 Completely Balanced Incomplete Block Designs

Definition 2.16

A (completely) *balanced incomplete block design* (BIB) is a proper and equi-replicated incomplete block design with the additional property that all treatment pairs occur in the same number λ of blocks. If a BIB has v treatments occurring with r replications in b blocks of size $k < v$, it will be denoted by $B(v, k, \lambda)$.

In the symbol $B(v, k, \lambda)$ only three of the five parameters v, b, k, r, λ of a BIB can be found. This is sufficient because only three of these five parameters can be chosen independently, the others are then also fixed. To show this we first determine the number of possible treatment pairs in the design. It is given by $\binom{v}{2} = \dfrac{v(v-1)}{2}$. On the other hand there are in each of the b blocks exactly $\binom{k}{2} = \dfrac{k(k-1)}{2}$ treatment pairs and therefore we obtain:

$$\lambda v(v-1) = bk(k-1)$$

because each of the $\binom{v}{2}$ treatment pairs occurs λ times in the experiment.

Using formula (2.5) we replace bk by vr in the last equation and get (after division by v):

$$\lambda(v-1) = r(k-1) \tag{2.6}$$

The equations (2.5) and (2.6) are *necessary* conditions for the existence of a BIB. These necessary conditions reduce the set of quintuples of five positive integers v, b, r, k, λ to the subset of those integers for which a BIB could be constructed. The latter subset corresponds to a set of three positive integers, for instance $\{v, k, \lambda\}$. From the three elements v, k, λ, the remaining two parameters of the BIB can be calculated using (2.5) and (2.6).

It should be noted that the necessary conditions are not always *sufficient*; it may so happen that for five positive integers fulfilling (2.5) and (2.6) no BIB exists. To show this a single example will be sufficient.

Example 2.8

In this example it can be seen that the conditions, necessary for the existence of a BIB need not always be sufficient. Consider the values $v = 16, r = 3, b = 8, k = 6$, $\lambda = 1$. Because $16 \times 3 = 8 \times 6$ and $1 \times 15 = 3 \times 5$, the necessary conditions for the existence of a BIB are met. Nevertheless no BIB exists for this combination of parameters.

Besides (2.5) and (2.6) there is another necessary condition given by Fisher's inequality, which states that the following inequality must always be satisfied:

$$b \geq v \tag{2.7}$$

This inequality does not hold in Example 2.8. There are further examples where (2.5), (2.6) and (2.7) hold and yet no BIB exists.

Example 2.8 - Continued

We need a BIB having $v = 16$ treatments; blocks with $k = 6$ experimental units are available, and we are looking for a BIB with as few blocks as possible. We can construct this "smallest" BIB using the Experimental Design option in the CL window in Figure 2.1, where we continue by choosing "Balanced Block Design". We fill in the dialogue box appropriately as in Figure 2.5 and obtain the results in Figure 2.6.

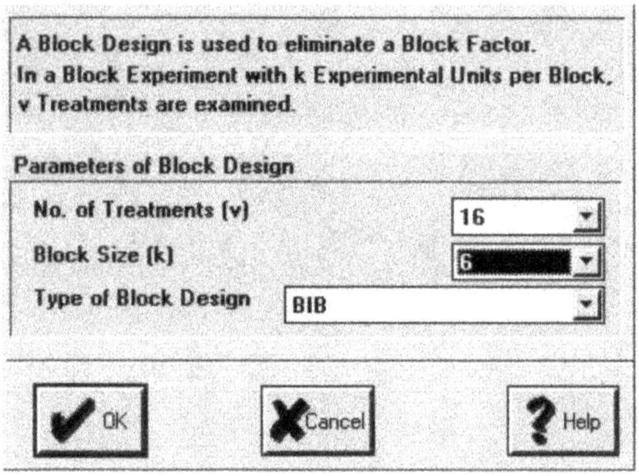

A Block Design is used to eliminate a Block Factor.
In a Block Experiment with k Experimental Units per Block,
v Treatments are examined.

Parameters of Block Design

No. of Treatments (v)	16
Block Size (k)	6
Type of Block Design	BIB

OK   Cancel   Help

Figure 2.5 *Dialogue box for the Random Allocation of v=16 Treatments in 16 Blocks of Size k=6*

Decision:
Construction of a Completely Balanced
Incomplete Block Design

Allocation Table

Block	Treatments
1	2 3 4 5 6 11
2	3 4 10 12 15 16
3	1 3 6 7 8 14
4	3 5 8 9 13 15
5	1 2 6 9 10 15
6	1 4 5 7 14 15
7	1 5 7 9 11 12
8	4 6 7 9 13 16
9	1 4 8 10 11 13
10	5 6 8 10 12 16
11	1 2 3 12 13 16
12	2 7 8 11 15 16

Figure 2.6 *Output Window for the Specification in Figure 2.5 with b = 16, r = 6 and λ = 2*

A BIB (a so called unreduced or trivial BIB) can always be constructed for any positive integer v and k by forming all possible combinations of the v numbers in groups of size $k < v$. Hence $b = \binom{v}{k}$, $r = \binom{v-1}{k-1}$ and $\lambda = \binom{v-2}{k-2}$. Often a BIB can be found as a part of such an unreduced BIB and this is a reduced BIB. One case for which such a reduction is not possible is that with $v = 8$ and $k = 3$. There is no other case for $v \leq 25$ and $2 < k < v - 1$ where no unreduced BIB exists. More about the existence and methods of constructing BIB and other designs can be found in RASCH and HERRENDÖRFER (1986) and RAGHAVARAO (1971, 2005).

Occasionally so-called partially balanced incomplete block designs (PBIB) are used which are designed analogously to BIBs, but which allow two or even more classes of treatment groups which each occur in the same number of blocks. They can be constructed using CL; see also VB1/21/4150 - 1/21/4162.

2.7 Factorial Designs

The classical method for studying the effect of several factors consists in varying one factor at a time while keeping the others constant. Apart from being very expensive, this method does not permit interactions between factors to be analysed. These drawbacks induced R. A. Fisher and F. Yates to develop the basics of the theory of factorial experiments.
Experiments of this kind are used to study the effects of several factors simultaneously. The following is an example.

Example 2.9
The effects of varying amounts of phosphate and nitrogenous fertilisers on the yield y of a crop are to be studied. In an experiment, factor P (phosphate) is applied at the levels P_1, P_2 and P_3, and factor N (nitrogenous fertiliser) at the levels N_1 and N_2, each of the six plots in an experimental field being "treated" (fertilised) with one of the factor level combinations P_1N_1, P_1N_2, P_2N_1, P_2N_2, P_3N_1 and P_3N_2. To improve accuracy, this can be done r times, i.e. using a total of $r \cdot 6$ plots. In this case, one would speak of r (complete) replications. The choice of r will depend on the precision requirements and will be determined using the methods in chapter 3 (and chapter 4 or 5). All $6 \cdot r$ plots must have the same kind of soil to avoid the disturbing effects of soil differences. If no homogeneous field of the necessary size is available, then at least each replication should have the same kind of soil. The different soils will then act as levels of a disturbing or block factor, the effects of which must be eliminated during analysis. The combinations of factor levels tested on one kind of soil form a block (in the sense of section 2.5), while all six possible combinations of levels correspond to the $v=6$ treatments.

We can use Example 2.9 to illustrate the concept of interaction. An interaction is present if the effect on the characteristic being observed when we move from one level to another of a certain factor depends on the level(s) of one or more of the other factors. The number of other factors involved defines the order of the interaction. In example 2.9 a first order interaction is present if the effect on the yield caused by changing from phosphate level P_1 to P_2 is affected by whether the nitrogen level is N_1 or N_2.

In general, the factors are denoted by A, B, C, ..., and their levels A_1, A_2, ..., B_1, B_2, ..., and so on. The factors being studied are treatment factors, and the combinations of levels of all treatment factors are the treatments (strictly treatment combinations). Other factors that are of no interest, but whose possible effects mean that they have to be taken into account by blocking or other means, are called noise factors. The purpose of factorial experiments is to estimate the effects of the treatment factors and the interactions between factors, using a statistical model whose parameters can be tested or estimated. The number of factors and their levels are settled beforehand. The factors may be either qualitative or quantitative.

Definition 2.17

A factorial experiment with $p > 1$ factors $A, B, \ldots$ and the corresponding numbers of factor levels $s_a, s_b, \ldots$ is called a *factorial experiment of type* $s_a \cdot s_b \cdot \ldots$. If $s_a = s_b = , \ldots, = s$, the experiment is a *symmetric factorial experiment of type* s^p, otherwise it is *asymmetric*.

For simplicity we will restrict ourselves to the case with $p = 3$ factors A, B, C for our further discussions; for the general case we refer you to VB 1/21/4800-1/21/4825.
In the case $p = 3$ we denote the levels of A, B and C, by A_i, B_j, and C_k ($i = 1, \ldots, s_a$; $j = 1, \ldots, s_b$; $k = 1, \ldots, s_c$) respectively.

Definition 2.18

The *experimental design* of a factorial experiment with $p = 3$ factors specifies for each possible combination (A_i, B_j, C_k) of the levels of all factors the number n_{ijk} of experimental units assigned to that combination of levels (i.e. the number of units "treated" with that combination). The total number $N = \sum_{ijk} n_{ijk}$ of experimental units

is the *size of the experiment*.

Definition 2.19

A factorial experiment is called *complete* if $n_{ijk} > 0$ for all combinations (A_i, B_j, C_k) of the levels of all factors, otherwise it is called *incomplete*.

Fractional factorial designs are an important class of incomplete factorial designs, especially useful when the factors are qualitative. They consist of one k-th ($k = 2, 3, \ldots$) of all the possible treatment combinations. Fractional factorial designs are used when there are many factors to be considered in an experiment. Since the number of treatment combinations rises sharply with the number of factors, most of the time there are insufficient experimental units available for a full factorial experiment, An incomplete factorial has the consequence that not all the definable main and interaction effects can be estimated separately from each other, but in part only their sum. We call this *confounding*. One strives as far as possible to avoid confounding main effects and lower order interactions with each other. It is general assumed that higher order interaction effects are negligible and so can be confounded with lower order effects, if necessary. For more information about factorial design see WU and HAMADA(2000).

3 Design and Analysis of Completely Randomised Designs

In this chapter we give the sample size calculations and analysis procedures for various problems and precision requirements.

We will give formulae which can be handled by a pocket calculator, but we will also give solutions using computer packages such as Cademo-*light* and SPSS. For the analysis we will nearly always demonstrate the formulae by numerical examples. Some of the examples will be based on data which will now be described and set up in an SPSS data file.

Example 3.1 - A data set

We will use the data set in Table 3.1 to illustrate the analysis in several parts of this chapter. The table gives the litter weights of mice (in g). The values x_i and y_i will be interpreted in two ways.

First interpretation:

Each of thirteen mice gave birth to two litters. The x_i are the weights of the first litter and the y_i the weights of the second litter of these mice, which are considered to be a random sample from a population of mice.

Second interpretation:

Independent samples of 13 mice are drawn from two mouse populations (26 mice in all). The x_i and the y_i are the litter weights of the first litters of the mice in populations 1 (x_i) and 2 (y_i) respectively.

Table 3.1 *The litter weights of mice (in g).*

i	x_i	y_i
1	7.6	7.8
2	13.2	11.1
3	9.1	16.4
4	10.6	13.7
5	8.7	10.7
6	10.6	12.3
7	6.8	14.0
8	9.9	11.9
9	7.3	8.8
10	10.4	7.7
11	13.3	8.9
12	10.0	16.4
13	9.5	10.2

We will now create this data as an SPSS-data file. First we need to rename var in the first column as x and var in the second column as y. Then we need three digits in each column and one decimal place. To do these we change from Data View to Variable View (see Fig. 3.1 below left). Now we can change the variable names to x and y, and the number of decimal places to 1. Having returned to Data View we now enter the data values. We save the file under the name Litterweights.sav. The SPSS file is shown in Figure 3.1.

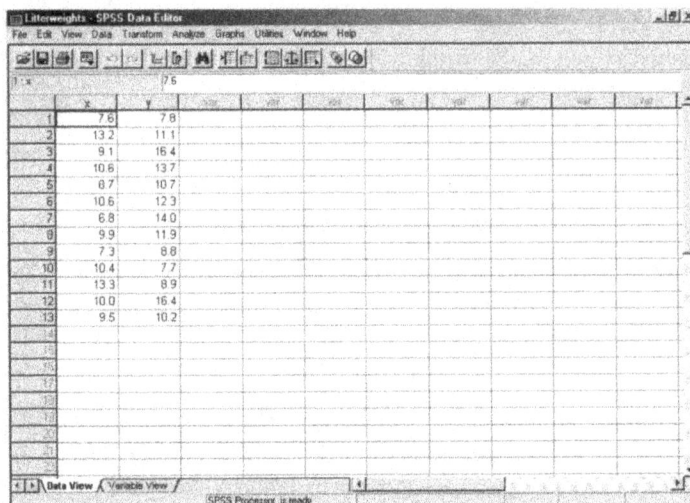

Figure 3.1 *SPSS data file for Example 3.1*

We will denote observations resulting from a simple experimental design by real numbers $y_1, ..., y_n$, which are *realizations of* the *random variables* $y_1, ..., y_n$ respectively, and we assume that within each group these random variables are identically and independently distributed (if we have two groups, we use x_i for one group and y_i for the other, and if we have more than two groups we use a subscript for the group number as in the ANOVA models in chapter 4). These random variables are components of a random sample $(y_1, ..., y_n)$, i.e. we use the mathematical definition of a random sample (or a sample for short) as a random vector with *identically and independently distributed* components. From time to time the realisation of a *random sample* is also called a (random) sample, as is also the case for a set of objects or individuals chosen randomly from a population.

In a random sample thus defined it is assumed that all the y_i have the same distribution, and that this distribution comes from a certain *family of distributions*. In many applications we use *normal distributions* with expectation μ ($-\infty < \mu < \infty$) and variance $\sigma^2 > 0$ as the parameters; the parameter vector $\theta^T = (\mu, \sigma^2)$ lies in the upper half of R^2, the two dimensional Euclidian plane (as defined in Appendix C, θ^T is the transpose (T) of the vector θ; a vector is a column, its transpose is a row (vector)). An experiment will form the basis on which we draw statistical conclusions about the unknown part of θ.

In this chapter we will discuss some examples of simple experimental designs.

Example 3.1 - continued

The two interpretations of the data in Table 3.1 require different models and types of analysis. In interpretation 2 each of the groups is regarded as a realization of a random sample (of xs or ys). Furthermore we assume that we have **two** samples which are independent of each other. In the first interpretation we must accept that there is a dependence between the two litter weights from the same animal (of genetic origin, for example). Thus independent samples give an inadequate model in this case. The data are properly modelled by a vector of observations having two elements (x and y) from **one** sample.

3.1 Point Estimation of Parameters.

Suppose that we have a situation in which we have to plan and carry out an experiment to estimate the unknown parameter(s) of a distribution. First we consider so-called point estimation, and in section 3.2 we discuss interval estimation.

The idea of point estimation is to assign a value calculated from observations as an "estimate" of an unknown parameter of a distribution. Thus in statistics the word "estimate" does not have the subjective and inexact connotations that it does in everyday speech.

Let us first explain what we mean by a *parameter*.

The normal distribution with expectation μ and variance σ^2 depends on μ and σ^2 and on nothing more. This can be seen by looking at the *density function*.

A normal distribution with *expectation (mean)* μ and *variance* σ^2 (written $N(\mu;\ \sigma^2)$ for short) has density function given by

$$f(y) = \frac{1}{\sigma\sqrt{2\pi}}\exp\{-\frac{1}{2\sigma^2}(y - \mu)^2\}, \quad (\sigma > 0)$$

We call μ and σ^2 the parameters of the distribution and the vector $\theta = (\mu,\sigma^2)^T$ the *parameter vector*.

The set of all possible values of θ is called the *parameter space* Ω. In the case of the normal distribution μ is any real number i.e. $-\infty < \mu < \infty$ and σ^2 is any positive number i.e. $0 < \sigma^2 < \infty$. Therefore Ω is given by the positive half plane Ω: $\{-\infty < \mu < \infty,\ \sigma^2 > 0\}$.

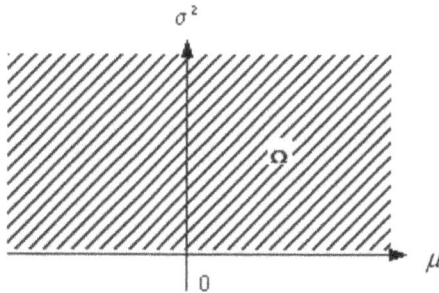

Figure 3.2 *Parameter Space Ω for the Parameter (Vector) $\theta = (\mu,\ \sigma^2)^T$ of Normal Distributions*

If we fix a point θ in Ω, we have **a** (single) normal distribution out of the set of all normal distributions. If we consider the set of all normal distributions (for any $\theta \in \Omega$) we call this set the *family of normal distributions*.

In general a family of distributions is the set of all distributions with the same density (or probability) function and any parameter θ from the corresponding parameter space Ω. In this text we consider the following families of distributions

Name	Parameters θ	Ω	Symbol	P-quantile
Normal	$(\mu; \sigma^2)$	$\{-\infty < \mu < \infty, \sigma^2 > 0\}$	$N(\mu; \sigma^2)$	$u(P), z(P)$
Binomial (n known)	p	$(0,1)$	$B(n; p)$	-
t	f	$\{1,2,3,...\}$	$t(f)$	$t(f; P)$
χ^2(Chi-squared)	f	$\{1,2,3,...\}$	$\chi^2(f)$	$\chi^2(f; P)$
F	$(f_1; f_2)$	$\{1,2,...\}\times\{1,2,...\}$	$F(f_1; f_2)$	$F(f_1; f_2; P)$

If the distribution is not specified in detail (as a member of a family), for example let say we only know that it is continuous, then we use moments or functions of the moments to characterise the distribution. Usually not more than the first four moments are used. The first moment of the distribution of a random variable y is the expectation $E(y) = \mu$, and the second (central) moment is the variance $var(y) = \sigma^2$. The third (central) moment is $\mu_3 = E[(y-\mu)^3]$ and the fourth (central) moment is $\mu_4 = E[(y - \mu)^4]$.
The corresponding sample moments of a sample $y_1, ..., y_n$ of size $n \geq 4$ are

the sample mean $\bar{y} = \dfrac{1}{n}\sum_{i=1}^{n} y_i$, the sample variance $s^2 = \dfrac{1}{n-1}\sum_{i=1}^{n}(y_i - \bar{y})^2$,

$$m_3 = \frac{1}{n}\sum_{i=1}^{n}(y_i - \bar{y})^3 \quad \textit{(third sample moment)}$$

and

$$m_4 = \frac{1}{n}\sum_{i=1}^{n}(y_i - \bar{y})^4 \quad \textit{(fourth sample moment)}.$$

We frequently use the following *standardised moments*. Firstly the *skewness*, which is

$$\gamma_1 = \frac{\mu_3}{\sigma^3}$$

and the *kurtosis*, which is

$$\gamma_2 = \frac{\mu_4}{\sigma^4} - 3.$$

The *sample skewness* (estimate of γ_1) is calculated by SPSS as

$$g_1 = \frac{m_3 n^2}{s^3(n - 1)(n - 2)},$$ with estimated variance of the corresponding estimator

$$\hat{var}(g_1) = \frac{6n(n-1)}{(n-2)\cdot(n+1)\cdot(n+3)}$$

and the *sample kurtosis* (estimate of γ_2) is calculated by SPSS as

$$g_2 = \frac{[(n + 1)m_4 - 3(n - 1)^3 s^4 / n^2]n^2}{(n - 1)(n - 2)(n - 3) s^4},$$

with estimated variance of the corresponding estimator

$$\text{vâr}(g_2) = \frac{24n(n-1)^2}{(n-3)\cdot(n-2)\cdot(n+3)\cdot(n+5)}.$$

Example 3.1 - continued

Using SPSS and the data in Table 3.1, we now calculate the sample moments that we have just introduced. To do this we choose the following command sequence: Analyze - Descriptive Statistics, click the button "Options", und tick Mean, Variance, Skewness and Kurtosis. Figure 3.3 contains the results.

Descriptive Statistics

	N	Mean	Variance	Skewness		Kurtosis	
	Statistic	Statistic	Statistic	Statistic	Std. Error	Statistic	Std. Error
x	13	9.769	3.947	.412	.616	-.090	1.191
y	13	11.531	8.714	.409	.616	-.840	1.191
Valid N (listwise)	13						

Figure 3.3 *SPSS results for the data in Table 3.1*

The standard error (Std. Error) given in Figure 3.3 is the square root of the estimated variance. After these preliminaries about parameters and moments of distributions, we will return to the main theme of estimating these quantities.

Usually some function of θ, $\psi = g(\theta)$ say, has to be estimated. In the normal and binomial distributions, the following functions are of interest:

$N(\mu, \sigma^2)$: $g_1(\theta) = \mu$, $g_2(\theta) = \sigma^2$, $g_3(\theta) = \sigma$, $g_4(\theta) = \sigma/\mu$ (called the coefficient of variation),

$B(n; p)$: $g(\theta) = p$

Statistical inferences are based on *abstract random samples* $(y_1, y_2, ..., y_n)$ of size $n > 1$. The realization $(y_1, y_2, ..., y_n)$ of $(y_1, y_2, ..., y_n)$ is a model for the experimental results, which are also denoted by $(y_1, y_2, ..., y_n)$ (we may of course use x or other symbols in place of y).

Point estimation is concerned with calculating an estimate for either the parameter (vector) θ or for a function $g(\theta)$ using the observations $y_1, ..., y_n$ on the experimental units. We must distinguish carefully between the estimation function $\hat{\psi}$, the "estimator" as a function of the random vector $(y_1, ..., y_n)$, and the value of a realization of $\hat{\psi}$ for actual measurements $y_1, ..., y_n$. The latter is called the "estimated value" or "estimate" $\hat{\psi}$.

The *precision requirement* for the estimation of $\psi = g(\theta)$ is usually given as an upper bound for the distance of the estimator from the true value $\psi = g(\theta)$. If we want to estimate ψ by an unbiased estimator, i.e. if the expectation of the estimator is equal to the true value (so that $E(\hat{\psi}) = \psi$), the precision requirement is usually that the variance $\text{var}(\hat{\psi})$ of the estimator should lie below a specified upper bound. In cases where it is unknown whether the estimator is unbiased or not, or when it is known that the estimator is biased, then the expected squared deviation (or "mean squared error") $MSE(\hat{\psi})$ is commonly used as a measure of the distance of the estimator from $\psi = g(\theta)$. If we define the bias of the estimator $\hat{\psi}$ by $E(\hat{\psi}) - \psi$, then it is known that

$$MSE(\hat{\psi}) = var(\hat{\psi}) + \{E(\hat{\psi}) - \psi\}^2 \qquad (3.1)$$

From this it follows that for unbiased estimators the two criteria - mean squared error and variance - are equal, because in this case $E(\hat{\psi}) - \psi = 0$.

Instead of placing an upper bound on the variance or the MSE as a precision requirement we sometimes demand that the probability that $|\psi - \hat{\psi}|$ is larger than a given value d does not exceed a given α, i.e. that $P(|\psi - \hat{\psi}| \geq d) \leq \alpha$.

The difference between an estimator and an estimate can be likened to the difference between a gun and a gun-shot. If you want to hit a target you can select one of several guns. Some may be guns which produce very consistent shots, but these are all offset from the target. Others may have a wide variation between the shots but the results are scattered around the target. Another analogy is that of a balance (estimator) and the weight registered by a balance (estimate). A biased balance registers weights which deviate systematically from the true weight.

In Figure 3.4 we show the behaviour of three balances when weighing the same object repeatedly. Which of the three balances would you select? Balance 1 and 2 are unbiased but balance 1 has a large variation.

Balance 3 has the smallest variation but unfortunately not around the true weight of the object. The decision between the three balances is analogous to the choice between different estimators.

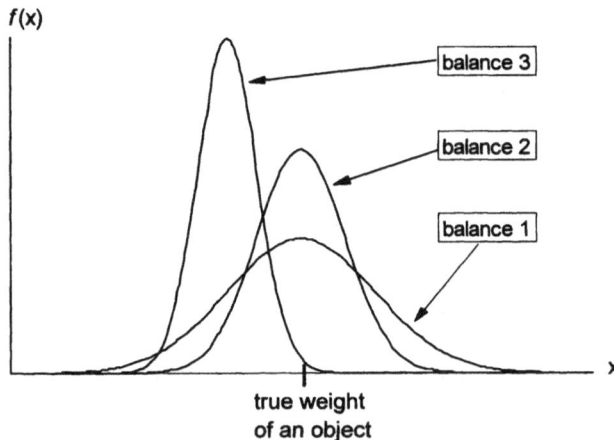

Figure 3.4 *Characteristics of three balances*

3.1.1 Point Estimation of the Parameters of a Normal Distribution

Consider a sample from a univariate normal distribution with parameters $\theta^T = (\mu, \sigma^2)$. (For brevity we say the y_i are distributed as $N(\mu; \sigma^2)$).

Suppose that the function $E(y) = \mu = \psi = g(\theta)$ has to be estimated. It can be shown that for a random sample with $E(y_i) = \mu$, $var(y_i) = \sigma^2$ the arithmetic mean (or sample average, or mean for short - we shall also use the word mean as an abbreviation for the expectation (expected value) of a random variable; the context will make the meaning clear)

$$\hat{\mu} = \bar{y} = \frac{1}{n}\sum_{i=1}^{n} y_i$$

is an *unbiased estimator* of μ (this is in general the case for all distributions having an expectation).

Because the y_i are independent in an abstract random sample, it follows that

$$var(\bar{y}) = MSE(\bar{y}) = \frac{1}{n}\sigma^2 \tag{3.2}$$

But how do we actually arrive at the function $\hat{\mu}$ as an estimator for μ?

In this book we consider two methods for the construction of estimating functions, the method of Maximum Likelihood and the method of Least Squares. The method of least squares will be used frequently in chapters 4 and 5.

We shall now describe the method of least squares; the method of maximum likelihood will be dealt with in section 3.1.2.

The *method of ordinary least squares* (*OLS*) does not need any knowledge of the distribution. However what it does need is a model for the random variable in which the parameter to be estimated appears. The simplest model for the components y_i of the random sample is given by

$$y_i = \mu + e_i \qquad (i = 1, ..., n)$$

where $\mu = E(y_i)$ is the expectation of y_i and $var(e_i) = \sigma^2$ of the independent errors e_i is a constant. The random variable e_i models the deviation of y_i from μ. We now estimate μ, squaring and then summing the observed deviations

$$y_i - \mu$$

and then minimising this "*error sum of squares*" (ESS)

$$S = \sum_{i=1}^{n}(y_i - \mu)^2$$

The value $\hat{\mu}$ which minimises S is called the *least squares estimate* (*LSE*) of μ. Since

$$\frac{dS}{d\mu} = -2\sum_{i=1}^{n}(y_i - \mu)$$

it follows that

$$\sum_{i=1}^{n}(y_i - \hat{\mu}) = 0 \text{ and } \sum_{i=1}^{n} y_i - n\hat{\mu} = 0.$$

Thus $\hat{\mu} = \dfrac{\sum\limits_{i=1}^{n} y_i}{n} = \bar{y}$ is the least squares estimate.

In terms of random variables we thus have $\hat{\mu} = \bar{y} = \dfrac{1}{n}\sum\limits_{i=1}^{n} y_i$ as least squares estimator.

Since $\dfrac{d^2 S}{d\mu^2} = 2n > 0$ we really have a minimum.

If we have the *precision requirement* in the form

$$\text{var}(\bar{y}) = \frac{1}{n}\sigma^2 \le K,$$

with a positive upper bound K it follows that

$$n \ge \frac{\sigma^2}{K}.$$

If σ^2/K is an integer then we use it as the sample size n. In all other cases we round σ^2/K up to the next larger integer i.e. we write $n = \text{CEIL}(\sigma^2/K)$.

We will use the symbol CEIL (from ceiling) throughout the text. We define it as follows.

Definition 3.1

By the modified integer symbol CEIL(x) of a non-negative number x we define the following integer

$$\text{CEIL}(x) = \begin{cases} x, & \text{if } x \text{ is an integer} \\ 1 + \text{the integer part of } x, & \text{if } x \text{ is not an integer} \end{cases} \tag{3.3}$$

For example if $x = 8.001$, then CEIL(8.001) $= 9$; but if $x = 8$, then CEIL(8) $= 8$.
Assume now we have an $N(\mu; \sigma^2)$ distribution and wish to estimate $\psi = g(\theta) = \sigma^2$ to satisfy var($\hat{\psi}$) $\le K$. Now,

$s^2 = \sum\limits_{i=1}^{n}(y_i - \bar{y})^2 / (n-1)$ is an unbiased estimator of σ^2 and $\bar{y} = \dfrac{1}{n}\sum\limits_{i=1}^{n} y_i$ is an unbiased estimator of μ.

We know that $(n-1)s^2/\sigma^2$ has a central χ^2-distribution with $(n-1)$ degrees of freedom (FREUND, 1992), therefore var(s^2) $= 2\sigma^4/(n-1)$. From var(s^2) $\le K$ we obtain

$$n = \text{CEIL}(2\sigma^4/K) + 1 \tag{3.4}$$

If we wish to estimate $\psi = \sigma^2$ optimally so that $\mathrm{MSE}(\hat\psi) \le K$, then the unbiased estimator s^2 is not MSE-optimal. In this case the estimator[1]

$$\tilde\sigma^2 = \frac{1}{n+1}\sum_{i=1}^{n}(\,y_i-\bar y\,)^2 = \frac{n-1}{n+1}\,s^2$$

has to be used. Because the variance of this estimator is

$$\mathrm{var}(\tilde\sigma^2) = \frac{(n-1)^2}{(n+1)^2}\,\mathrm{var}(s^2) = \frac{2\sigma^4(n-1)}{(n+1)^2}$$

and its bias is

$$\mathrm{E}(\tilde\sigma^2) - \sigma^2 = \frac{-2s^2}{n+1},$$

it follows that

$$\mathrm{MSE}(\tilde\sigma^2) = \frac{2\sigma^4(n\text{-}1)}{(n\text{+}1)^2} + \frac{4\sigma^4}{(n\text{+}1)^2} = \frac{2\sigma^4}{n\text{+}1} \tag{3.5}$$

which is smaller than $\mathrm{MSE}(s^2) = \mathrm{var}(s^2) = 2\sigma^4/(n\text{-}1)$ and from this it follows that

$$n = \mathrm{CEIL}\!\left(\frac{2\sigma^4}{K}\right) - 1 \tag{3.6}$$

satisfies the precision requirement for this estimator.

Sample size determination and analysis for the estimation of the mean of a truncated normal distribution can be found in VB 3/21/0052 and 3/21/0053, for censored samples see 3/21/0161. Robust estimators can be found in 3/21/3400, 3/21/3401 (trimmed mean), 3/21/3402 (Winsorised mean), 3/21/3403 (Anderson's M-estimator), 3/21/3404 (Huber estimator), 3/21/3405 (Hampel estimator). Estimation of the mean of a log-normal distribution is described in procedure 3/21/3121.

3.1.2 Point Estimation of the Parameter p of a Binomial Distribution

A random variable x with *probability function*

$$P(x = k) = \binom{n}{k}p^k(1\text{-}p)^{n\text{-}k}, \tag{3.7}$$

$k = 0,1,2,...,n$, $0 < p < 1$ is called a *binomial variable* with *parameter* p, and x is said to have a *binomial distribution*. If we have n independent trials in each of which a particular outcome (event) has the same probability p then the number of occurrences of the outcome in all n trials is binomially distributed with parameter p. The binomial distribution has expectation np and variance $np(1\text{-}p)$.

---

[1]   In this book we denote an unbiased estimator by ^ and any other estimator by a ~.

We now introduce the *Maximum Likelihood Principle* which means that we take as our estimate of the parameter, that value in the parameter space which maximises the likelihood function. The likelihood function is the probability (in the discrete case) or the probability density function (in the continuous case) of the random sample. It is now regarded as a function of the parameters, with the other arguments being given. Thus we substitute the observed values in this function and regard the parameters as unknown. In place of the likelihood function we may also maximise its logarithm which leads to the same result, but is easier to differentiate. We then obtain the estimator by replacing the observations in the formula by the elements of the random sample, by simply emboldening the corresponding letters.

In the binomial case the natural logarithm of the probability function (3.7) with $k = x$ being the frequency of occurrence of the event is

$$\ln L = \text{const.} + x\ln(p) + (n-x)\ln(1-p), \tag{3.8}$$

where the constant is independent of p. Differentiating with respect to p and putting the derivative equal to zero we obtain $\dfrac{d \ln L}{dp} = \dfrac{x}{p} - \dfrac{n-x}{1-p} = 0$ and so $\hat{p}$ satisfies $(1-\hat{p})x = (n-x)\hat{p}$. Thus the estimate is $\hat{p} = x/n$ and the estimator is

$$\hat{p} = x/n. \tag{3.9}$$

Since $d^2 \ln L / dp^2 = -x/p^2 - (n-x)/(1-p)^2 < 0$, we really have a maximum.
We can thus say that the probability of an event is estimated by its *relative frequency*.
The estimation of the parameter of a Poisson distribution may be found in VB 3/21/3201-3205.

3.1.3 Point Estimation in Surveys

In the case of experiments we model the population from which the experimental units are sampled as being essentially an infinite set. In *sample surveys* we often sample from relatively small populations.

The characteristic to be observed on the elements of the sample should be measurable on each element of the population. The measurement is denoted by Y and the *population* of the measurements is the set $\{Y_1, Y_2, ..., Y_N\}$, where N is the population size. The distribution of the N values of this population has population mean

$\mu = \overline{Y} = \displaystyle\sum_{i=1}^{N} Y_i / N$ (also called *expectation* or expected value), *population variance*

$\sigma^2 = \displaystyle\sum_{i=1}^{N} (Y_i - \overline{Y})^2 / N$, *skewness* $\gamma_1 = \mu_3/(\sigma^2)^{3/2}$ where the *third moment*

$\mu_3 = \displaystyle\sum_{i=1}^{N} (Y_i - \overline{Y})^3 / N$, and the *kurtosis* $\gamma_2 = \mu_4/(\sigma^2)^2 - 3$ using the *fourth moment*

$\mu_4 = \displaystyle\sum_{i=1}^{N} (Y_i - \overline{Y})^4 / N$.

Often the research worker is only interested in the population mean μ, the population total $\Sigma Y_i = N\bar{Y}$, and the population variance σ^2. On the basis of a *sample* of n sampling units, we wish to get good estimates of μ and σ^2.

Note that the *population total* $\Sigma Y_i = N\bar{Y}$ can easily be dealt with by multiplying the estimate for the population mean $\bar{Y}$ by N.

The *sample* must of course be a random sample, but when the population is finite, we can draw the sample either *with replacement (wr)* or *without replacement (wor)*.

In sampling *wr* the sampling procedure is very simple, and each element of the population has the same probability $1/N$ of being chosen. Each sampled unit is put back into the population before the next unit is drawn and the next element is taken at random from the whole population. This procedure is repeated till the n elements are drawn. This is called a *simple random sampling scheme with replacement*. This is only possible in non-destructive sampling, i.e. when the observation process does not modify the sampled unit (examples when sampling with replacement is not possible are tearing experiments, investigations on slaughtered animals, cutting fruit from trees, harvests etc.). In random sampling without replacement, the first random chosen element is not put back in the population. In this case clearly $n < N$, but in the case of sampling *wr* the same element can appear several times in the sample and it is possible for n to be larger than N.

Let the observations in the sample be $y_1, y_2, \ldots, y_n$. From this sample the sample mean

$$\bar{y} = \sum_{i=1}^{n} y_i / n \text{ and the sample variance}$$

$$s^2 = \sum_{i=1}^{n}(y_i - \bar{y})^2 / (n - 1) = \left[\sum_{i=1}^{n} y_i^2 - \left(\sum_{i=1}^{n} y_i\right)^2 / n\right] / (n - 1) \qquad (3.10)$$

are calculated.

The corresponding estimator $\bar{y}$ is unbiased for μ both for sampling *wr* and *wor*. In the case of sampling *wr* the distribution of $\bar{y}$ has variance $\text{var}(\bar{y}) = \sigma^2/n$ and in the case of sampling *wor* $\text{var}(\bar{y}) = (\sigma^2/n)[(N-n)/(N-1)]$.

For sampling *wr* the distribution of the sample variance s^2 has expectation $E(s^2) = \sigma^2$ and variance $\text{var}(s^2) = \sigma^4[(\mu_4/(\sigma^2)^2 - 3)/n + 2/(n-1)]$.

Hence for sampling *wr* s^2 is an unbiased estimator for σ^2 and an unbiased estimator for $\text{var}(\bar{y})$ is s^2/n.

In the case of sampling *wor* the distribution of the sample variance s^2 has mean $E(s^2) = \sigma^2(N/(N-1)) = S^2$ and variance $\text{var}(s^2) = \sigma^4[\{(\mu_4/(\sigma^2)^2 - 3)/n\} \cdot c_1 + (2/(n-1)) \cdot c_2]$ where

$$c_1 = \frac{N}{N-1}(1 - \frac{N-1}{n-1} \cdot \frac{n-2}{N-2} \cdot \frac{n-3}{N-3}) \text{ and}$$

$$c_2 = \frac{N}{N-1}(1 - \frac{1}{2} \cdot \frac{n-1}{N-1} - \frac{1}{2} \cdot \frac{N}{n} \cdot \frac{n-2}{N-2} \cdot \frac{n-3}{N-3}).$$

Hence for sampling *wor*

$$s^2(N-1)/N \qquad (3.11)$$

is an *unbiased estimator* for σ^2 and an unbiased estimator for $\text{var}(\bar{y}) = (S^2/n)\cdot(N-n)/N$ is $(s^2/n)\cdot(N-n)/N = (s^2/n)\cdot(1 - n/N)$ where $1 - n/N$ is called the finite population correction. In practice simple *random sampling without replacement* is the usual procedure.

Example 3.2

Let the population be $\{Y_1 = 10,\ Y_2 = 12,\ Y_3 = 16,\ Y_4 = 18,\ Y_5 = 24\}$ with $N = 5$. This gives:

$$\mu_1 = \mu = \sum_{i=1}^{N} Y_i/N = 16 \qquad \text{Population mean}$$

$$\mu_2 = \sigma^2 = \sum_{i=1}^{N} (Y_i-\mu)^2/N = 24 \qquad \text{Population variance}$$

$$\mu_3 = \sum_{i=1}^{N} (Y_i-\mu)^3/N = 48$$

$$\text{and } \gamma_1 = \mu_3/(\sigma^2)^{3/2} = 0.40825$$

$$\mu_4 = \sum_{i=1}^{N} (Y_i-\mu)^4/N = 1132.8$$

$$\text{and } \gamma_2 = \mu_4/(\sigma^2)^2 - 3 = -1.03333.$$

Random sampling with replacement with sample size $n = 2$ gives 25 possible samples.

ordered sample	$\bar{y}$	s^2	ordered sample	$\bar{y}$	s^2
(10,10)	10	0	(16,18)	17	2
(10,12)	11	2	(16,24)	20	32
(10,16)	13	18	(18,10)	14	32
(10,18)	14	32	(18,12)	15	18
(10,24)	17	98	(18,16)	17	2
(12,10)	11	2	(18,18)	18	0
(12,12)	12	0	(18,24)	21	18
(12,16)	14	8	(24,10)	17	98
(12,18)	15	18	(24,12)	18	72
(12,24)	18	72	(24,16)	20	32
(16,10)	13	18	(24,18)	21	18
(16,12)	14	8	(24,24)	24	0
(16,16)	16	0			

By an unordered sample we mean a set containing all samples having the same particular elements in any possible order. For example $\{10,24\}$ contains (10,24) and (24,10), while $\{16,16\}$ includes only the one case (16,16).

Direct calculation from the distribution or from the formulae gives the same results:

$$E(\bar{y}) = \bar{\bar{y}} = \sum_{i=1}^{25} \bar{y}_i\,/25 = 16 \ ; \ E(\bar{y}) = \mu = 16;$$

$$\text{var}(\bar{y}) = \sum_{i=1}^{25} (\bar{y}_i - \bar{\bar{y}})^2 / 25 = 12 \ ; \ \text{var}(\bar{y}) = \frac{\sigma^2}{n} = \frac{24}{2} = 12;$$

$$E(s^2) = \bar{s}^2 = \sum_{i=1}^{25} s_i^2 / 25 = 24 \ ; \ E(s^2) = \sigma^2 = 24;$$

$$\text{var}(s^2) = \sum_{i=1}^{25} (s_i^2 - \bar{s}^2)^2 / 25 = 854.4;$$

$$\text{var}(s^2) = \sigma^4 \left(\frac{1}{n}(\gamma_2) + \frac{2}{n-1} \right) = 24^2 \left(\frac{1}{2}\left(\frac{1132.8}{24^2} - 3 \right) + \frac{2}{2-1} \right) = 854.4.$$

The unbiased estimator for μ is $\bar{y}$, for σ^2 is s^2 and for var $(\bar{y})$ is s^2/n.

Random sampling without replacement with sample size $n = 2$ gives 20 possible samples, namely the same samples as sampling with replacement with $n = 2$ omitting the 5 samples (10,10), (12,12), (16,16), (18,18) and (24,24).

Again direct calculations from the distribution or from the formulae give the same results:

$$E(\bar{y}) = \bar{\bar{y}} = \sum_{i=1}^{20} \bar{y}_i / 20 = 16 \ ; \ E(\bar{y}) = \mu = 16$$

$$\text{var}(\bar{y}) = \sum_{i=1}^{20} (\bar{y}_i - \bar{\bar{y}})^2 / 20 = 9 \ ; \ \text{var}(\bar{y}) = \frac{\sigma^2}{n}\left(\frac{N-n}{N-1} \right) = \frac{24}{2}\left(\frac{5-2}{5-1} \right) = 9;$$

$$E(s^2) = \bar{s}^2 = \sum_{i=1}^{20} s_i^2 / 20 = 30 \ ; \ E(s^2) = \frac{N}{N-1}\sigma^2 = \frac{5}{4} \cdot 24 = 30;$$

$$\text{var}(s^2) = \sum_{i=1}^{20} (s_i^2 - \bar{s}^2)^2 / 20 = 888;$$

$$\text{var}(s^2) = \sigma^4 \left(\frac{1}{n}(\gamma_2)c_1 + \frac{2}{n-1}c_2 \right)$$

with $\gamma_2 = \mu_4 / (\sigma^2)^2 - 3 = 1132.8 / 24^2 - 3 = -1.0333, \ n = 2,$

$$c_1 = \frac{N}{N-1}\left(1 - \frac{N-1}{n-1} \cdot \frac{n-2}{N-2} \cdot \frac{n-3}{N-3} \right) = \frac{5}{4}(1-0) = \frac{5}{4}, \ \text{and}$$

$$c_2 = \frac{N}{N-1}\left(1 - \frac{1}{2}\frac{n-1}{N-1} - \frac{1}{2}\frac{N}{n} \cdot \frac{n-2}{N-2} \cdot \frac{n-3}{N-3} \right) = \frac{5}{4}(1 - \frac{1}{2}\cdot\frac{1}{4} - 0) = \frac{35}{32},$$

hence

$$\text{var}(s^2) = 24^2 \left(\frac{1}{2}(\frac{1132.8}{24^2} - 3)\frac{5}{4} + \frac{2}{1}\cdot\frac{35}{32} \right) = 888 .$$

The unbiased estimators are:

for μ: $\bar{y}$,

for σ^2: $s^2(N-1)/N$

and for var($\bar{y}$): $(s^2/n)(1-n/N)$.

If we take a random sample *without replacement* of size $n = 4$ the following samples are possible

unordered sample	frequency f	$\bar{y}$	s^2
{10,12,16,18}	24	14	13.33333
{10,12,16,24}	24	15.5	38.33333
{10,12,18,24}	24	16	40
{10,16,18,24}	24	17	33.33333
{12,16,18,24}	24	17.5	25

For example the unordered sample {10,12,16,18} consists of the 24 ordered samples (10,12,16,18), (10,12,18,16), ..., (18,16,12,10).

$$E(\bar{y}) = \bar{\bar{y}} = \Sigma\, f_i\bar{y}_i/\Sigma f_i = 16 \;;\; E(\bar{y}) = \mu = 16$$

$$\text{var}(\bar{y}) = \Sigma\, f_i(\bar{y}_i - \bar{\bar{y}})^2/\Sigma\, f_i = \frac{\Sigma\, f_i\bar{y}_i^2 - (\Sigma\, f_i\bar{y}_i)^2/120}{120} = 1.5$$

$$\text{var}(\bar{y}) = \frac{\sigma^2}{n}(\frac{N-n}{N-1}) = \frac{24}{4}\cdot\frac{5-4}{5-1} = 1.5.$$

$$E(s^2) = \bar{s}^2 = \Sigma\, f_i s_i^2/120 = 30.$$

$$E(s^2) = \frac{N}{N-1}\sigma^2 = \frac{5}{4}\cdot 24 = 30.$$

$$\text{var}(s^2) = \Sigma\, f_i(s_i^2 - \bar{s}^2)^2/120 = 96.66667.$$

$$\text{var}(s^2) = \sigma^4\left(\frac{1}{n}(\gamma_2)c_1 + \frac{2}{n-1}c_2\right)$$

with $\gamma_2 = -1.0333$, $n = 4$,

$$c_1 = \frac{N}{N-1}(1 - \frac{N-1}{n-1}\cdot\frac{n-2}{N-2}\cdot\frac{n-3}{N-3}) = \frac{5}{4}(1 - \frac{4}{3}\cdot\frac{2}{3}\cdot\frac{1}{2}) = \frac{5}{4}\cdot\frac{5}{9} = \frac{25}{36}$$

$$c_2 = \frac{N}{N-1}(1 - \frac{1}{2}\frac{n-1}{N-1} - \frac{1}{2}\frac{N}{n}\cdot\frac{n-2}{N-2}\cdot\frac{n-3}{N-3}) = \frac{5}{4}(1 - \frac{1}{2}\cdot\frac{3}{4} - \frac{1}{2}\cdot\frac{5}{2}\cdot\frac{2}{4}\cdot\frac{3}{2}\cdot\frac{1}{2})$$

$$= \frac{5}{4}\cdot\frac{10}{24} = \frac{5}{4}\cdot\frac{5}{12} = \frac{25}{48}$$

$$\text{var}(s^2) = 24^2\left(\frac{1}{4}(\frac{1132.8}{24^2} - 3)\frac{25}{36} + \frac{2}{3}\cdot\frac{25}{48}\right) = 96.66667.$$

If we wish to determine the minimum sample size n which will ensure that $\text{var}(\hat{\mu}) \le K$, then for random sampling with replacement the formula is

$$n = \text{CEIL}\left(\frac{\sigma^2}{K}\right)$$

and for sampling without replacement it becomes

$$n = \text{CEIL} \left[\frac{N}{N-1} \frac{\sigma^2}{K + \dfrac{\sigma^2}{N-1}} \right] \approx \text{CEIL} \left[\frac{\sigma^2}{K + \dfrac{\sigma^2}{N}} \right]$$

Further special cases are described in VB 3/21/5000 - 3/21/5090.

3.2   Interval Estimation

Interval estimation means the construction of a *random region* in the *parameter space* (this region will be an interval if the parameter space is the real line), whose boundaries are functions of the y_i, in such a way that the probability that this region includes the unknown parameter θ or a function $\psi = g(\theta)$ is $1-\alpha$. The probability $1-\alpha$ is called the *confidence coefficient*. In the case of an interval we call the boundaries *confidence limits*. If we take a sample and calculate the boundaries of the interval from realisations of the components of the random sample, then we must regard our actual confidence interval as a "realised" interval.   According to our understanding it is not possible to make a *probability statement* about the coverage of the parameter by such in interval.   The parameter is a real number even if it is unknown, and our *confidence interval* is a real interval. Thus either it includes the parameter or it does not. If a researcher frequently quotes confidence intervals with confidence coefficient 0.95, then a frequency interpretation is possible, and we can say that on about 95% of occasions the interval will include the parameter, and in about 5% of cases it will not. The situation is analogous to a clinic where the chance of success of a particular operation is 95%. We would prefer to go to this clinic than to one where the success rate is 80%, although for a particular patient a failure is possible in both cases, and if that happens the patient is not interested in whether he is in a good or bad clinic.

3.2.1   Confidence Intervals for the Parameters of a Distribution

If ψ is a real function, then the confidence region is a real interval, a so-called *confidence interval*. We restrict ourselves to such cases, i.e. to confidence intervals for ψ, where ψ by a proper choice of $g(\theta)$ is always a real number.

If only one of the boundaries of the interval is random and thus dependent on the outcome of the experiment, and the other is one or other of the boundaries of the parameter space, then we call the interval a one-sided confidence interval, otherwise it is two-sided. In this book we shall mostly consider only two-sided confidence intervals, which are usually more appropriate in practical situations. The procedures in VB give the one-sided confidence intervals (upper and lower) as well as a two-sided one.

In the following sections we present formulae for the evaluation of confidence limits from samples of size n. The determination of the n for such a sample is part of the experimental planning process.

3.2.1.1 Confidence Intervals for the Expectation of the Normal Distribution

Case (a) σ^2 *known:*

Suppose that σ^2 is known for a particular normal distribution, and that we need a confidence interval for μ. For this we use the fact that

$$u = \frac{\bar{y}-\mu}{\sigma}\sqrt{n} \qquad\qquad (3.12)$$

follows an $N(0;1)$ distribution. Defining $u(1-\alpha/2)$ as the $(1-\alpha/2)$-quantile of the standardised normal distribution, we have

$$P\{-u(1-\frac{\alpha}{2}) \le u \le u(1-\frac{\alpha}{2})\} = 1-\alpha$$

and from this, by using $u = \frac{\bar{y}-\mu}{\sigma}\sqrt{n}$ it follows that the interval

$$[\bar{y}-u(1-\frac{\alpha}{2})\frac{\sigma}{\sqrt{n}} \;\; ; \;\; \bar{y}+u(1-\frac{\alpha}{2})\frac{\sigma}{\sqrt{n}}] \qquad\qquad (3.13)$$

is a $(1-\alpha)$-confidence interval for μ.
This interval is optimal; it can be shown that under the assumptions above this interval has the smallest expected width of all $(1-\alpha)$-confidence intervals. The expected half-width E(H) is

$$E(H)=u(1-\frac{\alpha}{2})\frac{\sigma}{\sqrt{n}}.$$

If the precision requirement states that the expected half-width must be less than or equal to d, then, for a given α, n has to be determined so that

$$u(1-\frac{\alpha}{2})\frac{\sigma}{\sqrt{n}} \le d,$$

it follows that

$$n = \text{CEIL}\left(u^2(1-\frac{\alpha}{2})\frac{\sigma^2}{d^2}\right), \qquad\qquad (3.14)$$

with d as the upper bound for the expected half-width.

If on the other hand the precision requirement states that both confidence limits must not differ by more than d from the parameter μ with given probability $1-\beta$, then, following (BOCK, 1998) we must choose

$$n = \text{CEIL}\left[\frac{\sigma^2}{d^2}\cdot\left[u(1-\alpha/2)+u(1-\beta/2)\right]^2\right]. \qquad\qquad (3.14a)$$

Case (b) σ^2 *unknown:*

Assume now that σ^2 is unknown and again that under the requirements mentioned above a confidence interval for μ has to be constructed. The unknown σ in the denominator of u will then be replaced by the square root s of the sample variance s^2. The resulting statistic

$$t = \frac{\bar{y}-\mu}{s}\sqrt{n}$$

has a (central) t-distribution with $n-1$ degrees of freedom. If $t(n-1; 1-\alpha/2)$ is the

$(1-\alpha/2)$-quantile of the central t-distribution with n-1 degrees of freedom, then a $(1-\alpha)$-confidence interval for μ is given by

$$[\bar{y}-t(n-1;1-\frac{\alpha}{2})\frac{s}{\sqrt{n}} \quad ; \quad \bar{y}+t(n-1;1-\frac{\alpha}{2})\frac{s}{\sqrt{n}}] \tag{3.15}$$

The expected half-width of the interval (3.15) is

$$t(n-1;1-\frac{\alpha}{2})\frac{E(s)}{\sqrt{n}} \tag{3.16}$$

We use the approximation $E(s) \cong \sigma$, which works well if $n \geq 20$.
In accordance with our first precision requirement we have to determine the smallest integer n so that

$$t(n-1;1-\frac{\alpha}{2}).\frac{\sigma}{\sqrt{n}} \leq d \tag{3.17}$$

The CADEMO-*light* program uses the exact formula for $E(s)$.

For the calculation of the sample size n we have to solve two problems:

Problem 1:
The inequality (3.17) cannot be solved explicitly for n, but we can write (3.17) as follows:

$$n \geq h(n) \tag{3.18}$$

with

$$h(n) = \mathrm{CEIL}\left(\frac{\sigma^2}{d^2} \cdot t^2(n-1;1-\frac{\alpha}{2})\right) \tag{3.19}$$

We can try to find the smallest value of n (starting with $n = 2, 3, ...$) which fulfils the requirement (3.18) and at the same time also (3.17). This can be inefficient and time consuming. For simplification we propose the following iterative algorithm A. Because $h(n)$ is a monotonic decreasing function in n, this algorithm always leads to the required result.

Algorithm A
Choose a certain starting value n_0 and calculate iteratively the values $n_1, n_2, n_3, ...$ by the recursive relation $n_{i+1} = h(n_i)$ until either $n_i = n_{i-1}$ or $|n_i - n_{i-1}| \geq |n_{i-1} - n_{i-2}|$. In the first case $n = n_i = n_{i-1}$ is the solution. In the second case we can find a solution by systematic search starting with $n = \min (n_{i-1}, n_{i-2})$.
This algorithm often converges to the solution after one or two steps; we will use it in subsequent sections and chapters.

Problem 2:
The smallest n for the inequality (3.17) depends on the unknown variance σ^2.

To solve problem 2 we use algorithm B.

1. We look for some *a priori* information (an experiment in the past, results from the literature) $\tilde{\sigma}^2$ about σ^2 and use this as a rough estimate of σ^2. Of course such an approach gives only an estimate of the sample size n we are looking for.

2. If step 1 is not possible because we cannot get such information, then we can obtain an estimate of the unknown variance by estimating the smallest possible and the largest possible observation and calculating the difference between them. We divide this difference by 6 (or by 5 or 4 as some authors recommend) to estimate σ.

3. If even step 2 will not work or seems to be too heuristic, we can get a better solution for this problem by using a sequential procedure based on a two stage method of STEIN (1945). In the first stage of an experiment with between 10 and 30 units the variance σ^2 is estimated. The estimate is then used to calculate the total sample size. If the total sample size is smaller than or equal to the number used in the first step, then our chosen size for the first stage is sufficient, otherwise the rest of the experimental units must be used to generate a second sample in the procedure.

By using this procedure we assume that experimental conditions for both stages are the same. Also Algorithm B will be used in subsequent sections and chapters.

Often it is difficult to calculate the expected length d of a confidence interval. In our case we replace (3.16) by the approximation

$$H(E[s]) = t(n\text{-}1;1\text{-}\frac{\alpha}{2})\sqrt{\frac{s^2}{n}} \ .$$

This corresponds to the approximation already used above: $E(s) \approx \sigma$.

For the second precision requirement referred to above (3.14a), there is the following approximation analogous to (3.14a)

$$n = \text{CEIL}\left[\frac{\sigma^2}{d^2}\cdot\left[t(n-1;1-\alpha/2)+t(n-1;1-\beta/2)\right]^2\right] \qquad (3.19a)$$

Example 3.1 – continued

In Table 3.1 we calculate a (realised) 95% confidence interval ($\alpha = 0.05$) for the mean of the population from which the y_i have been drawn. From Figure 3.3 we know that

$$\bar{y} = 11.531$$

and we calculate the standard error of the mean $\dfrac{s}{\sqrt{n}} = \dfrac{2.952}{\sqrt{13}} = 0.819$.

From Table A1 we find

$$t(12; 0.975) = 2.1788$$

and the (realised) 95% confidence interval becomes

$$[11.531 - 0.819 \cdot 2.1788;\ 11.531 + 0.819 \cdot 2.1788] = [9.75;\ 13.31].$$

To do the calculation in SPSS we use the menu sequence Analyze - Compare Means - One-Sample T Test and choose y as the Test Variable (we will describe the test in section 3.4).

If we use the Options button we obtain a screen where we can choose $(1-\alpha)$ 100%. Here we accept the default value 95%.
The result is given in the output in Figure 3.5 (after deleting some irrelevant information).

One Sample Test

Variable	Mean Difference	95% Confidence Interval for the Difference	
		Lower	Upper
y	11.53077	9.7469	13.3146

Figure 3.5 *Confidence interval for the mean of the y-values in Table 3.1*

Denoting the expected half-width of the $(1-\alpha)$ confidence interval by $E(H)$ we can express the given precision requirement as $E(H) \le d$ or

$$t(n-1; 1-\frac{\alpha}{2}) \cdot E(s)/\sqrt{n} \le d.$$

Here s again denotes the sample standard deviation. Approximating its expected value by σ and solving the inequality for n we get

$$n = \text{CEIL}\left[\frac{t^2(n-1;1-\frac{\alpha}{2})\sigma^2}{d^2}\right] \qquad (3.20)$$

For this equation to be useful, d, α, and σ^2 have to be known. For α we usually choose one of the values $0.01; 0.05; 0.1$ and hence: $(1-\alpha) = 0.99; 0.95; 0.90$.
Since the percentile of the t-distribution requires knowledge of n, the equation (3.20) will be solved by the iterative Algorithm A.
From (3.20) it can also be seen that n increases with σ^2 and decreases with d^2. It actually depends only on the ratio d/σ. Therefore the precision requirement may sometimes be defined in terms of d/σ. This has the advantage that σ need not be known in advance, and it is not necessary to use Algorithm B. If we put $d = c \cdot \sigma$ (typically $c \le 1$) the necessary sample size is calculated from:

$$n = \text{CEIL}\left[\frac{t^2(n-1;1-\frac{\alpha}{2})}{c^2}\right] \qquad (3.21)$$

Table 3.2 gives the *minimal sample size n* for selected values of α and $d = c \cdot \sigma$

The numbers in braces are the values obtained according to (3.19a) for $\beta = 0.2$.

Table 3.2   *Sample size n for selected values of α and c.*

$d = c \cdot \sigma$	$\frac{1}{2}\sigma$	$\frac{1}{3}\sigma$	$\frac{1}{4}\sigma$	$\frac{1}{5}\sigma$
$\alpha = 0.01$	31(63)	64(137)	110(242)	170(375)
$\alpha = 0.05$	18(45)	38(97)	64(171)	99(265)
$\alpha = 0.10$	13(36)	27(79)	46(139)	70(216)

Example 3.3

We will verify the entry 64 in Table 3.2 for $\alpha = 0.05$ and $d = 0.25\sigma$.
From Table A1 we find for $n_0 = \infty$

$$t(\infty; 0.975) = 1.96,$$

and from (3.21) we obtain

$$n_1 = \text{CEIL}\left[\frac{1.96^2}{0.25^2}\right] = \text{CEIL}[61.47] = 62.$$

Now we look up

$$t(61; 0.975) = 1.9996$$

and this gives

$$n_2 = \text{CEIL}\left[\frac{1.9996^2}{0.25^2}\right] = \text{CEIL}[63.97] = 64.$$

Finally with

$$t(63; 0.975) = 1.9983$$

n_3 becomes

$$n_3 = \text{CEIL}\left[\frac{1.9983^2}{0.25^2}\right] = \text{CEIL}[63.89] = 64$$

and thus $n = 64$ is the solution.

The CEIL operator accelerates the convergence of the iteration algorithm.

We will now calculate this value from table 3.2 using the CADEMO-*light* programme. When CL starts up, a decision must be made whether we want to calculate a sample size or construct an experimental design. We choose the first option, and we then have the choice between:
One-sample problem
Two sample problem with dependent and
                                   with independent samples[2]
k Sample problem (k>2)
We choose the one-sample problem option for this example, and use the menu sequence -mean - estimation. If we enter the precision requirements given above, we obtain a sample size of 64 as before.

---

[2]   Both SPSS and CADEMO use the misleading expression "dependent samples" for random samples of paired observations.

Example 3.1 - continued

Let us use the variance estimated $s^2 = 3.947$ for the litter weight in the first litter as shown in Figure 3.3 to calculate the sample size needed to construct a 0.9-confidence interval for this character with an expected length not larger than 2 g. The precision requirements are shown in Figure 3.6 and the result in Figure 3.7.

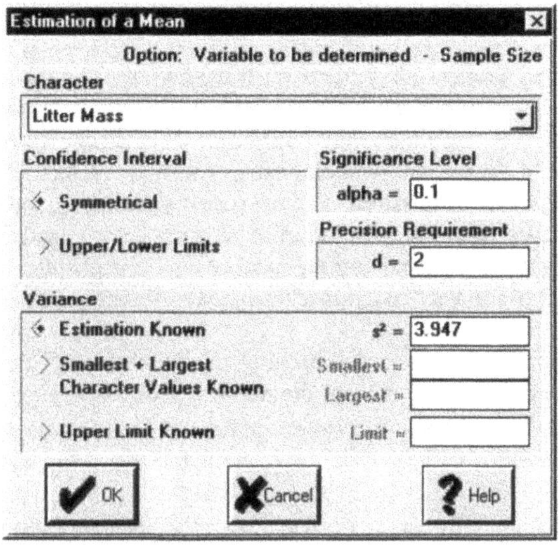

Figure 3.6 *Using CL to calculate a sample size*

```
Decision:
One Sample Problem
Estimation of a Mean
Determination of Sample Size
```

```
Character:
Litter Mass

 For the specified parameters
       s² = 3.9470,
        d = 2.0000,
        α = 0.1000
 and a symmetrical Confidence Interval
 a necessary sample size of
        n = 5
 results.
```

Figure 3.7 *Sample size corresponding to a given d*

Conversely CADEMO-*light* allows us to calculate the upper bound for the expected length of a 0.9-confidence interval if $s = 2$ and $n = 13$ as in Example 3.1. We do this using the menu item "Option" and defining the expected length (in place of the sample size) as the value which has to be calculated. The result is for $s^2 = 3.947$, $n = 13$ and $\alpha = 0.1$ as in Example 3.1 a d-value of 0.9821.

3.2.1.2 Confidence Intervals for the Expectation of the Normal Distribution in the Presence of a Noise Factor

The mean μ of a normally distributed variable may have to be estimated when the observations depend on a noise factor. The following example illustrates this.

Example 3.4

Returning to the scenario described in example 2.1, the average fuel consumption of a certain type of a lorry has to be estimated using data on the performance obtained from different vehicles which may have come from different production runs. The factor "lorry" is thus a random noise factor (or block factor) and should therefore be eliminated as far as possible. For the investigation a random sample of vehicles is to be drawn from the population of all such lorries produced. An adequate model for this situation is the model equation (2.1) (in chapter 4 we will call this model a Model II one-way analysis of variance and use equation (4.7)).
The design:
Planning this experiment thus means determining the number a of cars as the levels of the noise factor (block factor) and the number n_i of journeys by vehicle i ($i = 1, ..., a$). The required precision for the estimation of the mean μ is defined by the expected half-width d of a confidence interval for μ and the confidence coefficient $(1-\alpha)$.
For an optimal design of experiment we need estimates s_a^2 and s_R^2 of the variance components σ_a^2 (between the cars) and σ_R^2 (residual variance) or an estimate $\hat{\theta}$ of the intraclass-correlation coefficient $\theta = \sigma_a^2/(\sigma_a^2+\sigma_R^2)$.
If no costs are taken into account, we define a design as optimal if it minimises $N = \Sigma n_i$. Without any restrictions on n_i and a, this leads to $n_i = n = 1$ and N defined by

$$N = \text{CEIL}\left[\frac{t^2(N-1;1-\frac{\alpha}{2})}{c^2}\right] \tag{3.22}$$

where

$$c = \frac{d}{\sqrt{s_a^2 + s_R^2}}. \tag{3.23}$$

If, on the other hand a lower bound, n_0 for n_i is given, then we let $n_i = n_0$, ($i = 1, ..., a$) and calculate a iteratively from

$$a = \text{CEIL}\left[\frac{\left(\hat{\theta} - \frac{1-\hat{\theta}}{n_0}\right)t^2(a-1;1-\frac{\alpha}{2})}{c^2}\right]$$

where c is as in (3.23) and $\hat{\theta}=s_a^2/(s_a^2+s_R^2)$.

If a is fixed in advance (for example as an upper limit), we must first check the condition

$$c^2 > \frac{\hat{\theta}}{a} \cdot t^2(a-1;1-\frac{\alpha}{2}).$$

If this is fulfilled, then the value n^* is calculated from

$$n^* = \text{CEIL}\left[\frac{\left(1-\hat{\theta}\right)t^2\left(a-1;1-\frac{\alpha}{2}\right)}{c^2a - \hat{\theta}t^2\left(a-1;1-\frac{\alpha}{2}\right)}\right]$$

A cost-optimal design can be found in HERRENDÖRFER and SCHMIDT (1978). Experiment sizes and cost-optimal plans can be determined using CADEMO-MEANS.

Analysis:
An exact confidence interval can be calculated if the number n of journeys made by each lorry is constant. Let

$$\bar{y}.. = \frac{1}{an}\sum_{i=1}^{a}\sum_{j=1}^{n}y_{ij} \qquad (3.24)$$

be the average of all $N = an$ observations. We obtain the $(1-\alpha)$-confidence interval

$$[\bar{y}.. - t(a-1;1-\frac{\alpha}{2})\sqrt{\frac{MS_A}{N}}; \bar{y}.. + t(a-1;1-\frac{\alpha}{2})\sqrt{\frac{MS_A}{N}}] \qquad (3.25)$$

with MS_A from table 4.2 in chapter 4

Example 3.4 - continued
We want to construct the optimum design for the estimation of the average fuel consumption in example 3.4. In equation (2.1), a is the number of lorries used in the experiment, and n_i the number of trips made by the i-th lorry. We want to find a 95% confidence interval for μ having an expected half-width no greater than 0.3 (y_{ij} is the fuel consumption in litres per 100km).
If we know beforehand that the sum of the variance components is 0.36, then using equation (3.23) we find that $c = 0.5$. We want to find the design ($a, n_1, ..., n_a$) which minimises $N = \Sigma n_i$.
As we shell see, we must now use each selected vehicle for one journey only ($n_i=1$ for all i), and use equation (3.22) to determine the number of vehicles. We start with $a = \infty$ and find that $t(\infty;0.975) = 1.96$, giving $a = 16$. Then $t(15;0.975) = 2.1314$ gives the value $a = 19$, and $t(18;0.975) = 2.1009$ which leads to $a = 18$. Since $t(17;0.975) = 2.1098$ the final value of a is 18.
We will now repeat this Example using CADEMO-MEANS.
In MEANS we select Estimation – of a Mean – Confounding factor influence, and after entering the prerequisites for the example, in which we have given the sum of the components of variance as 0.3 + 0.06 (all divisions lead to the same result) we obtain Figure 3.8.

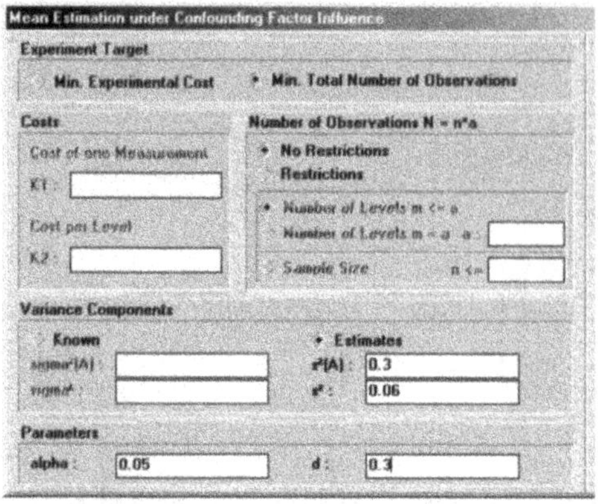

Figure 3.8 *Predetermined precision requirements for Example 3.4*

After clicking OK, the result is 18 levels, each with one observation. If we can only manage a maximum of 16 levels, we enter this in Figure 3.8 after clicking the "Restrictions" button. In this case 4 replications are needed in each of the 16 levels. If we wish to minimise the costs of the experiment, we select the option in the top left hand corner of Figure 3.8.

3.2.1.3 Confidence Intervals for the Mean and Total from a Survey.

For random sampling without replacement with samples with size n we found in section 3.1.3 that an unbiased estimator for the Population Mean $\mu = \overline{Y}$ is $\overline{y}$ and for its variance var($\overline{y}$) the unbiased estimator is

$$\hat{var}(\overline{y}) = (s^2/n)(1-n/N)$$ or equivalently the *standard error* of this estimator is

$$SE(\overline{y}) = \sqrt{(s^2/n)(1-n/N)}.$$ If $n < 0.1 \cdot N$ the finite population correction $1-n/N$ can be replaced by 1. An approximate $(1-\alpha)$-confidence interval for the population mean $\mu = \overline{Y}$ is given by

$$[\overline{y}-SE(\overline{y}) \cdot t(n-1; 1-\alpha/2); \ \overline{y} + SE(\overline{y}) \cdot t(n-1; 1-\alpha/2)] \tag{3.26}$$

For the Population Total $N\overline{Y} = N\mu$ the unbiased estimator is $N\overline{y}$. The standard error of $N\overline{y}$ is $SE(N\overline{y}) = \sqrt{N^2\hat{var}(\overline{y})} = N \cdot SE(\overline{y})$. The approximate $(1-\alpha)$-confidence interval for the Population Total is then given by

$$[N\overline{y} - N \cdot SE(\overline{y}) \cdot t(n-1; 1-\alpha/2); \ N\overline{y} + N \cdot SE(\overline{y}) \cdot t(n-1; 1-\alpha/2)]. \tag{3.27}$$

We now discuss the sample size determination problem in a simple random sampling *without replacement* scheme when we have prior information about $S^2 = \sigma^2 N/(N-1)$ in a population; the information is in the form of an estimate s^2.

Usually one wishes to control the *relative* error r in the estimated population mean, and we shall use this specification. If our simple random sample *wor* has mean $\overline{y}$, then we require (assuming $\overline{Y} > 0$)

$$P(|(\overline{y}-\overline{Y})/\overline{Y}| \geq r) = P(|\overline{y}-\overline{Y}| \geq r\overline{Y}) = \alpha \quad \text{i.e.} \quad P(|\overline{y}-\overline{Y}| < r\overline{Y}) = 1-\alpha.$$

From equation (3.26) for the approximate $(1-\alpha)$-confidence interval for $\overline{Y}$ it follows:

$$P(|\,\overline{y}-\overline{Y}\,| < SE(\overline{y}) \cdot t(n-1;\, 1-\alpha/2)) = 1-\alpha$$

hence

$$r\overline{Y} = \sqrt{[(s^2/n)(1-n/N)]} \cdot t(n-1;\, 1-\alpha/2).$$

We use the iterative Algorithm A from section 3.2.1.1 to solve the equation
$$n = \text{CEIL}\{[t(n-1;\, 1-\alpha/2)]^2 \cdot s^2/(r\cdot\overline{Y})^2\}.$$

If we wish to limit the expected width of the $(1-\alpha)$-confidence interval by saying it must not be larger than $2d$ or $P(|\,\overline{y}-\overline{Y}\,| < d) = 1-\alpha$, the formula is then $n = n_0/[1+(n_0/N)]$ where $n_0 = \text{CEIL}\{[t(n-1;\, 1-\alpha/2)]^2 \cdot s^2/d^2\}$ or $d = r\overline{Y}$ where the expected half-width of the $(1-\alpha)$-confidence interval is expressed as the relative error r times $\overline{Y}$.

3.2.1.4 Confidence Interval for the Variance of the Normal Distribution

The parameter space for a variance is the positive real line. The precision requirement for this parameter differs somewhat from those for the location parameter. Firstly we work with the length of the interval and not the half-length. This is because of the property of the chi-squared distribution which results in the interval not being symmetrical about the unknown parameter. Moreover we regard the ratio of this length to the expected middle point of the interval as representing the closeness to the real parameter value.
We can find a confidence interval for σ^2 using s^2, the sample variance from a random sample, and also the $(1-\alpha)$-quantile of the chi-square distribution on $n-1$ degrees of freedom (Table A2). The interval is given by

$$\left[\frac{(n-1)s^2}{\chi^2\left(n-1;\, 1-\dfrac{\alpha}{2}\right)};\, \frac{(n-1)s^2}{\chi^2\left(n-1;\, \dfrac{\alpha}{2}\right)} \right] \tag{3.28}$$

Unlike the intervals (3.13) and (3.15), this interval does not have the shortest expected length τ of all intervals with the same confidence coefficient. To obtain this optimal interval we must separate α into two parts α_1 and α_2 so that the relative expected length attains a minimum. Since the improvement is slight and the computations heavy (and for hand calculations the relevant tables are not available) equation (3.28) is generally used, even in computer packages, where the difficulties would not arise.
Depending on $1-\alpha$ and the relative expected length τ, the required sample size is obtained by a systematic search to find n which satisfies

$$\tau = \frac{\chi^2(n-1;\, 1-\dfrac{\alpha}{2}) - \chi^2(n-1;\, \dfrac{\alpha}{2})}{\chi^2(n-1;\, 1-\dfrac{\alpha}{2}) + \chi^2(n-1;\, \dfrac{\alpha}{2})} \tag{3.29}$$

Example 3.1 -continued

We will again presume that the normality assumption for our litter weights is justified, and we wish to construct a 90% confidence interval for the variance σ^2 of the x-values. The expected relative deviation of the confidence limits from the mid-interval value should not exceed ± 0.25. How large must the sample size be? We will use the CL-program (the hand calculations are very tedious); the command sequence is Sample size - One sample problem - Variance - Estimation. After entering the parameters we obtain the output in Figure 3.9

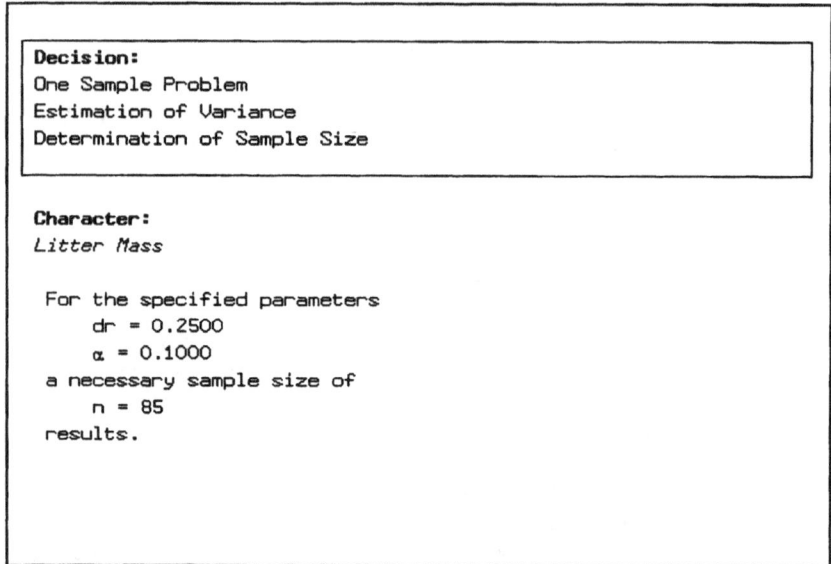

```
Decision:
One Sample Problem
Estimation of Variance
Determination of Sample Size


Character:
Litter Mass

  For the specified parameters
       dr = 0.2500
       α = 0.1000
  a necessary sample size of
       n = 85
  results.
```

Figure 3.9 *Calculation of the sample size for estimating a variance*

We see that $n = 85$, which we also find from Table 3.3. If we substitute $n = 85$ in (3.29), we quickly find that if $\tau(=dr$ in CADEMO) equals 0.25, the equation is approximately satisfied.

For the $n = 13$ x-values in example 3.1 we have $s^2 = 3.947$ (see Figure 3.3). From Table A2 we find $\chi^2(12; 0.05) = 5.226$ and $\chi^2(12; 0.95) = 21.03$, and a 90% confidence interval is

$$\left[\frac{12 \cdot 3.947}{21.03} ; \frac{12 \cdot 3.947}{5.226} \right] = [2.25 ; 9.06],$$

whose mid-point is 5.66; the relative deviation of the limits from this mid-point is 0.6, which is very large.

Table 3.3 contains solutions for n from (3.29) for various values of α and τ.

Table 3.3   Sample size n in relation to τ and α.

τ	α 0.05	α 0.10	τ	α 0.05	α 0.10	τ	α 0.05	α 0.10
0.04	4800	3382	0.24	131	93	0.44	37	27
0.05	3071	2164	0.25	120	85	0.45	35	25
0.06	2132	1503	0.26	111	79	0.46	34	24
0.07	1566	1104	0.27	103	73	0.47	32	23
0.08	1199	843	0.28	95	68	0.48	31	22
0.09	945	665	0.29	89	63	0.49	29	21
0.10	764	538	0.30	83	59	0.50	28	20
0.11	631	444	0.31	77	55	0.51	27	19
0.12	530	373	0.32	72	52	0.52	26	19
0.13	450	318	0.33	68	48	0.53	25	18
0.14	388	274	0.34	64	45	0.54	24	17
0.15	337	239	0.35	60	43	0.55	23	16
0.16	297	210	0.36	57	40	0.60	18	14
0.17	263	185	0.37	53	38	0.65	15	11
0.18	234	165	0.38	50	36	0.70	13	10
0.19	210	149	0.39	48	34	0.75	11	8
0.20	189	134	0.40	45	32	0.80	9	7
0.21	171	121	0.41	43	31	0.85	7	6
0.22	156	110	0.42	41	29	0.90	6	5
0.23	143	101	0.43	39	28	1.00	2	2

3.2.1.5 Confidence Intervals for Probabilities

We already know (section 3.1.2) that the parameter p of a *binomial distribution* can be estimated by the method of maximum likelihood as the relative frequency $\frac{y}{n}$ of the occurrence of the event A in n independent trials.

In n independent trials the absolute frequency y of the occurrence of the event A, whose probability is $p = P(A)$, follows a binomial distribution exactly. From this we can deduce that either there is an infinite population of objects, which each have a probability p of presenting the event A (and a probability $1-p$ of not presenting it), or we have a finite population of size N, in which Np objects present the event A and $N(1-p)$ do not. However y only follows a binomial distribution if we select the elements with replacement from this finite population. We will only consider this case. We now seek a confidence interval (having confidence coefficient $1-\alpha$) for the parameter p of a binomial distribution. An exact $(1-\alpha)$ confidence interval has the form:

$$[P_l(n, y, \alpha); P_u(n, y, \alpha)] \tag{3.30}$$

where P_l and P_u are the lower and upper limits, n is the sample size and y the number of elements in the sample which present the event A.
It can be shown that

$$P_l(n,y,\alpha) = \frac{y}{y+(n-y+1)F[2(n-y+1);2y;1-\frac{\alpha}{2}]} \qquad (3.31)$$

and

$$P_u(n,y,\alpha) = \frac{(y+1)F[2(y+1);2(n-y);1-\frac{\alpha}{2}]}{n-y + (y+1)F[2(y+1);2(n-y);1-\frac{\alpha}{2}]} \qquad (3.32)$$

where $F(f_1; f_2; P)$ is the *P-quantile* of the *F*-distribution (Table A3).

This interval is exact but often unnecessarily large.

Generally, for large n and with p close to 0.5, there is a shorter approximate $(1-\alpha)$-confidence interval. It is given by

$$[P_{Al} ; P_{Au}] \qquad (3.33)$$

where

$$P_{Al} = \frac{y + \frac{1}{2}u^2(1-\frac{\alpha}{2}) - K}{n + u^2(1-\frac{\alpha}{2})} \qquad (3.34)$$

and

$$P_{Au} = \frac{y + \frac{1}{2}u^2(1-\frac{\alpha}{2}) + K}{n + u^2(1-\frac{\alpha}{2})} \qquad (3.35)$$

where

$$K = \sqrt{\left(y+\frac{1}{2}u^2\left(1-\frac{\alpha}{2}\right)\right)^2 - \frac{y^2}{n}\left(n+u^2\left(1-\frac{\alpha}{2}\right)\right)}$$

If we wish to determine the minimum sample size such that for a given α the interval will have a maximum expected width of $2d$, then if possible an *a-priori* estimate of p should be used. The value of p for which the minimum sample size is greatest is $p = 0.5$. If we have some prior information about p, we could use this value. In both cases we can calculate n using the programme CADEMO-*light*.

Example 3.5

We require a confidence interval for the probability $p = P(A)$ of the event A: "an iron casting is faulty". The confidence coefficient is specified as 0.90. How many castings would be tested if the expected width of the interval shall be:

a) not greater than $2d = 0.1$, and nothing is known about p?

b)   not greater than $2d = 0.1$, when we know that at most 10% of castings are faulty?

Also we would like to know:

c)   What is the interval when out of 300 tested castings $y = 25$ faulty ones are found, taking $\alpha = 0.1$?

For case a) CL gives the required sample size as $n = 270$.

If from prior knowledge we can put an upper limit of $p = 0.1$ (case b)), then we get a smaller minimum sample size of $n = 116$ as in Figure 3.10.

We thus see how useful it is to have prior information; in our example the sample size has been reduced to less than a half.

In case c) we have $n = 300$ and $y = 25$, so we can obtain an exact interval using a package, because it will calculate the exact quantiles of the F-distribution, (whereas by hand we can only approximate it by interpolation in Table A3) as follows:

$$F[552; 50; 0.95] = 1.455 \text{ and } F[52; 550; 0.95] = 1.367.$$

From (3.30), (3.31) and (3.32) we obtain

$$\left[\frac{25}{25 + 276 \cdot 1.455} ; \frac{26 \cdot 1.367}{276 + 26 \cdot 1.367} \right] = [0.0586 ; 0.1145]$$

```
Decision:
One Sample Problem
Estimation of a Probability
Determination of Sample Size


Character:
Quality of iron casting

  For the specified parameters
       p* = 0.1000
       α = 0.1000
       d = 0.0500
  a necessary sample size of
       n = 116
  results.

Note:
  The probability to be estimated P is supposed to be smaller than p*
```

Figure 3.10   CL output giving sample size

The approximate interval (3.33), using $u(0.95) = 1.645$ and

$$K = \sqrt{(25 + \frac{1}{2} 1.645^2)^2 - \frac{625}{300}(300 + 1.645^2)} = 7.990$$

is given by

$$\left[\frac{25+\frac{1}{2}1.645^2-7.99}{300+1.645^2} \; ; \; \frac{25+\frac{1}{2}1.645^2+7.99}{300+1.645^2}\right]=[0.0606 \; ; \; 0.1135]$$

and is slightly shorter than the exact one, but it should not be used here. The reason is that for small values of p ($p < 0.1$) it is better to use a Poisson approximation than the normal approximation.

In the case of sample surveys from finite populations of size N let N_A elements present the event A or possess the characteristic (or attribute) A and $N - N_A$ not. Then we use the following notation:

Number of elements with the characteristic A		Relative frequency of the elements with the characteristic A	
Population N_A	Sample n_a	Population $P = p = N_A/N$	Sample $\hat{p} = n_a/n$

We set Y_i (and y_i) equal to 1, if the element of the population (and also the sample) possesses the characteristic A and equal to 0 otherwise. Then $p = \dfrac{N_A}{N} = \dfrac{1}{N}\sum\limits_{i=1}^{N} Y_i$

and $\hat{p} = \dfrac{1}{n}\sum\limits_{i=1}^{n} y_i$ and $\hat{p}$ is an unbiased estimator for p. Sampling *wor* we have

$\hat{var}(\hat{p}) = \dfrac{\hat{p}(1-\hat{p})}{n-1}(1 - \dfrac{n}{N})$ and the estimated standard deviation $SD(\hat{p})$ is $\sqrt{\hat{var}(\hat{p})}$.

A $(1-\alpha)$ confidence interval for p is given by

$$[\hat{p} - SD(\hat{p}) \cdot u(1-\alpha/2), \; \hat{p} + SD(\hat{p}) \cdot u(1-\alpha/2)]$$

In the case of sampling *wr* the formulae are the same as those based on the binomial distribution when sampling from an infinite population. Since the length of a $(1-\alpha)$ confidence interval for p in the case of sampling *wor* is given by

$$2\sqrt{\frac{\hat{p}(1-\hat{p})}{n-1}}(1-\frac{n}{N}) \cdot u(1-\frac{\alpha}{2})$$

the minimal sample size for a given expected length of $2d$ is found approximately as in the case of infinite populations.

3.2.2 Confidence Intervals for the Difference between the Means of Two Normal Distributions

When we introduced Example 3.1 we gave two possible interpretations of the data set. In the first interpretation the litter weights of the first and the second litters of the same mouse are expected to be dependent on each other. This fact must be taken into consideration in any statistical model, and must be modelled using paired observations.

Let us suppose that we have two random variables y_1 and y_2 representing two observations on the same experimental unit at different times, as in the first interpretation in example 3.1. Then we must assume that there will be a dependence between the random variables. We model y_1 and y_2 as components of a two-dimensional normally distributed random vector with variances σ_1^2 and σ_2^2, and a given covariance $cov(y_1,y_2)$. Then the difference $\Delta = y_1 - y_2$ has variance:

$$\sigma_\Delta^2 = \sigma_1^2 + \sigma_2^2 - 2cov(y_1,y_2) = \sigma_1^2 + \sigma_2^2 - 2\sigma_{12} = \sigma_1^2 + \sigma_2^2 - 2\rho \cdot \sigma_1 \cdot \sigma_2.$$

where ρ is the correlation coefficient as defined in chapter 5 and also in appendix B 2.6.

In the second interpretation the independence between the two variables may be a reasonable assumption.
The method of construction of confidence intervals (and also of tests as in section 3.3) depends very much on whether the variables are dependent or independent.

3.2.2.1 The Difference Between the Means of Normal Distributions - Paired Observations

Let us assume that we wish to construct a confidence interval for the difference between the means $\mu_1 - \mu_2$ of the two components of a two-dimensional normally distributed random variable with unknown covariance matrix

$$\Sigma = \begin{pmatrix} \sigma_1^2 & \rho \cdot \sigma_1 \cdot \sigma_2 \\ \rho \cdot \sigma_1 \cdot \sigma_2 & \sigma_2^2 \end{pmatrix}.$$

Again the precision requirement is given by specifying the expected half-width d of a confidence interval for the difference $\mu_1 - \mu_2$ and the confidence coefficient $(1-\alpha)$.

For the determination of the minimal sample size an estimate s_d^2 for the variance σ_Δ^2 of the difference $y_1 - y_2$ with

$$\sigma_\Delta^2 = \sigma_1^2 + \sigma_2^2 - 2\rho \cdot \sigma_1 \cdot \sigma_2$$

is needed. If necessary we use Algorithm B from section 3.2.1.1. Depending on d and α the sample size n for the first form of the precision requirement is determined analogously to (3.14) using the iterative Algorithm A from 3.2.1.1 from:

$$n = \text{CEIL} \left[\frac{t^2\left(n-1;1-\dfrac{\alpha}{2}\right) \cdot \sigma_\Delta^2}{d^2} \right],$$

and for the second form of the precision requirement, analogously to (3.14a) from

$$n = \text{CEIL} \left[\frac{\left[t\left(n-1;1-\dfrac{\alpha}{2}\right) + t\left(1-\dfrac{\beta}{2}\right)\right]^2 \cdot \sigma_\Delta^2}{d^2} \right].$$

The confidence interval for $\mu_1 - \mu_2$ is constructed as follows. Firstly we need the following quantities:

$$d_i = x_i - y_i, \bar{d} = \frac{1}{n}\sum_{i=1}^{n} d_i, \ s_d^2 = \frac{1}{n-1}\sum_{i=1}^{n}(d_i - \bar{d})^2 \text{ and the } (1-\alpha)\text{-confidence interval for } \mu_1 -$$

μ_2 is given by

$$\left[\bar{d} - t\left(n-1;1-\frac{\alpha}{2}\right)\frac{s_d}{\sqrt{n}}, \bar{d} + t\left(n-1;1-\frac{\alpha}{2}\right)\frac{s_d}{\sqrt{n}}\right] \tag{3.36}$$

Example 3.1 - continued

To calculate the $(1-\alpha)$-confidence interval for $\alpha = 0.1$ for our data set using the first interpretation, The 13 differences $d_i = x_i - y_i$ between the x and y values are - 0.2; 2.1; -7.3; -3.1; -2.0; -1.5; 2.7; 4.4; -6.4; -0.7. We find $\bar{d} = \bar{x} - \bar{y} = -1.7615$ with standard deviation $s_d = 3.653$.

Using $t(12; 0.95) = 1.7823$ from Table A1 we substitute in (3.36) and obtain

$$[-1.7615 - 1.7823 \cdot \frac{3.653}{\sqrt{13}}; \ -1.7615 + 1.7823 \cdot \frac{3.653}{\sqrt{13}}]$$

$= [-3.567; 0.044]$ as the required confidence interval.

We can obtain this result in SPSS using the menu sequence Analyze - Compare Means - Paired Samples T Test and use "Options" to change $(1-\alpha)$ 100% from the default 95% to 90%. The output in Figure 3.11 shows the results. (As already mentioned, both SPSS and CADEMO use the term "paired (dependent) samples" but in fact we have **one** sample of paired observations).

		Paired Differences				
		Mean	Std. Deviation	Std. Error Mean	90% Confidence Interval of the Difference	
					Lower	Upper
Pair 1	x - y	-1.76154	3.65252	1.01303	-3.56704	.04397

Figure 3.11 *SPSS output for Example 3.1*

If in this situation we want to determine the size of another experiment under the same conditions except that the expected half-width of the interval must not be greater than 1.2, then we use as prior information the estimate of the standard deviation $s_d = 3.653$ of the $d_i = x_i - y_i$ obtained in Figure 3.11 above. The result from the CL program is shown in Figure 3.12.

```
Decision:
Two Sample Problem - Dependent Samples
Estimation of the Difference of two Means - Two dependent Samples
Determination of Sample Size


Character:
Difference of litter masses

 For the specified parameters
        s²(6) = 13.3400,
        d = 1.2000
        α = 0.1000
 and for a symmetrical Confidence Interval
 minimum sample sizes of
        n1 = n2 = 27
 result.
```

Figure 3.12   *CL output*

Performing this calculation by hand we start with $n_0 = \infty$, $t(\infty;0.95)=1.6449$. Then we find $n_1= 26$, $t(25;0.95)=1.7081$, $n_2=28$, $t(27;0.95)=1.7033$ $n_3=27$; $t(26;0.95)=1.7056$; $n_4=27$, so that both methods indicate that 27 data pairs will be required.

3.2.2.2 The Difference between the Means of Normal Distributions - Two Independent Samples

Consider two normally distributed populations with means μ_1 and μ_2 and variances σ_1^2 and σ_2^2. The sizes n_1 and n_2 of two independent samples from these two distributions have to be determined to allow the construction of a confidence interval for the difference μ_1 - μ_2 with a given precision. The precision requirement is again expressed in terms of the half expected width d of a $(1-\alpha)$-confidence interval for μ_1-μ_2.
In the case of equal variances $\sigma_1^2 = \sigma_2^2 = \sigma^2$, a $(1-\alpha)$-confidence interval for μ_1-μ_2 is,

$$\left[\bar{x}-\bar{y}-t\left(n_1+n_2-2;1-\frac{\alpha}{2}\right)s\sqrt{\frac{n_1+n_2}{n_1n_2}};\bar{x}-\bar{y}+t\left(n_1+n_2-2;1-\frac{\alpha}{2}\right)s\sqrt{\frac{n_1+n_2}{n_1n_2}}\right] \quad (3.37)$$

where $\bar{x}$ and $\bar{y}$ are the two sample means. We use the pooled estimator of the common variance

$$s^2 = \frac{1}{n_1+n_2-2}\ [\Sigma(x_i - \bar{x})^2 + \Sigma(y_i -\bar{y})^2] \text{ to calculate } s = \sqrt{s^2}.$$

At this point we would like to indicate how one-sided confidence intervals can be constructed. In an upper (lower) confidence interval, the lower (upper) limit is the boundary of the parameter space (here ∞ (-∞)).
The upper $(1-\alpha)$-confidence interval is given by

$$[\bar{x}-\bar{y}-t(n_1+n_2-2;1-\alpha)s\sqrt{\frac{n_1+n_2}{n_1n_2}};\infty) \quad (3.38)$$

and the lower one by

$$(-\infty; \bar{x} - \bar{y} + t(n_1 + n_2 - 2; 1 - \alpha)s \sqrt{\frac{n_1 + n_2}{n_1 n_2}}]. \tag{3.39}$$

In the case of equal variances it can be shown that optimal plans require the two sample sizes n_1 and n_2 to be equal. Thus $n_1 = n_2 = n$, and in the case where the expected half-width must be less than d, we find n iteratively using Algorithms A and B from

$$n = \text{CEIL}\left[2\sigma^2 \frac{t^2(2n - 2; P)}{d^2}\right] \tag{3.40}$$

If on the other hand the precision requirement states that both confidence limits must not differ by more than d from the parameter difference $\mu_1 - \mu_2$ with given probability $1-\beta$, then

$$n = \text{CEIL}\left[\frac{\left[t(2n-2;P) + t\left(2n-2;1-\frac{\beta}{2}\right)\right]^2 \cdot \sigma^2}{d^2}\right] \tag{3.40a}$$

For *two-sided (1-α)-confidence intervals* we set $P = 1 - \alpha/2$ in (3.40) and in (3.40a) and for one-sided intervals $P = 1 - \alpha$. For two-sided intervals d is the upper bound for the expected half-width of the interval. For *one-sided intervals* the first precision requirement is defined by

$$P\{\mu_1 - \mu_2 \geq \bar{y}_1 - \bar{y}_2 - d\} = 1 - \alpha$$

or

$$P\{\mu_1 - \mu_2 \leq \bar{y}_1 - \bar{y}_2 + d\} = 1 - \alpha$$

and the interpretation of d follows from these.

In the case of one-sided intervals with the second precision requirement, as well as taking $P = 1 - \alpha$, we must replace $1 - \beta/2$ by $1 - \beta$ and the probability statements simply refer to the distance of the final limits from $\mu_1 - \mu_2$.

If the variances are unequal the confidence interval is based on the usual estimators s_1^2 and s_2^2 of σ_1^2 and σ_2^2 respectively. The confidence interval (3.41) is only approximately a (1-α)-confidence interval (see WELCH (1947)). It is given by

$$\left[\bar{x} - \bar{y} - t\left(f^*; 1 - \frac{\alpha}{2}\right)\sqrt{\frac{s_1^2}{n_1} + \frac{s_2^2}{n_2}}; \bar{x} - \bar{y} + t\left(f^*; 1 - \frac{\alpha}{2}\right)\sqrt{\frac{s_1^2}{n_1} + \frac{s_2^2}{n_2}}\right] \tag{3.41}$$

with f^* from (3.42)

$$f^* = \text{CEIL}\left[\dfrac{\left(\dfrac{s_1^2}{n_1} + \dfrac{s_2^2}{n_2}\right)^2}{\dfrac{s_1^4}{(n_1-1)n_1^2} + \dfrac{s_2^4}{(n_2-1)n_2^2}}\right] \tag{3.42}$$

To determine the necessary sample sizes n_1 and n_2 we will need information about the two variances. Suppose that estimates s_1^2 and s_2^2 are available for the variances σ_1^2 and σ_2^2 which are known to be unequal. We can calculate n_1 and n_2 for a two-sided confidence interval iteratively from:

$$n_1 = \text{CEIL}\left[\dfrac{s_1(s_1+s_2)}{d^2} \cdot t^2\left(f^*; 1-\dfrac{\alpha}{2}\right)\right] \text{ and}$$

$$n_2 = \text{CEIL}\left[\dfrac{s_2}{s_1} \cdot n_1\right]$$

with f^* from (3.42).

Example 3.1 - continued

Let us calculate 95%-confidence intervals for our data set using interpretation 2 i.e. two independent samples from normal distributions. We already know from Figure 3.3 that $\bar{x} = 9.7692$, $\bar{y} = 11.5308$, $s_1^2 = 3.947$, $s_2^2 = 8.714$ and we know that $n_1 = n_2 = 13$. We will assume for the moment that $\sigma_1^2 = \sigma_2^2$ (how to test this will be shown in section 3.4.3). Then from (3.37) we find that the pooled variance is $s^2 = \dfrac{12 \cdot 3.947 + 12 \cdot 8.714}{24} = 6.332$ giving $s = 2.516$. The confidence interval is

$$\left[9.77 - 11.53 - t(24;0.975)\sqrt{\dfrac{26}{169}} \cdot 2.516 ; 9.77 - 11.53 + t(24;0.975) \cdot \sqrt{\dfrac{26}{169}} \cdot 2.516\right]$$

Using $t(24; 0.975) = 2.0639$ we obtain the interval $[-3.80; 0.28]$.

To do this calculation using SPSS we arrange the 26 observations in one column (starting with the 13 x-values followed by the 13 y-values) calling the variable "value" and to define a variable "group" with the number 1 for the 13 x-values and the number 2 for the 13 y-values. From case 14 on we thus have the 13 y-values. (To arrange the 26 values in one column we select the y-values by click-and-drag and choose Edit - Cut from the menus. Then we click in the cell immediately below the last x-value and choose Edit – Paste). Finally we save the data under "Litterweights II". Figure 3.13 shows an extract from this new file.

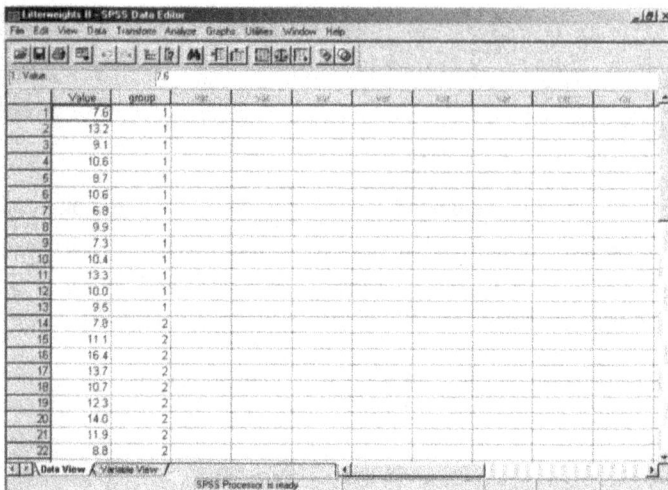

Figure 3.13 *SPSS Data File for Example 3.1 with Group Membership*

With **Analyze – Compare Means - Independent Samples T-Test** we reach a dialog box in which we define "value" as the Test Variable, and "Group" as the Grouping Variable". Under "Define Groups" we define the *x*-values as Group 1 and the *y*-values as Group 2. The following schema shows the result (after deleting irrelevant columns).

		df	95% Confidence Interval for the Difference	
			Lower	Upper
Value	Equal variances assumed	24	-3.7984	.2753
	Equal variances not assumed	21 .0 21	-3.8138	.2907

The confidence interval in the top row is calculated for equal variances in both mouse populations as in (3.37): [-3.80; 0.28].

The interval in the row below gives the confidence interval as in (3.41) assuming unequal variances: [-3.81; 0.29], with the degrees of freedom $(df)\, f^*$ from (3.42), namely $f^* = 21.02$.

3.3 Selection Procedures

The aim of research in empirical science is very often to select the best one out of a given set of possibilities. In clinical research for instance we may want to find out which of a given number of therapies is the one with the best chance of curing the patient, or we may want to find out the most effective drug amongst several available drugs. In industrial research we can find similar situations when we look for the best technology or the best mixture of different components in a particular product. Agricultural researchers may be looking for the best variety, fertiliser, pesticide etc. There are many examples

66

from different areas where the aim of an investigation or experiment is to find out which is "best" out of a number of possibilities. In each particular case we have to define exactly what we mean by "best", as part of the problem formulation. If we model each of the possibilities by a population, and the characteristic of interest by a random variable whose distributions in the various populations differ only in the value of one of the parameters, then we can define "best" in terms of this parameter. The best case can be the one with the largest probability (for instance of leading to a cure), or the one with the largest expectation (for instance for the harvest of a particular fruit), or the one with the smallest variance (for instance for the udder size of cows in connection with the use of a special milking technology).

Although there are very many practical examples which are essentially the same as the examples above, the statistical selection methods developed during the last 45 years (see MIESCKE and RASCH, 1996) are almost never applied. Indeed, even in most statistical text books neither theoretical nor practical aspects of *statistical selection procedures* are discussed. Another handicap is the small number of good computer programs in this field (RASCH, 1996).

We discuss statistical selection procedures before statistical tests, in order to draw attention to the fact that in many cases they are more appropriate to the research objective than are multiple comparison tests as described in Section 4.3, and should therefore be used more frequently.

Statistical selection procedures can be divided into two groups: the ones based on the formulation of an indifference zone, and subset selection methods. We restrict ourselves in this book to the indifference zone formulation of selection problems. For subset selection procedures we recommend GUPTA and PANCHAPAKESAN (1972, 1979).

The basis for the indifference zone formulation of selection problems can be found in a paper by BECHHOFER (1954). The formulation of the problem is as follows. We are given a "independent" treatments, procedures or populations which will be modelled by a finite set $S = \{P_{\theta_1}, ..., P_{\theta_a}\}$ of size a with elements from a family of distributions. "Independent" means that the samples to be drawn from these distributions are assumed to be mutually independent. From this set we have to select the t "best" elements. To define what we understand by "best" we use the parameter transformation $\psi = g(\theta)$ defined in 3.1 as a selection criterion (evaluation function). Restricting ourselves to real functions g we say that P_{θ_i} is better than P_{θ_j} when

$$\psi_i = g(\theta_i) > \psi_j = g(\theta_j).$$

Since the parameters are initially unknown, the aim of an experiment is to select the t best distributions from the a distributions being investigated, with $1 \le t < a$. In what follows we will use the term "population" instead of "distribution" - the terms may be used synonymously. An absolutely correct selection is only possible if the θ_i and thus also the ψ_i are known, but in this case we do not need an experiment. Therefore we assume that the parameters are unknown.

We clarify these ideas with the aid of an example.

Example 3.6

> We choose a situation where we know the true facts. We use modified dice to define two populations. For the first population we ignore every throw which results in a "6", so that we effectively have a "five-sided" die giving the values {1,2,3,4,5}. Similarly for the second population we ignore all the "1"s, giving a die with faces labelled {2,3,4,5,6}. If we throw one of the dice, each face has the same probability of appearing (one fifth); the expectation in the first population is 3, in the second it is 4.

We wish to draw random samples of size two from both these populations by throwing each die twice (of course as well as performing this experiment practically in this way, we could also simulate it using a computer-based random number generator).

We calculate the sample mean of the results of the throws of each die, and we define the best population as the one which gives the larger sample mean (of course in a real situation we would not know which population is actually best). In order to calculate the probability of a correct selection we need to know how frequently the second population (which is actually the best one) will be chosen as best by the sampling procedure. We list all the possible outcomes in the form (a,b), where "a" is the result from the first throw, and "b" the one from the second:

Population 1:   (1,1); (1,2); (1,3); (1,4); (1,5);
(2,1); (2,2); (2,3); (2,4); (2,5);
(3,1); (3,2); (3,3); (3,4); (3,5);
(4,1); (4,2); (4,3); (4,4); (4,5);
(5,1); (5,2); (5,3); (5,4); (5,5);

Population 2:   (2,2); (2,3); (2,4); (2,5); (2,6);
(3,2); (3,3); (3,4); (3,5); (3,6);
(4,2); (4,3); (4,4); (4,5); (4,6);
(5,2); (5,3); (5,4); (5,5); (5,6);
(6,2); (6,3); (6,4); (6,5); (6,6);

In both populations each event (a,b) has the same probability of occurring. Moreover each result from the first population can be combined with each result from the second population to give **one** possible outcome of the experiment.

That a false selection is by no means impossible can be seen from the example above. If we throw a 3 and a 4 with the first die (throw number 14 above), and a 3 and a 2 with the second one (throw 6), then as a result of this experiment we shall erroneously choose the first population as being the best. We leave it as an exercise for the reader to calculate in how many of the 25·25 possible outcomes the mean of the 2 numbers from the second population is greater than the mean of the two drawn from the first population. This number divided by 25·25 gives the probability of a correct selection. (Hint: you don't have to calculate the means. Beginning with (6,6), (6,5) and (5,6) from population 2, each of these leads to a correct selection for all 25 outcomes from population 1. Continue in this way as far as (2,2) from population 2, which only gives a correct selection when combined with (1,1), (2,1) and (1,2) from population 1.

How can we increase the chance of a correct selection? We can achieve this in our example - and also quite generally - by increasing the sample size, just as in the case of point and interval estimation. But the probability of a correct selection depends not only on the sample size, but also on the "distance" between the t best populations and the remaining $a - t$ inferior populations. This fact is the motivation for BECHHOFER's introduction of the concept of *indifference zones*. He demanded that the probability that a population is erroneously denoted as one of the t best populations is not larger than β, if the difference between the smallest of the t best populations and the largest one of the a-t remaining populations is larger than a specified difference d. This d is the smallest difference of practical interest to the experimenter; it characterises the indifference region as the smallest distance between the t best and the a-t "non-best" populations.

This can be better demonstrated if we assume for the moment that the ψ-values are known. In that case we denote by $\psi_{[1]} < \psi_{[2]} < ... < \psi_{[a]}$ the ordered values of ψ. A population will be called better than another if it has the larger parameter value. The value $\psi_{[a-t+1]}$ belongs to the worst of the t best populations, whereas $\psi_{[a-t]}$ belongs to the best one of the remaining populations. When $\psi_{[a-t+1]} - \psi_{[a-t]} < d$ then the distance between both groups lies in the indifference zone in which BECHHOFER states that we do not need to restrict the probability of an incorrect selection (However GUIARD (1996) has made another proposal for statement to be made in this case).

The precision requirement in BECHHOFER's indifference zone formulation is:

In the case $\psi_{[a-t+1]} - \psi_{[a-t]} \geq d$ the probability of an incorrect selection is at most β.

The *precision requirement* for the determination of the necessary size of an experiment is given by the four values (a, t, d, β), and they suffice to determine the minimum sizes for all a samples. Since the formulae involved are more complicated than in previous sections, we refer you to a program [RASCH (1996)], which calculates the sample sizes amongst other things for the following cases:
- selection of the t normal distributions with the largest (smallest) expectations with known or unknown, equal or unequal variances
- selection of the normal distribution with the largest (smallest) variance (using a modified precision requirement for the ratio of scale parameters)
- selection of the t binomial distributions with the largest (smallest) probability p_i.

Example 3.7

We consider the case of selecting the normal distribution with the largest expectation, if the variances are known.

From a normal populations with known equal variances $\sigma_i^2 = \sigma^2$ and unknown expectations μ_i the best ($t = 1$) population has to be selected using $\psi_i = \mu_i$ as evaluation function. Mutually independent samples $(y_{i1}, y_{i2}, ..., y_{in_i})$ of size n_i ($i=1, ..., a$) will be taken from the populations. How can we choose the sample sizes satisfying the precision requirement given by (a,1,d,β), if we apply BECHHOFER's selection rule: "Choose as the best population the one which had the largest sample mean"? Here, thankfully, the analysis is simple, which is perhaps one reason why selection procedures do not appear in most statistical analysis programmes. What is more troublesome here is finding the n_i ($i = 1, ..., a$).

We choose $n_i = n$ and using the (1-β) quantile $u_{[a-1]}(1-\beta)$ of the (a-1)-dimensional normal distribution we calculate

$$c^2 = \frac{d^2}{2(u_{(a-1)}(1-\beta))^2} \tag{3.43}$$

and then n from

$$n = \text{CEIL}(\sigma^2/c^2) \tag{3.44}$$

69

Tables with the quantiles $u_{[a-1]}(1-\beta)$ are available for instance in VB 1/51/1012.

We choose $d = \sigma$, $\beta = 0.05$ and in order to calculate the required minimum sample sizes for the selection from $a = 5$, $a = 10$ and $a = 20$ populations, we look up the quantiles $u_{[4]}(0.95) = 2.160$; $u_{[9]}(0.95) = 2.417$; $u_{[19]}(0.95) = 2.631$ and obtain the n-values $n = 10$, 12 and 14. The larger number of populations is, from which we want to choose the best, the larger the minimal sample size has to be. In the CADEMO Module SELPRO we enter the requirements as shown in Figure 3.14, and obtain the output in Figure 3.15.

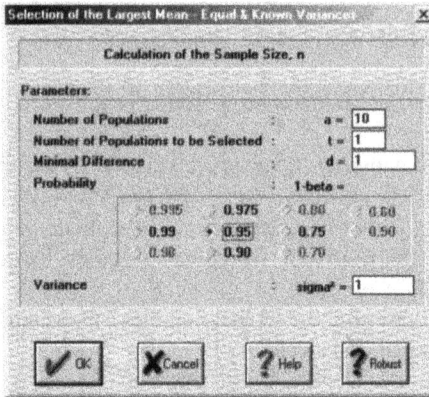

Figure 3.14 *Precision Requirements in SELPRO*

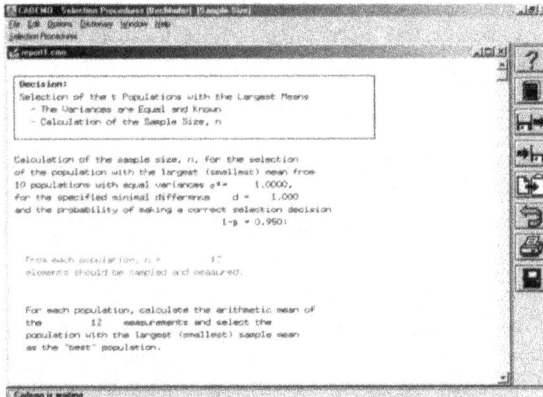

Figure 3.15 *The Necessary Size of Each Sample in the Case a = 10*

In VB can be found selection procedures for the following problems:

3/27/1101 - Selection of the largest mean from a normal distributions with equal variances,

3/27/1102 - Selection of the t largest means from a normal distributions with equal known variances,

3/27/1202 - Sequential selection of the largest mean from a normal distributions with unknown equal variances,

3/27/1301 - Selection of the t largest means from a normal distributions with arbitrary unknown variances,

3/27/3101 –   Selection of a subset from a normal distributions which contains the largest mean (equal known variances),

3/27/3201 –   Selection of a subset of size $r \geq t$ from a normal distributions which contains the largest mean (equal known variances),

3/27/4201 –   Selection of a subset from a normal distributions which contains all the populations which are better than a standard.

3/31/0001 –   Selection of the t populations having the smallest variances,

3/33/0010 –   Selection of a subset from a populations which contains the population with the smallest variance.

3/63/0001 –   Selection of the population with the greatest probability.

3.4 Hypothesis Testing

This section describes the problems of the analysis and sample size determination in situations where hypotheses are to be tested. We deal with cases concerning the means and variances of normal distributions, and we also consider hypotheses about probabilities. First we will introduce the basic ideas of hypothesis testing.

Hypotheses about the parameters of statistical models can be subjected to statistical tests. A *statistical test* is a rule by which, based on a random sample, a choice can be made between two mutually exclusive hypotheses concerning the parameter θ of the distribution of the elements of the random sample. A statistical test, or a test for short, can be considered as the solution of a two-choice problem. However in mathematical statistics and especially in many applications, solutions for three- (or more) choice problems are sometimes also called tests. Examples for this are the Tukey-test and the Dunnett-test used for multiple comparisons of means, which we shall meet in chapter 4.

We must emphasise here that the result of a statistical test is never a statement about the truth of one of the two hypotheses. A hypothesis will either be accepted or rejected - this simply provides suggestions for action but has little to do with whether the accepted hypothesis is true or not. This is so because it is impossible to derive such a statement from the realisation of a random sample. The acceptance of any hypothesis may be correct or may be an error. From this it follows that there exist two kinds of errors depending on which of the two hypotheses is accepted erroneously. We call them errors of the first and of the second kind. This reflects the lack of symmetry of the two hypotheses. One of these we call the *null hypothesis* H_0 and the other we call *alternative hypothesis* H_A.

The name null hypothesis comes from the fact that in many applications the hypothesis that there is no difference between means (i.e. that the difference of two expectations is zero or null) is taken as the null hypothesis. The probability of wrongly rejecting the null hypothesis can be controlled by the test in a very easy manner. Whenever we reject the null hypothesis when it is true, we commit an *error of the first kind* or *Type I error*. If we wrongly accept the null hypothesis or equivalently reject a true alternative hypothesis we commit an *error of the second kind* or *Type II error*.

Example 3.8

Assume that a random variable y with expectation μ and known variance σ^2 is normally distributed (to be brief we write $y \sim N(\mu, \sigma^2)$). Given a certain value μ_0 we have to test the null hypothesis

$H_0 : \mu = \mu_0$

against the alternative hypothesis

$H_A : \mu \neq \mu_0$

A Type I error is made if $\mu = \mu_0$ and the null hypothesis is rejected. A Type II error is made if the null hypothesis is accepted but in fact $\mu \neq \mu_0$. This error becomes more serious as the difference between μ and μ_0 increases. On the other hand, we will see later that the probability of this error occurring decreases with increasing $|\mu - \mu_0|$.

Definition 3.2

A hypothesis is called *simple* if it refers to a single point in the parameter space; otherwise it is *composite*. If the alternative hypothesis region lies entirely to one side of the null hypothesis region (here we consider only the real-line parameter space) then the hypothesis is called one-sided, and the corresponding test is called one-tailed; otherwise they are called two-sided and two-tailed respectively.
The rejection of a null-hypothesis which is true, is called an *error of the first kind* or *Type I error*, the rejection of the alternative hypothesis, if it is true, is called an *error of the second kind* or *Type II error*. The probability that an error of the first kind occurs is called the *risk of the first kind* (*Type I error probability*) $\alpha(\theta)$; the maximum α attained by $\alpha(\theta)$ in the null hypothesis space is called the *significance level*. The probability of an error of the second kind is called the *risk of the second kind* (*Type II error probability*) $\beta(\theta)$.
The probability $\pi(\theta)$ of the rejection of the null-hypothesis as a function of the unknown parameter θ of a distribution is called the *power function*.

Example 3.8 - continued

In the situation of example 3.8 above, the null hypothesis has to be tested against a (one sided) alternative hypothesis, i.e.:

$H_0 : \mu = \mu_0$ (null hypothesis)
$H_A : \mu > \mu_0$ (alternative hypothesis),

with σ^2 known. Let $\bar{y}$ be the mean of the n elements y_i of the random sample $y^T = (y_1,..., y_n)$, with $y_i \sim N(\mu; \sigma^2)$, then the test can be performed using the test statistic

$$u = \frac{\bar{y} - \mu_0}{\sigma}\sqrt{n}$$

with a significance level α defined in advance. To do this for a specified significance level (which in this case equals the unique value of the Type I error probability α because the null hypothesis region is degenerate consisting of only a single point μ_0), we have to know the distribution of u. But this can easily be derived because it is assumed that the elements of the random sample follow an $N(\mu; \sigma^2)$-distribution. Therefore $\bar{y}$ is distributed as $N(\mu; \sigma^2/n)$ and u is distributed as

$N(\frac{\mu - \mu_0}{\sigma}\sqrt{n}; 1)$. We call the value

$$\lambda = \frac{\mu - \mu_0}{\sigma}\sqrt{n} \tag{3.45}$$

the *non-centrality parameter* of the distribution of the test statistic $\boldsymbol{u}$.
If the null hypothesis is actually true, then the non-centrality parameter equals zero. Test statistics usually have a distribution that is simpler to handle under the null hypothesis than under the alternative hypothesis, and tables are published for such applications (as for example Tables A1-A6 in the Appendix). In our example $\boldsymbol{u}$ is distributed as $N(0;1)$ under the null hypothesis. The probability that an $N(0;1)$-distributed random variable is larger than the $(1-\alpha)$-quantile $u(1-\alpha)$ of the standard normal distribution is exactly equal to α. In other words, the probability that the null hypothesis is rejected when it actually is true is exactly equal to the risk of the first kind α chosen in advance if we reject H_0 if the realisation u of $\boldsymbol{u}$ exceeds $u(1-\alpha)$.

We will now calculate the power function of this test and to keep the arithmetic simple we assume that σ^2 is an integer so that we can choose $n = \sigma^2$. Let us further assume that $\mu_0 = 6$. Then the probability $P(\boldsymbol{u} > u)$ can easily be calculated for each real u as a function of μ. (Table 3.4) .

Table 3.4   *Values of the power function $\pi(\mu) = P(\boldsymbol{u} > u(1-\alpha))$ in example 3.8 ($\mu_0=6$).*

μ	$\pi(\mu)$
6	0.05
7	0.26
8	0.64
9	0.91
10	0.99
11	$\cong 1.00$

In this example $\pi(\theta)$, starting from its minimum value $\alpha = 0.05$ when $\theta = \mu = 6$, increases monotonically with μ. For μ-values outside the region of the null hypothesis (therefore inside the region of the alternative hypothesis) we have $\pi(\theta) = 1-\beta(\theta)$; the probability of rejecting the null hypothesis when it is not true. Notice that $\pi(\theta)$ is defined only in the union of both regions. The further the actual μ-value deviates from the value for the null hypothesis, the smaller is $\beta(\theta)$ (and the larger $1-\beta(\theta)$). This means that the chance of failing to notice a large deviation of the actual mean from the null hypothesis value is relatively small.

This is true for all statistical tests in this text; such tests are called unbiased. However there exist tests whose power functions take their smallest values in the alternative hypothesis region; such tests are called biased.
Tests with a monotone power function allow us to use the following precision requirements as a basis of the determination of sample sizes:

- The Type I error probability for a composite null hypothesis will not exceed the upper bound α, or in the case of a simple null hypothesis, it will equal α.
- The Type II error probability will not exceed a fixed value β_0 as long as (after defining a proper distance measure) the distance between the actual value of the parameter (in the region of the alternative hypothesis) and the value of the parameter under the null hypothesis is at least equal to a value d given in advance, i.e. if $d \leq |\mu - \mu_0|$. The symbol d is mainly used if hypotheses about location

parameters have to be tested. For scale parameters the symbols dr or τ are commonly used.

The *precision requirement* is given by the triple (α, β_0, d) and possibly by *a priori* knowledge about parameters of the distribution (e.g. σ^2).

We will discuss this using example 3.8.

Example 3.8 - continued

Assume $\mu_0 = 6$, as was the case for calculating Table 3.4. We specify $\alpha = 0.05$ and $\pi(\theta) \geq 0.8 = 1 - \beta_0$, if $\mu \geq 8$ (and therefore that $\beta(\theta) \leq 0.2$ if $\mu \geq 8$). This requirement for μ means that $\beta(\theta) \leq 0.2$ if there is a distance of at least 2 units between μ and μ_0. Based on the monotonicity of the power function the requirement is fulfilled if $\beta(8) \leq 0.2$. It is now sufficient to determine the minimum n that guarantees that $\beta(8) = \beta_0 = 0.2$. This means we have to choose n in such a way that for $\mu = 8$ the probability of a (wrong) acceptance of the null-hypothesis equals 0.2 and this means that $\beta(8) = P(u < u(1-\alpha)|\mu = 8) = 0.2$. For $\alpha = 0.05$, $u(0.95) = 1.645$ and we have

$$\beta(8) = P(u < 1.645|\mu=8) = 0.2 .$$

But with $\mu = 8$ we have

$$u = \frac{\bar{y} - \mu_0}{\sigma}\sqrt{n} = \left(\frac{\bar{y} - 8}{\sigma} + \frac{8 - 6}{\sigma}\right)\sqrt{n} = u_0 + \frac{2}{\sigma}\sqrt{n} ,$$

where u_0 is a random variable with an $N(0;1)$ distribution. Hence our requirement can be written as:

$$\beta(8) = P(u_0 < 1.645 - \frac{2}{\sigma}\sqrt{n}) = 0.2$$

This means that the term in the middle [after the $<$ sign] between parentheses has to be equal to the 0.2-quantile of the standard normal distribution, which is -0.842. Let us now assume that σ is equal to 2, then the equality

$$1.645 - \sqrt{n} = -0.842$$

can be solved for the sample size n using the CEIL operator:

$$n = \text{CEIL}\left[(1.645 + 0.842)^2\right] = 7.$$

In general for $d = \mu - \mu_0$ the equation for n, using the identity $u(\beta) = -u(1-\beta)$:

$$n = \text{CEIL}\{[u(1-\alpha) - u(\beta)]^2 \frac{\sigma^2}{d^2}\} = \text{CEIL}\{[u(1-\alpha) + u(1-\beta)]^2 \frac{\sigma^2}{d^2}\}. \tag{3.46}$$

For a two-sided alternative hypothesis we replace α by $\alpha/2$ in (3.46) and reject H_0 if

$$|u| > u\left(1 - \frac{\alpha}{2}\right).$$

3.4.1 Testing Hypotheses about the Mean of a Normal Distribution

A random sample $y_1, y_2, ..., y_n$ of size n will be drawn from a normally distributed population with mean μ and variance σ^2, with the purpose of testing the null hypothesis:

$H_0 : \mu = \mu_0$ (μ_0 is given constant)

against one of the following alternative hypotheses:

a) $H_A : \mu > \mu_0$ (one-sided alternative)
b) $H_A : \mu < \mu_0$ (one-sided alternative)
c) $H_A : \mu \neq \mu_0$ (two-sided alternative)

In the known variance case we have already described the procedure in the previous section.

If σ is unknown we replace the test statistic u by Student's test statistic t, which formally can be obtained from u by replacing σ by the sample standard deviation s. This test statistic is

$$t = \frac{\bar{y} - \mu_0}{s}\sqrt{n} \qquad\qquad (3.47)$$

If the Type I error probability is α, H_0 will be rejected if:
in case a), $t > t(n\text{-}1;1\text{-}\alpha)$,
in case b), $t < -t(n\text{-}1;1\text{-}\alpha)$,
in case c), $|t| > t(n\text{-}1;1\text{-}\alpha/2)$.

SPSS always calculates the so-called significance level (or P-value) for the two-sided alternative (case c), called Sig.(2-tailed) in the output. This is the value of the probability $P(\ t(n\text{-}1) < - |t|\ ) + P\ (t(n\text{-}1) > |t|\ ) = 2\ P\ (t(n\text{-}1) > |t|\ )$. Thus H_0 is rejected whenever the P-value is smaller than the chosen α. For one-sided hypotheses, we simply double our chosen α, and compare 2α with Sig.(2-tailed).

This test statistic (3.47) is distributed as a non-central t-variate with $n\text{-}1$ degrees of freedom and non-centrality parameter $\lambda = [(\mu - \mu_0)\sqrt{n}]/\sigma$ as in the case where the variance is known. Under the null hypothesis $\mu = \mu_0$ we have $\lambda = 0$. Denoting the $(1\text{-}\alpha)$-quantile of the central t-distribution with $n\text{-}1$ degrees of freedom by $t(n\text{-}1;1\text{-}\alpha)$ and the β-quantile of the corresponding non-central t-distributed by $t(n\text{-}1;\lambda;\beta)$ we obtain by analogy with example 3.8 from

$$1 - \pi(\theta) = P(t < t(n-1;1-\alpha)|\lambda) = \beta$$

the requirement:

$$t(n\text{-}1;1\text{-}\alpha) = t(n\text{-}1;\lambda;\beta) \qquad\qquad (3.48)$$

In words: The $(1\text{-}\alpha)$-quantile of the central t-distribution (the distribution if the null hypothesis is true) has to be equal to the β-quantile of the non-central t-distribution (the distribution if an alternative hypothesis is true) with non-centrality parameter λ. Here λ depends on the minimal difference d. This requirement is illustrated in Figure 3.16.

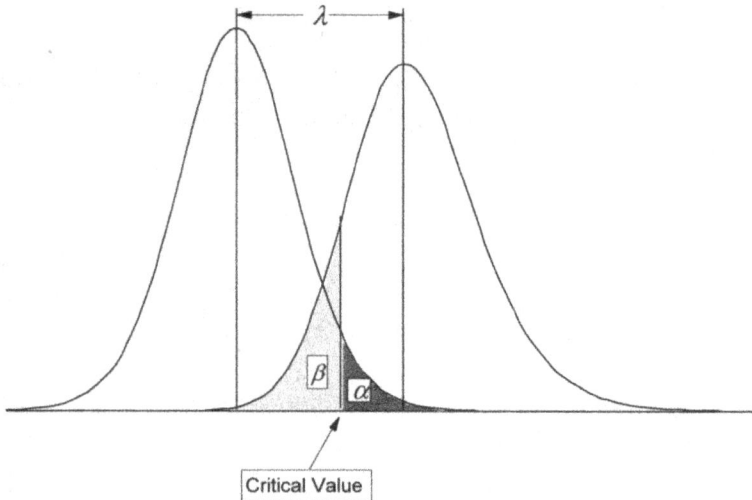

Figure 3.16 *Graphical representation of the two risks (α and β) of (3.48)*

For the determination of sample sizes we use an approximation which is sufficiently accurate. It is:

$$t(n\text{-}1;\lambda;\beta) \approx t(n\text{-}1;\beta) + \lambda = t(n\text{-}1;\beta) + \frac{\mu - \mu_0}{\sigma}\sqrt{n} \qquad (3.49)$$

The requirement (3.48) by analogy with (3.46) gives the minimum sample size n as:

$$n = \text{CEIL}\{[t(n\text{-}1;1\text{-}\alpha) - t(n\text{-}1;\beta)]^2 \frac{\sigma^2}{d^2}\}$$

$$= \text{CEIL}\{[t(n\text{-}1;1\text{-}\alpha) + t(n\text{-}1;1\text{-}\beta)]^2 \frac{\sigma^2}{d^2}\} \qquad (3.50)$$

Example 3.1 - continued

We will use the values from the first litter in example 3.1 (the x-values in table 3.1) to test the hypothesis that the population mean of the litter weight equals 8 g against each of the three alternatives (this is only for demonstrating the method - in practical problems we must select exactly one alternative!). We choose $\alpha = 0.05$. From Figure 3.3 we find

$$\bar{y} = 9.769 \text{ and } s^2 = 3.947 \text{, so that } s_{\bar{y}} = \frac{\sqrt{3.947}}{\sqrt{13}} = 0.551 \text{ and}$$

$$t = \frac{9.769 - 8}{1.987}\sqrt{13} = \frac{9.769 - 8}{0.551} = 3.21.$$

Using SPSS we choose the menu sequence Analyze - Compare Means - One-sample T Test which leads to Figure 3.5. Here we insert 8 for the test value (μ_0) (not 0 as in Figure 3.5) and obtain the same t-value $t = 3.21$ as above. Since $t(12; 0.95) = 1.7823$ and $t(12; 0.975) = 2.1788$, our decisions are in:
case a): reject H_0 (3.21 > 1.78)
case b): accept H_0 (3.21 not < -1.78)
case c): reject H_0 (3.21 > 2.18).

Let α and β denote the risks of the first and second kind respectively (i.e. the probabilities of Type I and Type II errors). Our aim is to determine the size n of the required sample for a given α so that β as a function of ($\mu - \mu_0$) for:

$\mu - \mu_0 \geq d$ in the case of the alternative hypothesis a),

$\mu - \mu_0 \leq -d$ in the case of the alternative hypothesis b), and

$|\mu - \mu_0| \geq d$ in the case of the alternative hypothesis c),

does not exceed a predetermined value β_0.
The value d is called the minimal difference of practical interest.
The determination of the minimal sample size n requires information about the precision requirements defined by α, β_0 and d as well as an estimate s^2 for the variance σ^2 of the underlying distribution.
The optimal sample size is then calculated iteratively from

$$n = \text{CEIL}\left[\frac{\sigma^2}{d^2} \cdot \left[t(n-1; P) + t(n-1; 1 - \beta_0)\right]^2\right] \tag{3.51}$$

where $P = 1 - \alpha$ for the one-sided alternatives and $P = 1 - \alpha/2$ for the two-sided alternative. If no estimate of σ^2 is available and a two-stage approach as in Algorithm B is not possible, then d may instead be defined relative to σ by $d = c \cdot \sigma$. This yields:

$$n = \text{CEIL}\left[\frac{\left[t(n-1; P) + t(n-1; 1 - \beta_0)\right]^2}{c^2}\right] \tag{3.52}$$

In Table 3.5 sample sizes are given for $\alpha = 0.05$, $\beta_0 = 0.20$ and for selected values of c.

Table 3.5 *Values of n depending on $d = c \cdot \sigma$ for $\alpha = 0.05$, $\beta_0 = 0.20$, for a two-sided alternative hypothesis (i.e. $P = 1 - \alpha/2$).*

d	0.04σ	$1/10\sigma$	$1/5\sigma$	$1/4\sigma$	$1/3\sigma$	$1/2\sigma$	1σ
n	4908	787	199	128	73	34	10

Remark: Because $t(df; 0.5) = 0$ for all values of df the following connection between a two-sided $(1-\alpha)$-confidence interval (CI) for μ and a two-sided test of H_0: $\mu = 0$ with a Type I error risk α is given:
(i)   Formulae (3.20) and (3.51) are identical if we put $P = 1 - \alpha/2$ and $\beta_0 = 0.5$.
(ii) H_0 is accepted if and only if zero is covered by CI.
(iii) If we use (ii) as the test, the power is $1-\beta = 0.5$ if $\mu = 2d$ or $\mu = -2d$ with $2d$ the expected length of the CI.

Example 3.9

Let us calculate the value 73 in Table 3.5 for $d = 1/3\sigma$. Starting with $n^{(0)} = \infty$ we obtain $t(\infty; 0.975) = 1.96$ and $t(\infty; 0.8) = 0.84162$ and from this

$$n^{(1)} = \text{CEIL}[70.64] = 71.$$

Since $t(70; 0.975) = 1.99444$ and $t(70; 0.8) = 0.846786$ we have

$$n^{(2)} = \text{CEIL}[72.65] = 73$$

which remains unchanged in the next step ($\text{CEIL}(72.60) = 73$).

In CADEMO-*light* we use the menu sequence: "Test - mean against constant - mean of a normal distribution" which gives the same result.

Example 3.1 - continued

Returning to the litter weights of mice given in the first column of Table 3.1, we will test the hypothesis

$$H_0: \mu = E(x_i) = 10$$

against

$$H_A: \mu \neq 10$$

using a significance level $\alpha = 0.05$.
The sample size of the data set is already fixed with $n = 13$.

If $\alpha = 0.05$ and we accept a Type II error probability 0.2, what is the difference of practical interest (detectable with a probability $1-\beta = 0.8$) $d = |\mu - 10|$, if the estimate $\hat{\sigma}^2 = 2$?

We use CADEMO-*light* , and use the OPTION command in the menu bar (at the top of the screen). The sequence OPTIONS-MODULE SETTINGS leads us to Figure 3.17.

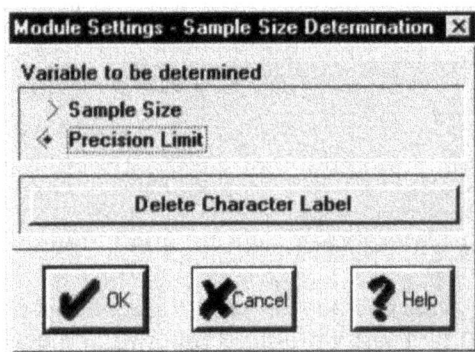

Figure 3.17 *Module Settings*

Then when we insert our predetermined values and set $n = 13$ as the sample size, we get the result $d = 1.2$

This means that the power function for testing H_0: $\mu = 10$ with a sample of size 13 and variance $\sigma^2 = 2$ takes the value $\alpha = 0.05$ for $\mu = 10$ and the value 0.8 (= 1-β) for the two values $\mu = 8.8$ and $\mu = 11.2$. The complete power function is shown in Figure 3.18.

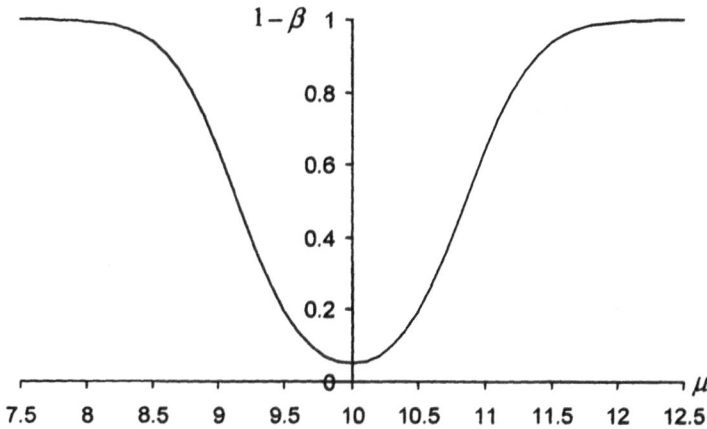

Figure 3.18 *The Power Function for H_0: $\mu = 10$ for $n = 13$ and $\alpha = 0.05$ and $\beta = 0.2$ in the case $|\mu - 10| = 1.2$*

3.4.2 Testing Hypotheses Concerning the Difference between the Means of Two Normal Distributions

Two cases occur in the comparison of means of two normal distributions. Firstly we can compare the means of the two components of a two-dimensional normal distribution. Or, we draw two samples independently of each other, one from each of two normal distributions – the situation already discussed when finding confidence intervals in section 3.2.2. We begin with the case of a two-dimensional distribution.

3.4.2.1 Paired Observations

The scenario is the one described in section 3.2.2.1. In this case we can use the *t*-Test for paired observations (often misleadingly called paired samples). This is the one-sample test introduced in section 3.4.1 applied to the *n* differences between the paired observations *x* and *y*. In fact the pairs of values (*x*, *y*) must be regarded as **one** sample from a *two-dimensional* distribution.

The present problem is solved by analogy with the one in section 3.4.1. Using the terminology of section 3.2.2.1, we replace μ by Δ, μ_0 by 0 and σ^2 by σ_Δ^2. This is completely analogous to the confidence interval construction for paired observations (Figure 3.11).

The sample size is obtained from:

$$n = \text{CEIL}\left[\frac{\sigma_\Delta^2}{d^2} \cdot \left[t(n-1;P) + t(n-1;1-\beta_0)\right]^2\right]$$ (3.53)

79

Example 3.1 - continued

Taking the first interpretation of the data in Example 3.1, we shall test the null hypothesis: $\mu_1 = \mu_2$ ($\mu_x = \mu_y$). We use the same SPSS program as we did for the construction of confidence intervals for the difference $\mu_1 - \mu_2$ between the two population means. In Figure 3.19 we show the relevant part of the SPSS output.

Paired Samples Statistics

		Mean	N	Std. Deviation	Std. Error Mean
Pair 1	x	9.769	13	1.9868	.5510
	y	11.531	13	2.9519	.8187

Paired Samples Test

		t	df	Sig. (2-tailed)
Pair 1	x - y	-1.739	12	.108

Figure 3.19 *Part of the SPSS output for Example 3.1*

In the lower part we find the t-value $t = -1.739$ with 12 degrees of freedom. Since the value of Sig. (2-tailed). in the last column is greater than $\alpha = 0.05$, the null hypothesis is accepted.

3.4.2.2 Independent Samples

Here we discuss the situation already considered in section 3.2.2.2. We have two normally distributed populations with means μ_1, μ_2 and variances σ_1^2, σ_2^2. Our purpose is to take two independent random samples $(y_{11}, ..., y_{1n_1})$ and $(y_{21}, ..., y_{2n_2})$ of sizes n_1 and n_2 from the two populations in order to test the null hypothesis

$$H_0 : \mu_1 = \mu_2$$

against one of the following one- or two-sided alternative hypotheses

a) $H_A : \mu_1 > \mu_2$
b) $H_A : \mu_1 < \mu_2$
c) $H_A : \mu_1 \neq \mu_2$

The sample sizes n_1 and n_2 should be determined in such a way that for a given risk of the first kind α, the risk of the second kind β as a function of $(\mu_1 - \mu_2)$ does not exceed a predetermined upper bound β_0 as long as, for the respective alternative hypothesis, we have either

a) $\mu_1 - \mu_2 \geq d$,
b) $\mu_1 - \mu_2 \leq -d$, or
c) $|\mu_1 - \mu_2| \geq d$.

As before, the value of d is called the minimal difference of practical interest between μ_1 and μ_2.

Because there are different tests for the cases $\sigma_1^2 = \sigma_2^2$ and $\sigma_1^2 \neq \sigma_2^2$; we will have different formulae for the analysis and for determining the necessary sample sizes.

Case A: Population variances are equal: $\sigma_1^2 = \sigma_2^2 = \sigma^2$.

In the case of equal (or nearly equal) variances the hypotheses above are best tested either by the one-sided t-test (cases a) and b)) or the two-sided t-test (case c)). The test is based on the *pooled estimator of the common variance* σ^2 given by

$$s_p^2 = \frac{\sum_{i=1}^{n_1}(y_{1i}-\bar{y}_{1.})^2 + \sum_{i=1}^{n_2}(y_{2i}-\bar{y}_{2.})^2}{n_1+n_2-2}.$$

$$(3.54)$$

The test statistic is:

$$t = \frac{\bar{y}_1-\bar{y}_2}{s_p}\sqrt{\frac{n_1 n_2}{n_1+n_2}}$$

$$(3.55)$$

and H_0 is rejected:

in case a) if $t > t(n_1+n_2-2; 1-\alpha)$,

in case b) if $t < -t(n_1+n_2-2; 1-\alpha)$ and

in case c) if $|t| > t(n_1+n_2-2; 1-\dfrac{\alpha}{2})$, and otherwise accepted.

When using SPSS, we reject H_0 in case c), whenever Sig.(2-tailed) is smaller than α. In case a) we reject H_0 if Sig.(2-tailed) is less than 2α. In case b) we reject H_0, when ever, for a negativen t-value, Sig.(2-tailed) is smaller than 2α. If the t-value is positive, we reject H_0, if α is less than $1-\dfrac{\text{Sig}(2-\text{tailed})}{2}$.

Example 3.1 - continued

Taking the second interpretation of the data, we test the hypothesis: $\mu_1 = \mu_2$ ($\mu_x = \mu_y$) using the file Litterweights II. The SPSS program is the same as for the construction of confidence intervals for the difference $\mu_1-\mu_2$ between the means of independent samples. We give the relevant extracts from the SPSS output in Figure 3.20.

Independent Samples Test

Levene's Test for Equality of Variances						
F	Sig.	t	df	Sig. (2-tailed)	Mean Difference	Std. Error Difference
2.601	.120	-1.785	24	.087	-1.7615	.9869
		-1.785	21.021	.089	-1.7615	.9869

Figure 3.20 *Extract from the SPSS Output for the example*

In the first line we find the t-value $t = -1.785$ with 24 degrees of freedom..

81

For $\alpha = 0.05$ and $f = 24$ we find from Table A1
$t(24; 0.95) = 1.7109$
$t(24; 0.975) = 2.0639$.

In a practical problem exactly one of the three possible alternative hypotheses will be used. Here we show the procedures for all the possible choices.
Case 1: The experimenter tests H_0 against
$H_A: \mu_1 > \mu_2$
Decision: Accept H_0 because
$-1.78 < 1.71$

Case 2: The experimenter tests H_0 against
$H_A: \mu_1 < \mu_2$
Decision: Reject H_0, because
$-1.78 < -1.71$

Case 3: The experimenter tests H_0 against
$H_A: \mu_1 \neq \mu_2$
Decision: Accept H_0, because $|-1.78| < 2.06$.

In Case 3 we accept H_0, because in the SPSS output Sig.(2-tailed) = 0.087, which is greater than 0.05. In Case 1 we accept H_0, because 1 - Sig.(2-tailed) = 0.913, which is greater than 0.10. In Case 2 we reject H_0, because Sig.(2-tailed) = 0.087, which is less than 0.10.
When the variances are equal this test leads to the smallest possible sample sizes for a given precision requirement.
Given the total number of observations $n_1 + n_2$ then $\text{var}(\bar{y}_1 - \bar{y}_2)$ is minimised for $n_1 = n_2 = n$, i.e. when the two sample sizes are equal.
The value of n can be determined iteratively from:

$$n = \text{CEIL}\left[\frac{2\sigma^2}{d^2} \cdot \left[t(2n-2; P) + t(2n-2; 1-\beta_0) \right]^2 \right] \qquad (3.56)$$

where $P = 1-\alpha$ for a one-sided alternative, and $P = 1-\alpha/2$ for the two-sided alternative hypothesis. If no a-priori information concerning the common variance σ^2 is available, we can use Algorithm B, which has already been described.

Example 3.10
We wish to determine the *minimal sample size* to test the hypothesis of the equality of two means from independent normal distributions with common variances against a two-sided alternative. We choose $\alpha = 0.05$, $\beta = 0.1$ and $d = 3$. An estimate of σ^2 from earlier experiments is $\tilde{\sigma}^2 = 25$.
Using CL we obtain the result $n = 60$.

Case B: Population variances are different : $\sigma_1^2 \neq \sigma_2^2$.

This is known as the Behrens-Fisher problem. An approximate solution was proposed by WELCH (1947) and uses the following test statistic:

82

$$t = \frac{\bar{y}_1 - \bar{y}_2}{\sqrt{\frac{s_1^2}{n_1} + \frac{s_2^2}{n_2}}} \tag{3.57}$$

where s_1^2 and s_2^2 are the two sample variances. Taking f^* from (3.42) we reject H_0:
in case 1, if $t > t(f^*; 1 - \alpha)$,
in case 2 if $t < - t(f^*; 1 - \alpha)$ and
in case 3, if $|t| > t(f^*; 1 - \alpha/2)$ and accept it otherwise (the three cases correspond to those in Case A for equal variances).

Example 3.1 - continued
In SPSS outputs analogous to Figure 3.20 will depend upon whether the Levene Test of the equality of variances was significant or not, and if it is, then always on the result of the Welch test. Here the Levene Test gave an F-value of 2.6 and a Sig.-value of 0.12, which with $\alpha = 0.05$ is not significant, so the Welch test need not be used. Anyway we do not know the Type II error probability (and that is very relevant here). However as a precaution we can use the Welch test. The results do not change, except that the degrees of freedom reduce somewhat.

The two sample sizes can be determined as follows:

$$n_1 = \text{CEIL}\left[\frac{\tilde{\sigma}_1(\tilde{\sigma}_1 + \tilde{\sigma}_2)}{d^2}\left[t\left(f^*; P\right) + t\left(f^*; 1 - \beta_0\right)\right]^2\right] \text{ and}$$

$$n_2 = \text{CEIL}\left[n_1 \cdot \frac{\tilde{\sigma}_2}{\tilde{\sigma}_1}\right], \tag{3.58}$$

with f^* as in (3.42). The case of unknown variances can be handled separately using Algorithm B.

Example 3.11
Prior information is available for two normal distributions with unequal variances, namely $\tilde{\sigma}_1 = s_1 = 4$ and $\tilde{\sigma}_2 = s_2 = 5$.
We wish to test H_0: $\mu_1 = \mu_2$ against the two-sided alternative with $\alpha = 0.05$, $\beta = 0.1$ and $d = 2$. How large should the samples be?
With $\dfrac{\tilde{\sigma}_1(\tilde{\sigma}_1 + \tilde{\sigma}_2)}{d^2} = \dfrac{4(4 + 5)}{4} = 9$ the iteration procedure gives the following results

$$f^{(0)} = \infty$$

$$n_1^{(1)} = \text{CEIL}[9 \cdot [1.96 + 1.2816]^2] = \text{CEIL}[94.57] = 95,$$

$$n_2^{(1)} = \text{CEIL}[\frac{5}{4} \cdot 94.57] = 119, \quad f^{(1)} = 21, \quad n_1^{(2)} = 96, \quad n_2^{(2)} = 120$$

which remain unchanged in further iterations. Thus $n_1 = 96$, $n_2 = 120$.

We obtain this value quicker with CL or CADEMO-MEANS using the command sequence Test – Two Means – Normal Distributions – Independent Samples – Unknown Variances. Figure 3.21 shows the results.

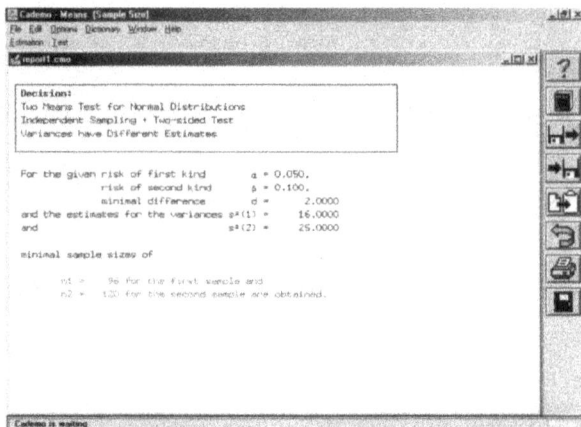

Figure 3.21. Sample size determination for unequal variances

At this point we will compare the above fixed-sample-size procedures with the alternative *sequential tests*. Sequential experiments were first published by WALD (1947). These experiments were so called open-ended experiments – they end at some point with probability 1, but one cannot say when. Under some circumstances they can last a very long time. In our mouse example we must continue taking measurements until a decision to accept either the null or alternative hypothesis is taken. Later so-called closed experiments were developed. In these there is an upper limit to the number of observations. This limit is greater than that required for the corresponding fixed sample size test, but the full number will seldom be needed. On average all sequential procedures require smaller numbers than fixed sample size procedures. SCHNEIDER (1992) describes the underlying triangular sequential tests, which are available in the CADEMO module TRIQ. Readers interested in the theoretical background, which lies outside the scope of this book, can refer to SCHNEIDER or WHITEHEAD (1992).

Again we wish to test the null hypothesis

$$H_0 : \mu_1 = \mu_2$$

against the two-sided alternative hypothesis

$$H_A : \mu_1 \neq \mu_2$$

- but now by using a sequential test. We describe the procedure as applied to our mouse example.

Example 3.1 - continued

First we must carry out the steps File New in CADEMO-TRIQ, and in the dialogue box which appears (Figure 3.22) we enter the scale of measurement (here quantitative). Then for each type of scale a further dialogue box appears; in the case of quantitative data it is Figure 3.23.

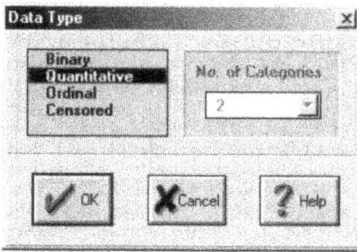

Figure 3.22 *Entering the scale of measurement in CADEMO-TRIQ*

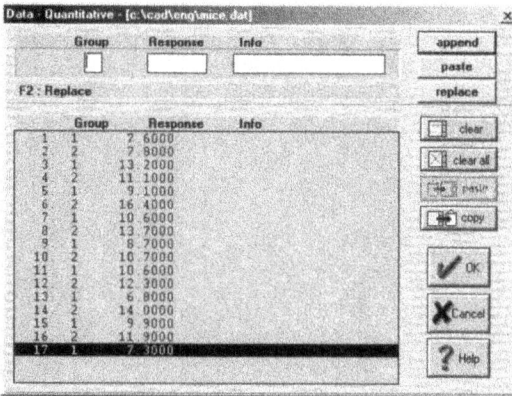

Figure 3.23 *The data used in Example 3.1*

The existing data are now entered, analysed, and the file saved under a new name (here mice.dat). If the test cannot be terminated using the already available data, then further data is collected and we call up the original data file with **File Open** and choose the file from the list which appears (in Figure 3.24 the data for Example 3.1 is highlighted). The new data are entered and analysed, and either data collection continues, or the procedure ends with a so-called "terminating decision" (i.e. we accept either the null or the alternative hypothesis).

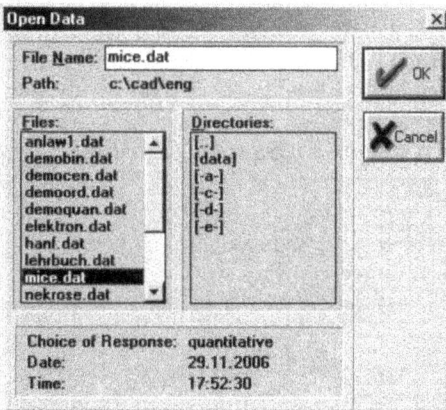

Figure 3.24 *Calling up a required data file*

In a sequential test we first of all decide on the precision requirements. Usually we begin by taking two observations from each of the two groups, and then we take new values alternately from Groups 1 and 2. Thus the allocation rate between the two groups is 1:1. Of course one set the allocation differently from 1:1, for example on ethical grounds (especially in clinical trials comparing two therapies). This often happens according to the "play the winner rule", in which one of the two therapies continues to be used so long as it is successful. As soon as it results in a failure, we switch to the other therapy.

Example 3.1 – continued

When we confirm the data with OK, Figure 3.25 appears, which we show here already filled in. The values $\alpha = 0.05$, $\beta = 0.2$ und $d = 2.5$ have been entered, and also the value 3 as an estimate for σ^2.

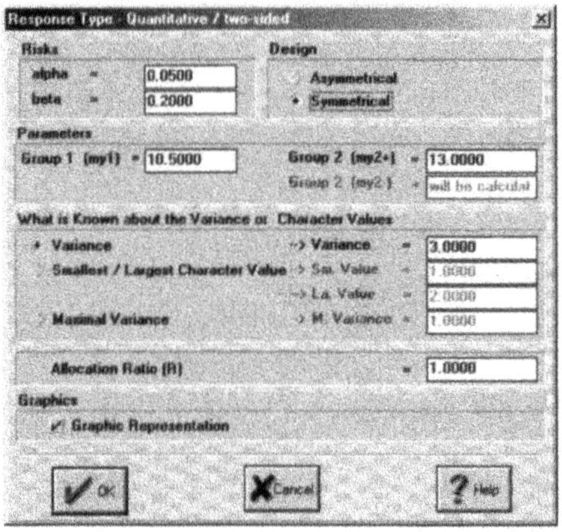

Figure 3.25 *Entering the precision requirements*

After a total of 17 values (alternating between Groups 1 and 2) from Table 3.1 have been entered, we come to a terminating decision; the null hypothesis is rejected, because the path of the line showing the observations has crossed a boundary of one of the hatched triangles in Figure 3.26. So long as it remains in the hatched area, the experiment continues. Had the line reached the region between the two triangles, then the null hypothesis would have been accepted. That is rather difficult to discern in the picture, so we must always look at the numerical part of the results as in Figure 3.27, where the result is clear. We will not deal with all the numbers round the edge of Figure 3.26 (a detailed description and further examples can be found in RASCH and KUBINGER (2006)), the value N+ max = 24 is interesting, it means that the experiment will terminate after at most 24 observations. For the same precision requirements, CL would have used 18 observations (the value 16 under 'fix' for fixed sample sizes was calculated by TRIQ under the assumption of known variances).

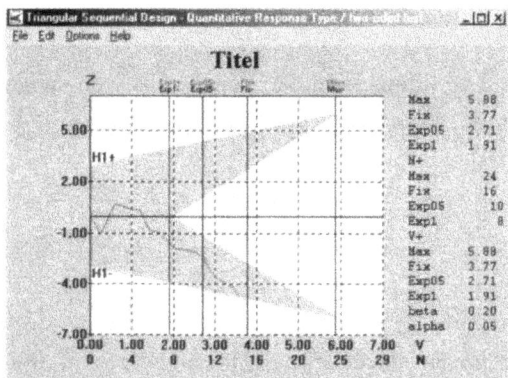

Figure 3.26 *Graphical output from a sequential test*

Figure 3.27 *Numerical output of a sequential test*

3.4.3 Comparison of the Variances of Two Normal Distributions

We wish to compare the variances σ_1^2 and σ_2^2 of two normal populations and for this purpose we will take a random sample from each population. Let the sample sizes be n_1 and n_2. If n_1 and n_2 can be freely chosen, then we choose $n_1 = n_2 = n$. For the analysis we allow for $n_1 \neq n_2$ (a situation which can occur through drop outs even with optimal planning). In most textbooks the F-test is recommended for the analysis.

However simulation experiments have shown that this test is very sensitive to even small deviations from the assumed normality of the underlying distributions of the variables. The F-Test is the best (optimal) test if the two variables really are normally distributed, but in practice we can never be sure that the distributions do not deviate slightly from normality. This does not matter in the case of confidence intervals or tests about means, because the procedures based on the t-test have shown themselves to be extremely robust. However for the comparison of two variances we only use the F-test for the calculation of the sample size n; for the analysis we use Levene's test, which is also available in SPSS.

Experimental design:

Independent samples of size n will be drawn from two populations with variances σ_1^2 and σ_2^2 in order to test the hypothesis

$$H_0:\ \sigma_1^2 = \sigma_2^2$$

against the alternative hypothesis

$$H_A:\ \sigma_1^2 \neq \sigma_2^2$$

How do we choose n if, for a significance level of α and for a given $\tau > 1$, the Type II error probability when

$$\frac{\sigma_{max}^2}{\sigma_{min}^2} \geq \tau \text{ must not be greater than } \beta_0?$$

Here σ_{max}^2 is the larger, and σ_{min}^2 the smaller of the two variances.
The required n is the solution of

$$\tau = F(n-1; n-1; 1 - \frac{\alpha}{2}) F(n-1; n-1; 1 - \beta_0)$$

involving the quantiles of the F-distribution with n-1 and n-1 degrees of freedom. Here Table A3 is not very useful, since it only gives the 95%-quantiles and we can only find n for the case $\alpha = 0.1$, $\beta_0 = 0.05$.
Therefore we recommend the use of CADEMO-*light* taking the menu sequence **Sample Size - Two Sample Problem -Variances**, or table 3.6, which is an extract from VB 3/32/0102.
For a β_0-value not contained in Table 3.6 we use CL and enter $\alpha = 0.05$, $\beta_0 = 0.2$ and $\tau = 5.5$ (=Q in CL) and obtain the value of $n = 13$ (see Figure 3.28), which can also be calculated approximately from Table 3.6 by interpolation.
This is the sample size in Example 3.1.

```
Decision:
Two Sample Problem - Independent Samples
Test of Two Variances
Determination of Sample Size
```

```
Character:
Litter Mass

For the specified parameters
    Q = 5.5000 (quotient of both variances)
    α = 0.0500
    β = 0.2000
for a two-sided test
minimum sample sizes of
    n₁ = 13 and
    n₂ = 13
result.
```

Figure 3.28 *CL Output*

Table 3.6 *Values of τ corresponding to sample sizes $n_1 = n_2 = n$ for the comparison of two variances for $\alpha = 0.05$ and 3 values of β_0.*

n	$\beta_0 = 0.05$	$\beta_0 = 0.1$	$\beta_0 = 0.25$
3	741.0000	351.0000	117.0000
4	143.2214	83.2286	36.3666
5	61.3564	39.4486	19.8256
6	36.0915	24.6765	13.5403
7	24.9310	17.7769	10.3713
8	18.9157	13.9103	8.4968
9	15.2418	11.4789	7.2687
10	12.7983	9.8246	6.4050
11	11.0694	8.6326	5.7659
12	9.7864	7.7340	5.2728
13	8.8048	7.0377	4.8838
14	8.0245	6.4778	4.5652
15	7.3955	6.0220	4.3025
16	6.8791	5.6446	4.0822
19	5.7519	4.8096	3.5841
21	5.2351	4.4208	3.3468
25	4.5018	3.8621	2.9987
31	3.8178	3.3317	2.6594
41	3.1743	2.8233	2.3247
49	2.8616	2.5720	2.1550
61	2.5574	2.3255	1.9855
121	1.9369	1.8118	1.6210
∞	1.0000	1.0000	1.0000

Analysis

Suppose that we have two independent random samples $(x_1, x_2, ..., x_{n_1})$ and $(y_1, y_2, ..., y_{n_2})$ from each of two continuous distributions, in which

$$\text{var}(x_i) = \sigma_1^2$$

and

$$\text{var}(y_j) = \sigma_2^2.$$

The null hypothesis H_0 given above concerning the equality of the variances is tested with the Levene Test. For this we use the realised observations x_i and y_j to calculate the quantities

$$|x_i - \bar{x}| \text{ or } u_i = (x_i - \bar{x})^2$$

and

$$|y_j - \bar{y}| \text{ or } v_j = (y_j - \bar{y})^2$$

and carry out an independent samples t-test with the $|x_i - \bar{x}|$ and $|y_j - \bar{y}|$ or with the u_i and v_j (in section 3.4.2.2 replace the x_i by the $|x_i - \bar{x}|$ or the u_i and the y_j by $|y_j - \bar{y}|$ or the

v_j). SPSS automatically carries out a Levene test as part of the procedure in an independent samples t-test. The version it uses to compare the variances is the one involving the absolute values $|x_i\text{-}\bar{x}|$ and $|y_i\text{-}\bar{y}|$. Unfortunately there is no reference (neither in the on-line help nor in the manual) to this test. You find it only by chance, if you happen to compare means.

Example 3.1 - continued

We will compare the variances of the litter weights of the two strains of mice using the data from Table 3.1.

First we will use the values $\bar{x} = 9.769$ and $\bar{y} = 11.531$ already obtained (see Figure 3.3) to calculate the values of u_i and v_i

i	$|x_i\text{-}\bar{x}|$	u_i	$|y_i\text{-}\bar{y}|$	v_i
1	2.169	4.7046	3.731	13.9204
2	3.431	11.7718	0.431	0.1858
3	0.669	0.4476	4.869	23.7072
4	0.831	0.6906	2.169	4.7046
5	1.069	1.1428	0.831	0.6906
6	0.831	0.6906	0.769	0.5914
7	2.969	8.8150	2.469	6.0960
8	0.131	0.0172	0.369	0.1362
9	2.469	6.0960	2.731	7.4584
10	0.631	0.3982	3.831	14.6766
11	3.531	12.4680	2.631	6.9222
12	0.231	0.0534	4.869	23.7072
13	0.269	0.0724	1.331	1.7716

and carry out a two-sample t-test with $\alpha = 0.05$ both for the pairs $|x_i\text{-}\bar{x}|$ and $|y_i\text{-}\bar{y}|$ and also u_i and v_i.

Using SPSS we get the $|t|$-value to be 1.642 for the u_i and v_i and a t-value of $|t|=1.613$ for the absolute deviations. The t-value $|t| = 1.613$ for the deviations is the positive square root of the Levene F-value 2.601 which appears in Figure 3.20. The hypothesis of equality of the two variances is not rejected.

3.4.4 Comparison between two Proportions using Independent Samples

To introduce the problem we make use of the following example from VB 3/62/2005.

Example 3.12

In an experiment to compare two breeds (B_1, B_2) of carrier pigeons, the proportions of the two breeds who successfully returned home were observed. We denote the return of a pigeon by A_1 and the loss of a pigeon by A_2. The results are shown in the following layout, which is known as a four-fold (or (2×2)) table.

Breed	A_1 (Return)	A_2 (Loss)	Total
B_1	289	27	316
B_2	274	42	316

As can be seen from the Total column, 316 pigeons of each breed were released. We wish to establish whether the difference between the proportions observed is statistically significant.

In the above example we can assume that the two samples are independent of each other, and we will only deal with this case in this book. For the case of paired observations we refer the reader to the McNemar Test in VB 3/62/2020.

Using independent samples from two populations, we wish to test the null hypothesis

H_0: $p_1 = p_2$

against one of the alternative hypotheses:

a) H_A: $p_1 > p_2$
b) H_A: $p_1 < p_2$
c) H_A: $p_1 \neq p_2$.

In each population it is also assumed that, out of n_i observations, the number y_i of those which result in a certain event A follows a binomial distribution with parameter p_i. In the above example A is the event that the pigeon returns, there are $n_1 = n_2 = n = 316$ released pigeons, and we have

$p_1 = P(A_1|B_1), \; p_2 = P(A_1|B_2).$

To design an experiment, we would also have to determine n_1 and n_2 so that pre-assigned precision requirements were satisfied.
In contrast to the other parts of Section 3.4, in the case of two independent proportions it is not possible to give a generally applicable recommendation for the test to be used and for the best formula for calculating the sample size. Most often one uses one of the numerous approximate formulae discussed in, for example, SARHAI and KURSCHID (1996).
Also the test itself is frequently carried out in an approximate form (apart from Fisher's exact test (which is conservative)). We give here the formulae which, following BOCK (1998), are recommended for the test and also for the sample size calculation, when the conditions

$0.05 \leq p_1, p_2 \leq 0.95,$
$n_1 = n_2 = n$

are satisfied.

First of all we generalize the four-fold table of the example, and (as in Appendix B.2.2.1) we denote a certain event by A and its complementary event by $\overline{A}$ (not-A). Then the results of an experiment can be laid out as follows:

	Event		
Sample from:	A	$\overline{A}$	Total
Population1	a	b	$n_1 = a + b$
Population 2	c	d	$n_2 = c + d$

Estimates for $p_1 = P(A|\text{Pop1})$ and $p_2 = (P(A|\text{Pop2})$ [Pop = Population] are obtained as in (3.9):

$$\hat{p}_1 = \frac{a}{n_1}, \qquad \hat{p}_2 = \frac{c}{n_2}.$$

In the case where the hypothesis $p_1 = p_2 = p$ is true, we would estimate the common p from

$$\hat{p} = \frac{a+c}{n_1 + n_2}.$$

Under the null hypothesis

$$u = \frac{\hat{p}_1 - \hat{p}_2 + \dfrac{x}{n_1 n_2}}{\sqrt{\hat{p}(1-\hat{p})}} \sqrt{\dfrac{n_1 n_2}{n_1 + n_2}} \tag{3.59}$$

approximately follows an $N(0;1)$ distribution. In (3.59) x is a correction factor, which is required in order to allow us to approximate the discrete binomial distribution by the continuous normal distribution, so that the type I error probability is approximately attained (in Fisher's exact test the actual type I risk is nearly always slightly smaller than α - therefore we call this test *conservative*). The sign of x depends on the alternative hypothesis. We use the following decision rules:

a) H_A: $p_1 > p_2$
       Reject H_0 whenever

$$u_a = \frac{\hat{p}_1 - \hat{p}_2 - \dfrac{\min(n_1,n_2)}{2 n_1 n_2}}{\sqrt{\hat{p}(1-\hat{p})}} \sqrt{\dfrac{n_1 n_2}{n_1 + n_2}} > u(1-\alpha)$$

       holds.

b) H_A: $p_1 < p_2$
       Reject H_0 whenever:

$$u_b = \frac{\hat{p}_1 - \hat{p}_2 + \dfrac{\min(n_1,n_2)}{2 n_1 n_2}}{\sqrt{\hat{p}(1-\hat{p})}} \sqrt{\dfrac{n_1 n_2}{n_1 + n_2}} < u(\alpha)$$

       holds.

c) H_A: $p_1 \neq p_2$.
       Reject H_0 whenever

$$u_c = \frac{|\hat{p}_1 - \hat{p}_2| - \dfrac{\min(n_1,n_2)}{2 n_1 n_2}}{\sqrt{\hat{p}(1-\hat{p})}} \sqrt{\dfrac{n_1 n_2}{n_1 + n_2}} > u(1-\frac{\alpha}{2})$$

       holds, taking the P-quantiles $u(P)$ from Table A1.
       u_c can also be written as follows:

$$u_c = \frac{\left[|ad - bc| - \frac{\min(n_1, n_2)}{2}\right]\sqrt{n_1 + n_2}}{\sqrt{n_1 n_2 (a + c)(b + d)}}.$$

When there is no reason (ethical or economic) to take a larger sample from one of the two populations than the other, we choose $n_1 = n_2 = n$ when planning the experiment. As in the previous sections, the precision requirements stipulate the values of both risks α und β as well as a minimal difference of practical interest

$$\begin{array}{ll} d = p_1 - p_2 & \text{in case a)} \\ d = p_2 - p_1 & \text{in case b)} \\ d = |p_1 - p_2| & \text{in case c).} \end{array}$$

In addition n depends on prior information about the values of p_1 und p_2. Following FLEISS (1981) we have

$$n = \text{CEIL}\left[\frac{1}{d^2}\left[u(P)\sqrt{(p_1 + p_2)(1 - \frac{1}{2}(p_1 + p_2))} + u(1 - \beta)\sqrt{p_1(1 - p_1) + p_2(1 - p_2)}\right]^2\right]$$

(3.60)

In cases a) and b) we set $P = 1 - \alpha$ in (3.60) and in case c) we set $P = 1 - \frac{\alpha}{2}$.

We then use the following modification, following CASAGRANDE, PIKE and SMITH (1978), which takes the form

$$n_{\text{corr}} = \text{CEIL}\left[\frac{n}{4}\left[1 + \sqrt{1 + \frac{4}{nd}}\right]^2\right]$$

(3.61)

where n is taken from (3.60).

Example 3.12 – Continued

Using the data from Example 3.12 we wish to test the hypothesis
$H_0: p_1 = p_2$ against
$H_A: p_1 \neq p_2$
where we have chosen $\alpha = 0.05$.
The value of u_c (using the second version of the formula) is

$$u_c = \frac{\left(|289 \cdot 42 - 27 \cdot 274| - \frac{316}{2}\right)\sqrt{632}}{316\sqrt{563 \cdot 69}} = 1.8495$$

and since $u_c < u(0.975) = 1.96$, H_0 is accepted.
How large must the sample size be, if we want to test the above hypothesis and $\alpha = 0.05$, $\beta = 0.20$, $d = 0.1$, and also we have $p_1 = 0.95$, $p_2 = 0.85$ given as prior estimates?

Using (3.60) we obtain

$$n = \text{CEIL}\left[100\left[1.96\sqrt{1.8 \cdot 0.1} + 0.8416 \cdot \sqrt{0.95 \cdot 0.05 + 0.85 \cdot 0.15}\right]^2\right] = 141,$$

and using (3.61)

$$n_{\text{corr}} = \text{CEIL}\left[\frac{141}{4}\left(1 + \sqrt{1 + \frac{4}{14.1}}\right)^2\right] = 161.$$

In CADEMO-*light* we choose the command sequence **Sample Size Determination** - **Two Sample Problem** –**Independent Samples** - **Probabilities Test** and a dialogue box appears, in which we enter the above precision requirements, which gives Figure 3.29

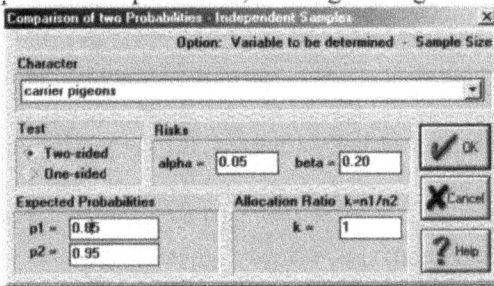

Figure 3.29 *Dialogue box in CADEMO-light for Example 3.12*

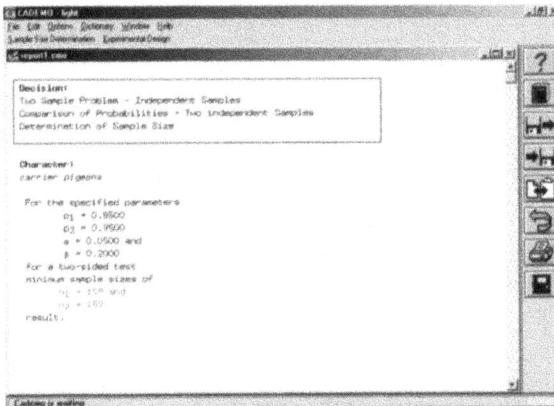

Figure 3.30 *Results for Example 3.12*

The result *n* =159 given by CADEMO lies between the corrected and uncorrected values given by formulae (3.60) and (3.61).

Now we will compare the fixed-sample-size procedures described above with the alternative sequential tests.

In Figure 3.22 we now choose the option "binary" and instead of Figure 3.23 we now have Figure 3.31, in which we have already entered the first observations, here called "Return" and "Loss".

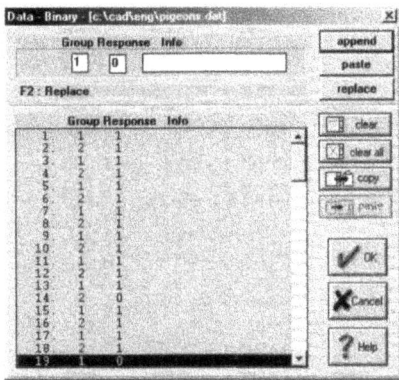

Figure 3.31 *The first data from Example 3.12*

We do not need to enter all the data again, but merely notice that in Group 1 (breed B_1) the experimental units 10, 23, 29, 43, 48 and in Group 2 (breed B_2) experimental units 7, 11, 14, 18, 25, 28, 31, 36, 37, 44, 46, 49, 50, 53 give rise to a zero, otherwise a 1 always occurs. On the 53rd observation of a pigeon from Group 2, the sequential investigation ends with the rejection of the null hypothesis that the probabilities of Return are the same in both breeds against the one-sided alternative that breed B_1 has a higher probability of return, as we can see in Figure 3.32.

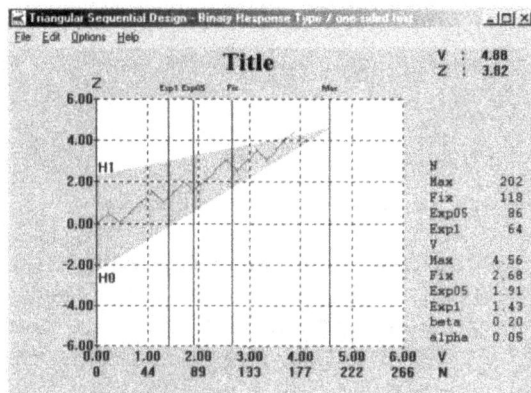

Figure 3.32 *Graphical output from the one-sided sequential test.*

Had we stipulated a two-sided alternative hypothesis, when entering the pre-set precision requirements in Figure 3.33, the experiment would have continued as in Figure 3.34.

95

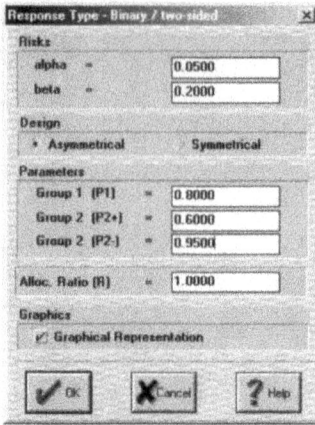

Figure 3.33 *Asymmetrical predetermined precision requirements*

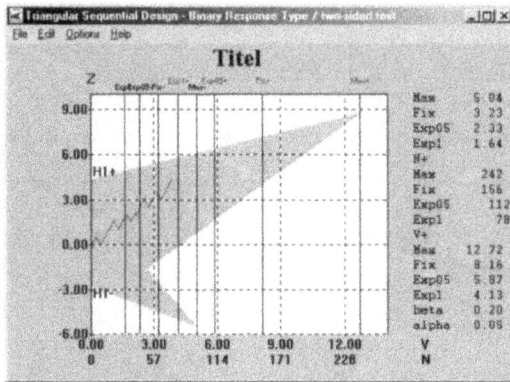

Figure 3.34 *The progress in the case of a two-sided asymmetrical alternative*

In Figure 3.33 the distances from the null hypothesis value were not chosen to be the same on both sides (the asymmetrical case). As a result, the two overlapping triangles are not equally large. Had we entered a distance of 0.18 on both sides, we would have had two big triangles as in Figure 3.35.

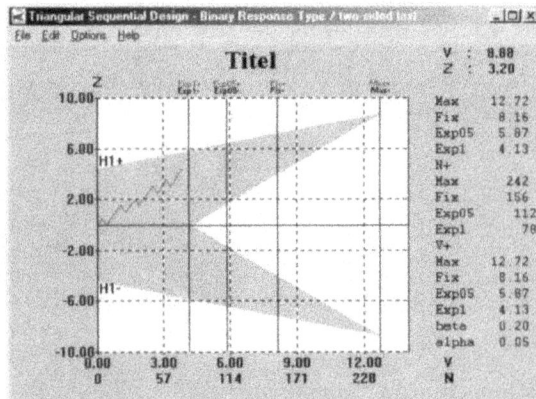

Figure 3.35 *The progress in the case of a two-sided symmetrical alternative*

It is good to see that the path here is also leading to the rejection of the null hypothesis, and is moving in the direction of the area denoted by H1+. This means that an eventual rejection of the null hypothesis will indicate that breed B_1 has the greater probability of return.

3.4.5 Equivalence Tests

In most applications of statistical tests the null hypothesis takes the form of a statement that two quantities are equal. In the one-sample problem concerning the mean of a normal distribution, the null hypothesis is (for known variance) a so-called "simple" hypothesis, which contains only one point on the real line, while the alternative hypothesis is "composite" and describes an interval (or two intervals) on the real line. But since one can reasonably start from a position that says that no two things in nature are equal, these null hypotheses describe situations that in reality are impossible. Equivalence tests eliminate this asymmetry, and by the interchange of the null and alternative hypotheses, replace the concept of complete equality by "practical equality" or even equivalence. As a consequence the interpretation of the risks alters.

We will illustrate these ideas using the scenario described in section 3.4.2.2. By means of two independent random samples $(y_{11}, ..., y_{1n_1})$ and $(y_{21}, ..., y_{2n_2})$ of sizes n_1 and n_2 drawn from the corresponding populations, in section 3.4.2.2 we tested the null hypothesis

$$H_0 : \mu_1 = \mu_2$$

against the two-sided alternative hypothesis

$$H_A : \mu_1 \neq \mu_2.$$

A corresponding *equivalence test* tests the hypothesis

$$H_0 : \text{either } \mu_1 - \mu_2 < -d \text{ or } \mu_1 - \mu_2 > d,$$

i.e. the null hypothesis assumes that the means differ by at least d. This is the symmetrical formulation. In the unsymmetrical case different positive and negative limits for the difference can be chosen. The alternative hypothesis of the equivalence test now says: H_0 does not hold, i.e.

$$H_A : -d \leq \mu_1 - \mu_2 \leq d$$

or the difference, in the language of section 3.3, lies in an indifference region.
The problem just described can now be solved very simply.

As in section 3.2.2.2 we form an upper and lower (one-sided) $(1-\alpha)$-confidence interval. If both finite limits of the intervals lie in the alternative hypothesis region, then we reject H_0 and accept the alternative hypothesis, and we consider the two expectations to be practically equivalent.
In VB can be found the following equivalence tests (EQ for short):

6/13/5110 one-sided EQ for means
6/13/5120 one-sided EQ for probabilities
6/13/5221 EQ for the mean of a normal distribution
6/13/5222 EQ for the mean of two normal distributions
6/13/5230 two-sided EQ for probabilities.

Example 3.1 - continued

Taking the second interpretation of the data (two independent samples from normal distributions), we calculate upper and lower 95% one-sided confidence intervals for the difference between the population means. We already know (Figure 3.3), that $\bar{x} = 9.7692$, $\bar{y} = 11.5308$, $s_1^2 = 3.947$, $s_2^2 = 8.714$ and we know that $n_1 = n_2 = 13$.

We can assume $\sigma_1^2 = \sigma_2^2$. Then it follows from (3.38) and (3.39), using $t(24;0.95)=1.7109$ that the upper interval is [-3.45; ∞) and the lower one (-∞; -0.073].

For $d = 2$ only one of the finite limits lies in the interval - $2 \le \mu_1 - \mu_2 \le 2$ (the alternative hypothesis region), and H_0 is not rejected, i.e. our decision is "the population means are not equivalent". If $d = 4$ the hypothesis H_A of equivalence will be accepted.

WELLEK (2003) gives a detailed description of equivalence tests.

4   Analysis of Variance

The *analysis of variance* (*ANOVA*) comprises several linear statistical models for the description of the influence of one or more qualitative factor(s) on a quantitative character y. For all models in the analysis of variance, the linear model equation has the form

$$y = E(y) + e \qquad (4.1)$$

In this equation the random variable y models the observed character. The observation y is the sum of the expectation (mean) $E(y)$ of y and an error term e, containing observational errors with $E(e) = 0$, and the variability in $E(y)$ between experimental units depends linearly on model parameters. The models for the analysis of variance differ in the number and the nature of these parameters.

The observations in an analysis of variance are allocated to at least two classes which are determined by the levels of the factors.

Each of the models of the analysis of variance contains the general mean μ, i.e. we write $E(y)$ in the form:

$$E(y) = \mu + EC(y) \qquad (4.2)$$

where $EC(y)$ is the mean deviation from μ within the corresponding class. In the case of p factors the analysis of variance is called p-way.

Later in this chapter we describe the models for the one- and two-way classifications and give the corresponding ANOVA tables.

It follows from (4.2) that the total set of the y_i does not constitute a random sample because not all the y_i have the same expectation. Furthermore in models with random factors the y-values within a class are not independent.

The overall mean μ and the non-random components of $EC(y)$ are estimated by the method of (ordinary) least squares (OLS) described in section 3.1.1; in the case of correlated errors OLS will be generalised and becomes the generalised least squares method (GLS).

The theoretical background can be found in many statistical textbooks, and special books on ANOVA (for instance: SCHEFFÉ (1959), LINDMAN (1991), and RASCH (1995)). Also, in section 4.2.3 we give guidelines as to how the reader should deal with a problem in which an analysis of variance involves more than 2 factors.

4.1 One-way Analysis of Variance

If the influence of only one factor is considered in the analysis of variance, we call this a *one-way analysis of variance*. The number of levels of the treatment factor will be denoted by a, the factor itself is A and its a levels are written as A_1, ..., A_a. We need to consider two basic situations depending on how we select the levels of A:

Situation 1:   There are exactly a levels, all included in the experiment. We call this *Model I analysis of variance* or the *fixed effects model*.

Situation 2:   There are many levels, whose number is in theory considered to be infinite. The levels to be included in the experiment have to be selected randomly from the universe of levels; we call this *Model II analysis of variance* or the *random effects model*.

In this book both fixed and random models are considered. For two-way classifications so-called *mixed* models are also considered, where one factor is fixed and the other random.

The difference between models I and II can be illustrated by the following simple examples. If the treatment factor is the time in years and if we observe the differences in a country's steel production in five specially selected years, a fixed model has to be chosen. However if yearly differences in the yield of 8 particular wheat varieties are of interest, a two-way analysis of variance with a fixed factor "variety" (because just these 8 varieties are of interest and no others) and a random factor "years" (we are interested in the variability between years in general, not just particular years) should be chosen as a model.

For both model I and model II analysis of variance a linear model equation of the form defined above is assumed, but the nature of the parameters depends on whether the model is fixed or random.

We use at least two suffixes for the observations in the model, for example i for the factor levels and j for the observations within the level i. The suffix i runs from 1 to a and j runs from 1 to n_i, where n_i is the number of observations made in factor level A_i.

In the analysis of variance hypotheses can be tested and parameters estimated. If the factors are fixed we estimate their effects and generally test hypotheses about whether different effects are equal.

In the case of random factors we estimate the components of variance associated with each factor and/or test whether these variance components are zero.

4.1.1   One-way Analysis of Variance - Model I

The model equation is written in the form:

$$y_{ij} = E(y_{ij}) + e_{ij} = \mu + a_i + e_{ij} \tag{4.3}$$

The a_i are called the main effects of the *factor levels* A_i, they are real numbers, i.e. not random. The model is completed by the following constraints (sometimes called side conditions): the e_{ij} are mutually independent with $E(e_{ij}) = 0$ and $var(e_{ij}) = \sigma^2$. We assume either that the sum of the a_i is zero, or that the sum of the products $n_i a_i$ equals zero (which are equivalent if the n_i are all equal).

Table 4.1 gives the *analysis of variance* (ANOVA) table for the model, with
$$N = \sum_{i=1}^{a} n_i = an,$$ since we shall restrict ourselves to the case where $n_i = n$ and
$$\sum_{i=1}^{a} a_i = 0 \; [SS = \text{Sum of Squares}, \; MS = \text{Mean Square}].$$

Table 4.1   ANOVA Table: One-way classification, Model I ($n_i = n$).

Source of variation	SS	df	MS	E(MS)
Main effect A	SS_A $= \frac{1}{n}\sum_i Y_{i.}^2 - \frac{Y_{..}^2}{N}$	a-1	$MS_A = \frac{SS_A}{a-1}$	$\sigma^2 + \frac{n}{a-1}\sum a_i^2$
Residual	SS_R $= \sum_{i,j} y_{ij}^2 - \frac{1}{n}\sum_i Y_{i.}^2$	N-a	$MS_R = \frac{SS_R}{N-a}$	σ^2
Total	SS_T $= \sum_{i,j} y_{ij}^2 - \frac{Y_{..}^2}{N}$	N-1		

If y has a normal distribution we can test the following null hypothesis:
H_0:   "The factor A has no effect on the dependent variable y". In other words: "All the a_i are equal". If it is assumed that the sum of the a_i is zero, this is the same as "All the a_i are zero".

The alternative hypothesis is:
H_A: "At least two of the a_i are different".

The test statistic for this test is a variate F which (if the null hypothesis is true) follows a (central) F-distribution with f_1 and f_2 degrees of freedom. The $(1-\alpha)$-quantile of the distribution of $F(f_1;f_2)$ is denoted by $F(f_1;f_2; 1-\alpha)$.

This test statistic is generally calculated by following the next 8 steps - here "generally" means that these steps should be used for all situations and models in this chapter (and subsequently).

1.   Define the null hypothesis.
2.   Choose the appropriate model (I, II, or mixed).
3.   Find the E(MS) column in the ANOVA table (if there are several such columns, find the one that corresponds to your model). In our case we use the E(MS) column of Table 4.1.
4.   In the same table find the row for the factor that appears in your null hypothesis.
5.   Change the E(MS) in this row to what it would be if the null hypothesis were true.
6.   Search in the same table (in the same column) for the row which now has the same E(MS) as you found in step 5.
7.   The F-value is now the value of the MS of the row you found in step 4 divided by the value of the MS of the row you found in step 6.
8.   Note: in ANOVA with higher classifications, step 6 may not be successful, in which case one can use the so-called Satterthwaite approximation (see VB 3/24/2003, 3/42/3000, 3/42/3001, 3/42/3002).

To carry out the test, we have to compare the calculated F-value with the $(1-\alpha)$-quantile of the F distribution with f_1 and f_2 degrees of freedom for the given α. The value of f_1 is the number of degrees of freedom associated with the MS of the numerator of the calculated F value and f_2 is the number of degrees of freedom for the MS of the denominator of F. Table A3 contains the 0.95-quantiles of F for various degrees of freedom.

The decision rule is as follows:

If $F > F(f_1; f_2; 1 - \alpha)$ reject the null hypothesis, otherwise accept it.
Using the SPSS output, we reject the null hypothesis whenever it gives the significance (p-value, i.e. $P(F(f1; f_2) > F)$) is less than 0.05.

These general rules will now be applied to our very simple case. The null hypothesis (step 1) has already been defined above; our model is a Model I (step 2). Step 3 is unnecessary, as there is only one E(MS) column in Table 4.1. Step 4 leads us to the "Main effect A" row in table 4.1. If the null hypothesis that all the a_i are equal, is true, then the E(MS) for this row reduces to σ^2 (step 5), and this is the E(MS) for the residual (step 6). Therefore

$$F = \frac{MS_A}{MS_R}$$

is the required test statistic (step 7). It is distributed as $F(a - 1; N - a)$ i.e. it follows an F-distribution with $f_1 = a - 1$ and $f_2 = N - a$ degrees of freedom.

To determine the minimum sample size to test the above null hypothesis H_0, we saw in chapter 3 that we have to specify α and β, and we also need an estimate of σ^2. In chapter 3 we fixed β for a given least difference (of practical interest) from H_0. If we had $a = 2$ in the present case, then the F-test would be identical with the two-sample t-test for independent samples in 3.4.2.2.
The power of the F-test depends on the non-centrality parameter λ which is a generalisation of the square of the λ in (3.45), for more than one sample. For the one-way Model I analysis of variance in this section it is proportional to

$$\sum_{i=1}^{a}(a_i - \bar{a})^2 \quad \text{where } \bar{a} = \frac{1}{a} \sum a_i \tag{4.4}$$

If we use the side condition $\sum_{i=1}^{a} a_i = 0$ we have $\sum_{i=1}^{a}(a_i - \bar{a})^2 = \sum_{i=1}^{a} a_i^2$. Of course

when H_0 is true λ equals zero. If the a_i are not all equal, the value of λ depends on their values. The least favourable case from the point of view of the sample size required (leading to the maximum number n for each factor level) is the case with the smallest possible λ-value if at least two of the a_i are different. Let $a_{max} = \max(a_i)$ be the largest and $a_{min} = \min(a_i)$ be the smallest of the a effects a_i of the levels A_i of A. Then (4.4) is minimised if the a-2 remaining effects are equal to

$$\frac{1}{2}(a_{min} + a_{max}) \tag{4.5}$$

If we use this case when we calculate the *minimal sample size* fulfilling the precision requirement $a_{max} - a_{min} = d$ we are always on the safe side. We call the corresponding minimal sample size the *maxi-min* size. It may also be useful to know the minimal sample size for the most favourable case which minimises (4.4). This is the case where a_I of the a_i equal a_{min} and a_{II} of the a_i equal a_{max} and $a = a_I + a_{II}$ and $|a_I-a_{II}| \leq 1$. This means that a_I and a_{II} differ by not more than 1 and for even a it means $a_I = a_{II} = \dfrac{a}{2}$. We call the corresponding minimal sample size for this case the *mini-min* size. The total size of the experiment is minimised if all n_i are equal; this means that we design the experiment so that

$$n_i = n.$$

We denote the mini-min size by n_l and the maxi-min size by n_u. The experimenter now has to choose the number of observations n per factor level (class) between the lower bound n_l and the upper bound n_u:

$$n_l \leq n \leq n_u \qquad (4.6)$$

All that remains to be done is to calculate the bounds n_l and n_u. Since the calculations are long, we will only use CADEMO-*light* (CL), the CADEMO-module MEANS (for the one-way classification) or CADEMO-ANOV (for one up to three-way classifications) (see also section 4.2.3). Whilst CL and MEANS calculate maxi-min and mini-min sizes, in ANOV only maxi-min sizes are obtainable.

The estimation of the effects of the factor levels can be obtained by the Method of Least Squares described in Section 3.1.1. This gives the following equations (with $\sum a_i = 0$):

$$\hat{\mu} = \bar{y}_{..} \; ; \; \hat{a}_i = \bar{y}_{i.} - \bar{y}_{..} \; (i = 1, ..., a).$$

Example 4.1

We plan to perform an experiment with 4 levels of a fixed factor A and measure the yield in dt per ha. The levels are the four varieties of a cereal crop. We formulate the null hypothesis:

H$_0$:   All the varieties have the same mean yield, i.e.

$$a_1 = a_2 = a_3 = a_4$$

and the alternative hypothesis:

H$_A$:   At least two varieties differ in their average yield, that is to say

$$a_i \neq a_j \text{ for at least one pair } i \neq j.$$

Suppose the number n of plots per variety has to be determined, to satisfy the following conditions: Type I error probability $\alpha = 0.05$, and Type II error probability $\beta \leq 0.2$ if $a_{max} - a_{min} \geq 2\sigma$.

Using CL and following the menu sequence Sample Size Determination - k-sample Problem (k>2) – Means Test – Test of k Means against – Each Other, we input the appropriate values and choose the F-test. The output is shown in Figure 4.1.

Decision:
k Sample Problem (k>2)
Test of k Means against Each Other
Determination of Sample Size

Character:
Yield

4 means shall be compared with each other (F-Test).

To met the accuracy demands
α = 0.0500 (experimentwise),
β = 0.2000 (experimentwise)
and d = 2.0000
with an estimated variance of s^2 = 1.0000 you have to realize
n = 7 (in the most unfavorable case)
n = 6 (in the medium case)
n = 4 (in the most favorable case)
measurements in each of the 4 universes.

Figure 4.1 *CL output for Example 4.1*

We select $n = 5$.
Let us now assume that the experiment has been done with five replications, and the values in Figure 4.2 were obtained.

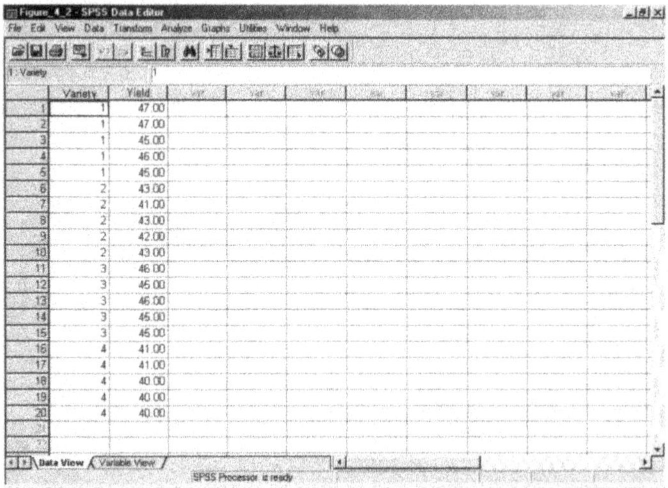

	Variety	Yield
1	1	47.00
2	1	47.00
3	1	45.00
4	1	46.00
5	1	45.00
6	2	43.00
7	2	41.00
8	2	43.00
9	2	42.00
10	2	43.00
11	3	46.00
12	3	45.00
13	3	46.00
14	3	45.00
15	3	46.00
16	4	41.00
17	4	41.00
18	4	40.00
19	4	40.00
20	4	40.00

Figure 4.2 *Results of Example 4.1*

We can either carry out the analysis by hand or use SPSS. The menu sequence Analyze - Compare Means - One-way ANOVA leads to Figure 4.3; the results are shown in Figure 4.4.

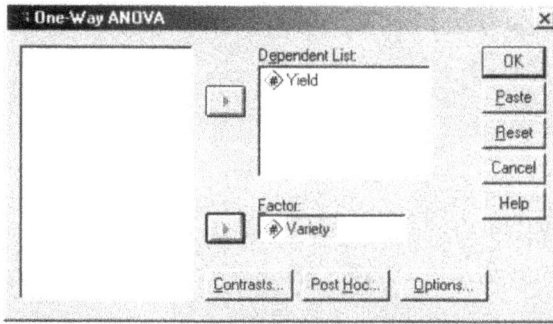

Figure 4.3 *SPSS dialogue box for one-way ANOVA*

Oneway

ANOVA

Yield

	Sum of Squares	df	Mean Square	F	Sig.
Between Groups	103.350	3	34.450	57.417	.000
Within Groups	9.600	16	.600		
Total	112.950	19			

Figure 4.4 *ANOVA Table of the data in Figure 4.2*

The output contains all the entries in Table 4.1 except the column for E(*MS*), which is only of theoretical interest. This column is used to find the test statistic in accordance with steps 1 to 7 - it does not depend on the data. The test statistic is

$$F = \frac{34.45}{0.6} = 57.417$$

We have to compare this (using for example $\alpha = 0.05$ as in the design phase) with (from Table A3) $F(3; 16; 0.95) = 3.24$; H_0 will be rejected.

In the SPSS output we compare our given α with the Sig. value in the last column of Figure 4.4, and reject the null hypothesis when, as in our case here, it is smaller than α.

We estimate the fixed effects by the method of least squares, which leads to the results: $\hat{\mu} = 43.55$; $\hat{a}_1 = 46 - 43.55 = 2.45$;

$\hat{a}_2 = 42.4 - 43.55 = -1.15$; $\hat{a}_3 = 45.4 - 43.55 = 1.85$;

$\hat{a}_4 = 40.4 - 43.55 = -3.15$; $(\hat{a}_1 + \hat{a}_2 + \hat{a}_3 + \hat{a}_4 = 0)$.

4.1.2 One-way Analysis of Variance - Model II

The model equation now takes the form

$$y_{ij} = \mu + a_i + e_{ij} \ (i = 1, \ldots, a, \ j = 1, \ldots, n_i) \tag{4.7}$$

The a_i are again called the main effects of the factor levels A_i; they are now random variables. The model is completed by the following constraints: $E(a_i) = 0$, $\mathrm{var}(a_i) = \sigma_a^2$, $E(e_{ij}) = 0$, $\mathrm{var}(e_{ij}) = \sigma^2$, and all random variables are mutually independent. σ_a^2 and σ^2 are called variance components.

Table 4.2 is the analysis of variance table for this model with $n_i = n$, and $N = an$.

Table 4.2 ANOVA table: One-way Classification, Model II ($n_i = n$).

Source of variation	SS	df	MS	E(MS)
Main effect A	SS_A $= \dfrac{1}{n}\sum_i Y_{i.}^2 - \dfrac{Y_{..}^2}{N}$	$a-1$	$MS_A = \dfrac{SS_A}{a-1}$	$\sigma^2 + n\sigma_a^2$
Residual	SS_R $= \sum_{i,j} y_{ij}^2 - \dfrac{1}{n}\sum_i Y_{i.}^2$	$N-a$	$MS_R = \dfrac{SS_R}{N-a}$	σ^2
Total	SS_T $= \sum_{i,j} y_{ij}^2 - \dfrac{Y_{..}^2}{N}$	$N-1$		

The null hypothesis in case of a random factor is the following:

H_0: "The variance component of factor A is equal to zero" i.e. $\sigma_a^2 = 0$.

H_A: "The variance component of factor A is larger than zero" i.e. $\sigma_a^2 > 0$.

The F-test statistic when the variables in (4.7) are normally distributed can be found as described in 4.1.1 using Table 4.2. It is identical with that in 4.1.1.

In model II we are very often interested in estimating the variance components σ^2 and σ_a^2. There are several methods of doing this. If all the n_i are equal ($n_i = n$) most of the methods are identical. We explain here the simplest method of variance component estimation, the so-called ANOVA method.

To use the ANOVA method for the estimation of the variance components, we go to the E(MS) column in the ANOVA table and replace the variance components by their estimates (σ^2 by s^2 and σ_a^2 by s_a^2) and put the results equal to the calculated MS for the corresponding row.

In our case of a one-way classification we thus get:

$$MS_A = s^2 + n s_a^2$$

$$MS_R = s^2$$

We now have to solve these equations for the *components of variance*. This gives

$$s^2 = MS_R \qquad (4.8)$$

$$s_a^2 = \frac{MS_A - MS_R}{n}, \qquad (4.9)$$

which are the ANOVA estimates for σ^2 and σ_a^2 respectively. If we now switch over to random variables we obtain the estimators s^2 and s_a^2 respectively and we find that both are unbiased:

$$E(s^2) = \sigma^2$$

$$E(s_a^2) = \sigma_a^2.$$

For the determination of the minimum sample size we must first decide whether we want to find the size appropriate for estimating the variance components or as in Example 2.1 for estimating the population mean, or for the testing of a hypothesis. Note that the precision (in all cases where we are testing a hypothesis) is affected by the number a of the factor levels.

Example 4.2

Let us assume that we have calculated the SS and MS of a one-way ANOVA with 400 levels of the factor A (boar) and measured the fattening days (time to attain a certain weight) of 12 offspring (piglets) per boar. The ANOVA Table which was obtained using the same SPSS program as in Example 4.1 is given in Table 4.3.

Table 4.3   *ANOVA Table of Example 4.2.*

Source of variation	SS	df	MS
Between Boars	23022.3	399	57.7
Residual	90200	4400	20.5

From this we obtain directly from (4.8)

$$s^2 = 20.5$$

and from (4.9)

$$s_a^2 = \frac{57.7 - 20.5}{12} = 3.1.$$

The estimate for μ obtained by the method of least squares is $\hat{\mu} = \bar{y}_{..}$.

4.2 Two-way Analysis of Variance

In any model of a *two-way analysis of variance* the linear model equation is of the form:

$$y = E(y) + e = \mu + EC(y) + e$$

The two factors are denoted by A and B respectively. We distinguish between two kinds of combinations of the levels of the two factors:

Cross-classification ($A \times B$):
Observations can (but do not have to) be made in all combinations of A- and B-levels.
If observations are available for all of the $a \cdot b$ factor level combinations of the a levels A_i of the factor A with the b levels B_j of B then the cross-classification is called complete (e.g. a complete block design); otherwise it is called incomplete (for instance an incomplete block design such as a BIB or a PBIB (as in section 2.6.2)). We always assume that incomplete cross-classifications are connected (see section 2.6.1).
A typical example of a two-way classification occurs if the effect of a treatment factor A is investigated in a block experiment. Then the blocks are the levels of a further (noise) factor B.

Nested (or hierarchical) classification:
The levels of B can only occur jointly with exactly one level of A ($B \prec A$).

4.2.1 Two-way Analysis of Variance - Cross-classification

In the *two-way cross-classification* the classes are defined by the factor level combinations (i,j) of the levels A_i of A and the levels B_j of B. Let y_{ijk} be the k-th observation in the class (i,j). Then we get:

$$y_{ijk} = \mu + a_i + b_j + w_{ij} + e_{ijk} \ (i = 1, ..., a; \ j = 1, ..., b; \ k = 1, ..., n_{ij})$$

In this equation μ is the general mean; a_i are the main effects of levels A_i of A, b_j the main effects of levels B_j of B; w_{ij} the interactions between A_i and B_j, (they are defined only if observations are available for the class (i,j). k runs in class (i,j) from 1 to n_{ij}. If $n_{ij} = n$, we have the case of equal class numbers (replications); we call this a balanced ANOVA. Optimal experimental designs in the two-way analysis of variance often require equal class numbers. The main effects and interactions are not at the moment defined as being fixed or random - these differences will be discussed in the following paragraphs. For all the subsequent models we assume that the e_{ijk} are mutually independent with expectation zero and have a common variance σ^2; and $n_{ij} = n$.
The ANOVA Table for all models (without the column $E(MS)$) is given for this balanced case in Table 4.4. Because $n_{ij} = n$ for all i, j, we have $N = abn$.

Table 4.4 *ANOVA Table for the Two-way Cross-classification ($n_{ij} = n > 1$).*

Sources of Variation	SS	df	MS
Main effect A	$SS_A = \dfrac{1}{bn}\sum_i Y_{i..}^2 - \dfrac{1}{N}Y_{...}^2$	$a-1$	$MS_A = \dfrac{SS_A}{a-1}$
Main effect B	$SS_B = \dfrac{1}{an}\sum_j Y_{.j.}^2 - \dfrac{1}{N}Y_{...}^2$	$b-1$	$MS_B = \dfrac{SS_B}{b-1}$
Interaction $A{\times}B$	$SS_{AB} = \dfrac{1}{n}\sum_{i,j} Y_{ij.}^2 - \dfrac{1}{bn}\sum_i Y_{i..}^2$ $\qquad - \dfrac{1}{an}\sum_j Y_{.j.}^2 + \dfrac{Y_{...}^2}{N}$	$(a-1)\cdot$ $(b-1)$	MS_{AB} $= \dfrac{SS_{AB}}{(a-1)(b-1)}$
Residual	$SS_R = \sum_{i,j,k} y_{ijk}^2 - \dfrac{1}{n}\sum_{i,j} Y_{ij.}^2$	$ab(n-1)$	$MS_R = \dfrac{SS_R}{ab(n-1)}$
Total	$SS_T = \sum_{i,j,k} y_{ijk}^2 - \dfrac{1}{N}Y_{...}^2$	$N-1$	

If there is only one replication, so that $n = 1$, only the sum of $w_{ij} + e_{ijk} = e'_{ijk}$ can be defined; the individual components cannot be separated. The ANOVA table then reduces to the form given in Table 4.4a.

Table 4.4a *ANOVA Table for the Two-way Cross -classification ($n_{ij} = 1$).*

Source of Variation	SS	df	MS
Main effect A	$SS_A = \dfrac{1}{b}\sum_i Y_{i..}^2 - \dfrac{1}{N}Y_{...}^2$	$a-1$	$MS_A = \dfrac{SS_A}{a-1}$
Main effect B	$SS_B = \dfrac{1}{a}\sum_j Y_{.j.}^2 - \dfrac{1}{N}Y_{...}^2$	$b-1$	$MS_B = \dfrac{SS_B}{b-1}$
Residual	$SS_R = \sum_{i.jk} y_{ijk}^2 - \dfrac{1}{b}\sum_i Y_{i..}^2 - \dfrac{1}{a}\sum_j Y_{.j.}^2 + \dfrac{1}{N}Y_{..}^2$	$(a-1)$ $(b-1)$	$MS_R = \dfrac{SS_R}{(a-1)(b-1)}$
Total	$SS_T = \sum_{i,j,k} y_{ijk}^2 - \dfrac{1}{N}Y_{...}^2$	$N-1$	

4.2.1.1 Two-way Analysis of Variance - Cross-classification - Model I

A Model I cross-classified two-way analysis of variance is specified as follows:
The model with equal subclass numbers equation is given by

$$y_{ijk} = \mu + a_i + b_j + w_{ij} + e_{ijk} \ (i = 1, ..., a; j = 1, ..., b; k = 1, ..., n) \tag{4.10}$$

All main effects a_i and b_j and interactions w_{ij} are real numbers i.e. they are not random. The model is completed by the side conditions that the sums of the a_i and of the b_j and of the w_{ij} (separately over each index) all equal zero.

The expected mean squares can be found in Table 4.5 for the case of $n_{ij} = n > 1$.
The estimates of the fixed effects are obtained by the method of least squares and are given by the following equations:

$$\hat{\mu} = \bar{y}_{...}, \ \hat{a}_i = \bar{y}_{i..} - \bar{y}_{...}, \ \hat{b}_j = \bar{y}_{.j.} - \bar{y}_{...}, \ \hat{w}_{ij} = \bar{y}_{ij.} - \bar{y}_{i..} - \bar{y}_{.j.} + \bar{y}_{...}.$$

Table 4.5 The Expected Mean Squares for the Models of the Two-way Cross-classification ($n_{ij} = n > 1$).

Sources of Variation	Model I	Model II	Mixed model, (A fixed, B random)
		E(MS)	
Main effect A	$\sigma^2 + \dfrac{bn}{a-1}\sum_i a_i^2$	$\sigma^2 + n\sigma_{ab}^2 + bn\sigma_a^2$	$\sigma^2 + n\sigma_{ab}^2 + \dfrac{bn}{a-1}\sum_i a_i^2$
Main effect B	$\sigma^2 + \dfrac{an}{b-1}\sum_j b_j^2$	$\sigma^2 + n\sigma_{ab}^2 + an\sigma_b^2$	$\sigma^2 + \kappa n\sigma_{ab}^2 + an\sigma_b^2$
Interaction A×B	$\sigma^2 + \dfrac{n}{(a-1)(b-1)}\cdot\sum_{i,j} w_{ij}^2$	$\sigma^2 + n\sigma_{ab}^2$	$\sigma^2 + n\sigma_{ab}^2$
Residual	σ^2	σ^2	σ^2

The value κ in Table 4.5 depends on the side condition about interaction effects. For the condition $cov(w_{ij}, w_{ij'}) = 0$ (if $j \neq j'$) we have $\kappa = 1$ and for the side condition $\sum_{i=1}^{a} w_{ij} = 0$

for each j we have $\kappa = 0$.

The null hypotheses that can be tested (under the assumption that the e_{ijk} are independently distributed as $N(0; \sigma^2)$) are:
H_{01}: "All a_i are zero"
H_{02}: "All b_j are zero"
H_{03}: "All w_{ij} are zero"

To find the minimum class size (number of replications) n which will satisfy given precision requirements, we can in principle proceed as in section 4.1, but we must first decide on one of the three null hypotheses. We limit ourselves here to one example which we handle using the CADEMO program ANOV, see section 4.2.3 for the general approach.

Example 4.3

We want to test the null hypothesis that six wheat varieties do not differ in their yields. For the experiment we can use a number of plots for each of the varieties at each of four experimental stations (farms for short). The varieties are the levels of a fixed factor A and the four farms are also considered as fixed levels of a (block) factor B.

First we select the appropriate branch in the ANOV module in CADEMO (Figure 4.5) namely:

Design - Two way Analysis of Variance - $A \times B$ Cross-classification which leads us to Figure 4.6.

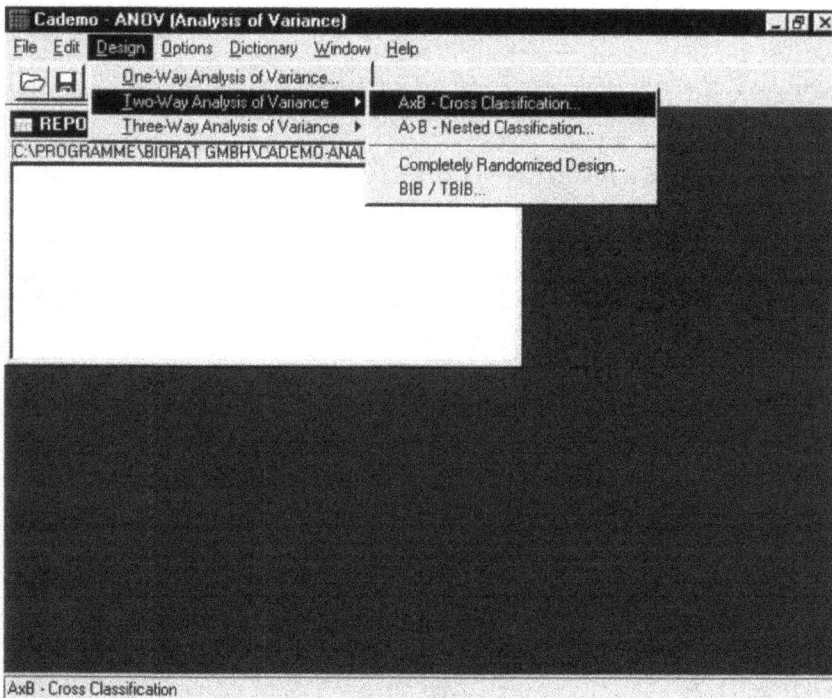

Figure 4.5 *The CADEMO-ANOV menu*

111

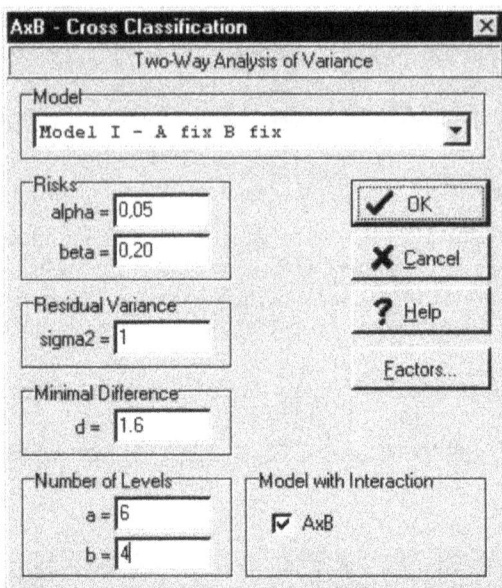

Figure 4.6 *The precision requirements for Example 4.3*

Here, as in section 4.1, we have to input α, β, and an estimate $\tilde{\sigma}^2$ for σ^2, $d = a_{max} - a_{min}$, a and b. Next we select a model with interactions between A and B. We have $a = 6$, $b = 4$ and we choose $\alpha = 0.05$, $\beta = 0.2$. To input $d = 1.6\sigma$ we can set $\sigma^2 = 1$ and $d = 1.6$ without loss of generality.

From the result shown in Figure 4.7 we find that $n = 3$ is the *maxi-min size* and this means that just 3 plots have to be used for each variety at each farm. In total we have $N = a \cdot b \cdot n = 6 \times 4 \times 3 = 72$ plots.

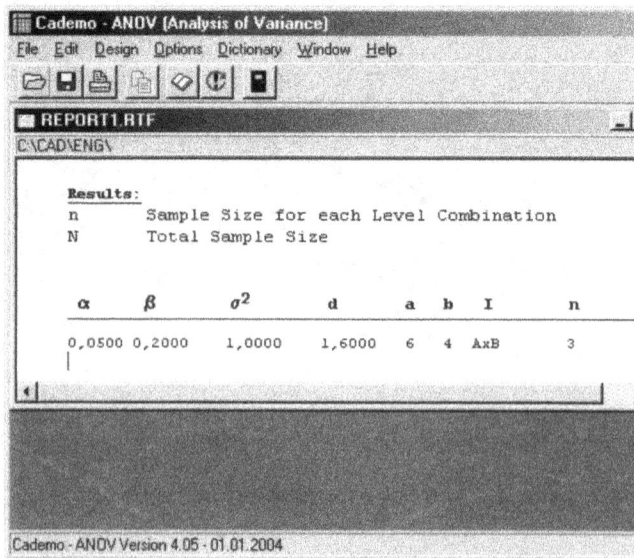

Figure 4.7 *The maxi-min sample size for the precision given in Figure 4.6*

We now assume that an experiment has been done at each of the four farms in a Completely Randomised Design (CRD) with six varieties on three plots each. The yield in dt/ha was measured. The results are shown in Table 4.6 below.

Table 4.6   *Results of a CRD with 6 varieties tested on 4 farms with three plots each.*

B: Farms	Plots	A: Varieties					
		1	2	3	4	5	6
1	1	32	48	25	33	48	29
	2	28	52	25	38	27	27
	3	30	47	34	44	38	31
2	1	44	55	28	39	21	31
	2	43	53	26	38	30	33
	3	48	57	33	37	36	26
3	1	42	64	40	53	38	27
	2	42	64	42	41	29	33
	3	39	64	47	47	23	32
4	1	44	59	34	54	33	31
	2	40	58	27	50	36	30
	3	42	57	32	46	36	35

We can perform the Two-way Analysis of Variance with SPSS by using the procedure: Analyze – General Linear Model - Univariate.
We input Variety and Farm as fixed factors and Yield as the dependent variable. The results of the SPSS calculations are shown in Figure 4.8.

Tests of Between-Subjects Effects

Dependent Variable: YIELD

Source	Type III Sum of Squares	df	Mean Square	F	Sig.
Corrected Model	7368.986[a]	23	320.391	17.436	.000
Intercept	110842.014	1	110842.014	6032.218	.000
FARM	602.708	3	200.903	10.933	.000
VARIETY	5696.236	5	1139.247	62.000	.000
FARM * VARIETY	1070.042	15	71.336	3.882	.000
Error	882.000	48	18.375		
Total	119093.000	72			
Corrected Total	8250.986	71			

a. R Squared = .893 (Adjusted R Squared = .842)

Figure 4.8 *ANOVA Table for Example 4.3*

The three hypotheses mentioned above might be written in contextual language as follows:

H_{01}: "There is no difference in yield between the varieties" or "all a_i are equal to zero"
(according to the model assumption that the sum of the a_i is zero)

H_{02}: "There is no difference in yield between the farms" or "all b_j are equal to zero"
(similarly the sum of the b_j is also zero).

H_{03}: "There is no interaction between farms and varieties" or "all w_{ij} are equal to zero"
(here the assumption is that the sums of the w_{ij} (separately over each subscript) equal zero).

With the help of the 7 steps defined in 4.1 and by using Tables 4.4 and 4.5 we get:

$$F_{01} = \frac{MS_{Varieties}}{MS_R} = 1139.25/18.37 = 62.00$$

$F((a-1); ab(n-1); 1-\alpha) = F(5; 48; 0.95) = 2.409$ (2.418 after linear interpolation)
$F_{01} > F(5; 48; 0.95)$, therefore we reject H_{01} that there is no difference in yield between the varieties.
This follows directly from Figure 4.8 because sig. < 0.05.

$$F_{02} = \frac{MS_{Farms}}{MS_R} = 200.90/18.37 = 10.93$$

$F((b-1); ab(n-1); 1-\alpha) = F(3; 48; 0.95) = 2.798$ (if we do linear interpolation between 40 and 60 degrees of freedom we get 2.808)
$F_{02} > F(3; 48; 0.95)$, therefore we reject H_{02} that there is no difference in yield between the farms.
This also follows directly from Figure 4.8 because sig. < 0.05.

$F_{03} = MS_{Varieties \times Farms} / MS_R = 71.34/18.37 = 3.88$
$F((a-1)(b-1); ab(n-1); 1-\alpha) = F(15; 48; 0.95) = 1.880$ (1.888 after linear interpolation)
$F_{03} > F(15; 48; 0.95)$, therefore we reject H_{03} that there is no interaction between the varieties and farms.
Again this follows directly from Figure 4.8 because sig. < 0.05.

4.2.1.2 Two-way Analysis of Variance - Cross-classification - Model II

The situation for model II of the cross-classified two-way analysis of variance is in the balanced case as follows:
A character (and its model, a variate y) depends on a randomly selected levels $A_1, ..., A_a$ of the factor A, on b randomly selected levels $B_1, ..., B_b$ of the factor B and further on random error terms e by the equation

$$y_{ijk} = \mu + a_i + b_j + w_{ij} + e_{ijk} \ (i = 1, ..., a; j = 1, ..., b; k = 1, ..., n) \qquad (4.11)$$

For both A-levels and B-levels the existence of a population of factor levels is assumed from which the levels in the experiment are sampled.

The meanings of the symbols are: μ is the general mean; a_i are the main effects of the levels of A, b_j the main effects of levels of B and the w_{ij} the interactions between A_i and B_j (these are defined only if observations are available in (i,j)).

All effects (except μ) are random. The model is completed by the following conditions: $E(a_i) = E(b_j) = E(w_{ij}) = E(e_{ijk}) = 0$ and $\text{var}(e_{ijk}) = \sigma^2$, $\text{var}(a_i) = \sigma_a^2$, $\text{var}(b_j) = \sigma_b^2$, $\text{var}(w_{ij}) = \sigma_{ab}^2$ for all i,j,k and the mutual independence of all random variables on the right hand side of the model equation. σ^2, σ_a^2, σ_b^2 and σ_{ab}^2 are called components of variance or variance components.
The analysis of variance table for this model is given in Table 4.4. Table 4.5 gives the $E(MS)$.

The null hypotheses that can be tested under the assumption that all random components are normally distributed are:
H_{01}: "$\sigma_a^2 = 0$"
H_{02}: "$\sigma_b^2 = 0$"
H_{03}: "$\sigma_{ab}^2 = 0$".

We determine the F-ratios following the 7 steps given in Section 4.1 with the help of the $E(MS)$ column for model II in Table 4.5.
If H_{01} is correct the $E(MS_A)$ equals $E(MS_{A \times B})$ and we test H_{01} by

$$F_A = \frac{MS_A}{MS_{A \times B}},$$

which has an F-distribution with $a-1$ and $(a-1)(b-1)$ degrees of freedom. Similarly H_{02} is tested by

$$F_B = \frac{MS_B}{MS_{A \times B}}$$

which has an F-distribution with $b-1$ and $(a-1)(b-1)$ degrees of freedom.
If H_{03} is true, then $E(MS_{A \times B})$ equals $E(MS_R)$ and therefore the F-ratio for testing H_{03} is

$$F_{A \times B} = \frac{MS_{A \times B}}{MS_R}$$

which has an F-distribution on $(a-1)(b-1)$ and $ab(n-1)$ degrees of freedom.
For estimating the variance components we can use the ANOVA method explained in section 4.1.2. This leads to the following system of equations:

$$s^2 + n s_{ab}^2 + bn s_a^2 = MS_A$$
$$s^2 + n s_{ab}^2 + an s_b^2 = MS_B$$
$$s^2 + n s_{ab}^2 = MS_{A \times B}$$
$$s^2 = MS_R$$

From these we obtain

$$s^2 = MS_R \tag{4.12}$$

$$s_{ab}^2 = \frac{1}{n}(MS_{A\times B} - MS_R) \tag{4.13}$$

$$s_b^2 = \frac{1}{an}(MS_B - MS_{A\times B}) \tag{4.14}$$

$$s_a^2 = \frac{1}{bn}(MS_A - MS_{A\times B}) \tag{4.15}$$

In planning for the minimum sample size in this model we must decide on the number of factor levels to select from the corresponding population of levels. According to the null hypothesis of interest these are either the A- or the B-levels or both. The estimate for μ is $\hat{\mu} = \bar{y}_{...}$.

Example 4.4

Let us assume that we have randomly selected 20 levels A_i of a factor A and also randomly selected 10 levels B_j of a factor B. The existence of interactions cannot be excluded in advance, and will be allowed for in the model. We choose $n = 2$ observations for each combination of factor levels as the minimal class size. This allows us to test and estimate the interactions. We could analyse the data by SPSS as described in 4.2.1.1 and the ANOVA table in Table 4.7 might be obtained.

Table 4.7   *ANOVA Table for Example 4.4.*

Source of variation	SS	df	MS	F
Between A-levels	1027.9	19	54.1	2.94
Between B-levels	703.8	9	78.2	4.25
Interaction $A \times B$	3146.4	171	18.4	1.29
Residual	2860	200	14.3	

Let us first estimate the variance components.
From (4.12) we get

$$s^2 = 14.3$$

and from (4.13)

$$s_{ab}^2 = \frac{1}{2}(18.4 - 14.3) = 2.05.$$

From (4.14) we obtain

$$s_b^2 = \frac{1}{40}(78.2 - 18.4) = 1.495$$

and from (4.15)

$$s_a^2 = \frac{1}{20}(54.1 - 18.4) = 1.785$$

SPSS offers further procedures for estimating variance components within the Analysis of Variance module. Figure 4.9 gives the overview of the options available; we follow the command sequence Analyze-General Linear Model –Variance Components and obtain after specifying the dependent variable and Random Factors:

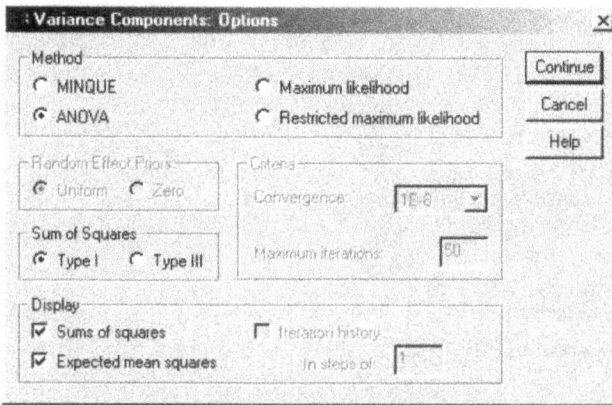

Figure 4.9 *Dialogue box for the selection of methods for variance components estimation in SPSS*

Here we have chosen the Analysis of Variance option (ANOVA), (the default is MINQUE). A detailed description of the methods available in SPSS (and many more) can be found in SARHAI and OJEDA (2004, 2005); a briefer overview containing an evaluation of the methods is given in RASCH and MAŠATA (2006).

Example 4.4 - continued

If we assume that the observations can be modelled by normally distributed random variables we can test the three hypotheses mentioned above ($\alpha = 0.05$).
We test

H_{01}: " $\sigma_a^2 = 0$" by

$$F = \frac{54.1}{18.4} = 2.94$$

and this is larger than $F(19; 171; 0.95) = 1.648$; so we reject the null hypothesis.

We test

H_{02}: " $\sigma_b^2 = 0$" by

117

$$F = \frac{78.2}{18.4} = 4.25$$

and this exceeds $F(9; 171; 0.95) = 1.935$; and again we reject the null hypothesis.

We test
$$H_{03}: "\sigma_{ab}^2 = 0" \text{ by}$$

$$F = \frac{18.4}{14.3} = 1.29.$$

Here Table A3 is not very helpful. The value $F(120; 120; 0.95) = 1.35$ exceeds our calculated F but it is not certain what the value $F(171; 200; 0.95)$ is. For this a more extended table is needed. In VB1/51/0042 we find $F(150; 200; 0.95) = 1.28$ and $F(200; 200; 0.95) = 1.26$. The exact value for $F(171; 200; 0.95)$ is 1.2732 and this null hypothesis must also be rejected.

In SPSS we find the "Significance" (p-value) as follows::
1. for H_{01} using **Compute Significance = 1 – CDF.F(2.94,19,171) Execute** we get 0.00010;
2. for H_{02} we get similarly 0.00005;
3. for H_{03} we get 0.04149;
so that all 3 null hypotheses are rejected.

4.2.1.3 Two-way Analysis of Variance - Cross-classification - Mixed Model

The situation in a mixed model of the cross-classified two-way analysis of variance is as follows. Without loss of generality we assume that the levels of A are fixed and those of B are random. The model equation is in the balanced case given by

$$y_{ijk} = \mu + a_i + b_j + w_{ij} + e_{ijk} \ (i = 1, ..., a; j = 1, ..., b; k = 1, ..., n) \tag{4.16}$$

All effects except μ and the a_i are random. The model is completed by the following conditions: $E(b_j) = E(w_{ij}) = E(e_{ijk}) = 0$ and $var(e_{ijk}) = \sigma^2$, $var(b_j) = \sigma_b^2$, $var(w_{ij}) = \sigma_{ab}^2$, the mutual independence of all random variables except eventually the w_{ij} and that the a_i sum to zero. σ^2, σ_b^2 and σ_{ab}^2 are called variance components.

The expected mean squares for this model are given in Table 4.5 for $n_{ij} = n$.
The value κ in Table 4.5 depends on the side condition about interaction effects. For the condition $cov(w_{ij}, w_{ij'}) = 0$ (if $j \neq j'$) we have $\kappa = 1$ and for the side condition $\sum_{i=1}^{a} w_{ij} = 0$

for each j we have $\kappa = 0$.
The user has to select just one of these two conditions.
The null hypotheses that can be tested are:
H_{01}: "All a_i are zero"

H_{02}: " $\sigma_b^2 = 0$ "

H_{03}: " $\sigma_{ab}^2 = 0$ ".

We determine the F-ratios using the 7 steps from 4.1 under the condition $\sum_{i=1}^{a} w_{ij} = 0$ for each j, hence $\kappa = 0$ in the E(MS) column for the mixed model (A fixed, B random) in Table 4.5. If H_{01} is true, then E(MS_A) equals E($MS_{A\times B}$) and we test H_{01} using

$$F_A = \frac{MS_A}{MS_{A\times B}},$$

which has an F-distribution with $(a-1)$ and $(a-1)(b-1)$ degrees of freedom. If H_{02} is true E(MS_B) equals E(MS_R) and we test H_{02} by

$$F_B = \frac{MS_B}{MS_R},$$

which has an F-distribution with $(b-1)$ and $ab(n-1)$ degrees of freedom. If H_{03} is true E($MS_{A\times B}$) equals E(MS_R) and the F ratio for testing H_{03} is

$$F_{A\times B} = \frac{MS_{A\times B}}{MS_R},$$

which has an F-distribution with $(a-1)(b-1)$ and $ab(n-1)$ degrees of freedom.
The fixed effects can be estimated by the method of least squares, which gives the following equations:

$$\hat{\mu} = \bar{y}_{...}, \quad \hat{a}_i = \bar{y}_{i..} - \bar{y}_{...}.$$

To estimate the variance components we can use the ANOVA method explained in paragraph 4.1.2. This leads to the following system of equations:

$$
\begin{aligned}
s^2 &+ & an\, s_b^2 &= MS_B \\
s^2 &+ n\, s_{ab}^2 & &= MS_{A\times B} \\
s^2 & & &= MS_R.
\end{aligned}
$$

From which we obtain:

$$
\begin{aligned}
s^2 &= MS_R \\
s_{ab}^2 &= \frac{1}{n}(MS_{A\times B} - MS_R) \\
s_b^2 &= \frac{1}{an}(MS_B - MS_R).
\end{aligned}
$$

We illustrate hypothesis testing and variance component estimation by an example:

Example 4.5

Next, for the purpose of comparison, we wish to determine the maxi-min size for the precision requirements in Example 4.3, but this time for the mixed model with B a random factor. Again we shall test the null hypothesis that the six wheat varieties have equal effects. When we look at the appropriate test statistic F_A on the previous page, we realise that this has an F-distribution with a-1 and $(a$-1$)(b$-1$)$ degrees of freedom. The number of replications does not affect the validity of the test. Since $a = 6$ is already determined, we can only arrive at a given precision through the number b of the sampled levels of the factor B. We call up ANOV, but this time, in Figure 4.6 we select **Design-Two Way Analysis of Variance** $-A \times B$ **Cross Classification**, and the option **mixed** $-$ A **fixed,** B **random**. After this, Figure 4.6 alters very simply, the window for the input of b disappears, and b is immediately determined. We obtain the result given in Figure 4.10.

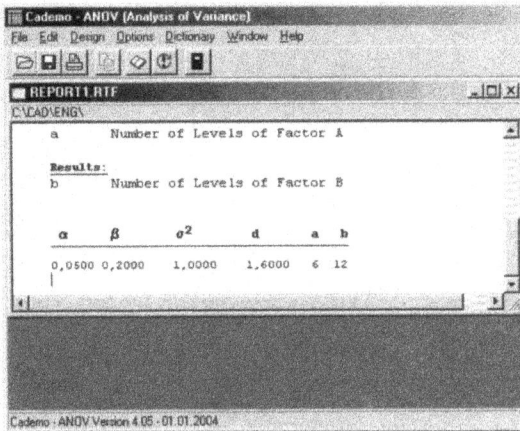

Figure 4.10 *Result given by ANOV for Example 4.5*

In order to be able also to test and estimate interactions, we choose $n = 2$ in each of the $6 \cdot 12 = 72$ cells.

We want to test 6 varieties at a yet to be determined number of randomly chosen farms, using three plots for each variety at each farm. How many farms do we need, if $d = 1.6$; $\sigma^2 = 1$, $\alpha = 0.05$ and $\beta = 0.2$ have been specified? To answer this question we enter the above values in the CADEMO ANOV module dialog box (Figure 4.6) and get 12 farms (see Figure 4.10) for the maxi-min size as the answer to our question. However we only want to use 4 farms; this leads to a much lower precision with an attainable least difference of $d = 4$.

The varieties are the levels of a fixed factor (A) and the four farms are randomly chosen levels of a random factor B. We use the same data of Example 4.3. The ANOVA-table in Figure 4.8 can be used to obtain the SS and MS but *not* all the F-values.

We get

$$F_A = \frac{MS_A}{MS_{A \times B}} = 1139.25 / 71.34 = 15.97$$

$F((a\text{-}1);(a\text{-}1)(b\text{-}1);1\text{-}\alpha) = F(5;15;0.95) = 2.90;$
$F_A > F(5;15;0.95)$, therefore we reject H_{01} that there is no difference in yield between the varieties.

We get

$$F_B = \frac{MS_B}{MS_R} = 200.90 / 18.37 = 10.93$$

$F((b\text{-}1);ab(n\text{-}1);1\text{-}\alpha) = F(3;48;0.95) = 2.789$, so that
$F_B > F(3;48;0.95)$, and we reject H_{02} that $\sigma_b^2 = 0$. Therefore the variability among farms is significant.

We get

$$F_{AB} = \frac{MS_{A \times B}}{MS_R} = 71.34 / 18.37 = 3.88$$

$F((a\text{-}1)(b\text{-}1);ab(n\text{-}1);1\text{-}\alpha) = F(15;48;0.95) = 1.880$
$F_{AB} > F(15;48;0.95)$, therefore we reject H_{03} that $\sigma_{ab}^2 = 0$.

The estimates of the variance components are

$$s^2 = 18.37$$
$$s_{ab}^2 = (71.34 - 18.37)/3 = 17.66$$
$$s_b^2 = (200.90 - 18.37)/18 = 10.14.$$

The reader should now rework Example 4.5 but with the condition $\text{cov}(w_{ij}, w_{ij'}) = 0$ for $j \neq j'$.

We find the significance in the SPSS analysis of variance table corresponding to that in Figure 4.8, but with A fixed, B random. We get this table when (as an exercise) we enter, in **Analyze-General-Linear Model-Univariate**, the factor VARIETY as Fixed and the factor FARM as Random.

If a (fixed) treatment factor is investigated in a block design, a cross-classified two-way ANOVA is usually used as the underlying model. In models with interactions more than one replication is needed. If the blocks are fixed, we can use the approach in section 4.2.1.1, for example the 4 farms in Example 4.3 can be interpreted as fixed blocks. If the blocks are randomly selected from a population of possible blocks, then the approach described in section 4.2.1.3 must be used.

In many applications however incomplete blocks must be used (as for example the BIB designs described in chapter 2). This means that some of the n_{ij} are equal to 1 and others equal to zero. In this case we must use generalised least squares (GLS). Its use for this particular purpose will be briefly described below. This description will use matrix notation, and the reader not familiar with this may refer to Appendix C, or simply use the SPSS approach without learning about the principles behind the method.
We shall restrict ourselves to an illustration of the method in one example.

Example 4.6

An experiment had to be designed to investigate the effect of four different diets A_1, A_2, A_3 and A_4 on lysine in the milk of Holstein-Friesian cows. Blocks were used to eliminate the genetic variability between the cows. Genetic identity only occurs between identical twins (triplets etc. hardly ever occur) so that the block size was limited to $k = 2$ and only an incomplete block design was possible. Firstly we use the CADEMO module ANOV to determine the required number of blocks in a BIB.

For the precision requirement $\alpha = 0.05$, $\beta = 0.20$; $a_{max} - a_{min} \geq 2\sigma$ it turns out that we need 6 replications of each treatment as the maxi-min size and therefore 12 blocks. Hence 12 pairs of identical twins B_1, B_2, ..., B_{12} were used. The observations are the quantity of lysine in the milk (mg/100 ml) after the cows had been given the diets for a certain period. The data are given in the table below

	B_1	B_2	B_3	B_4	B_5	B_6	B_7	B_8	B_9	B_{10}	B_{11}	B_{12}
A_1	268	279	286				293	296	292			
A_2	253			318	278		277			306	303	
A_3		262		310		314		284		302		291
A_4			280		283	311			285		299	292

We assume that the 12 pairs of twins represent a random sample from the population of Holstein-Friesians, so that the blocks are a random factor, and we set up a mixed model as in (4.16) but without any interaction terms.
We assume that the remaining effects satisfy the conditions in 4.2.1.3.
We write $\gamma_i = \mu + \alpha_i$ to denote the mean effect of diet A_i, so that the mixed model becomes:

$$y_{ij} = \gamma_i + b_j + e_{ij}$$

In matrix notation (see Appendix C) this model is written

$$y = X\gamma + Zb + e$$

where $y = (y_{1,1}, ..., y_{4,12})^T$

$\gamma = (\gamma_1, \gamma_2, \gamma_3, \gamma_4)^T$, $b = (b_1, ..., b_{12})^T$ and $e = (e_{1,1}, ..., e_{4,12})^T$, X is the 24×4 design matrix for the diets, Z is the 24×12 design matrix for the block effects.

We denote a vector with n zeros by O_n, $O_{m \times n}$ is an $(m \times n)$-matrix of zeros, I_n is the identity matrix of order n. We have $E(b) = O_{12}$, $var(b) = \sigma_b^2 I_{12}$ where $var(b)$ is the variance-covariance matrix (or dispersion matrix) of b; $E(e) = O_{24}$, $var(e) = \sigma_e^2 I_{24}$ and $E(be^T) = O_{12 \times 24}$. Hence the variance-covariance matrix of y is

$$var(y) = Z\,var(b)Z^T + var(e) = \sigma_e^2 \left((\sigma_b^2/\sigma_e^2) ZZ^T + I_{24}\right) = \sigma_e^2 V.$$

The GLS solution for the estimate of the parameter γ is the solution of the (generalised) normal equations:

$$X^T V^{-1} X \hat{\gamma} = X^T V^{-1} y.$$

Using the identity

$$V^{-1} = \left((\sigma_b^2/\sigma_e^2) ZZ^T + I_{24}\right)^{-1} = I_{24} - Z(Z^T Z + (\sigma_b^2/\sigma_e^2)^{-1} I_{12})^{-1} Z^T$$

the solution is obtained by solving the so-called *Mixed Model Equations*.

$$\begin{pmatrix} X^T X & X^T Z \\ Z^T X & Z^T Z + \left(\sigma_b^2/\sigma_e^2\right)^{-1} I_{12} \end{pmatrix} \begin{pmatrix} \hat{\gamma} \\ \hat{b} \end{pmatrix} = \begin{pmatrix} X^T y \\ Z^T y \end{pmatrix} \tag{4.17}$$

For hypothesis testing and the construction of 95%-confidence intervals for the differences between the diet effects γ_h-γ_i, b and e must have *multivariate normal distributions*:

$$\begin{pmatrix} b \\ e \end{pmatrix} \sim N\left(\begin{pmatrix} O_{12} \\ O_{24} \end{pmatrix}; \begin{pmatrix} var(b) & O_{12 \times 24} \\ O_{24 \times 12} & var(e) \end{pmatrix} \right).$$

We can obtain this solution using SPSS as follows.
First we set up the following fixed effects model:

$$\tilde{y} = \tilde{X}\gamma + \tilde{Z}\beta + \tilde{e} \tag{4.18}$$

where $\tilde{y} = \begin{pmatrix} y \\ O_{12} \end{pmatrix}$, $\tilde{X} = \begin{pmatrix} X \\ O_{12 \times 4} \end{pmatrix}$.

$$\tilde{Z} = \begin{pmatrix} Z \\ 1/\sqrt{(\sigma_b^2/\sigma_e^2)} I_{12} \end{pmatrix}; \tilde{e} = \begin{pmatrix} e \\ O_{12} \end{pmatrix}.$$

We now create a data file in the SPSS data editor having three columns A, B, Y.

1 1 268

$$1 \quad 2 \quad 279$$
$$\vdots$$
$$4 \quad 12 \quad 292.$$

and save it as 'C: Lysin.sav'.

Next we must estimate the variance components σ_b^2 and σ_e^2 using the ANOVA method described in 4.2.1.3.

The ANOVA method gives $MS_B = 534.610$ with $E(MS_B) = 1.8182 \ \sigma_b^2 + \sigma_e^2$ and $MS_R = 11.069$ with $E(MS_R) = \sigma_e^2$.

The ANOVA method estimate for σ_b^2 is thus $(534.610 - 11.069)/1.8182 = 287.945$ and for σ^2 it is 11.069.

In SPSS we follow the menu sequence Analyze - General Linear Model - Variance Components and specify a Model without interactions. Then under Options we activate the ANOVA - Method.

The SPSS output gives 287.947 for σ_b^2 and 11.069 for σ_e^2.

To solve the equation system (4.17) we replace the variance components in the term $1/\sqrt{(\sigma_b^2/\sigma_e^2)}$ in (4.18) by their ANOVA estimates:

$$1/\sqrt{(287.947/11.069)} \ = \ 0.1961$$

The SPSS output gives the estimated means (MEAN) for the diets and their Standard Error (SE) based on 9 degrees of freedom (SPSS gives 20 degrees of freedom. due to the extra zero observations which we have added in the data file). The 95% confidence interval limits are found as MEAN $\pm$ SE $\cdot$ $t(9; 0.975)$ with $t(9; 0.975) = 2.262$.

	MEAN	SE	Lower CI-limit	Upper CI-limit
A_1:	298.829	5.365	286.692	310.966
A_2:	287.628	5.365	275.491	299.765
A_3:	285.450	5.365	273.313	297.587
A_4:	288.427	5.365	276.290	300.564

The covariance-matrix in the SPSS output gives the estimate of the variance of these diet means as 28.784 (based on 9 degrees of freedom) and the estimate of the covariance between two such means as 25.806. Hence the estimate of the variance of MEAN (A_h)-MEAN (A_i) is $28.784 + 28.784 - 2 \times 25.806 = 5.956$ and standard error $\sqrt{5.956} = 2.4405$ based on 9 degrees of freedom. Hence the 95% confidence intervals for the $\gamma_h - \gamma_i$ can be constructed.

SPSS-Programm 1

```
          COMPUTE X1=0.
          COMPUTE X2=0.
          COMPUTE X3=0.
          COMPUTE X4=0.
          EXECUTE.
          COMPUTE Z1=0.
          COMPUTE Z2=0.
          COMPUTE Z3=0.
          COMPUTE Z4=0.
          COMPUTE Z5=0.
          COMPUTE Z6=0.
          COMPUTE Z7=0.
          COMPUTE Z8=0.
          COMPUTE Z9=0.
          COMPUTE Z10=0.
          COMPUTE Z11=0.
          COMPUTE Z12=0.
          EXECUTE.
          IF (A=1) X1=1.
          IF (A=2) X2=1.
          IF (A=3) X3=1.
          IF (A=4) X4=1.
          EXECUTE.
          IF (B=1) Z1=1.
          IF (B=2) Z2=1.
          IF (B=3) Z3=1.
          IF (B=4) Z4=1.
          IF (B=5) Z5=1.
          IF (B=6) Z6=1.
          IF (B=7) Z7=1.
          IF (B=8) Z8=1.
          IF (B=9) Z9=1.
          IF (B=10) Z10=1.
          IF (B=11) Z11=1.
          IF (B=12) Z12=1.
          EXECUTE.
          SAVE OUTFILE = 'C: Lysin1.sav'.
          DATA LIST FREE
            /X1 X2 X3 X4  Z1 Z2 Z3 Z4 Z5 Z6 Z7 Z8 Z9 Z10 Z11 Z12  Y.
          BEGIN DATA.
          0 0 0 0    0.1961 0 0 0 0 0 0 0 0 0 0 0    0
          0 0 0 0    0 0.1961 0 0 0 0 0 0 0 0 0 0    0
          0 0 0 0    0 0 0.1961 0 0 0 0 0 0 0 0 0    0
          0 0 0 0    0 0 0 0.1961 0 0 0 0 0 0 0 0    0
          0 0 0 0    0 0 0 0 0.1961 0 0 0 0 0 0 0    0
          0 0 0 0    0 0 0 0 0 0.1961 0 0 0 0 0 0    0
          0 0 0 0    0 0 0 0 0 0 0.1961 0 0 0 0 0    0
          0 0 0 0    0 0 0 0 0 0 0 0.1961 0 0 0 0    0
          0 0 0 0    0 0 0 0 0 0 0 0 0.1961 0 0 0    0
          0 0 0 0    0 0 0 0 0 0 0 0 0 0.1961 0 0    0
          0 0 0 0    0 0 0 0 0 0 0 0 0 0 0.1961 0    0
          0 0 0 0    0 0 0 0 0 0 0 0 0 0 0 0.1961    0
          END DATA.
          SAVE OUTFILE = 'C: Lysin2.SAV' .
          NEW FILE.
          ADD FILES  FILE = 'C: Lysin1.SAV' / FILE = 'C:Lysin2.SAV'.
          REGRESSION
            /VARIABLES=X1 X2 X3 X4
               Z1 Z2 Z3 Z4 Z5 Z6 Z7 Z8 Z9 Z10 Z11 Z12 Y
            /STATISTICS = R ANOVA BCOV COEFF CI
            /ORIGIN
            /DEPENDENT Y
            /METHOD = ENTER X1 X2 X3 X4
               Z1 Z2 Z3 Z4 Z5 Z6 Z7 Z8 Z9 Z10 Z11 Z12.
```

4.2.2 Two-way Analysis of Variance - Nested Classification

A typical example of a two-way *nested* (or *hierarchical*) classification would occur if a survey was conducted in UN member states, which would represent the levels of a factor A. Within each state the largest administrative units, like for example the Federal Regions in Germany, the Provinces in the Netherlands or the States in the USA would be the levels of a second factor B, but each level of B belongs uniquely to (is nested in) one of the countries. The level of A is defined uniquely by the level of B.

We write B nested in A as: $B \prec A$ (or $A \succ B$). If all UN member states with all their sub-units are included in an investigation, we have a model I. If we take a sample member states but surveys are conducted in all the sub-units of the selected countries, then we have (approximately) a mixed model.

In a poultry experiment, if several hens are associated with exactly one cock, then we have a nested situation: hens $\prec$ cocks. If the hens and the cocks are chosen randomly from the appropriate populations, then we have a model II.

In the two-way nested classification the classes are defined by the factor level combinations (i,j) of level A_i of A and level B_{ij} of B within A_i. Let y_{ijk} be the k-th observation in the factor combination (i,j), i.e. in B_{ij}. Then we have:

$$y_{ijk} = \mu + a_i + b_{ij} + e_{ijk} \quad (i = 1, ..., a, j = 1, ..., b_i, k = 1, ..., n_{ij}) \tag{4.19}$$

In this equation the symbols are: μ is the general mean; a_i the main effects of the a levels A_i of A, b_{ij} the main effects of the b_i levels B_{ij} of B within A_i; interactions do not occur in this classification. In A_i, j runs from 1 to b_i; in class (i,j), k runs from 1 to n_{ij}. If $n_{ij} = n$ for all (i,j), we have the case of equal class numbers (replications). Optimal experimental designs in the two-way hierarchical analysis of variance often need equal replications and moreover equal b_i (this is the balanced case).

The following conditions hold independently of any particular model: $var(e_{ijk}) = \sigma^2$ and the e_{ijk} are mutually independent, with expectation zero.

The Analysis of Variance table is independent of the particular model, and is given in Table 4.8 for the balanced case (all $n_{ij} = n$ and all $b_i = b$).

In the SPSS procedure Analyze - General Linear Model - Univariate we click the Model button, and then under "build terms" we enter both factors as "Main effects" under "sum of squares" choose "type I" After clicking Continue, click on Paste and in the Syntax window change "design a b" to "design a b(a)" (signifying B nested in A). Then start the program with "Run".

SPSS-Program 2

```
UNIANOVA
  y  BY a b
  /METHOD = SSTYPE(1)
  /INTERCEPT = INCLUDE
  /CRITERIA = ALPHA(.05)
  /DESIGN = a  b(a)  .
```

Table 4.8 *Analysis of Variance Table for the Two-way Nested Classification and the E(MS) for Model I - balanced case:* $n_{ij} = n$, $b_i = b$.

Source of variation	SS	df	MS	E(MS) Model I
Main effect A	SS_A $= \dfrac{1}{bn}\sum_i Y_{i..}^2 - \dfrac{Y_{...}^2}{N}$	a-1	$MS_A = \dfrac{SS_A}{a-1}$	$\sigma^2 + \dfrac{bn}{a-1}\sum_i a_i^2$
Main effect B within factor A	$SS_{B\ in\ A}$ $= \dfrac{1}{n}\sum_{i,j} Y_{ij.}^2$ $-\dfrac{1}{bn}\sum_i Y_{i..}^2$	$a(b$-1)	$MS_{BinA} = \dfrac{SS_{B\ in\ A}}{ab-a}$	$\sigma^2 + \dfrac{n}{a(b-1)}\sum_{i,j} b_{ij}^2$
Residual	SS_R $= \sum_{i,j,k} y_{ijk}^2 - \dfrac{1}{n}\sum_{i,j} Y_{ij.}^2$	N-ab	$MS_R = \dfrac{SS_R}{N-ab}$	σ^2
Total	SS_T $= \sum_{i,j,k} y_{ijk}^2 - \dfrac{Y_{...}^2}{N}$	N-1		

The ANOVA table for the unbalanced case is given in Table 4.9.

Table 4.9 *Analysis of Variance Table for the Unbalanced Two-way Nested classification* $(B_. = \sum b_i, N_{i.} = \sum_j n_{ij}, N_{..} = \sum n_{ij})$.

Source of variation	SS	df	MS
Main effect A	$SS_A = \sum_{i=1}^{a} \dfrac{Y_{i..}^2}{N_{i.}} - \dfrac{Y_{..}^2}{N_{..}}$	a-1	$MS_A = \dfrac{SS_A}{a-1}$
Main effect B within factor A	$SS_{B\ in\ A} = \sum_{i=1}^{a}\sum_{j=1}^{b_i} \dfrac{Y_{ij.}^2}{n_{ij}} - \sum_{i=1}^{a} \dfrac{Y_{i..}^2}{N_{i.}}$	$B_.$-a	$MS_{BinA} = \dfrac{SS_{BinA}}{B_.-a}$
Residual	$SS_R = \sum_{i=1}^{a}\sum_{j=1}^{b_i}\sum_{k=1}^{n_{ij}} y_{ijk}^2 - \sum_{i=1}^{a}\sum_{j=1}^{b_i} \dfrac{Y_{ij.}^2}{n_{ij}}$	$N_{..}$-$B_.$	$MS_R = \dfrac{SS_R}{N_.-B_.}$

4.2.2.1 Two-way Analysis of Variance - Nested Classification - Model I

The representation of a model I two-way nested analysis of variance is given by the model equation (4.19). Here all the effects are real numbers i.e. not random. The model is completed by the following conditions: the sums of the a_i and of the b_{ij} (for each i) equal zero.

Table 4.8 contains a column containing the expected mean squares E(MS) for model I. With the aid of this table we can use the methods described in section 4.1 to derive the F-tests for the testing of various hypotheses - we will illustrate these in an example below. The least squares estimates of the effects are the following:

$$\hat{\mu} = \bar{y}_{...}, \ \hat{a}_i = \bar{y}_{i..} - \bar{y}_{...}, \ \hat{b}_{ij} = \bar{y}_{ij.} - \bar{y}_{i..}.$$

We test the null hypothesis that factor A has no effect with the test statistic

$$F_A = \frac{MS_A}{MS_R},$$

which under the null hypothesis has an F-distribution with $(a-1)$ and $(N-ab)$ degrees of freedom.

The null hypothesis that factor B has no effect is tested with the test statistic

$$F_B = \frac{MS_B}{MS_R},$$

which has an F-distribution with $a(b-1)$ and $(N-ab)$ degrees of freedom.

How the maxi-min size is determined is shown in the example.

Example 4.7

> The data are given in Table 4.10
> We consider an example of the balanced case with $a = 6$ levels of the factor A, $b = 4$ levels of factor B within each level of the factor A, and wish to determine the number of observations required to test the null hypothesis on the factor A so that $\alpha = 0.05$; $\beta = 0.2$ $d = 1.3\sigma$.
>
> In ANOV we choose the command sequence that leads to Figure 4.11, where the precision requirements have already been entered.

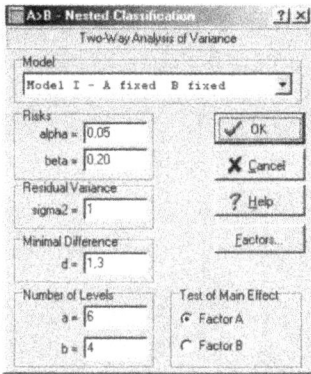

Figure 4.11 *Precision requirements for Example 4.7*

The result is given in Figure 4.12; we need 5 observations in every cell.

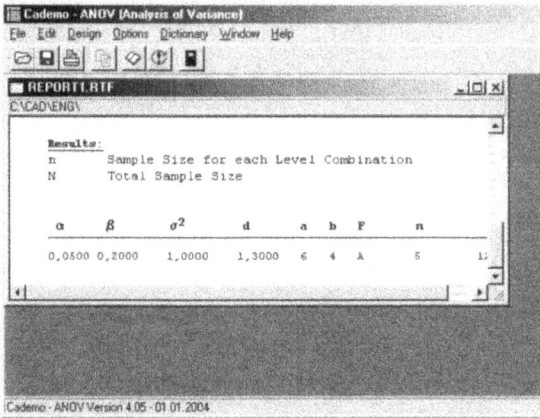

Figure. 4.12 *Size of Experiment for Example 4.7*

Table 4.10 *Observations from Example 4.7.*

Observation	Levels of A											
	A_1				A_2				A_3			
	Levels of B											
	B_{11}	B_{12}	B_{13}	B_{14}	B_{21}	B_{22}	B_{23}	B_{24}	B_{31}	B_{32}	B_{33}	B_{34}
1	30	0	7	28	24	14	20	20	14	14	18	-25
2	-19	20	5	15	16	11	18	-12	-18	8	16	13
3	-31	32	3	20	-18	27	8	0	33	-19	7	36
4	-14	11	-5	20	11	11	32	-5	-9	6	-4	18
5	-14	13	8	-48	-10	8	-25	44	-7	-38	21	-7
$Y_{ij.}$	-48	76	18	35	23	71	53	47	13	-29	58	35
$Y_{i..}$	81				194				77			

Table 4.10 continued.

Observation	Levels of A											
	A₄				A₅				A₆			
	Levels of B											
	B₄₁	B₄₂	B₄₃	B₄₄	B₅₁	B₅₂	B₅₃	B₅₄	B₆₁	B₆₂	B₆₃	B₆₄
1	12	-9	8	2	17	-3	17	13	0	-19	-6	-11
2	2	-41	16	-20	-4	15	9	30	-15	-28	-14	-17
3	2	-34	23	11	-20	10	-29	-19	1	16	-44	2
4	7	-12	17	8	22	6	12	15	4	9	-12	-22
5	-3	-6	-7	-10	26	16	-8	8	-6	-2	-9	-45
$Y_{ij.}$	20	-102	57	-9	41	44	1	47	-16	-24	-85	-93
$Y_{i..}$	-34				133				-218			

From Table 4.10 we obtain

$$\frac{1}{N}Y^2_{...} = \frac{(233)^2}{120} = 452.4$$

$$\frac{1}{bn}\sum_i Y^2_{i..} = \frac{1}{20}((81)^2 + (194)^2 + ... + (-218)^2) = 5824.8$$

$$\frac{1}{n}\sum_{i,j} Y^2_{ij.} = \frac{1}{5}((-48)^2 + (76)^2 + ... + (13)^2 + (-29)^2 + ... + (-85)^2 + (-93^2))$$

$$= 12496.6$$

$$\sum y^2_{ijk} = \sum_{i=1}^{6}\sum_{j=1}^{4}\sum_{k=1}^{5} y^2_{ijk} = (30)^2 + (-19)^2 + ... + (-22)^2 + (-45)^2 = 41445.0$$

and from this we get the ANOVA table in Table 4.11.

Table 4.11 ANOVA table for Example 4.7.

Source of variation	SS	df	MS
A-levels	5372.4	5	1074.5
B-levels in A	6671.8	18	370.7
Residual	28948.4	96	301.5

There is no direct access to hierarchical classifications in the Windows version of SPSS, but we can perform the analysis with SPSS-Program 2

The data has to be input as follows

observation no.	factor A	factor B	value
1	1	1	30
2	1	1	-19
3	1	1	-31
4	1	1	-14
5	1	1	-14
6	1	2	0
.	.	.	.
.	.	.	.
.	.	.	.
19	1	4	20
20	1	4	-48
21	2	1	24
.	.	.	.
.	.	.	.
.	.	.	.
120	6	4	-45

We proceed as described below Table 4.9 using "Paste" to change the program. When we run the modified program we get Figure 4.13.

Tests of Between-Subjects Effects

Dependent Variable: TRAIT

Source	Type I Sum of Squares	df	Mean Square	F	Sig.
Corrected Model	12044.192[a]	23	523.661	1.737	.034
Intercept	452.408	1	452.408	1.500	.224
A	5372.342	5	1074.468	3.563	.005
B(A)	6671.850	18	370.658	1.229	.254
Error	28948.400	96	301.546		
Total	41445.000	120			
Corrected Total	40992.592	119			

a. R Squared = .294 (Adjusted R Squared = .125)

Figure 4.13 *SPSS-output for Example 4.7*

4.2.2.2 Two-way Analysis of Variance - Nested Classification - Model II

The specification for a model II of the two-way nested analysis of variance is as follows. In the model equation

$$y_{ijk} = \mu + a_i + b_{ij} + e_{ijk} \ (i = 1, ..., a; j = 1, ..., b_i; k = 1, ..., n_{ij}) \tag{4.20}$$

all effects (except μ) are random. The model is completed by the following conditions: $\text{var}(a_i) = \sigma_a^2$, $\text{var}(b_{ij}) = \sigma_{bina}^2$, and all the random variables are mutually independent. σ^2, and σ_a^2 and σ_{bina}^2 are called *components of variance*.

The ANOVA tables 4.8 and 4.9 are (if we ignore the column with the E(*MS*)) indepen- dent of the model chosen, since only the E(*MS*) depend on the model. For model II (both factors random) we find these in the first column of Table 4.12. We will use the E(*MS*) both to estimate the variance components and also to find the appropriate F-tests for testing hypotheses using the 7 steps described in section 4.1. In the next example we will demonstrate the ANOVA method of estimating the components of variance. We use Table 4.8 and Table 4.9 to set up the equations for s_a^2, s_{bina}^2 and s^2 in Example 4.8 below.

We use the E(MS)-column for model II in Table 4.12.
Table 4.12 gives the E(MS) for all models with at least one random factor.

Table 4.12 E(MS) for mixed models and model II.

Source of variation	Model II	Mixed models	
		A fixed B random	A random B fixed
Between A-levels	$\sigma^2 + \lambda_1\sigma_{bina}^2 +$ $\lambda_2\sigma_a^2$	$\sigma^2 + \lambda_1\sigma_{bina}^2$ $+ \dfrac{\sum\limits_{i=1}^{a} N_i a_i^2}{a-1}$	$\sigma^2 + \lambda_2\sigma_a^2$
Between B-levels within A	$\sigma^2 + \lambda_3\sigma_{bina}^2$	$\sigma^2 + \lambda_3\sigma_{bina}^2$	$\sigma^2 + \dfrac{\sum\limits_{i=1}^{a}\sum\limits_{j=1}^{b_i} n_{ij} b_{ij}^2}{B_. - a}$
Residual	σ^2	σ^2	σ^2

Here $B_. = \sum\limits_{i=1}^{a} b_i$. We estimate μ by $\bar{y}_{..}$.

The factors λ_1, λ_2 and λ_3 in Table 4.12 are as follows:

$$\lambda_1 = \frac{1}{a-1}\sum_{i=1}^{a}\sum_{j=1}^{b_i} n_{ij}^2\left(\frac{1}{N_{i.}} - \frac{1}{N_{..}}\right),$$

$$\lambda_2 = \frac{1}{a-1}\left(N_{..} - \sum_{i=1}^{a}\frac{N_{i.}^2}{N_{..}}\right), \qquad (4.21)$$

$$\lambda_3 = \frac{1}{B_. - a}\sum_{i=1}^{a}\sum_{j=1}^{b_i}\left(n_{ij} - \frac{n_{ij}^2}{N_{i.}}\right).$$

If all $n_{ij} = n$ and $b_i = b$ the coefficients λ_1, λ_2, λ_3 simplify as follows. Because

$$\sum_{i=1}^{a} \sum_{j=1}^{b} n^2 = abn^2, N_{i.} = bn, N_{..} = abn \text{ we obtain } \frac{1}{N_{i.}} - \frac{1}{N_{..}} = \frac{1}{bn} - \frac{1}{abn} = \frac{a-1}{abn}$$

and therefore $\lambda_1 = n$, $\lambda_2 = bn$, $\lambda_3 = n$.

Example 4.8

Table 4.13 gives the number of days needed by piglets to grow up to a certain weight (110 kg). The data refer to the offspring of two boars paired with three sows each (six sows in all).

In SPSS after Analyze - General Linear Model we choose Variance Components. Under Options we click on ANOVA-method (the sums of squares are then automatically set to Type 1). Model and Paste are handled as described under Table 4.9; both factors are random. We get the same results as in the following hand calculations.

Table 4.13 *Fattening days of the offsprings from Example 4.8 (B =Boar, S = Sow).*

	B_1			B_2		
	$S_{1,1}$	$S_{1,2}$	$S_{1,3}$	$S_{2,1}$	$S_{2,2}$	$S_{2,3}$
	93	107	109	89	87	81
	89	99	107	102	91	83
	97		94	104	82	85
	105		106	97		91
n_{ij}	4	2	4	4	3	4
$N_{i.}$	10			11		

We find the ANOVA scheme in Table 4.9.

To estimate the variance components σ_a^2 and σ_{bina}^2 we need the values of λ_1, λ_2 and λ_3 in equations (4.21).

Because $a = 2, N_{1.} = 10, N_{2.} = 11, N = 21, B_{.} = 6$ we obtain

$$\lambda_1 = 4^2 (\frac{1}{10} - \frac{1}{21}) + 2^2 (\frac{1}{10} - \frac{1}{21}) + 4^2 (\frac{1}{10} - \frac{1}{21})$$

$$+ 4^2 (\frac{1}{11} - \frac{1}{21}) + 3^2 (\frac{1}{11} - \frac{1}{21}) + 4^2 (\frac{1}{11} - \frac{1}{21})$$

$$= \frac{36}{10} + \frac{41}{11} - \frac{77}{21} = 3.66,$$

133

$$\lambda_2 \; = \; 21 \; - \; \frac{1}{21}(10^2 \; + \; 11^2) \; = \; 10.47$$

and

$$\lambda_3 \; = \; \frac{1}{6 \; - \; 2}(21 \; - \; \frac{36}{10} \; - \; \frac{41}{11}) \; = \; 3.42$$

From the ANOVA table we get the equations

$$s^2 \; + \; 3.66\,s_{bina}^2 \; + \; 10.47\,s_a^2 \; = \; 568.54$$
$$s^2 \; + \; 3.42\,s_{bina}^2 \qquad\qquad = \; 132.84$$
$$s^2 \qquad\qquad\qquad\qquad = \; 36.04 \; .$$

From these we obtain

$$s^2 = 36.04$$

$$s_{sows\,in\,boars}^2 \; = \; s_{bina}^2 \; = \; \frac{132.84 \; - \; 36.04}{3.42} \; = \; 28.3$$

and

$$s_{boars}^2 \; = \; s_a^2 \; = \; \frac{568.54 \; - \; 3.66\cdot28.3 \; - \; 36.04}{10.47} \; = \; 40.97.$$

4.2.2.3 Two-way Analysis of Variance - Nested Classification - Mixed Model, A Fixed and B Random

The model equation for this mixed model is:

$$y_{ijk} \; = \; \mu \; + \; a_i \; + \; b_{ij} \; + \; e_{ijk} \; (i \; = \; 1,...,a; j \; = \; 1,...,b_i; k \; = \; 1,...,n_{ij}) \qquad (4.22)$$

the effects μ and a_i are fixed, the remaining ones random. The model is completed by the following side conditions: $\mathrm{var}(b_{ij}) \; = \; \sigma_{bina}^2$, all the random variables are mutually independent with expectation zero and the a_i sum to zero.

The ANOVA table for this model is given in Table 4.8; the expected mean squares are in Table 4.12.

The fixed effects can be estimated from the following equations:

$$\hat{\mu} = \bar{y}_{...}, \hat{a}_i = \bar{y}_{i..} - \bar{y}_{...} \, .$$

For the random factors, the ANOVA method gives estimators for σ_{bina}^2 and σ^2 as follows:

$$\sigma_{bina}^2 = (MS_{B\,in\,A} - MS_R)/\lambda_3, \; s^2 = MS_R.$$

The null hypothesis that the effects of all the levels of factor A are equal, is tested using the test statistic:

$$F_A = \frac{MS_A}{MS_{B \text{ in } A}},$$

which has an F distribution with $(a-1)$ and $a(b-1)$ degrees of freedom.

Here we will also calculate the size of experiment necessary, using the precision requirements given in Figure 4.10 for the fixed effects model, for a model having B as a random factor. Using ANOV we obtain the result that $b = 17$ levels of factor B are required.

4.2.2.4 Two-way Analysis of Variance - Nested Classification - Mixed Model, B Fixed and A Random

The model equation for this mixed model is:

$$y_{ijk} = \mu + a_i + b_{ij} + e_{ijk} \quad (i = 1,...,a; j = 1,...,b_i; k = 1,...,n_{ij}) \qquad (4.23)$$

The effects μ and b_{ij} are fixed; the remaining effects are random. The model is completed by the following conditions: $\text{var}(a_i) = \sigma_a^2$, all the random variables are mutually independent with expectation zero and the b_{ij} sum to zero over j for each i.

The ANOVA table for this model is again table 4.8; the expected mean squares are found in Table 4.12.
The fixed effects are estimated using the following equations:

$$\hat{\mu} = \bar{y}_{...}, \quad \hat{b}_{ij} = \bar{y}_{ij.} - \bar{y}_{...}.$$

The estimates for σ_a^2 and σ^2 using the ANOVA method are given by:

$$s_a^2 = (MS_A - MS_R)/\lambda_2.$$

$$s^2 = MS_R,$$

The null hypothesis, that the effects of all the levels of factor B are equal, is tested using the test statistic:

$$F_B = \frac{MS_B}{MS_R},$$

which has an F-distribution with $a(b-1)$ and $N-ab$ degrees of freedom.

135

4.2.3 Notes on the Procedure for Higher Classifications

In applications we often meet analyses of variance with more than two factors. Their treatment is outside the scope of an introductory text because there are so many cases. Thus even in three-factor analysis of variance there are two mixed classifications as well as the cross- and nested classifications. Let the observations be the weights of newly hatched chicks with factors: A = father, B = mother and C = sex of the chick. Then B is nested in A, but C is cross-classified with the factor combination $A \succ B$. We write this $(A \succ B) \times C$. Also, each of the factors can be fixed or random. Consequently the number of possible cases increases rapidly, according as to which of the factors in the four classifications $A \times B \times C$, $A \succ B \succ C$, $(A \succ B) \times C$ and $(A \times B) \succ C$ are fixed or random. The possible models are listed in Table 4.14; the random factors are printed in bold. In the case of cross-classified factors, the first is/are chosen as fixed; the other(s) random, by renumbering the factors, any case can be put in one of the given forms, which is not the case for nested factors.

Table 4.14   *Models for Three-factor Analyses of Variance.*

Sequence Number	Model	Sequence Number	Model
1	$A \times B \times C$	14	$(A \times B) \succ C$
2	$A \times B \times \boldsymbol{C}$	15	$(A \times \boldsymbol{B}) \succ C$
3	$A \times \boldsymbol{B} \times C$	16	$(A \times \boldsymbol{B}) \succ C$
4	$A \times \boldsymbol{B} \times \boldsymbol{C}$	17	$(A \times \boldsymbol{B}) \succ \boldsymbol{C}$
5	$A \succ B \succ C$	18	$(\boldsymbol{A} \times \boldsymbol{B}) \succ \boldsymbol{C}$
6	$A \succ B \succ \boldsymbol{C}$	19	$(A \succ B) \times C$
7	$A \succ \boldsymbol{B} \succ C$	20	$(A \succ B) \times \boldsymbol{C}$
8	$A \succ \boldsymbol{B} \succ \boldsymbol{C}$	21	$(A \succ \boldsymbol{B}) \times C$
9	$A \succ \boldsymbol{B} \succ C$	22	$(A \succ \boldsymbol{B}) \times C$
10	$A \succ \boldsymbol{B} \succ \boldsymbol{C}$	23	$(A \succ \boldsymbol{B}) \times C$
11	$A \succ \boldsymbol{B} \succ \boldsymbol{C}$	24	$(A \succ B) \times C$
12	$A \succ \boldsymbol{B} \succ \boldsymbol{C}$	25	$(A \succ \boldsymbol{B}) \times \boldsymbol{C}$
13	$(A \times B) \succ C$	26	$(A \succ \boldsymbol{B}) \times \boldsymbol{C}$

The various cases for three-way classifications are also dealt with in VB; the necessary procedures appear in 1/61/0000. SPSS allows the analysis of numerous classifications. There, where no exact tests exist, approximate tests are used.

Up to the three-way analyses of variance, the maxi-min size can be calculated using ANOV, so long as an exact test exists. For example, no exact test exists for the three-way cross-classification with A fixed and $\boldsymbol{B}$, $\boldsymbol{C}$ random.

4.3 Multiple Comparisons of Means

When we reject the null hypothesis that the effects of all the levels of a fixed factor are equal in a one-way or higher way ANOVA, then we accept the hypothesis that at least two of the $a = k$ factor levels (or interactions) differ from each other. Often the experimenter would very much like to know which particular levels show significant differences between each other. The procedures which we will describe below have been developed to answer this question. If however the objective of the investigation is to discover the extreme levels (largest or smallest) then tests should not be done. Instead the selection procedures described in section 3.3, which are designed for just this purpose, should be used, particularly since they generally require smaller sample sizes.

If we want to test some or all of the pairwise differences between $k>2$ expected values (means) against the null hypothesis of equality, then we should use multiple comparison methods.

In this connection we distinguish between two types of risks of the first and second kind (error probabilities).

Individual Risk: the individual risk applies to every single comparison. The greater the number of pairwise comparisons in an experiment, the greater is the chance (assuming a fixed pairwise risk) of a false decision in at least one of these comparisons. The individual risk is also called the *per comparison*, or *comparisonwise risk*.

Simultaneous Risk: the simultaneous risk applies overall to several comparisons simultaneously; it is also called the *familywise risk*. Frequently we consider all the comparisons in the experiment, in which case the risk is called the *experimentwise risk*. Under the null hypothesis H_0: $\mu_1 = \mu_2 =.....= \mu_k$ the experimentwise risk of the first kind is the probability that at least one of the alternative hypotheses H_{Aij}: $\mu_i \neq \mu_j$ will be falsely accepted.

If the simultaneous risk of the first kind α^* applies only to a subset of size $m>1$ of all $\binom{k}{2}$ pairwise comparisons, its size can be assessed in terms of the per comparison risk of the first kind α with the aid of the *Bonferroni Inequality* as follows:

$$\alpha < \alpha^* < m\alpha \qquad (4.24)$$

Before an experiment is planned or analysed, a choice must be made between fixing the experimentwise or the per comparison risks of the first and second kind. To fix the experimentwise risk at a certain level is a stricter condition, and will require a larger experiment than if the same level is fixed for per comparison risk. For the F-test in the analysis of variance the risks of both kinds are defined experimentwise. In what follows the risk of the second kind β is chosen per comparison. We consider the following cases.

Case 1. Comparison of the means of the $k > 2$ populations pairwise with each other.
Methods:
Multiple t-Test: pairwise comparisons with per comparison risk of the first kind.

Tukey-Test: pairwise comparisons with experimentwise risk of the first kind.

Case 2. Comparison of each of the means of k-1 populations with that of a standard (control) population.
Methods:

Multiple t-Test: Comparison with per comparison risk of the first kind.
Dunnett-Test: Comparison with experimentwise risk of the first kind.

Further multiple comparison procedures for means are described by HOCHBERG and TAMHANE (1987) and in VB 3/26/0000 – 3/26/9104.

The experimental design for all cases and for the F-Test in the one-way classification can be found in the CADEMO-Module MEANS or *light*. In MEANS we choose the command sequence: Test – k > 2 Means and continue in case 1 with – against each other and in case 2 with - against Standard or Control.

The following assumptions hold for all cases:
- pairwise independent random samples will be taken from all k populations; the sample from the i-th population is denoted by $(y_{i1}, y_{i2}, ..., y_{in_i})$.
- The y_{ij} ($i = 1, ..., k; j = 1, ..., n_i$) are distributed independently of each other as $N(\mu_i; \sigma^2)$ with the same variance σ^2. $N = \sum\limits_{i=1}^{k} n_i$ is the total number of observations.

Example 4.9

We wish to test the expectations of 9 Normal distributions; where if necessary the ninth population is the standard. We take $\alpha = 0.05$, $\beta_0 = 0.20$, $d = 4$ and assume that we have an estimate of σ^2, namely $\tilde{\sigma}^2 = 16$.

We use CADEMO- *light* for the determination of the sample size, selecting the option: "Test - k > 2 means" and either

        "Comparison with each other" (for Case 1) or
        "Comparison with a Standard" (for Case 2).

We use the following observed values for the analysis (yield of wheat varieties in dt/ha).

In the SPSS-Data Editor we define one variable as Variety and enter the numbers (1 to 9) and a second variable as Yield.

Then we select the menu sequence Analyze- Compare Means - One-way ANOVA. The output gives a significant F-value $F = 3.77$, which is greater than the corresponding table value which is $F(8; 81; 0.95) = 2.055$, with significance $0.001 < 0.05$. This means that at least 2 of the observed means are significantly different from each other. We will use these data to illustrate all the comparison procedures that we have introduced, in order to establish which groups of means differ significantly.

Table 4.16   *Observations (yield in dt/ha) from nine varieties (T_1, ..., T_9) and their sample means.*

Plot	T_1	T_2	T_3	T_4	T_5	T_6	T_7	T_8	T_9
1	50.1	50.0	46.8	39.0	48.6	45.4	52.8	50.2	44.7
2	45.6	55.3	39.0	31.3	56.3	64.5	46.9	54.9	60.7
3	57.6	43.1	47.1	49.0	55.8	53.8	44.8	61.4	57.9
4	48.7	48.6	49.0	52.0	45.4	58.3	44.7	53.4	47.5
5	49.9	46.1	47.6	50.3	59.8	55.6	38.8	56.7	44.6
6	56.8	48.4	45.4	47.0	53.4	49.0	46.6	46.3	53.2
7	48.9	44.3	51.1	40.1	47.7	60.4	39.2	47.8	52.2
8	48.4	55.7	47.3	42.7	50.4	53.6	40.4	47.8	46.0
9	53.5	56.8	47.3	57.0	56.7	51.5	50.9	51.9	56.3
10	45.1	43.9	48.5	41.6	56.2	46.1	52.5	54.3	50.1
Mean	50.46	49.22	46.91	45.00	53.03	53.82	45.76	52.47	51.32

4.3.1 Pairwise Comparisons between the Means of k Populations

For **each** of the $\binom{k}{2}$ pairs (i,j) with $i<j$ $(i,j = 1, ..., k)$ the null hypothesis

$$H_{0ij} : \mu_i = \mu_j$$

will be tested against the alternative

$$H_{Aij} : \mu_i \neq \mu_j.$$

When the risk of the first kind α is fixed per comparison, the probability that each null hypothesis H_{0ij} will be falsely rejected is equal to α, and we use the *multiple t-Test*.

4.3.1.1 The Multiple t-Test

Sample Size Determination

It is optimal to take equal sized samples for each treatment: $n_1 = n_2 = ... = n_k = n$. For given d, α and β_0, n is calculated from:

$$n = \text{CEIL}\left[\frac{2\sigma^2}{d^2}\left\{t\left[f;1-\frac{\alpha}{2}\right]+t[f;1-\beta_0]\right\}^2\right]. \tag{4.25}$$

Where f is the number of degrees of freedom for MS_R (MS-Residual). For example in the one-way ANOVA with k levels $f = df = k(n-1)$.

Example 4.10

Taking the values from Example 4.9, we apply equation (4.25) with $k = 9$, $d = 4$. Prior information for σ^2 is given in the form of an estimate $\tilde{\sigma}^2 = 16$. We fix $\alpha = 0.05$, $\beta_0 = 0.20$ and start an iteration with $n^{(0)} = \infty$. We find:
$n^{(1)} = \text{CEIL}[2(1.9602 + 0.841657)^2] = \text{CEIL}[15.7] = 16$.
For $f = 9 \cdot 15 = 135$ degrees of freedom we have:
$n^{(2)} = \text{CEIL}[2(1.7769 + 0.84429)^2] = \text{CEIL}[15.93] = 16$.
Therefore $N = 9 \cdot 16 = 144$.
CADEMO MEANS gives the same result as follows. After the menu sequence Test – $k > 2$ Means, against each other, Figure 4.14 appears.

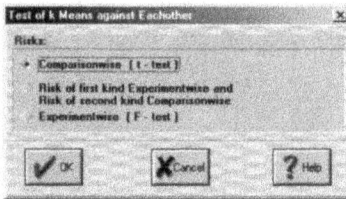

Figure 4.14 *CADEMO (MEANS) – branch for the comparison between means*

From Figure 4.14 we arrive at either the multiple t–test, the Tukey test (2nd Option) or the F –test for the model I one-way analysis of variance. In our case, with comparisonwise, we select the multiple t-test. In the dialogue box which follows, we enter the precision requirements, as shown in Figure 4.15.

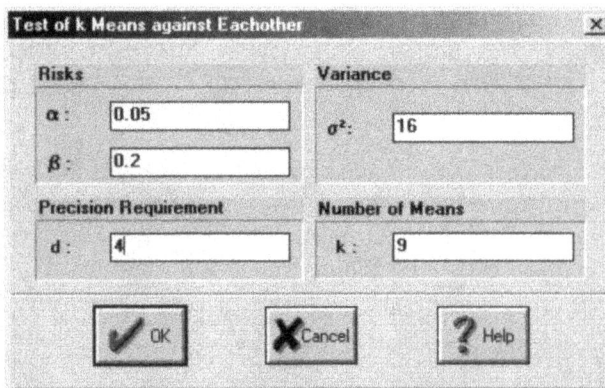

Figure 4.15 *Precision requirements for Examples 4.9 and 4.10*

The result is the same as with hand calculation.

Analysis

In **one-way** ANOVA the test statistic for H_{0ij} is

$$t_{ij} = \frac{\bar{y}_{i.} - \bar{y}_{j.}}{s} \sqrt{\frac{n_i n_j}{n_i + n_j}} \tag{4.26}$$

where s is the square root of MS_R from the ANOVA table.

$$s^2 = \frac{1}{\sum n_i - k} \sum_{i=1}^{k} \sum_{j=1}^{n_i} (y_{ij} - \bar{y}_{i.})^2 \tag{4.27}$$

In **multifactorial** analysis of variance with equal class numbers $(n_i = n_j)$ we can also use (4.26). If the class sizes are unequal then the SPSS procedure GLM is used.

We compare every value $|t_{ij}|$ with $t(f;1 - \frac{a}{2})$ and reject H_0 whenever $|t_{ij}|$ exceeds the appropriate quantile (with $f = k(n-1)$ degrees of freedom) The difference between (4.26) and the t-test statistics in chapter 3 lies in the fact that s has been estimated from all $k > 2$ samples (to do this we need to assume equal population variances) and this increases the degrees of freedom in comparison with the t-test in the one or two sample problem.

In SPSS we select the sequence Analyze - Comparison of Means - oneway ANOVA and click on "Post hoc... " we get Figure 4.16.

Note!

These post-hoc procedures are only used in balanced two- and higher way classifications. They use the simple class means and not the least squares estimators.

We shall return to this figure several times, but for our present purpose we click on LSD (least significant difference).

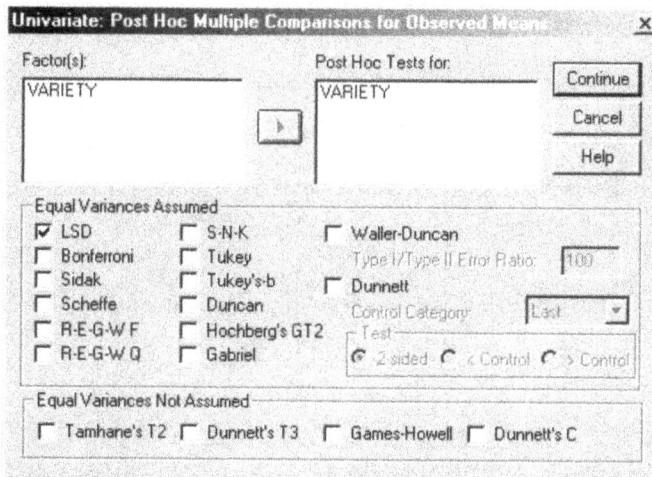

Figure 4.16 *Multiple comparisons in SPSS*

Instead of comparing the t-value for a pairwise difference with the tabulated quantile, we can of course compare each observed difference between means with that difference Δ which would just lead to the rejection of the null hypothesis. In our case with $n_1 = ... = n_k = n$ this value Δ is given by the relation

$$\frac{\Delta}{s}\sqrt{\frac{n}{2}} = t(f; 1 - \frac{\alpha}{2}).$$

Example 4.9 - continued

The SPSS results for the Data from Table 4.16 is very extensive - an extract is shown in Figure 4.17. There each pair whose means are significantly different are indicated by the symbol *. The null hypothesis is accepted when the confidence interval includes the value 0.

Multiple Comparisons

Dependent Variable: YIELD
LSD

(I) VARIETY	(J) VARIETY	Mean Difference (I-J)	Std. Error	Sig.	95% Confidence Interval	
					Lower Bound	Upper Bound
1	2	1.2400	2.36833	.602	-3.4722	5.9522
	3	3.5500	2.36833	.138	-1.1622	8.2622
	4	5.4600(*)	2.36833	.024	.7478	10.1722
	5	-2.5700	2.36833	.281	-7.2822	2.1422
	6	-3.3600	2.36833	.160	-8.0722	1.3522
	7	4.7000	2.36833	.051	-.0122	9.4122
	8	-2.0100	2.36833	.399	-6.7222	2.7022
	9	-.8600	2.36833	.717	-5.5722	3.8522

Based on observed means.
   * The mean difference is significant at the .05 level.

Figure 4.17 *SPSS output for Example 4.9*

A graphical summary of the results from the SPSS output is shown in Figure 4.18. Pairs of varieties which stand on the same line do not differ significantly; those which do not stand together on the same line lead to the rejection of the null hypothesis.

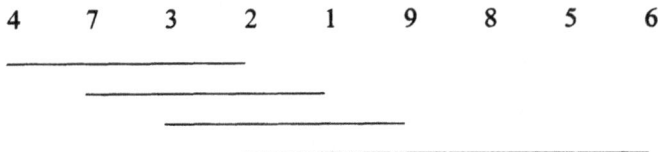

Figure 4.18 *Results of the multiple t-test*

The Tukey test tests all differences between means with an experimentwise risk of the first kind α_e (the risk of the second kind is still pairwise). An additional assumption required for this test is that all means are obtained from the same number of observations.

Sample Size Determination

The null and alternative hypotheses are the same as for the *t*-test. We again take $f = df$, $n_1 = n_2 = ... = n_k = n$ (here this is not just optimal but is a prerequisite for an exact test). The minimum sample size depends on d, α_e and β_0 is obtained iteratively from

$$n = \text{CEIL}\left[\frac{2\sigma^2}{d^2}\left(\frac{1}{\sqrt{2}}q(k;f;1-\alpha_e)+t(f;1-\beta_0)\right)^2\right]$$

(4.28)

The q-quantiles $q(k;f;1-\alpha_e)$ of the studentised range for the Tukey test can be found in Table A4 for $\alpha = 0.05$ and $f = df$. In fact $q(2;f;1-\alpha) = \sqrt{2} \cdot t(f; 1 - \alpha/2)$.

Example 4.11

In (4.28) let $k = 9$, $d = \sigma$, $\alpha = 0.05$ and $\beta_0 = 0.20$. Taking $n^{(0)} = \infty$ we obtain

$$n^{(1)} = \text{CEIL}\left[2(\frac{1}{\sqrt{2}}4.387+0.841657)^2\right]=\text{CEIL}[31.106]= 32 .$$

In the next iteration step with $f = 9 \cdot 31 = 279$ degrees of freedom we find $n^{(2)} = \text{CEIL}[31.7] = 32$ so that $n = 32$ is the solution. It follows that in all $N = 9 \cdot 32 = 288$ experimental units are required.
The same result is obtained with CADEMO, taking the middle option in Figure 4.14.

Analysis

We reject H_{0ij}: $\mu_i - \mu_j = 0$ with experimentwise risk of the first kind $\alpha = 0.05$ whenever

$$|\bar{y}_{i.} - \bar{y}_{j.}| > \sqrt{\frac{s^2}{2}}q(k;f;0,95)\sqrt{\frac{1}{n}+\frac{1}{n}}$$

(4.29)

holds, with the quantiles from Table A4.

Example 4.9 - continued

In the SPSS window shown in Figure 4.16 we now choose the Tukey test option, and we get the summarised results in Figure 4.19.

Treatment Means

| 4 | 7 | 3 | 2 | 1 | 9 | 8 | 5 | 6 |

Figure 4.19 *Results of the Tukey test*

For direct calculation we use the values in Table 4.16 and from the SPSS output
we find $s^2 = $ MS(Residual) $= 28.045$ on 81 df.
We reject H_{0ij}: $\mu_i - \mu_j = 0$ with an experimentwise $\alpha = 0.05$ whenever

$$|\bar{y}_i - \bar{y}_j| > \sqrt{\frac{s^2}{2}(\frac{1}{10} + \frac{1}{10})}q(9;81;0.95) \text{ or}$$

$$|\bar{y}_i - \bar{y}_j| > \sqrt{\frac{28.045}{2}\left(\frac{2}{10}\right)}4.51 = 7.55 \text{ holds.}$$

Remark: If $n_1 = n_2 = ... = n_k = n$ is not true, then in the case of one-way ANOVA one can
use the Tukey-Kramer approximation and reject

$$H_{0ij}: \mu_i - \mu_j = 0 \text{ if } |\bar{y}_{i.} - \bar{y}_{j.}| > \sqrt{\frac{s^2}{2}\left(\frac{1}{n_i} + \frac{1}{n_j}\right)}q(k;f;1-\alpha) \text{ holds.}$$

4.3.2 Multiple Comparisons with a Standard Population

The expected values of $k - 1 = p$ populations are each to be compared with the mean μ_k of
a so-called standard or control population. Thus the $(k - 1 = p)$ null hypotheses
$$H_{0i} : \mu_i = \mu_k \quad (i = 1, ..., k - 1 = p)$$
will each be tested against the corresponding alternative hypothesis
$$H_{Ai} : \mu_i \neq \mu_k.$$

4.3.2.1 The Multiple t-Test

For a per comparison risk of the first kind α we use the multiple t-test described in
section 4.3.1.1

Sample Size Determination

Here and in section 4.3.2.2 we meet a peculiarity; it is no longer optimal to have all
sample sizes equal. We set $n_i = n$ for $i = 1, ..., k-1 = p$ and $n_k = vn$. The total size of the
experiment N becomes minimal when $v = \sqrt{p}$ holds. We calculate N iteratively from:

$$N = \text{CEIL}\left[(\sqrt{p}+1)^2\frac{\sigma^2}{d^2}\left(t\left[f;1-\frac{\alpha}{2}\right]+t[f;1-\beta_0]\right)^2\right] \tag{4.30}$$

Example 4.12

In (4.30) we take $d = \sigma$, $\alpha = 0.05$ and $\beta_0 = 0.20$ and start with $N^{(0)} = \infty$. We find for $k = 9$, $p = 8$

$$N^{(1)} = \text{CEIL}[(\sqrt{8} + 1)^2(1.9602 + 0.841657)^2] = \text{CEIL}[115.06] = 116$$

With $116-9 = 107$ degrees of freedom we have

$$N^{(2)} = \text{CEIL}[(\sqrt{8} + 1)^2(1.98238 + 0.844993)^2] = \text{CEIL}[117.17] = 118$$

and this remains unchanged in subsequent iteration steps. Dividing 118 by $p + \sqrt{p} = 8 + \sqrt{8} = 10.82841$ gives 10.897, so we put $n = 11$ and $n_9 = \text{CEIL}[(\sqrt{8})\cdot 11] = \text{CEIL}[31.11] = 32$. This results in $N = 8\cdot 11 + 32 = 120$.

Another possibility is to put $n_9 = 118 - 8\cdot 11 = 30$ as is done in CADEMO. Following the menu sequence Test – k > 2 Means - against Standard or Control Figure 4.20 appears.

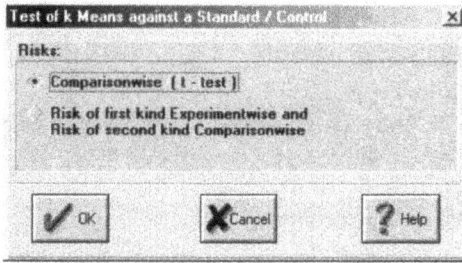

Figure 4.20 *Comparison with a standard*

From here we reach Figure 4.15 again. But this time we must not, as before, input the total number of means (here 9), but the number of means to be compared with the standard (this is 8). The output indicates that we need 30 observations for the standard, and 11 for each of the other means.

4.3.2.2 The Dunnett Test

If we take a per comparison risk of the first kind α_e for the $k-1 = p$ null hypotheses, then the *Dunnett Test* is used. We will only describe this test for the one-way ANOVA.

Sample Size Determination

Here again we set $n_i = n$ for $i = 1, ..., k-1 = p$ and $n_k = nv$ as in the t-test with $v = \sqrt{p}$. The total experiment size N is now obtained from:

$$N = \text{CEIL}\left[\left(\sqrt{p}+1\right)^2 \frac{\sigma^2}{d^2}\left(d[p; f; 1-\alpha_e] + t[f; 1-\beta_0]\right)^2\right] \tag{4.31}$$

with the quantiles $d(p; f; 1-\alpha_e)$ for the Dunnett tests for the optimal allocation from Table A5 (after BECHHOFER and DUNNETT (1988)).

Example 4.13

Putting $p = k-1 = 8$, $d = \sigma$, $\alpha = 0.05$, $\beta = 0.2$, and in CADEMO taking the second option in Figure 4.20, we find that we need 45 measurements for the standard and 18 for each of the other means. Thus $N = 8 \cdot 18 + 45 = 189$.

Analysis

We reject H_{0ik}: $\mu_i = \mu_k$ ($i = 1, ..., p = k - 1$) with experimentwise risk of the first kind α_e, whenever

$$|\bar{y}_{i.} - \bar{y}_k| > \sqrt{s^2 \left(\frac{1}{n_i} + \frac{1}{n_k} \right)} \cdot d^* \tag{4.32}$$

holds. The value of d^* is for $\alpha = 0.05$, $n_1 = n_2 = ... = n_p = n$ and $n_k = n\sqrt{p}$ the value $d(p;f;0.95)$ from Table A5 and for $n_l = n$ ($l = 1, ..., k$) it is $d(p;f;0.95)$ from Table A6.

Example 4.9 - continued

We go back to Table 4.16 with variety number 9 as standard. We have $s^2 = MS(\text{Residual}) = 28.045$ and $f = 81$. Since we have equal sample sizes we use Table A6 rather than Table A5. Table A6 contains the Dunnett-quantiles for equal class sizes.

We reject H_{0i}: $\mu_i - \mu_9 = 0$ with experimentwise $\alpha = 0.05$, if

$$|\bar{y}_{i.} - \bar{y}_9| > \sqrt{s^2 \left(\frac{1}{10} + \frac{1}{10} \right)} d(8;81;0.95) = \sqrt{28.045 \left(\frac{2}{10} \right)} \, 2.71 = 6.42.$$

In SPSS we select "Dunnett" in Figure 4.16 and get the results summary in Figure 4.21.

Multiple Comparisons

Dependent Variable: YIELD
Dunnett t (2-sided)ᵃ

(I) VARIETY	(J) VARIETY	Mean Difference (I-J)	Std. Error	Sig.	95% Confidence Interval Lower Bound	Upper Bound
1	9	-.8600	2.36833	1.000	-7.2814	5.5614
2	9	-2.1000	2.36833	.934	-8.5214	4.3214
3	9	-4.4100	2.36833	.311	-10.8314	2.0114
4	9	-6.3200	2.36833	.056	-12.7414	.1014
5	9	1.7100	2.36833	.978	-4.7114	8.1314
6	9	2.5000	2.36833	.854	-3.9214	8.9214
7	9	-5.5600	2.36833	.119	-11.9814	.8614
8	9	1.1500	2.36833	.998	-5.2714	7.5714

Based on observed means.
a. Dunnett t-tests treat one group as a control, and compare all other groups against it.

Figure 4.21 *SPSS output for Example 4.9*

4.3.3 Overview of Minimal Sample Sizes

Table 4.17 contains a summary of the minimal sample sizes obtained for the various methods used in the example:

Table 4.17 *Minimal Sample Sizes for Multiple Comparisons between Means for k = 9, $\alpha = 0.05$, $\alpha_e = 0.05$, $\beta_0 = 0.20$; $d = \sigma$.*

	Per comparison Risk of the first kind α	Experimentwise Risk of the first kind α_e
Pairwise Comparisons	Multiple t-Test $n = 16$ $N = 144$	Tukey-Test $n = 32$ $N = 288$
Comparison with a Standard	Multiple t-Test $n_i = 11 \quad (i=1, ..., 8)$ $n_9 = 32$ $N = 120$	Dunnett-Test $n_i = 18 \quad (i=1, ..., 8)$ $n_9 = 45$ $N = 189$

5 Regression Analysis

The focus of many research problems centres on the relationships between two or more variables. For example we may ask the question whether a dependence between shoe size and body height exists. We may also ask whether giving more fertiliser per acre of farm land changes the yield of a crop and if so, what is the best quantity of fertiliser to use?

Before starting to investigate the relationship between two (or more) variables, we should ask the following questions:
- what exactly are the variables?
- how and in which units are they measured (or counted)?
- are both variables quantitative or is at least one of them qualitative?
- if both variables are quantitative, then are both variables random or is one of them not random, and are its values therefore part of the experimental conditions (the design)?

Let us use the symbols x and y to denote two variables and consider the examples below.

Example 5.1
x: shoe size of students (in cm)
y: body height of the same students (in cm)

Example 5.2
x: age of hemp plants (in weeks)
y: height of these plants (in cm)

Example 5.3
y: the distance in cm a stone falls in vacuum if
x: is the time it falls in seconds

Example 5.4
x: name of bulls
y: average daily milk yield of daughters of the bulls (in kg)

Example 5.5
x: a variable with two values:
   x_1: a calf is treated with gammaglobulin
   x_2: a calf is not treated
y: a variable with two values:
   y_1: a calf observed during two weeks died
   y_2: a calf did not die during this time
Remark: The same set of calves is jointly classified by the two variables.

In Example 5.3 we may (as is usual in physics) assume that x and y can be determined with negligible measurement error. Then we have two quantitative non-random variables $y = h$, $x = t$ and we know (since the time of Galileo Galilei) that the relation between h and t can be described by a function of the form

$h = \alpha t^2$.

The value of the parameter α can easily be calculated by observing how much time t a stone takes to fall h units. The relation given by

$$h = \alpha t^2$$

is a quadratic function. Such relations are handled in a branch of mathematics called Analysis. The graph of a function is a curve and all pairs $(x_i, y_i) = (t_i, h_i)$ are represented by points which lie exactly on this curve. Such cases will not be discussed here because they do not include any stochastic element.

The aim of this chapter is to discuss problems similar to Examples 5.1 and 5.2, i.e. we consider the relationship between two quantitative variables. But before doing this let us discuss how to handle the other cases. Example 5.4 could be modelled by a one-way ANOVA model using bulls as levels of a factor and milk yields as observations in the cells for these levels. In Example 5.5 the observations are frequencies, which are usually displayed in a two-by-two table such as the following:

calves	survived	did not survive
treated	f_{11}	f_{12}
not treated	f_{21}	f_{22}

The question as to whether treatment with gammaglobulin has an effect on the survival probability, can be tested using the test for comparing two probabilities as described in Section 3.4.4. In other cases and if x and y have more than two outcomes, contingency table analysis may be used.

5.1 Scatter-plots

Example 5.1
> We will make use of data-pairs (shoe size, body height) collected from students on a statistics course in Wageningen in 1996 as given in Table 5.1 .
> Let us denote the pairs of observations by (x_i, y_i) with i running from 1 to n (n is the number of students).
> As a first step we display these pairs graphically as a *scatter-plot*, with each point on the plot representing a single student. The horizontal co-ordinate x_i is the shoe size. The vertical co-ordinate y_i is the body height.

Table 5.1   *Shoe sizes (x in cm) and body heights (y in cm) from 25 students on a statistics course in 1996.*

Shoe size	Height	Shoe Size	Height
42	165	40	162
43	185	41	163
43	178	40	160
41	170	38	151
39	157	42	170
44	170	41	170
36	159	43	178
40	180	42	163
40	168	38	160
39	165	39	166
42	172	40	170
40	158	42	178
43	180		

The scatter-plot for this group of students is shown in Figure 5.1.

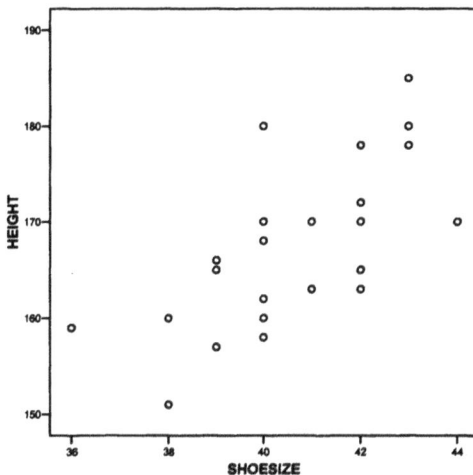

Figure 5.1   *Scatter-plot for the observations of Example 5.1*

To interpret a scatter-plot, we look first of all at the overall pattern. This should reveal the direction, form and strength of a possible relationship. From Figure 5.1 it is clear that students with a larger shoe size also tend to be the taller students. This means that the two quantitative characters are positively associated.

But unlike the situation in Example 5.3 there is no one-to-one correspondence between shoe size and body height. Each shoe size has several body heights associated with it. Therefore we do not use the term "function" for such a relationship. We use the term *regression* to describe such diffuse or stochastic relations between two quantitative variables. The *average relation* on the other hand is described by a function. The closer the points of the scatter-plot lie to the graph of this function, the stronger is the relation between x and y. If both quantitative variables are random and the function is a linear one, the *product-moment correlation coefficient* is used as a measure of the

151

strength of the linear association between the variables. If there is a monotonic but non-linear relation the *rank correlation coefficient* should be used.

For Example 5.2 we use the data in Table 5.2

Table 5.2 *The height of hemp plants (y in cm) during growth (x age in weeks).*

x_i	y_i	x_i	y_i
1	8,30	8	84,40
2	15,20	9	98,10
3	24,70	10	107,70
4	32,00	11	112,00
5	39,30	12	116,90
6	55,40	13	119,90
7	69,00	14	121,10

The scatter-plot for these data is shown in Figure 5.2.

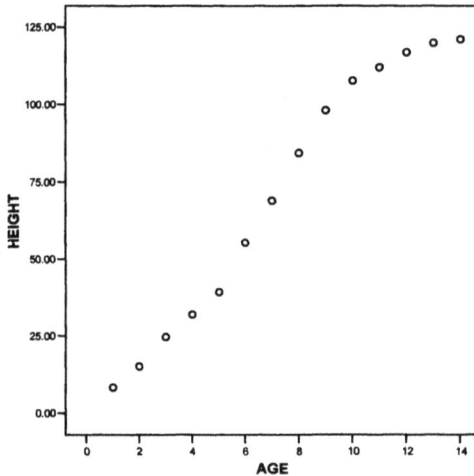

Figure 5.2 *Scatter-plot for the association between age and height of hemp plants*

Compared with the scatter-plot in Figure 5.1, we find a stronger relationship here, but it is evidently non-linear.

5.2   Model I and Model II in Regression Analysis

Examples 5.1 and 5.2 have it in common that both variables x and y are quantitative, but there is a difference in the way the data were collected. In example 5.1 we have a sample of n students, and from each student two measurements have been taken - shoe size x and body height y. If we model the characters x and y by two random variables x and y respectively, we can say that we observed a pair of random variables $(x, y)^T$ n

times (we can also refer to the vector $(x, y)^T$ as a *bivariate random variable*). The *regression model* can now be written in the form

$$y_i = f(x_i) + e_i \qquad\qquad (i = 1, ..., n) \qquad\qquad (5.1)$$

but also in the form

$$x_i = g(y_i) + \varepsilon_i \qquad\qquad (i = 1, ..., n) \qquad\qquad (5.2)$$

The function f is called the *regression function of y on x* and analogously the function g is called the regression function of x on y.
If both f and g are *linear functions* we obtain the *linear regression models*

$$y_i = \alpha + \beta x_i + e_i \qquad\qquad (i = 1, ..., n) \qquad\qquad (5.3)$$
and
$$x_i = \alpha' + \beta' y_i + \varepsilon_i \qquad\qquad (i = 1, ..., n) \qquad\qquad (5.4)$$

respectively, with the side conditions that all the e_i and ε_i have expectation 0 and are independently distributed, and also $\text{cov}(x_i, \varepsilon_i) = 0$ and $\text{cov}(y_i, e_i) = 0$.

Usually the two functions $y = \alpha + \beta x$ and $x = \alpha' + \beta' y$ differ from each other (they are identical only if the *correlation coefficient* $\rho = 1$).

A regression model as given by (5.1) or (5.3) [or (5.2) or (5.4)] is called a *Model II regression*. The value of n should never be smaller than the number p of unknown parameters of f (or g).

A different situation is given in Example 5.2. Here the values of x are determined by the experimenter in advance. She or he decided when the height of the plants should be observed. This means that the character x should not be modelled by a random variable but by a non-random one. The height y_i is measured for predetermined values x_i of x. This value must of course be modelled by a random y_i. This leads us to a regression model

$$y_i = f(x_i) + e_i \qquad\qquad (i = 1, ..., n) \qquad\qquad (5.5)$$

or in the linear case

$$y_i = \alpha + \beta x_i + e_i \qquad\qquad (i = 1, ..., n) \qquad\qquad (5.6)$$

The model (5.5) (and (5.6)) is called a *Model I regression*. In this case at least p of the x_i's must be different, where p is the number of parameters in f. In (5.6) $p = 2$. In all models all the e_i must be mutually independent and have expectation 0.

Example 5.6

Assume that the loss of carotene content of grass during storage between one and 303 days is of interest and that it is known that the relationship between the storage time and the carotene content is linear.

We use data collected by STEGER und PÜSCHEL (1960) for two kinds of storage (storage type 1 using glass containers, storage type 2 using bags). The data are given in Table 5.3.

Table 5.3 Relationship between carotene content Carotin1 (y_{1i}) and Carotin2 (y_{2i}) in mg/100 g dry mass of grass and storage time (x_i in days) for two types of storage (SPSS data file, data view).

It is clear that this is a model I regression - the y-values have been measured at values of x which have been determined by the experimenter in advance. Let us assume that the relationship really is linear. Then we can use the model equation (5.6) for each type of storage.

For type 1 we write:

$$y_{1i} = \alpha_1 + \beta_1 x_i + e_{1i} \quad (i = 1, ..., 5) \tag{5.6a}$$

with var$(e_{1i}) = \sigma_1^2$, E$(e_{1i}) = 0$ and independent e_{1i}'s

and for type 2 we write

$$y_{2i} = \alpha_2 + \beta_2 x_i + e_{2i} \quad (i = 1, ..., 5) \tag{5.6b}$$

with var$(e_{2i}) = \sigma_2^2$, E$(e_{2i}) = 0$ and independent e_{2i}'s.

The x_i-values are the same for both types.

The two residual variances σ_1^2 and σ_2^2 may or may not be equal; here we will assume that they are equal.

In model I situations, only one of the regression models (5.1) and (5.2) is meaningful. We shall always take x to be the predetermined variable. x is then called the *regressor* variable (or *predictor variable*, or *independent variable*) and *y* is called the *response variable* (or *dependent variable*).

Furthermore, even in the linear case (5.6) no correlation coefficient ρ is defined, because this is a measure of the strength of association between two *random* variables *x* and *y* based on the covariance between *x* and *y*. But in model I only *y* is random; *x* has no stochastic component.

In model II the *design problem* reduces to the choice of minimal *n* for given precision requirements. In model I the question is how to choose *n* and **also** how to choose the x_i in an optimal way.

Notwithstanding the above differences, the two models have some things in common. In particular the calculation of point estimates, confidence intervals and test statistics are identical (but not their properties). This may be the reason that statistical packages such as SPSS do not distinguish between the two models. As a consequence, the estimate *r* of ρ is always calculated. The reader should be careful to use *r* as a correlation coefficient only in cases where model II is applicable and to ignore this information when the regression is model I.

5.3   Parameter Estimation by the Method of Least Squares

If a regression model (I or II) has been chosen, we can write it in the form

$$y_i = f(x_i, \theta) + e_i \qquad\qquad (i = 1, ..., n) \qquad\qquad (5.7)$$

The errors e_i are assumed to be independently and identically distributed with expectation $E(e_i) = 0$ and variance $\mathrm{var}(e_i) = \sigma^2$.

The equation (5.7) can be interpreted directly as an equation for model I, but in the case of model II the x_i are realisations of the x_i, i.e. *f* is the conditional expectation

$$f(x_i, \theta) = E(y_i \mid x_i = x_i)$$

In (5.7) θ is a vector with *p* real components $\theta_1, \theta_2, ..., \theta_p$ where $p < n$.
The least squares method starts with $n > p$ observations (x_i, y_i) for which a realisation of (5.7) is given by

$$y_i = f(x_i, \theta) + e_i \qquad\qquad (5.8)$$

Estimating θ in (5.7) by the *least squares method* means defining an estimate $\hat{\theta}$ of θ in such a way that $\hat{\theta}$ is that value of θ which minimises the *sum of squares*

$$SS = \sum_{i=1}^{n} [y_i - f(x_i, \theta)]^2 \qquad\qquad (5.9)$$

Thus $\hat{\theta}$ is a function $\hat{\theta}(x_i, y_i)$ of the observations.

If we transfer over to random variables y_i (and in case of model II also x_i) the estimate $\hat{\theta}$ becomes the least squares estimator $\hat{\theta} = \hat{\theta}(x_i, y_i)$ [or $\hat{\theta} = \hat{\theta}(x_i, y_i)$].

Considering the case of a *simple linear regression*, the realisations for both model I and model II can be written as

$$y_i = \alpha + \beta x_i + e_i \qquad\qquad (i = 1, ..., n > 2) \qquad\qquad (5.10)$$

It is assumed that at least two of the x_i are different.
The SS in (5.9) now becomes

$$SS = \sum_{i=1}^{n} (y_i - \alpha - \beta x_i)^2 \qquad\qquad (5.11)$$

Later we shall need the following quantities:

$$\bar{x} = \frac{1}{n}\sum_{i=1}^{n} x_i, \quad \bar{y} = \frac{1}{n}\sum_{i=1}^{n} y_i,$$

$$SP_{xy} = \sum_{i=1}^{n} (x_i - \bar{x})(y_i - \bar{y}) = \sum_{i=1}^{n} x_i y_i - \frac{1}{n}\sum_{i=1}^{n} x_i \sum_{i=1}^{n} y_i \qquad\qquad (5.12)$$

and

$$SS_x = SP_{xx} \qquad\qquad (5.13)$$

To find the minimum of SS in (5.11) we differentiate SS partially with respect to α and β and put the derivatives equal to zero. The values of α and β which are solutions of these equations are denoted by a and b.

$$-2 \sum_{i=1}^{n} (y_i - a - b x_i) = 0$$

$$-2 \sum_{i=1}^{n} (y_i - a - b x_i) x_i = 0.$$

The first equation leads to:

$$a = \bar{y} - b\bar{x} \qquad\qquad (5.14)$$

and the second one to:

$$\sum_{i=1}^{n} x_i y_i - a \sum_{i=1}^{n} x_i - b \sum_{i=1}^{n} x_i^2 = 0$$

Replacing a by the right hand side of (5.14) leads to

$$b = \frac{SP_{xy}}{SS_x} \qquad\qquad (5.15)$$

It can be shown that these values of a and b do give a minimum of SS.

From these estimates a and b we obtain estimators by replacing the y_i by y_i, and for model II also the x_i by x_i. This gives

Model I $\qquad a = \bar{y} - b\,\bar{x}$

$$b = \frac{SP_{xy}}{SS_x}$$

Model II $\qquad a = \bar{y} - b\,\bar{x}$

$$b = \frac{SP_{xy}}{SS_x}.$$

We have (taking realisations of the x-values in the case of model II)

$$\sigma_a^2 = \text{var}(a) = \frac{\sigma^2}{n\,SS_x} \sum_{i=1}^{n} x_i^2 \tag{5.16}$$

$$\sigma_b^2 = \text{var}(b) = \frac{\sigma^2}{SS_x} \tag{5.17}$$

and $\qquad \sigma_{ab} = \text{cov}\,(a,b) = -\frac{\sigma^2 \cdot \bar{x}}{SS_x}. \tag{5.18}$

Thus the *covariance matrix* of $(a,b)^T$ for model I is given by

$$\text{var}\begin{pmatrix} a \\ b \end{pmatrix} = \frac{\sigma^2}{SS_x}\begin{pmatrix} \frac{1}{n}\sum_{i=1}^{n} x_i^2 & -\bar{x} \\ -\bar{x} & 1 \end{pmatrix} \tag{5.19}$$

and its determinant equals

$$D = \left| \text{var}\begin{pmatrix} a \\ b \end{pmatrix}\right| = \frac{\sigma^4}{SS_x^2}\left(\frac{1}{n}\sum_{i=1}^{n} x_i^2 - \bar{x}^2\right) = \frac{\sigma^4}{n\sum_{i=1}^{n} x_i^2 - \left(\sum_{i=1}^{n} x_i\right)^2}$$

or

$$D = \frac{\sigma^4}{n\,SS_x}. \tag{5.20}$$

Example 5.6 (continued)
We will illustrate the estimation of the parameters using the data of Example 5.6. We shall demonstrate the hand calculations, and as an exercise the reader may repeat the results using SPSS.
For hand calculation we need the values in Table 5.4 where $\hat{y}_{1i} = a_1 + b_1 x_i$ and $\hat{y}_{2i} = a_2 + b_2 x_i$.

Table 5.4   Steps in calculating the regression coefficients for Example 5.6.

i	x_i^2	$x_i y_{1i}$	$x_i y_{2i}$	$\hat{y}_{1i}$	$\hat{y}_{2i}$	$y_{1i} - \hat{y}_{1i}$	$y_{2i} - \hat{y}_{2i}$
1	1	31.25	31.25	31.160	32.104	0.09	-0.854
2	3600	1722.60	1828.20	27.942	27.326	0.768	3.144
3	15376	2935.08	2522.16	24.451	22.143	-0.781	-1.803
4	49729	4042.99	2640.32	19.059	14.126	-0.92	-2.286
5	91809	4705.59	2863.35	14.686	7.648	0.844	1.802
Total	160515	13437.51	9885.28	-	-	-	-

To calculate $\Sigma(y_i - \hat{y}_i)^2$ we use the relation

$$\Sigma(y_i - \hat{y}_i)^2 = SS_y - \frac{SP_{xy}^2}{SS_x}$$

This gives fewer rounding errors than squaring the residuals in the last two columns of Table 5.4.
From Table 5.4 and Table 5.3 we obtain:

	Type 1	Type 2
SS_x	59410.8	
SS_y	179.5845	411.9426
SP_{xy}	-3241.128	-4811.09
$\Sigma(y_i - y_i)^2$	2.7663	22.3403
$\bar{x}$	142.20	
$\bar{y}$	23.458	20.67

Using (5.15) for type 1 and 2 we obtain

$$b_1 = \frac{-3241.128}{59410.8} = -0.0545545$$

and

$$b_2 = \frac{-4811.09}{59410.8} = -0.0809801.$$

From (5.14) we obtain the *intercepts* for the two estimated regression lines as:

$$a_1 = \bar{y}_1 - b_1\bar{x} = 31.216$$

and

$$a_2 = \bar{y}_2 - b_2\bar{x} = 32.1854.$$

Thus we have the *estimated regression functions*

$$\hat{y}_1 = 31.216 - 0.0546x$$

and

$$\hat{y}_2 = 32.185 - 0.0810x.$$

The differences $y_{1i} - \hat{y}_{1i}$ and $y_{2i} - \hat{y}_{2i}$ are called the *residuals*. The estimates of the variances of the parameter estimates and the covariances can be calculated from (5.16), (5.17) and (5.18) respectively. For this we have to replace σ_1^2 by

$$s_1^2 = \frac{1}{n-2}\Sigma(y_{1i} - \hat{y}_{1i})^2 \text{ and } \sigma_2^2 \text{ by } s_2^2 = \frac{1}{n-2}\Sigma(y_{2i} - \hat{y}_{2i})^2. \text{ Because}$$

in our case $n = 5$ we have $n - 2 = 3$ and thus

$$s_1^2 = \frac{2.7663}{3} = 0.9221$$

$$s_2^2 = \frac{22.3403}{3} = 7.4468$$

are the estimates for σ_1^2 and σ_2^2 respectively.

These lead to:

$$s_{1a}^2 = \text{vâr}(a_1) = \frac{0.9221}{59410.8} \cdot \frac{160515}{5} = 0.4983,$$

$$s_{2a}^2 = \text{vâr}(a_2) = 4.0239,$$

$$s_{1b}^2 = \text{vâr}(b_1) = \frac{0.9221}{59410.8} = 1.5521 \cdot 10^{-5},$$

$$s_{2b}^2 = \text{vâr}(b_2) = 1.2534 \cdot 10^{-4},$$

$$s_{1ab} = \text{côv}(a_1, b_1) = -\frac{0.9221}{59410.8} \cdot 142.2 = -2.2071 \cdot 10^{-3},$$

$$s_{2ab} = \text{côv}(a_2, b_2) = -1.78239 \cdot 10^{-3}.$$

In Figure 5.3 the estimated regression lines are shown. Of course the carotene content decreases for both types of storage but storage in glass seems to lead to a lower rate of loss.

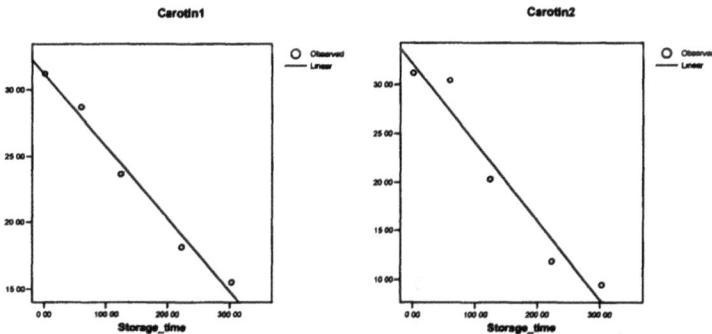

Figure 5.3 *The estimated regression lines from Example 5.6*

5.4 Simple Linear Regression

In this section we assume that the error terms e_i in the model equation (5.6) are independently and normally distributed as $N(0; \sigma^2)$. It can then be shown that the estimators a and b in section 5.3 are both normally distributed (with the covariance matrix given there). Furthermore $s^2(n - 2)$, is independent of a and b and is distributed as chi-squared with n-2 degrees of freedom. As we have already done in Example 5.6, we estimate σ^2 by the unbiased estimator

$$s^2 = \hat{\sigma}^2 = \frac{1}{n - 2} \sum_{i=1}^{n} (y_i - \hat{y}_i)^2 \tag{5.21}$$

and estimate $\sigma_a^2 = \text{var}(a)$, $\sigma_b^2 = \text{var}(b)$ and $\sigma_{ab} = \text{cov}(a, b)$ by replacing σ^2 by s^2 in (5.16), (5.17) and (5.18). This gives

$$s_a^2 = \frac{s^2 \cdot \Sigma x_i^2}{SS_x \cdot n} \tag{5.22}$$

$$s_b^2 = \frac{s^2}{SS_x} \tag{5.23}$$

$$s_{ab} = -\frac{s^2 \cdot \bar{x}}{SS_x} \tag{5.24}$$

5.4.1 Confidence Intervals

If $t(f;P)$ is the P-quantile of the t-distribution with f degrees of freedom and $\chi^2(f;P)$ the P-quantile of the chi-squared distribution with f degrees of freedom we obtain the following[1] $(1-\alpha^*) \cdot 100\%$ confidence intervals; (with s_a and s_b from (5.22) and (5.23) respectively).
For α:

$$[a - t(n - 2;1 - \frac{\alpha^*}{2}) s_a; \; a + t(n - 2;1 - \frac{\alpha^*}{2}) s_a] \tag{5.25}$$

For β:

$$[b - t(n - 2;1 - \frac{\alpha^*}{2}) s_b; \; b + t(n - 2;1 - \frac{\alpha^*}{2}) s_b] \tag{5.26}$$

For σ^2:

$$\left[\frac{s^2(n-2)}{\chi^2\left(n-2;1-\frac{\alpha^*}{2}\right)}; \frac{s^2(n-2)}{\chi^2\left(n-2;\frac{\alpha^*}{2}\right)} \right] \tag{5.27}$$

---

[1] We use α^* because α is now the intercept in the regression function.

Equation (5.27) is not the best solution, there is a shorter interval obtained by writing $\alpha^* = \alpha_1 + \alpha_2$ as a sum of positive components α_1 and α_2 different from $\alpha_1 = \alpha_2 = \alpha^*/2$ and then replacing $\alpha^*/2$ by α_1 and $1 - \alpha^*/2$ by $1 - \alpha_2$ in (5.27). The reason for this is the asymmetry of the chi-squared distribution.

For $E(y) = \alpha + \beta x$ for any x in the experimental region:

We need the value of the following quantity K_x:

$$K_x = \sqrt{\frac{\sum_{i=1}^{n} x_i^2 - 2x \sum_{i=1}^{n} x_i + nx^2}{nSQ_x}} = \sqrt{\frac{1}{n} + \frac{(x - \bar{x})^2}{SS_x}}$$

and then the $(1-\alpha^*)$-confidence interval for $E(y) = \alpha + \beta x$ is:

$$[a + bx - t(n - 2; 1 - \frac{\alpha^*}{2})s\,K_x;\ a + bx + t(n - 2; 1 - \frac{\alpha^*}{2})s\,K_x] \qquad (5.28)$$

If we calculate (5.28) for each x-value in the experimental region, and draw a graph of the upper and lower limits, the included region is called a confidence band.

Example 5.6 (continued)

Here we consider type 1 storage only (and we therefore for simplicity drop the suffix 1 in the notation). The values in (5.21) to (5.24) have been calculated earlier. We obtained

$$s_a = \sqrt{s_{1a}^2} = 0.7059$$

and

$$s_b = \sqrt{s_{1b}^2} = 0.0039397.$$

If we fix α^* at 0.05 we find from Table A1 in the appendix

$$t(3; 0.975) = 3.182,$$

and from Table A2 we find $\chi^2(3; 0.025) = 0.2158$, $\chi^2(3; 0.975) = 9.348$.

The (realised) 0.95-confidence interval for α is now (from 5.25)

$$[31.216 - 3.182 \cdot 0.7059;\ 31.216 + 3.182 \cdot 0.7059] = [28.97;\ 33.46].$$

Similarly we calculate a 95%-confidence interval for β as

$$[-0.0546 - 3.182 \cdot 0.0039397;\ -0.0546 + 3.182 \cdot 0.0039397] =$$
$$[-0.0671;\ -0.0421].$$

The 95%-confidence interval for the error variance σ^2 is:

$$\left[\frac{3 \cdot 0.9221}{9.348} ; \frac{3 \cdot 0.9221}{0.2158}\right] = [0.2959; 12.819].$$

The lower and upper bound of 95%-confidence intervals for $\alpha + \beta x$ can be found in Table 5.5.

Table 5.5 *Confidence Bounds ($\alpha^* = 0.05$) for $\alpha + \beta x$ and $x = x_i$ ($i = 1, ..., 5$) for Example 5.6 (type 1 storage).*

x	$\hat{y}$	K_x	lower bound	upper bound
1	31.16	0.73184	28.92	33.40
60	27.94	0.56012	26.23	29.65
124	24.45	0.45340	23.06	25.84
223	19.05	0.55668	17.35	20.75
303	14.69	0.79701	12.25	17.13

We can do the analysis using SPSS as follows.

Type the data from Table 5.3 into the SPSS Data Editor (using the "close" button) in the normal Data View. Then select the menu sequence **Graphs-Scatter-Simple**, and define y_1 as the Y-axis and x as the X-axis. This produces the scatter-plot shown in Figure 5.4.

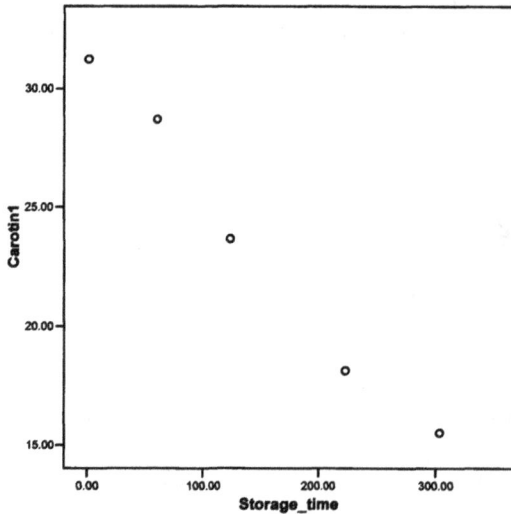

Figure 5.4 *Scatter-plot for storage type 1*

Enter **Graphs-Scatter-Simple** again and this time define y_2 as Y-axis and x as X-axis to give the scatter-plot of Figure 5.5.

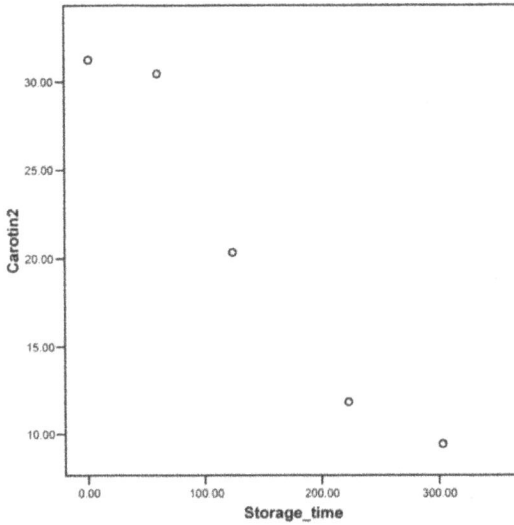

Figure 5.5   *Scatter-plot for storage type 2*

Using the menu sequence **Analyze-Regression-Linear** and using Carotin1 as Dependent and Time as Independent gives Figure 5.6

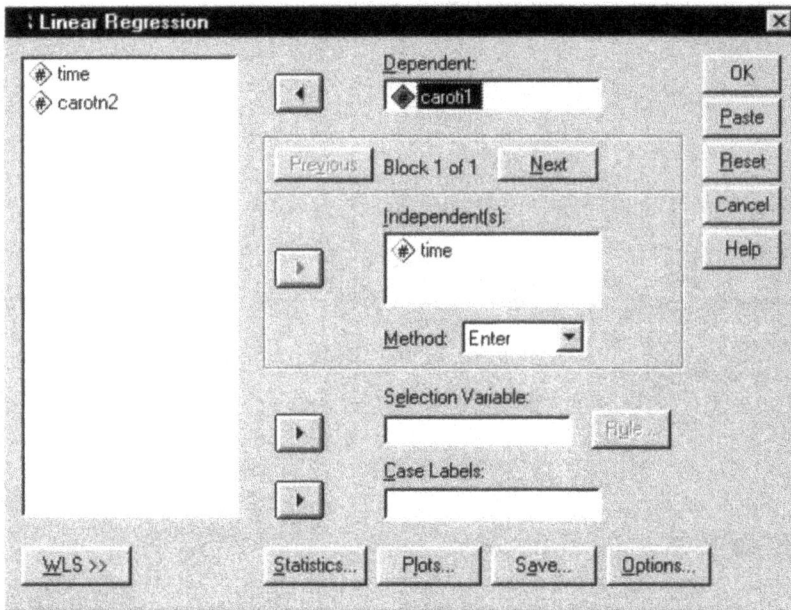

Figure 5.6   *Dialogue box "Linear Regression" for Example 5.6*

and clicking on the button Statistics brings up Figure 5.7 where we choose Confidence intervals as shown

163

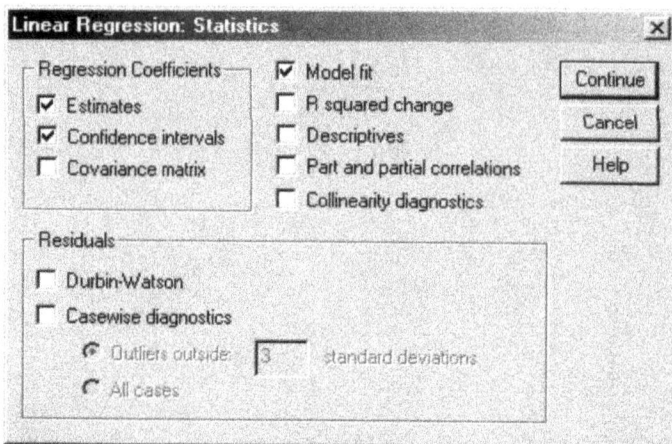

Figure 5.7 *SPSS dialog box "Statistics"*

After clicking on Continue, use the Save button (see Figure 5.8). As shown, ask for Predicted values-Unstandardised and S.E. of mean predictions. Also ask for Prediction Intervals-Mean and Unstandardised Residuals.

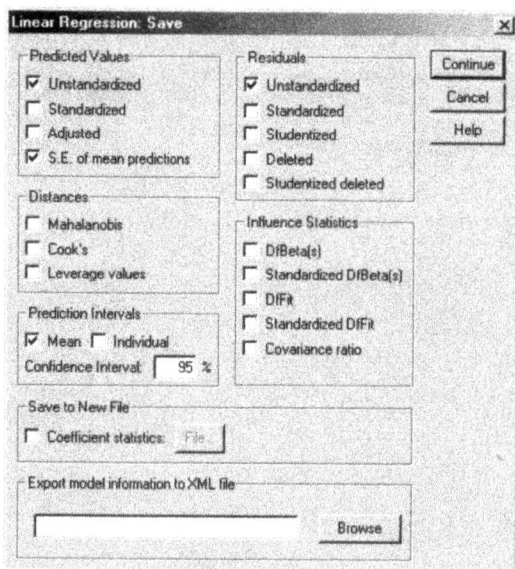

Figure 5.8 *SPSS dialog box "Save"*

After "Continue" and OK we get an output, which includes the regression coefficients with their 95%-confidence intervals as shown in Figure 5.9.

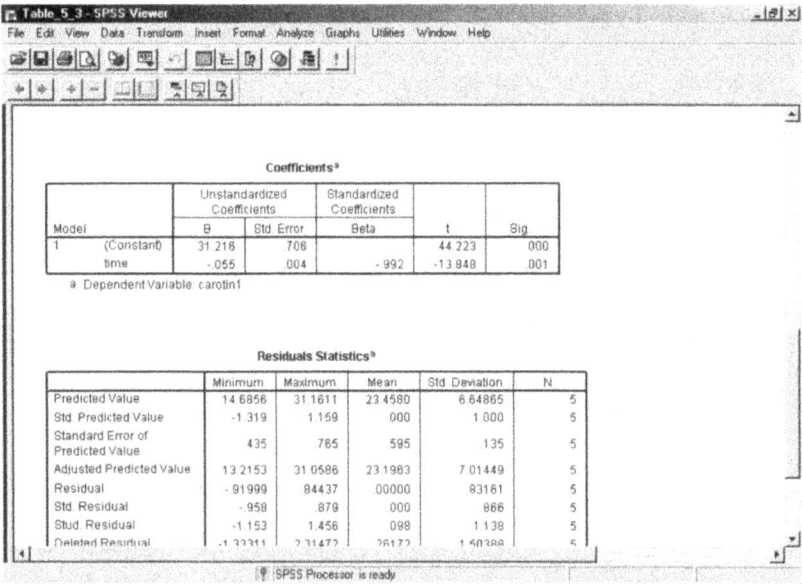

Figure 5.9 *SPSS output from Linear Regression procedure*

From the Data Editor we get Figure 5.10.

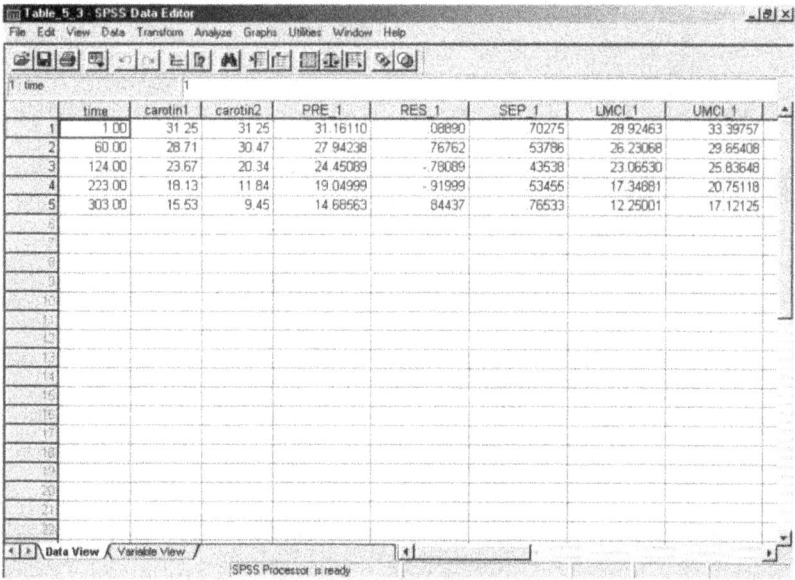

Figure 5.10 *SPSS Data Editor window showing predicted values and confidence intervals after running Linear Regression procedure*

Here PRE_1 is the predicted value $a + bx$ of the expected mean, SEP_1 is the standard error of the predicted value. RES_1 gives the so-called residuals, i.e. the differences $y - (a + bx)$. LMCI_1 is the 95%-lower confidence interval

165

limit and UMCI_1 is the 95%-upper confidence limit of the expected mean $\alpha + \beta x$.

Similarly we can do the same with the Carotin2 as dependent variable. The regression coefficients and their 95%-confidence intervals are shown in Figure 5.11.

ANOVA[b]

Model		Sum of Squares	df	Mean Square	F	Sig.
1	Regression	389.602	1	389.602	52.318	.005[a]
	Residual	22.340	3	7.447		
	Total	411.943	4			

a. Predictors: (Constant), time

b. Dependent Variable: carotin2

Coefficients[a]

Model		Unstandardized Coefficients		Standardized Coefficients	t	Sig.
		B	Std. Error	Beta		
1	(Constant)	32.185	2.006		16.045	.001
	time	-.081	.011	-.973	-7.233	.005

a. Dependent Variable: carotin2

Figure 5.11   *Regression results for storage type 2*

5.4.2   Optimal Designs in Model I

In a model I linear regression we determine the values of the predictor variable in advance. Clearly we would wish to do this so that a given precision can be reached using a minimal number of observations. In this context any selection of the x-values is called an experimental design. Before we can decide on the design we need to know what aspect of the analysis the precision requirement refers to: the variance of a point estimator, the expected width of a confidence interval or the power of hypothesis tests (as discussed in section 5.4.3). The value of the precision requirement is called the optimality criterion, and an experimental design that minimises the criterion for a given sample size is called an *optimal experimental design*.

Most optimal experimental designs are concerned with estimation criteria. Thus the x_i-values will often be chosen in such a way that the variance of an estimator is minimised (for a given number of measurements) amongst all possible allocations of x_i-values.

At first we have to define the so-called experimental region (x_l, x_u) in which measurements can or will be taken. Here x_l is the lower bound and x_u the upper bound of an interval on the x-axis.

A big disadvantage of optimal designs is their dependence on the accuracy of the chosen model, they are only certain to be optimal if the assumed model is correct. For example in the cases discussed in this chapter we must know that the chosen model is adequate, i.e. that the regression function actually is linear as given in (5.6). Optimal designs are often selected in a way that does not allow the model assumptions to be

166

tested; for example in the designs that we shall present below, we can only test whether a linear or quadratic function describes the relationship better for the G-optimal design if n is odd.

Often the following criteria are used:

- var(a) - (C_1-) optimality: minimise var(a) in (5.16)
- var(b) - (C_2-) optimality: minimise var(b) in (5.17)
- D-optimality: minimise the determinant D in (5.20)
- G-optimality: minimise the maximum [over (x_l, x_u)] of the expected width of the confidence interval (5.28).

To minimise var(b) in (5.17) we have to maximise SS_x in its denominator and at the same time this minimises D in (5.20). The two criteria give the same optimal design solution and they also minimise the *expected width of the confidence interval* for β in (5.26).

In the case of normally distributed errors the D-optimality criterion can be interpreted as follows. If we construct a confidence region for the vector of coefficients in the simple linear regression model, we get an ellipse. If the number of coefficients in the regression model is greater than 2 ($p > 2$) the region becomes a p-dimensional ellipsoid. The D-optimal experimental design minimises the volume of this ellipsoid, among all such ellipsoids arising from any design having the same number of observations. We restrict ourselves in this chapter to the D-optimality criterion, and thus also to var(b)-optimality and G-optimality.

We write experimental designs as two-line arrays (matrices); the first line contains the x-values at which the measurements are to be taken; the second line gives the number of measurements which are to be taken at each corresponding x-value in the line above.

The following theorem holds:

Theorem 5.1

If the experimental region is given as the interval (x_l, x_u) and if n is even ($n = 2r$), then the D-optimal and the G-optimal experimental designs are identical: - we take r measurements at each of the two boundaries of the region.

Thus these optimal designs take the form

$$\begin{pmatrix} x_l & x_u \\ r & r \end{pmatrix}.$$

If n is odd, with $n = 2r + 1$, then there are two D-optimal designs with r measurements at one boundary and $r + 1$ measurements at the other. Therefore the D-optimal designs are given by

$$\begin{pmatrix} x_l & x_u \\ r & r+1 \end{pmatrix} \text{ and } \begin{pmatrix} x_l & x_u \\ r+1 & r \end{pmatrix}.$$

The (unique) G-optimal design requires r readings at both end points of the interval and one at the interval mid-point. Therefore this design has the form

$$\begin{pmatrix} x_l & \frac{1}{2}(x_l + x_u) & x_u \\ r & 1 & r \end{pmatrix}.$$

We will now determine the D- and G-optimal designs for the carotene example 5.6. More theoretical background about D- and G-optimal designs can be found in MELAS (2006) and PUKELSHEIM(1993, 2006).

Example 5.6 (continued)

Given the experimental region (1, 303), what is the D-optimal design and at the same time the design minimising the variance var(b) of the estimator b of β and what is the G-optimal design minimising the maximum width of (5.28) in the experimental region (1, 303)?

Since n is an odd number $n = 2r+1$ with $r = 2$, it follows from theorem 5.1, that both

$$\begin{pmatrix} 1 & 303 \\ 2 & 3 \end{pmatrix} \text{ and } \begin{pmatrix} 1 & 303 \\ 3 & 2 \end{pmatrix}$$

are D-optimal designs. In both designs SS_x(optimal) = 109444.8 and the value of the D-criterion is $D = 1.8274 \cdot 10^{-6} \cdot \sigma^4$.
In general we would prefer the second design, in which we begin with three readings and take two readings at the end, because of the possibility that parts of the experimental material may become corrupted during the experiment. According to Theorem 5.1 the G-optimal design is given by

$$\begin{pmatrix} 1 & 152 & 303 \\ 2 & 1 & 2 \end{pmatrix}$$

This design is not D-optimal. After obtaining SS_x (G-optimal) = 91204 we find the D-value to be $D = 2.1929 \cdot 10^{-6} \cdot \sigma^4$. This design does however minimise the maximum of the expected width

$$E[2t(n-2;1 - \frac{\alpha^*}{2})sK_x] \approx 2\sigma t(n-2;1-\frac{\alpha}{2})K_x$$

of (5.28) and this means that it minimises the maximum of K_x (which can be found above formula (5.28)) in the experimental region (1, 303). It is known that for any design K_x takes its maximum at the border of the experimental region (this can be verified by reference to Table 5.5). In our case this is either at $x = 1$ or $x = 303$. Taking SS_x (G-optimal) = 91204 (see above), we insert $x = 1$ and $x = 303$ in the formula for K_x and, noting that:

$$\Sigma x_i^2 = 2 \cdot 1^2 + 152^2 + 2 \cdot 303^2 = 206724 \text{ and}$$
$$\Sigma x_i = 2 \cdot 1 + 152 + 2 \cdot 303 = 760,$$

we obtain

$$K_{x=1} = \sqrt{\frac{206724 - 2 \cdot 760 + 5}{5 \cdot 91204}} = \sqrt{0.45} = 0.671$$

and

$$K_{x=303} = \sqrt{\frac{206724 - 606 \cdot 760 + 5 \cdot 303^2}{5 \cdot 91204}} = \sqrt{0.45} = 0.671.$$

Using Table 5.5, this shows us that the maximum expected width of (5.28) is shorter in the G-optimal design by the factor

$$\frac{0.671}{0.797} = 0.84$$

than in the design actually used which has a maximum $K_x = 0.797$ for $x = 303$.

We now calculate the criterion value D for the original design as in Table 5.3, namely

$$\begin{pmatrix} 1 & 60 & 124 & 223 & 303 \\ 1 & 1 & 1 & 1 & 1 \end{pmatrix}$$

Using the value $SS_x = 59410.8$ already obtained, we find $D = 3.3664 \cdot 10^{-6} \cdot \sigma^4$.

We now compare the values of var(b) given by (5.17). For the original design in Table 5.3, var(b) $= \dfrac{\sigma^2}{SS_x} = \dfrac{\sigma^2}{59410.8} = 1.832 \cdot 10^{-5} \cdot \sigma^2$, and similarly for

the D-optimal design var(b) $= \dfrac{\sigma^2}{114005} = 8.7715 \cdot 10^{-6} \cdot \sigma^2$. Thus the variance for the C_2-optimal design is about half as large as that for the original heuristically chosen design in the example.

5.4.3 Hypothesis Testing

As mentioned above, we assume that the e_i in (5.6) follow independent $N(0; \sigma^2)$ distributions, and we use the notation introduced there.
To *test the hypothesis* that α has a given value α_0,

H_0: $\alpha = \alpha_0$

against the two-sided alternative

H_A: $\alpha \neq \alpha_0$

we use the test statistic

$$t_\alpha = \frac{a - \alpha_0}{s_a}.$$ (5.29)

and reject H_0 with a Type I error rate α^* if

$$|t_\alpha| > t(n - 2; 1 - \frac{\alpha^*}{2}).$$

To test the hypothesis that β has a given value β_0,

$$H_0: \beta = \beta_0$$

against

a) $H_A^+: \beta > \beta_0$

b) $H_A^-: \beta < \beta_0$

c) $H_A: \beta \neq \beta_0$

we use the test statistic

$$t_\beta = \frac{b - \beta_0}{s_b}$$ (5.30)

and reject H_0 with a first kind risk α^* if:

in case a) $t_\beta > t(n-2; 1-\alpha^*)$
in case b) $t_\beta < -t(n-2; 1-\alpha^*)$

in case c) $|t_\beta| > t(n-2; 1-\frac{\alpha^*}{2}).$

Example 5.6 -continued
     For the data on type 1 storage let us test the following two hypotheses
(independently of each other)

$$H_0: \alpha = 31 \qquad \text{against } H_A: \alpha \neq 31$$

and

$$H_0: \beta = 0 \qquad \text{against } H_A: \beta < 0$$

(we choose a one sided alternative because an increase in carotene during
storage is physically not possible).

The test statistics are

$$t_\alpha = \frac{31.216 - 30}{0.7059} = 1.7226$$

and

$$t_\beta = \frac{-0.0546}{0.0039397} = -13.86$$

respectively.

If we choose a *significance level* (*risk of the first kind*) of $\alpha^* = 0.05$ for each test we need the quantile $t(3; 0.975) = 3.182$ for the test on α, and the quantile $t(3; 0.95) = 2.353$ for the test on β.

This leads to the acceptance of H_0: $\alpha = 31$ and the rejection of H_0: $\beta = 0$, i.e. we conclude that the decrease in carotene during storage is significant.

Note that H_0: $\alpha = 31$ is not rejected at $\alpha^* = 0.05$ because the 0.95-confidence interval for α contains the value 31.

Note!

A two sided alternative hypothesis with significance level α^* will be rejected (and therefore the null hypothesis about the value of a parameter will be accepted) whenever the null hypothesis value of the parameter lies in the (two-sided) $(1-\alpha^*)$-confidence interval for the parameter.

Because of this relation, the calculation of confidence intervals is sufficient for the analysis. However for sample size determination for hypothesis tests the procedure is different; here the *Type II risk* is often incorporated into the *precision requirements*. This has already been treated in detail in chapter 3, and we can adapt the formulae given there. We merely replace the sample mean and its standard error by the (sample) regression coefficient and its standard error, and note that the degrees of freedom are now $n-2$ instead of $n-1$.

The determination of n will depend on the precision requirements, which by analogy with the tests on expectations in chapter 3 are given in terms of α^*, β_0^* and d and an estimate s^2 for the variance σ^2 of the distribution (or the use of Algorithm B).

Using the iterative procedure of Algorithm A we can find the optimum sample size for estimating the parameter α from

$$n = \text{CEIL}\left[\frac{\sigma^2}{d^2} \cdot \frac{\sum x_i^2}{SS_x} \left[t(n-2;P) + t(n-2;1-\beta_0^*)\right]^2\right] \tag{5.31}$$

where $P = 1 - \alpha^*$ for the one-sided alternative hypotheses and $P = 1 - \alpha^*/2$ for the two-sided alternative. The required minimal sample size depends on the experimental design, i.e. the planned range and allocation of the x-values.

The smallest minimal experiment for a test concerning β is obtained by using the D-optimal design in Theorem 5.1.

For such a design with n even, $n = 2r$ say, we obtain $\bar{x} = \dfrac{x_l + x_u}{2}$ and

$SS_x = \dfrac{n}{4}(x_u - x_l)^2$ and therefore n is obtained from

$$n = \text{CEIL}\left[\frac{4s^2}{d^2(x_u - x_l)^2} [t(n-2;P) + t(n-2;1-\beta_0^*)]^2\right] \tag{5.32}$$

171

If we wish to compare the slopes of two regressions, then we need two experiments which are independent of each other. The above assumptions must be satisfied in each of them.

We will take two independent sets of measurements $(y_{11}, ..., y_{1n_1})$ and $(y_{21}, ..., y_{2n_2})$ of sizes n_1 and n_2 from the two underlying populations, in order to test the null hypothesis

$$H_0 : \beta_1 = \beta_2$$

against one of the following one- or two-sided alternatives

    a) $H_A : \beta_1 > \beta_2$
    b) $H_A : \beta_1 < \beta_2$
    c) $H_A : \beta_1 \neq \beta_2$

By analogy with (5.6a) and (5.6b) we have the regression model
$y_{1i} = \alpha_1 + \beta_1 x_{1i} + e_{1i}$ $(i = 1, ..., n_1)$ in population 1, and the model
$y_{2i} = \alpha_2 + \beta_2 x_{2i} + e_{2i}$ $(i = 1, ..., n_2)$ in population 2. The sample sizes n_1 and n_2 are to be determined so that for a given risk of the first kind α^*, the risk of the second kind β^* as a function of $(\beta_1 - \beta_2)$ does not exceed an upper bound d, so long as, according to which is the alternative hypothesis, either

    a) $\beta_1 - \beta_2 \geq d$,
    b) $\beta_1 - \beta_2 \leq -d$, or
    c) $|\beta_1 - \beta_2| \geq d$

The value d is the least difference of practical interest between β_1 and β_2.

In the case of (approximately) equal variances, the above hypothesis is tested using the one-sided t-test (cases a) and b)) or with the two-sided t-test (case c)). The tests use the "pooled" estimate of the common variance σ^2 using the quantities s_1^2 and s_2^2 as in (5.21) from samples 1 and 2. The *pooled estimator* is

$$s^2 = \frac{1}{n_1 + n_2 - 4}[(n_1 - 2)s_1^2 + (n_2 - 2)s_2^2]$$

The test statistic is $t = \dfrac{b_1 - b_2}{s_d}$, where $s_d^2 = s^2\left[\dfrac{1}{SS_{x1}} + \dfrac{1}{SS_{x2}}\right]$ and SS_x is as in

(5.13).

H_0 is rejected if in case:

    a) $t > t(n_1+n_2-4; 1-\alpha^*)$,
    b) $t < -t(n_1+n_2-4; 1-\alpha^*)$ and
    c) $|t| > t(n_1+n_2-4; 1-\dfrac{\alpha^*}{2})$

and otherwise accepted.

If the total number of observations $n_1 + n_2$ is given, then it is optimal to make the two sample sizes equal.
The value of $n = n_1 = n_2$ is for D-optimal designs obtained iteratively from

$$n = \text{CEIL}\left[\frac{8\sigma^2}{(x_u - x_l)^2 d^2}[t(2n-4; P) + t(2n-4; 1-\beta_0^*)]^2\right] \qquad (5.33)$$

where $P = 1 - \alpha^*$ for a one-sided alternative and $P = 1 - \alpha^*/2$ for the two-sided alternative.

Example 5.6 - continuation

For a future experiment involving type 1 storage, the minimal size must be determined (assuming $\sigma^2 \approx 1$) so that a test with a significance level $\alpha^* = 0.05$ rejects the null hypothesis $\beta = \beta_0$ if $|\beta - \beta_0| > 0.01$ with a probability of at least 0.99 (two-sided alternative).

We obtain as the solution of the D-optimal design in [1, 303].

$$\begin{pmatrix} 1 & 303 \\ 6 & 6 \end{pmatrix}$$

with 12 measurements, 6 of them at day 1 and 6 of them at day 303.

To test against a two-sided alternative whether the slopes for both types (1, 2) of storage are equal with a risk of the first kind $\alpha^* = 0.05$, we assume we have prior estimates ($\tilde{\sigma}_1^2 \approx 1$, $\tilde{\sigma}_2^2 \approx 7.5$), and we take $\tilde{\sigma}_1^2 \approx \tilde{\sigma}_2^2 \approx \tilde{\sigma}^2 = 4$. We require that differences of at least 0.01 (i.e. $|\beta_1 - \beta_2| > 0.01$) can be detected with probability at least 0.9. If in spite of the very different sample variances we assume that the population variances are equal, we find, after applying (5.33) iteratively, that the minimal sample size (for the D-optimal design in [1, 303]) is $n = 38$ with 19 measurements at each of the two values $x = 1$ and $x = 303$.

If we assume unequal variances then just as with means in chapter 3 we have to use an approximate test. Since the calculations are very awkward, we use the CADEMO Module REA1 (regression analysis with one regressor variable) and obtain with $\tilde{\sigma}_1^2 = 1$ and $\tilde{\sigma}_2^2 = 7.5$ the results

$$\begin{pmatrix} 1 & 303 \\ 10 & 10 \end{pmatrix} \text{ for type 1}$$

and

$$\begin{pmatrix} 1 & 303 \\ 27 & 27 \end{pmatrix} \text{ for type 2.}$$

The higher number (54) of measurements for type 2 stems from the larger residual variance in the second population. Approximately we have

$$\frac{n_1}{n_2} \approx \frac{\sigma_1}{\sigma_2}.$$

5.4.4 Special Problems in Model II

We now turn to the case where model (5.3) must be used. The least squares estimates for the parameters, the realised confidence intervals and the test statistics can be calculated in the same way as described in sections 5.4.1 and 5.4.3
The differences between model (5.3) model (5.6) are:

- the expected half-width of the confidence intervals
- the power of the tests
- the design problems described in section 5.4.3 concerning the optimal choice of the x-values do not occur, but the sample size can be determined
- the product moment correlation coefficient can be used meaningfully in model (5.3).

The *correlation coefficient*

$$\rho = \frac{\sigma_{xy}}{\sigma_x \sigma_y} \qquad (5.34)$$

is estimated by

$$r = \frac{SP_{xy}}{\sqrt{SS_x \ SS_y}} \qquad (5.35)$$

We now choose one of the two linear regression models (5.3) or (5.4). The quotient

$$\Delta = \frac{\text{var}(\beta_0 + \beta_1 x)}{\text{var}(y)} = \frac{\text{var}(\beta_0^* + \beta_1^* y)}{\text{var}(x)}$$

is called the theoretical *coefficient of determination*.

We take the first quotient and using $\sigma_y^2 = \text{var}(y) = \text{var}(\beta_0 + \beta_1 x) + \sigma^2 = \beta_1^2 \sigma_x^2 + \sigma^2$

and $\beta_1^2 = \frac{\sigma_{xy}^2}{\sigma_x^4}$, we obtain

$$\Delta = \frac{\sigma_{xy}^2}{\sigma_x^2 \cdot \sigma_y^2} = \rho^2.$$ The value ρ^2 measures the proportion of the total variance of y

which is explained by the linear relationship between the two variables. Similarly it can be shown, using the SSs from the analysis of variance in Figure 5.11, that:

$$r^2 = \frac{SS_{\text{Regression}}}{SS_{\text{Total}}},$$ and this quotient is the sample coefficient of determination, or simply

coefficient of determination.

To test the hypothesis

$$H_0: \rho = 0$$
against
$$H_1: \rho \neq 0$$

we can use the test statistic (5.30) with $\beta_0 = 0$ and the decision rule described there. The null hypothesis

$$H_0: \rho = 0 \qquad\qquad\qquad (\sigma_{xy} = 0)$$
and
$$H_0: \beta = 0 \qquad\qquad\qquad (\sigma_{xy} = 0)$$

are equivalent (because $\beta = \frac{\sigma_{xy}}{\sigma_x^2}$ if (x,y) has a bivariate normal distribution).

Example 5.8

Let us calculate the correlation coefficient for the data given in Table 5.1. We find

n = 25
Σx_i = 1018
Σx_i^2 = 41542
Σy_i = 4198
Σy_i^2 = 706668
$\Sigma x_i y_i$ = 171216
SS_x = 89.04
SS_y = 1739.84
SP_{xy} = 273.44
and finally $r = 0.69473$

Using SPSS we choose Analyze-Correlate-Bivariate and get the results in Figure 5.12.

Correlations

		SHOESIZE	HEIGHT
SHOESIZE	Pearson Correlation	1	.695
	Sig. (2-tailed)		.000
	N	25	25
HEIGHT	Pearson Correlation	.695	1
	Sig. (2-tailed)	.000	
	N	25	25

Figure 5.12 *SPSS output with the correlation coefficient*

For the pair of hypotheses H_0: $\rho \leq \rho_0$ against H_A: $\rho > \rho_0 > 0$, only an approximate test is known. It has a test statistic u which is asymptotically distributed as $N(0;1)$. It is defined as follows. First we make the transformations $\zeta = \frac{1}{2} \ln \frac{1+\rho_0}{1-\rho_0}$ and $z = \frac{1}{2} \ln \frac{1+r}{1-r}$. Then $u = (z - \zeta)\sqrt{n-3}$ is the test statistic. We reject H_0 when $u = (z - \zeta)\sqrt{n-3} > u(1-\alpha)$. Two-sided alternatives are dealt with similarly. For the one-sided alternative KUBINGER et al. (2007) have shown, that for $\alpha = 0.05$ und $\rho_0 = 0.3$, the actual type I error probability α_{act} is always greater than the nominal α_{nom} (0.05). It falls from 0.0537 for $n = 10$ to 0.0503 for $n = 1500$. Table 5.6 contains results from this study for further values of ρ_0 und α

Table 5.6 *Values of α_{act} for the approximate test for selected values of α_{act} and ρ_0, for $n = 50$.*

ρ_0 \ α_{nom}	0.01	0.05	0.1
0.3	0.0117	0.0520	0.1025
0.7	0.0113	0.0545	0.1074

5.5 Multiple Linear Regression

In this section we consider special cases of the *general regression model*

$$y = f(x_1, ..., x_k) + e \qquad (5.36)$$

A character y (modelled by a random variable y) may depend on one or more *predictor variables* $x_1, x_2, ..., x_k$.

For the moment we assume that there is a linear dependence of the form $f(x_1, x_2, ..., x_k) = \beta_0 + \beta_1 x_1 + ... + \beta_k x_k$ with $k \geq 2$; so that equation (5.36) becomes

$$y_j = \beta_0 + \beta_1 x_{1j} + \beta_2 x_{2j} + ... + \beta_k x_{kj} + e_j, \quad (j = 1, ..., n) \qquad (5.37)$$

where y_j is the j-th value of y which depends on the j-th values $x_{1j}, ..., x_{kj}$ of $x_1, ..., x_k$. The e_j are error terms, as in simple linear regression, with $E(e_j) = 0$, $var(e_j) = \sigma^2$ (for all j) and $cov(e_j, e_{j'}) = 0$ for $j' \neq j$. When we construct confidence intervals and test hypotheses we also assume that the e_j are normally distributed.

The $x_1, ..., x_k$ may all be fixed by the experimenter, in which case we call (5.37) a *model I multiple linear regression*. On the other hand the $x_1, ..., x_k$ may all be random and merely observed by the experimenter, in which case (5.37) with x_{ij} printed bold is called a *model II multiple linear regression*. If some of the predictor variables are fixed and others random we have a *mixed model*. At this stage we will assume that the experiment has been performed and the data already collected - we will come back later to the question of experimental design. In the analysis we have to solve the following problems:

(i)   estimate the regression coefficients $\beta_0, \beta_1, ..., \beta_k$
(ii) estimate y by $\hat{y}(x_1, ..., x_k) = \hat{y}$ for given values $x_1, ..., x_k$.

Further problems can be solved under the additional assumption that the e_j are normally distributed:

(iii) construct confidence intervals for each regression coefficient or for functions of the regression coefficients
(iv) test hypotheses about the regression coefficients.

In the case of model I an optimal choice of the x_{ij} is possible during the design phase. For any model the number n of measurements required is determined in relation to the precision requirements corresponding to each type of analysis (i) - (iv).

Example 5.9

We consider body measurements of 30 cows (randomly chosen from the same population). The following three measurements have been taken (all in cm):
y_j body (withers) height
x_{1j} chest circumference
x_{2j} body (rump) length.

The observations are given in Table 5.7.

Table 5.7   *Measurements in cm of body height (y_j), chest circumference (x_{1j}) and body length (x_{2j}) of 30 cows.*

Identifi-cation j	y_j	x_{1j}	x_{2j}	Identifi-cation j	y_j	x_{1j}	x_{2j}
1	110	143	119	16	121	170	139
2	112	156	118	17	120	160	129
3	108	151	126	18	114	156	130
4	108	148	128	19	108	155	123
5	112	144	118	20	111	150	124
6	111	150	128	21	108	149	120
7	114	156	131	22	113	145	123
8	112	145	125	23	109	146	123
9	121	155	126	24	104	132	116
10	119	157	132	25	112	148	121
11	113	159	129	26	124	154	126
12	112	144	118	27	118	156	132
13	114	145	121	28	112	151	126
14	113	139	125	29	121	155	132
15	115	149	124	30	114	140	124

In this example $k = 2$ and if we assume that the dependence is linear, the model (5.37) takes the form

$$y_j = \beta_0 + \beta_1 x_{1j} + \beta_2 x_{2j} + e_j \qquad (j = 1, ..., 30) \tag{5.37a}$$

with $n = 30$. Of course this is a model II (all three variables y, x_1 and x_2 are measured and none could be fixed in advance). This means that any of the three may be chosen as the response variable.

5.5.1 Parameter Estimation

Independently of the model (I, II or mixed) the estimation of the regression coefficients is usually based on the Method of Least Squares (MLS).

In this method we use as estimates of β_0, β_1, ..., β_k, those values b_0, b_1, ..., b_k which minimise the sum of squared deviations

$$S = \sum_{j=1}^{n} (y_j - \beta_0 - \beta_1 x_{1j} - ... - \beta_k x_{kj})^2 \tag{5.38}$$

Because S is a convex function of the β_i, a solution is reached if we solve the set of $k+1$ equations

$$\frac{\partial S}{\partial \beta_l} = 0 \quad (l = 0, ..., k) \tag{5.39}$$

We will now use matrix notation to write down these solutions.

Example 5.9 -continued

The first step is to write (5.37a) in matrix notation (see appendix C).
We will start with the dependent variable. We write the y-values as a column vector y which is the transpose of the row vector given by

$$y^T = (110, 112, ..., 114)$$

with a in appendix C as $a = n = 30$ elements

$$y = \begin{pmatrix} 110 \\ \vdots \\ 114 \end{pmatrix}$$

The x_{ij} form a 30×2 matrix ($a = n = 30$, $b = k = 2$). We augment this by adding an indicator variable as the first column $x_{0j} = 1$ ($j = 1, ..., 30$). This enables us to include the intercept term β_0 in the matrix equation.
Thus we have:

$$X = \begin{pmatrix} 1 & 143 & 119 \\ 1 & 156 & 118 \\ 1 & 151 & 126 \\ \vdots & \vdots & \vdots \\ 1 & 140 & 124 \end{pmatrix}.$$

We also define a column vector

$$\beta = \begin{pmatrix} \beta_0 \\ \beta_1 \\ \beta_2 \end{pmatrix}$$

containing the 3 regression coefficients. Equivalently we can write $\beta^T = (\beta_0, \beta_1, \beta_2)$.
In order to write the system of n equations in (5.37a) in matrix notation we need to define $e^T = (e_1, ..., e_{30})$ as the realisation of the error vector.

In the general case we would have

$$y^T = (y_1, ..., y_n), \quad \beta^T = (\beta_0, ..., \beta_k),$$

$$X = \begin{pmatrix} 1 & x_{11} & \cdots & x_{k1} \\ 1 & x_{12} & \cdots & x_{k2} \\ \vdots & & & \\ 1 & x_{1n} & \cdots & x_{kn} \end{pmatrix}$$

and

$$e^T = (e_1, e_2, ..., e_n)$$

then (5.37a) becomes

$$y = X\beta + e \tag{5.37b}$$

and this is the general linear regression equation.

The normal equations for obtaining the estimators b are then

$$X^T X b = X^T y \tag{5.40}$$

Example 5.9 - continued

We have already defined the components of (5.37b) for this example if we put $k = 2$ and $n = 30$, for example $e^T = (e_1, ..., e_{30})$.

We will now show that the set of equations (5.37) and equation (5.37b) are identical.

The first element (110) of y is obtained by multiplying the first row (1, 143, 119) of X by β and adding e_1.

This gives the equation

$$110 = 1\beta_0 + 143\beta_1 + 119\beta_2 + e_1.$$

This corresponds to (5.37a) for $j = 1$.

For $j = 10$ for instance, $y_{10} = 119$ (Table 5.7), and we obtain

$$119 = 1\beta_0 + 157\beta_1 + 132\beta_2 + e_{10}$$

either by matrix multiplication (using the 10th row from X) or by putting $j = 10$ in (5.37a).

We can write the solution (5.40) of our Least Squares problem as the *least squares estimate* (assuming that $(X^T X)^{-1}$ exists - in model I this can always be achieved if we take at least $k + 1$ different design points; in model II it occurs nearly always (or more precisely with probability 1).

$$b = \hat{\beta} = (X^T X)^{-1} X^T y \tag{5.41}$$

The *least squares estimator* (*LSE*) is obtained by transferring to random variables, i.e. replacing y by y:

$$b = (X^T X)^{-1} X^T y \tag{5.42}$$

In the model assumptions we stated that $E(e_j) = 0$ which means that $E(e) = \begin{pmatrix} 0 \\ 0 \\ \vdots \\ 0 \end{pmatrix} = 0_n$

From this we find using (5.37b) that

$$E(y) = E(X\beta) + E(e) = X\beta + 0_n = X\beta$$

179

and

$$E(b) = (X^TX)^{-1} X^T E(y) = (X^TX)^{-1} X^TX\beta = \beta$$

and therefore b is an unbiased estimator of β.

The variance of b is given by the covariance (or variance-covariance) matrix

$$\mathrm{var}(b) = \sigma^2(X^TX)^{-1} \tag{5.43}$$

Note that in model I, X, and therefore $(X^TX)^{-1}$, is the result of the experimental design (in this case X is called the *design matrix*). Therefore information about σ^2 has to come from the y-data.

$\mathrm{var}(b)$ is the *covariance (or variance-covariance) matrix* of the estimator (vector) b

$$\mathrm{var}(b) = \begin{pmatrix} \mathrm{var}(b_0) & \mathrm{cov}(b_0, b_1) & \cdots & \mathrm{cov}(b_0, b_k) \\ \mathrm{cov}(b_1, b_0) & \mathrm{var}(b_1) & \cdots & \mathrm{cov}(b_1, b_k) \\ \vdots & & & \vdots \\ \mathrm{cov}(b_k, b_0) & \mathrm{cov}(b_k, b_1) & \cdots & \mathrm{var}(b_k) \end{pmatrix}$$

It is a symmetric matrix of order $k + 1$ with the variances of the estimators b_0, ..., b_k of the $k + 1$ regression coefficients in its main diagonal.

Example 5.9 - continued

Let us calculate b (the estimate of β) following (5.41) and var(b) following (5.43) for the data of Table 5.6. First we need the symmetric matrix

$$X^TX = \begin{pmatrix} n & \sum x_{1j} & \sum x_{2j} \\ \sum x_{1j} & \sum x_{1j}^2 & \sum x_{1j}x_{2j} \\ \sum x_{2j} & \sum x_{1j}x_{2j} & \sum x_{2j}^2 \end{pmatrix} = \begin{pmatrix} 30 & 4508 & 3756 \\ 4508 & 679034 & 565251 \\ 3756 & 565251 & 471044 \end{pmatrix}$$

In our case (5.40) becomes a system of 3 equations in 3 unknown estimates (b_0, b_1, b_2) of the form $(X^TX)b = X^Ty$:

$$
\begin{array}{llll}
30\ b_0 + 4508\ b_1 & + 3756\ b_2 & = 3403 & (= \Sigma y_j) \\
4508 b_0 + 679034 b_1 & + 565251 b_2 & = 511971 & (= \Sigma x_{1j}y_j) \\
3756 b_0 + 565251 b_1 & + 471044 b_2 & = 426491 & (= \Sigma x_{2j}y_j)
\end{array}
$$

The solution of this system of simultaneous equations using (5.42) or any other method is:

$$b_0 = 41.39,\ b_1 = 0.2037,\ b_2 = 0.3309.$$

We call these estimates the *sample regression coefficients*, and we use them to predict (estimate) the values of the response variable for any pair of values (x_1, x_2) from

$\hat{y} = b_0 + b_1 x_1 + b_2 x_2$ or $\hat{y} = 41.39 + 0.2037 x_1 + 0.3309 x_2$

var(**b**) in (5.43) is estimated by replacing σ^2 by s^2 given in (5.44). In SPSS these calculation are done in the procedure Analyze - Regression – Linear using height as "dependent" and circumference (= x_1) and length (= x_2) as "independent" variables. The output is given in Figure 5.13.

ANOVA[b]

Model		Sum of Squares	df	Mean Square	F	Sig.
1	Regression	269.075	2	134.538	9.653	.001[a]
	Residual	376.292	27	13.937		
	Total	645.367	29			

a. Predictors: (Constant), LENGTH, CIRCUMFERENCE
b. Dependent Variable: HEIGHT

Coefficients[a]

Model		Unstandardized Coefficients		Standardized Coefficients	t	Sig.
		B	Std. Error	Beta		
1	(Constant)	41.389	16.764		2.469	.020
	CIRCUMFERENCE	.204	.139	.324	1.466	.154
	LENGTH	.331	.199	.367	1.660	.108

a. Dependent Variable: HEIGHT

Figure 5.13   *SPSS output for Example 5.9*

In the SPSS output b_0 is denoted by (Constant).
From the SPSS output we can now find the estimated variances of the estimators b_0, b_1 and b_2 by squaring the standard errors of:
b_0 (Constant)
$$s_0^2 = 16.764^2 = 281.03,$$
b_1:
$$s_1^2 = 0.139^2 = 0.01932$$
and b_2:
$$s_2^2 = 0.199^2 = 0.0396$$
respectively. These are the estimates of the elements σ_0^2, σ_1^2 and σ_2^2 of the main diagonal of the variance matrix.

The error variance σ^2 of the e_j in the model (5.36) is estimated by
$$s^2 = \frac{1}{n-k-1} \sum_{j=1}^{n} (y_j - b_0 - b_1 x_{1j} - \dots - b_k x_{kj})^2$$

(5.44)

$$= \frac{1}{n-k-1} y^T (I_n - X(X^T X)^{-1} X^T) y$$

and is used to evaluate $s^2 (X^T X)^{-1}$, the estimate of $\sigma^2 (X^T X)^{-1}$.

Example 5.9 - continued

In the example we obtain

$$s^2 = \frac{1}{30-3} \sum_{j=1}^{30} (y_j - b_0 - b_1 x_{1j} - b_2 x_{2j})^2 = 13.93673,$$

which can be found in the SPSS output in Figure 5.13 as the Mean Square for the Residual)

5.5.2 Confidence Intervals and Tests

A (realised) (1-α) confidence interval for β_i ($i = 0, 1, ..., k$) can be obtained from the point estimate b_i of β_i and the standard error s_{b_i} by

$$[b_i - s_{b_i} \, t(n-k-1; \, 1-\frac{\alpha}{2}); \; b_i + s_{b_i} \, t(n-k-1; 1- \frac{\alpha}{2})] \tag{5.45}$$

Example 5.9 - continued

In this example we have $k = 2$ and thus $30-3 = 27$ *df* for the residual mean square. Taking $\alpha = 0.05$ we find $t(27; 0.975) = 2.0518$ in Table A1. The confidence intervals are therefore calculated:

for β_0:
$[41.3888-16.764 \cdot 2.0518; 41.3888+16.764 \cdot 2.0518] = [6.9919; 75.7857]$;
for β_1:
$[0.20372-0.13895 \cdot 2.0518; 0.20372+0.13895 \cdot 2.0518] = [-0.081384; 0.488820]$;
and
for β_2:
$[0.33093-0.19935 \cdot 2.0518; 0.33093+0.19935 \cdot 2.0518] = [-0.078; 0.7400]$.

The confidence intervals are included in the SPSS output if we click on the "Analyze" button and activate "confidence intervals". The differences between the SPSS output and our calculations are due to rounding errors.

To test null hypotheses such as
$\quad$ H_{00}: $\beta_0 = \beta_0'$
$\quad$ H_{01}: $\beta_1 = \beta_1'$

or generally

$\quad$ H_{0j}: $\beta_j = \beta_j'$ ($j = 0, 1, ..., k$)

against the two-sided alternative hypotheses

$\quad$ H_{A0}: $\beta_0 \neq \beta_0'$
$\quad$ H_{A1}: $\beta_1 \neq \beta_1'$ and

$\quad$ H_{Aj}: $\beta_j \neq \beta_j'$ ($j = 0, 1, ..., k$) respectively.

with a type I error probability α, we can, as was done in chapter 3 for means, set up the t-statistics in the form "difference between the estimate and the null hypothesis value divided by the standard error of the estimate". Alternatively we can construct the corresponding $(1-\alpha)$-confidence interval, and if this interval includes the null hypothesis value, we accept the null hypothesis; otherwise we reject it. We have $n-k-1$ df.

Example 5.9 -continued

We will test whether the regression coefficients β_0, β_1 and β_2 are different from $\beta_0' = \beta_1' = \beta_2' = 0$ respectively (with two-sided alternatives). Taking $\alpha = 0.05$ we reject H_{00}: $\beta_0 = 0$, but accept H_{01}: $\beta_1 = 0$ and H_{02}: $\beta_2 = 0$. The corresponding confidence intervals for β_1 and β_2 contain the value 0.

These confidence intervals can be found in SPSS output shown in Figure 5.14.

Coefficients(a)

Model		Unstandardized Coefficients		Standardized Coefficients	95% Confidence Interval for B	
		B	Std. Error	Beta	Lower Bound	Upper Bound
1	(Constant)	41.389	16.764		6.991	75.786
	CIRCUMFERENCE	.204	.139	.324	-.081	.489
	LENGTH	.331	.199	.367	-.078	.740

a Dependent Variable: HEIGHT

Figure 5.14 *SPSS output with Confidence Intervals for Example 5.9*

We obtain this by clicking the "Analyze" button and then choosing "Confidence Intervals".
The differences between the SPSS output and our hand calculations are due to rounding errors.

5.5.3 Special Problems in Model II

As in simple linear regression described in section 5.1, the analysis is formally the same for all models. In model II however it is meaningful to calculate measures of dependency between the random dependent variable and the random regressor variables (one can obtain these measures in model I, but they have no useful interpretation). For each pair of the $k + 1$ random variables $(y, x_1, ..., x_k)$ there is a correlation coefficient analogous to the correlation coefficient ρ_{xy} defined in B.2.6. Thus we have:

$$\rho_{yx_i} = \frac{\sigma_{yx_i}}{\sigma_y \sigma_{x_i}}$$

and

$$\rho_{ij} = \rho_{x_ix_j} = \frac{\sigma_{x_ix_j}}{\sigma_{x_i} \sigma_{x_j}}$$

These are estimated by replacing the covariances σ_{yx_i}, $\sigma_{x_ix_j}$ by the estimated covariances s_{yx_i}, $s_{x_ix_j}$ and the standard deviations σ_y, σ_{x_i} by the estimated standard deviations s_y and s_{x_i} respectively. The estimates of ρ_{yx} and ρ_{ij} are denoted by r_{yx} and r_{ij}.

However if there are more than two random variables involved, other measures of dependency can be defined. We restrict ourselves here to three variables as in Example 5.9 and will denote the response variable y by $x_{k+1} = x_3$ for our case $k = 2$. Then we have the random variables x_1, x_2 and x_3 with their *correlation coefficients* ρ_{12}, ρ_{13} and ρ_{23}. We may ask what is the correlation between x_1 and x_2 if x_3 is at a fixed level? A measure for this kind of conditional dependency is the *partial correlation coefficient*

$$\rho_{12\cdot3} = \frac{\rho_{12} - \rho_{13} \cdot \rho_{23}}{\sqrt{(1 - \rho_{13}^2)(1 - \rho_{23}^2)}} \tag{5.46}$$

which is estimated by

$$r_{12\cdot3} = \frac{r_{12} - r_{13} \cdot r_{23}}{\sqrt{(1 - r_{13}^2)(1 - r_{23}^2)}} \tag{5.47}$$

Furthermore we also can define the (sample) *multiple correlation coefficient R* as the square root of the *coefficient of determination* R^2 which is given by (using the identity $SS_y = SS_{regr.} + SS_{residual}$)

$$R^2 = \frac{SS_{regr}}{SS_y} = \frac{SS_{regr}}{SS_{regr} + SS_{residual}} \tag{5.48}$$

where

$$SS_{residual} = SS_y - \sum_{i=1}^{k} b_i \, SP_{x_iy}$$

writing SS as sum of squares and SP as the sum of products of the variables. R can also be shown to be the correlation coefficient between $\hat{y}$ and y.

Example 5.9 - continued

We will find all the partial correlation coefficients and the multiple correlation coefficient for the data in Table 5.7.

The usual correlation coefficients are:

$r_{12} = r_{21} = 0.7468$ (between chest circumference (x_1) and rump length (x_2))
$r_{13} = r_{31} = 0.5979$ (between x_1 and body height (x_3))
$r_{23} = r_{32} = 0.6087$ (between x_2 and x_3)

From these the partial correlation coefficient $r_{12\cdot3}$ between chest circumference (x_1) and the rump length (x_2) for given body height (x_3) is found using (5.47) to be

$$r_{12\cdot3} = \frac{0.7468 - 0.5979 \cdot 0.6087}{\sqrt{(1 - 0.5979^2)(1 - 0.6087^2)}} = 0.6020$$

Similarly we find

$$r_{13.2} = 0.2716$$

and

$$r_{23.1} = 0.3043.$$

To obtain these results using SPSS we use the procedure Analyze - Correlate, an then choose either Bivariate for the simple coefficients, and Partial for the partial ones. In the case of the partial coefficients the program must be used separately for each conditioning variable (which has to be entered first). The simple correlation coefficients are shown in Figure 5.15.

Correlations

		HEIGHT	CIRCUMFERENCE	LENGTH
HEIGHT	Pearson Correlation	1	.598	.609
	Sig. (2-tailed)		.000	.000
	N	30	30	30
CIRCUMFERENCE	Pearson Correlation	.598	1	.747
	Sig. (2-tailed)	.000		.000
	N	30	30	30
LENGTH	Pearson Correlation	.609	.747	1
	Sig. (2-tailed)	.000	.000	
	N	30	30	30

Figure 5.15   *The simple correlation coefficients for Example 5.9*

The SPSS procedure Analyze-Regression-Linear produces the multiple correlation coefficient automatically without prompting the user to specify that the analysis is model II. If the problem is model I, the user should simply ignore this information and should on no account publish it or use it in any other way. Its value can in fact be influenced by skilful choice of the design points. In this example of course we do have a meaningful value.

We find

$$R = 0.6457$$

and the coefficient of determination (R-squared in SPSS)

$$R^2 = 0.41693.$$

We can interpret R^2 as saying that about 42% of the variability, defined by $\sum_{j=1}^{n} (x_{3j} - \bar{x}_3)^2$, of the body height can be explained by the two predictor variables.

The quantity "Adjusted R-squared" in the SPSS output is defined as

$$R_{adj}^2 = 1 - \frac{MS_{res.}(n - 1)}{SS_y}$$

(i.e. R_{adj}^2 is adjusted for degrees of freedom).

185

Exercise

Repeat the calculations of R for Example 5.9 by using
  (i)   the chest circumference
  (ii)   the rump length
as response variable (and the others as predictor variables).

5.5.4   Optimal Designs in Model I

In multiple regression the experimental design problems are very complex. This stems from the fact that the experimental region (i.e. the region in which measurements can reasonably be taken) is not so easily determined as in simple linear regression. There most of the time the experimental region is an interval. However even in the two-dimensional case it is not always obvious that the experimental region is a rectangle, which is what we get if we define the experimental region to be an interval for each predictor variable separately. Often we find that certain values of the predictor variables cannot be used in combination. A natural experimental region could then be an ellipse. But even if a rectangle is taken as the basic region in which, say, a G-optimal design is to be found, we come up against technical problems. The solution can be found in VB 4/31/2110.

5.6   Simple Polynomial Regression

We go back to case $k = 1$ in the model (5.36) and therefore denote x_1 by x but we now take f to be *polynomial* in x.

$$f(x) = \beta_0 + \beta_1 x + \beta_2 x^2 + \dots + \beta_k x^k.$$

Here f is a k-th order polynomial.
In practice *quadratic* $(k = 2)$ or *cubic* $(k = 3)$ *functions* are usually sufficient.

Example 5.10
  The (withers) height (in cm) of 112 female cattle were measured at six monthly intervals between birth (age = 0) up until the age of 60 months. Table 5.8 contains the average measurements of the 112 animals.

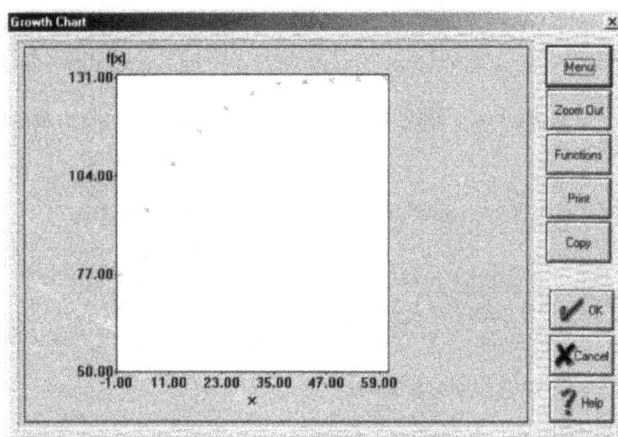

Figure 5.16   *Scatter-plot of the data in Example 5.10*

The scatter-plot in Figure 5.16 shows us that the relation between height and age is not linear. We shall therefore fit a second order polynomial (quadratic function) and a third order polynomial (cubic function) to these data.

Table 5.8 *Average withers heights of 112 cows in the first 60 months of life.*

j	Age (Months)	Height (cm)
1	0	77.20
2	6.00	94.50
3	12.00	107.20
4	18.00	116.00
5	24.00	122.40
6	30.00	126.70
7	36.00	129.20
8	42.00	129.90
9	48.00	130.40
10	54.00	130.80
11	60.00	131.20

With $k = 1$ and $f(x) = \beta_0 + \beta_1 x + \beta_2 x^2$ we obtain the following model equation for the y_j from (5.36):

$$y_j = \beta_0 + \beta_1 x_j + \beta_2 x_j^2 + e_j \quad (j = 1,...,n) \tag{5.49}$$

Where we assume the e_j are mutually independent and are distributed as $N(0; \sigma^2)$.

This is the model for a *simple* ($k = 1$ regressor) *quadratic* ($k = 2$ in (5.47)) regression. Formally we can handle this case like a multiple linear regression with two regressors. Let

$$x_1 = x$$

$$x_2 = x^2 .$$

In this case of course even if we have model II with random x, the partial correlation coefficients are not meaningfully defined.

Equation (5.49) gives us the following matrix expressions:

$$\beta^T = (\beta_0, \beta_1, \beta_2),$$

$$X = \begin{pmatrix} 1 & x_1 & x_1^2 \\ 1 & x_2 & x_2^2 \\ \vdots & \vdots & \vdots \\ 1 & x_n & x_n^2 \end{pmatrix}$$

with e and y as in (5.37b) and we obtain equation (5.37a). In (5.41) however we have the following:

$$X^T X = \begin{pmatrix} n & \sum x_j & \sum x_j^2 \\ \sum x_j & \sum x_j^2 & \sum x_j^3 \\ \sum x_j^2 & \sum x_j^3 & \sum x_j^4 \end{pmatrix}$$

and

$$X^T y = \begin{pmatrix} \sum y_j \\ \sum x_j y_j \\ \sum x_j^2 y_j \end{pmatrix}.$$

The structure of these matrix equations remains unchanged if we go over to a third order polynomial; we merely have an additional dimension in the X-matrix and the parameter vector.

We will now estimate β in the quadratic case from the values given in Example 5.10.

Example 5.10 - continuation.

From table 5.7 we find

$$\Sigma x_j = 330, \ \Sigma x_j^2 = 13860, \ \Sigma x_j^3 = 653400, \ \Sigma x_j^4 = 32831568, \ \Sigma y_j = 1295.5,$$

$$\Sigma x_j y_j = 41981.4 \text{ and } \Sigma x_j^2 y_j = 1791716.4.$$

Thus the estimate b of the parameter vector is given by

$$b = \begin{pmatrix} 11 & 330 & 13860 \\ 330 & 13860 & 653400 \\ 13860 & 653400 & 32831568 \end{pmatrix}^{-1} \begin{pmatrix} 1295.5 \\ 41981.4 \\ 1791716.4 \end{pmatrix} = \begin{pmatrix} 80.76 \\ 2.28 \\ -0.0248 \end{pmatrix}$$

The estimated quadratic regression function is therefore

$$\hat{y} = 80.76 + 2.28x - 0.0248x^2$$

We get these results in SPSS by following the sequence **Analyze - Regression - Curve Estimation**, if we click the **Quadratic** button (and at the same time activate the **Cubic** button). This leads to the results in Figure 5.17, in which the linear case appears automatically. The estimates s^2 of σ^2 for the three models "Linear", "Quadratic" and "Cubic" are:

Dependent Variable: HEIGHT

Equation	R-Squared	df 1	df 2	Constant	b1	b2	b3
Linear	.769	1	9	94.164	.787		
Quadratic	.983	2	8	80.762	2.276	-.025	
Cubic	1.000	3	7	77.427	3.159	-.063	.0004

Independent Variable: AGE

Figure 5.17 *(Linear) Quadratic and Cubic Regression for Example 5.10*

Model	s^2
Linear	82.0433
Quadratic	6.6816
Cubic	0.06258

From this it can be seen that the cubic regression with regression function

$\hat{y} = 77.43 + 3.159x - 0.06342x^2 + 0.000429x^3$

fits the data best out of the above models. We shall come back to this point again in Section 5.8.

D- and G-optimal designs for polynomials are given in Table 5.8. (For more information see PUKELSHEIM, (1993)).

Table 5.8 *D- and G-optimal designs for polynomial regression for $x \in [a,b]$ and $n = m(k + 1)$.*

k	optimal design
1	$\begin{pmatrix} a & b \\ m & m \end{pmatrix}$
2	$\begin{pmatrix} a & \dfrac{a+b}{2} & b \\ m & m & m \end{pmatrix}$
3	$\begin{pmatrix} a & 0.7236a+0.2764b & 0.2764a+0.7236b & b \\ m & m & m & m \end{pmatrix}$
4	$\begin{pmatrix} a & 0.82735a+0.17265b & \dfrac{a+b}{2} & 0.17265a+0.82735b & b \\ m & m & m & m & m \end{pmatrix}$
5	$\begin{pmatrix} a & 0.88255a+0.11745b & 0.6426a+0.3574b & 0.3574a+0.6426b & 0.11745a+0.88255b & b \\ m & m & m & m & m & m \end{pmatrix}$

For $k = 2$ and $k = 3$ an example is given in Section 5.8.

5.7 Multiple Quadratic Regression

In chapter 4 the analysis of variance was shown to be a method by which *factorial experiments*, as introduced in Definition 2.19, can be analysed, provided all the factors are *qualitative*. If all the factors are *quantitative* we can regard them as regressors in a *model I multiple regression*. In applications, factorial experiments with quantitative factors are mostly used to search for the optimum on a *response surface*. The description of such non-linear relationships can be achieved most simply by a quadratic function of the regressor variables. In this section we shall describe the design and analysis of such experiments, and we will also demonstrate the procedure for model II with random x-values in equation (5.50) with the aid of an example.

This section combines the ideas from sections 5.5 and 5.6. We assume that we have more than one regressor variable and also a quadratic regression function. In the case of $k = 2$ regressors (x_1, x_2) the complete regression model takes the form

$$y_j = \beta_0 + \beta_1 x_{1j} + \beta_2 x_{2j} + \beta_{11} x_{1j}^2 + \beta_{22} x_{2j}^2 + \beta_{12} x_{1j} x_{2j} + e_j \qquad (5.50)$$

If any of the βs on the right hand side of (5.50) is negligibly small, a reduced model can be employed having the corresponding terms omitted. Model (5.50) without the term $\beta_{12} x_1 x_2$ is called a *pure quadratic model* in x_1 and x_2 (without an *interaction term $x_1 x_2$*). The analysis proceeds as described in sections 5.5 and 5.6; we merely adapt X and the vector β accordingly.

We will now illustrate the analysis of a quadratic regression (model II) by SPSS, using the data from Example 5.9.
The analysis in SPSS requires an intermediate step. The functions (squares and products) of the original regressor variables must first be calculated as new variables in the Data Editor. We will illustrate this for Example 5.9 using the data in Table 5.7.

Example 5.9 – continued

We generate a new SPSS data file from the one already set up containing the values of the variables height, length and circumference from Table 5.7. We choose the length as the dependent variable and the two others as predictor variables in the full quadratic model (5.50). Choosing the option Compute in the Transform menu we create new variables which are circumference squared (cc) and height squared (hh), and also the product of circumference and height (hc). These appear in the Data Editor as shown in Figure 5.18. Choosing the procedure Analyze - Regression - Linear we get a dialog box that we have met before (Figure 5.6). But now we declare the length to be the dependent variable and all the 5 other variables as the independent variables. The results are shown in Figure 5.19.

	HEIGHT	CIRCUMFERENCE	LENGTH	CC	HH	HC			
1	110.00	143.00	119.00	20449.00	12100.00	15730.00			
2	112.00	156.00	118.00	24336.00	12544.00	17472.00			
3	108.00	151.00	126.00	22801.00	11664.00	16308.00			
4	108.00	148.00	128.00	21904.00	11664.00	15984.00			
5	112.00	144.00	118.00	20736.00	12544.00	16128.00			
6	111.00	150.00	128.00	22500.00	12321.00	16650.00			
7	114.00	156.00	131.00	24336.00	12996.00	17784.00			
8	112.00	145.00	125.00	21025.00	12544.00	16240.00			
9	121.00	155.00	126.00	24025.00	14641.00	18755.00			
10	119.00	157.00	132.00	24649.00	14161.00	18683.00			
11	113.00	159.00	129.00	25281.00	12769.00	17967.00			
12	112.00	144.00	118.00	20736.00	12544.00	16128.00			
13	114.00	145.00	121.00	21025.00	12996.00	16530.00			
14	113.00	139.00	125.00	19321.00	12769.00	15707.00			
15	115.00	149.00	124.00	22201.00	13225.00	17135.00			
16	121.00	170.00	139.00	28900.00	14641.00	20570.00			
17	120.00	160.00	129.00	25600.00	14400.00	19200.00			
18	114.00	156.00	130.00	24336.00	12996.00	17784.00			
19	108.00	155.00	123.00	24025.00	11664.00	16740.00			
20	111.00	150.00	124.00	22500.00	12321.00	16650.00			
21	108.00	149.00	120.00	22201.00	11664.00	16092.00			
22	113.00	145.00	123.00	21025.00	12769.00	16385.00			

Figure 5.18 *SPSS-Data Editor after creating new variables*

Coefficients[a]

Model		Unstandardized Coefficients		Standardized Coefficients			
		B	Std. Error	Beta	t	Sig.	
1	(Constant)	52.719	331.627		.159	.875	
	HEIGHT	4.381	6.131	3.952	.715	.482	
	CIRCUMFERENCE	-2.990	2.472	-4.290	-1.210	.238	
	CC	.007	.017	2.857	.393	.698	
	HH	-.026	.038	-5.417	-.692	.496	
	HC	.012	.045	3.347	.279	.783	

a. Dependent Variable: LENGTH

Figure 5.19 *SPSS-output for Example 5.9*

Before we deal with the problems of model I in detail, we will generalise the model equation (5.50) to more than two regressors. In matrix notation we obtain, just as in (5.37b) the regression model

$$y = X\beta + e \qquad\qquad (5.50a)$$

except that now:

$$y^T = (y_1, ..., y_n),$$

$$\beta^T = (\beta_0, \beta_1, ..., \beta_k, \beta_{11}, ..., \beta_{kk}, \beta_{12}, ..., \beta_{k-1, k}),$$

$$X = \begin{pmatrix} 1 & x_{11} & \cdots & x_{k1} & x_{11}^2 & \cdots & x_{k1}^2 & x_{11}x_{21} & \cdots & x_{k-11}x_{k1} \\ 1 & x_{12} & \cdots & x_{k2} & x_{12}^2 & \cdots & x_{k2}^2 & x_{12}x_{22} & \cdots & x_{k-12}x_{k2} \\ \vdots & & & & & & & & & \vdots \\ 1 & x_{1n} & \cdots & x_{kn} & x_{1n}^2 & \cdots & x_{kn}^2 & x_{1n}x_{2n} & \cdots & x_{k-1n}x_{kn} \end{pmatrix}$$

and

$$e^T = (e_1, e_2, ..., e_n).$$

To estimate the regression coefficients β_i, β_{ii} and β_{hi} of this model and to investigate a maximum, it is necessary that the levels of the factors are such that quadratic effects can be found, hence *at least three different* x_i values are needed for each quantitative factor A_i.

The equation (5.50a) of the response surface contains the linear terms $\{x_{ij}\}$ for $i = 1, 2, ..., k$; all corresponding quadratic terms $\{x_{ij}^2\}$ for $i = 1, 2, ..., k$; and all product terms of two factors $\{x_{hj} \cdot x_{ij}\}$ for $h = 1, 2, ..., k$ and $h < i$.

The product term $x_{hj} \cdot x_{ij}$ corresponds to the interaction between the factors x_h and x_i.
When the number of regressor variables increases, it is often not possible to include all the combinations of factor levels in the experiment. One must then use an incomplete factorial design, as mentioned in Definition 2.19 and the text following it. Having said that, we must ensure that in a quadratic model three different levels of each of the k factors are included. An especially efficient way of accomplishing this without including all 3^k possible factor level combinations is to use a *second order central composite*

191

design. The phrase second order means that it allows the analysis of the quadratic model (5.50a) (which can also be called a model of the second degree or second order). This experimental design consists of three components. The *kernel* is either a complete factorial design with two levels for each factor, or, when there is a large number of factors, a fractional two-level design. We therefore describe the kernel as a 2^{k-m} design, where we allow m to take the value 0 (when the design is complete). We can thus summarise the components of the full design as follows:

Basis design 1 (cube or kernel):

2^{k-m} design with levels +1 and −1 with n_k replicates, often we have $n_k = 1$.

Basis design 2 (star):

This design contains for each factor two "star points" with the levels $+\alpha$ and $-\alpha$ for the corresponding factor and zero for the remaining factors. (number of replicates = n_s, star point distance = α)

Basis design 3 (centre):

A design with the factor level combination $(0, 0, ..., 0)$ replicated n_c times

The total number of experimental units is therefore $n = 2^{k-m} \cdot n_k + 2 \cdot k \cdot n_s + n_c$.

The levels above are given in the standardised notation for the treatment factors, analogous to the notation for two level designs. In this notation the factors are transformed in such a way that the levels of the kernel correspond with the numbers +1 and -1. If $\alpha \leq 1$ the standardised experimental region for all factors is (-1; 1), otherwise it is $(-\alpha, \alpha)$. All basis designs have the origin as their centre of symmetry of the coordinates; hence the phrase central composite.

In practical applications, of course, the design is given in the non-standardised way, as shown in Example 5.11 below.

If $\alpha \neq 1$, each factor in a composite design occurs at five levels. The matrix of the coefficients of such a design with three factors and a complete kernel is given in Table 5.10.

Table 5.10   *Matrix of the coefficients of a composite design with three factors.*

I	x_a	x_b	x_c	$x_a x_b$	$x_a x_c$	$x_b x_c$	x_a^2	x_b^2	x_c^2	design component	number of replicates
1	1	1	1	1	1	1	1	1	1		
1	1	1	-1	1	-1	-1	1	1	1		
1	1	-1	1	-1	1	-1	1	1	1		
1	1	-1	-1	-1	-1	1	1	1	1	kernel	n_k
1	-1	1	1	-1	-1	1	1	1	1		
1	-1	1	-1	-1	1	-1	1	1	1		
1	-1	-1	1	1	-1	-1	1	1	1		
1	-1	-1	-1	1	1	1	1	1	1		
1	$-\alpha$	0	0	0	0	0	α^2	0	0		
1	α	0	0	0	0	0	α^2	0	0		
1	0	$-\alpha$	0	0	0	0	0	α^2	0	star	n_s
1	0	α	0	0	0	0	0	α^2	0		
1	0	0	$-\alpha$	0	0	0	0	0	α^2		
1	0	0	α	0	0	0	0	0	α^2		
1	0	0	0	0	0	0	0	0	0	centre	n_c

The construction of optimal second order designs is difficult and such designs need a relative large number of experimental units. Therefore in the place of D- or G-optimality, designs with other useful properties like *rotatability* and/or *orthogonality* have been used. The value of α can be chosen such that the variance of the estimator of $E(y)$ at all points equidistant from the centre point is constant. Such a design is called *rotatable*. One gets a rotatable design if

$$\alpha = 4\sqrt{\frac{n_k}{n_s} 2^{k-m}} = \alpha_R.$$

We get an orthogonal design (hence the columns of the matrix X in $E(y) = X\beta$ are orthogonal), if $\alpha = \dfrac{1}{\sqrt{2n_s}}\sqrt{\sqrt{n \cdot n_k \cdot 2^{k-m}} - n_k 2^{k-1}}$ and we get a rotatable and orthogonal

design by choosing $\alpha = \alpha_R$ and $n_c = 4\sqrt{n_k \cdot n_s \cdot 2^{k-m}} + 2n_s(2-k)$. More detailed definitions of these criteria can be found in VB 4/33/1250. For central composite rotatable designs and other designs for quadratic response surfaces, see COCHRAN and COX (1957), KHURI and CORNELL (1987) or MYERS (1976).

Table 5.11 contains parameters of the smallest D- and G-optimal designs for $k = 2, ..., 9$, but there are smaller designs which are either rotatable, orthogonal or both.

Table 5.11   *Smallest D- and G-optimal, second order central composite designs.*

k	m	n	n_c	n_k	n_s	$\alpha = \sqrt{k}$
2	0	48	8	5	5	1.414
3	0	400	40	27	24	1.732
4	0	180	12	7	7	2.000
5	1	588	28	25	16	2.236
6	1	3584	128	81	72	2.449
7	1	20736	576	245	320	2.646
8	2	900	20	11	11	2.828
9	2	38720	704	243	384	3.000

Using CADEMO (*light* or DESIGNS) we can obtain smaller central composite designs and we can choose between designs with several sizes. We will demonstrate this by an example.

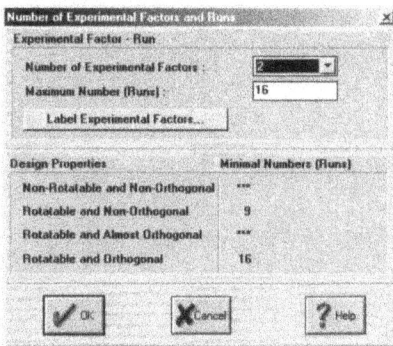

Figure 5.20 *Entry window in CADEMO for the construction of central composite designs*

But first we must follow in CADEMO-DESIGNS the command sequence: Experimental design – 2nd order Central Composite Design. This leads to Figure 5.20.

Example 5.11

In a laboratory experiment with a mini-harrow, the influence of 5 factors on the soil quality is to be investigated. The factors associated with adjustment of the harrow are speed (in the range (1; 3)), working depth (in (10; 30)) and tooth angle (in (–25; 25)). Soil factors are humidity (in (5; 20)), and density (in (0.5; 1.2)). For a D-optimal design we need, following Table 5.11, a total of 588 experimental units. For this CADEMO-DESIGNS constructs (non-optimal) central composite designs with 36, 27 and even 23 experimental units and informs us whether they are rotatable and/or orthogonal, or neither of these.

To do this, we choose the experimental designs option and activate "central composite designs".

In Figure 5.20 we have to enter the number of factors and the available number of experimental units, and if necessary the names of the factors and their units of measurement. Figure 5.21 gives an example.

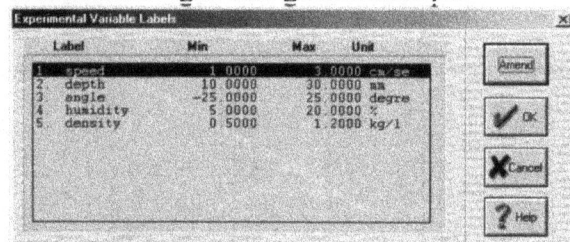

Figure 5.21 *CADEMO input for Example 5.11*

Then we obtain in Figure 5.22 the following experimental design and the associated plans.

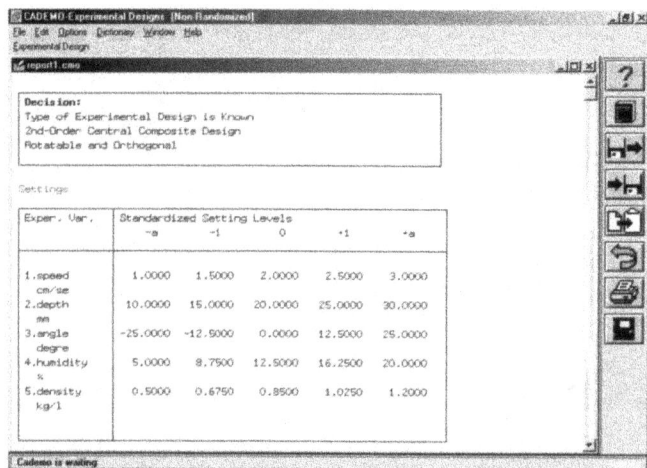

Figure 5.22 *First part of the CADEMO output for Example 5.11; the rest is in the accompanying text*

Design

Runs   Factors

	1	2	3	4	5
	Speed	Depth	Angle	Humidity	Density
	cm/se	cm	degree	%	kg/l
Cube Points					
1	1.5000	15.0000	-12.5000	8.7500	1.0250
2	2.5000	15.0000	-12.5000	8.7500	0.6750
3	1.5000	25.0000	-12.5000	8.7500	0.6750
4	2.5000	25.0000	-12.5000	8.7500	1.0250
5	1.5000	15.0000	12.5000	8.7500	0.6750
6	2.5000	15.0000	12.5000	8.7500	1.0250
7	1.5000	25.0000	12.5000	8.7500	1.0250
8	2.5000	25.0000	12.5000	8.7500	0.6750
9	1.5000	15.0000	-12.5000	16.2500	0.6750
10	2.5000	15.0000	-12.5000	16.2500	1.0250
11	1.5000	25.0000	-12.5000	16.2500	1.0250
12	2.5000	25.0000	-12.5000	16.2500	0.6750
13	1.5000	15.0000	12.5000	16.2500	1.0250
14	2.5000	15.0000	12.5000	16.2500	0.6750
15	1.5000	25.0000	12.5000	16.2500	0.6750
16	2.5000	25.0000	12.5000	16.2500	1.0250
Star Points					
17	1.0000	20.0000	0.0000	12.5000	0.8500
18	3.0000	20.0000	0.0000	12.5000	0.8500
19	2.0000	10.0000	0.0000	12.5000	0.8500
20	2.0000	30.0000	0.0000	12.5000	0.8500
21	2.0000	20.0000	-25.0000	12.5000	0.8500
22	2.0000	20.0000	25.0000	12.5000	0.8500
23	2.0000	20.0000	0.0000	5.0000	0.8500
24	2.0000	20.0000	0.0000	20.0000	0.8500
25	2.0000	20.0000	0.0000	12.5000	0.5000
26	2.0000	20.0000	0.0000	12.5000	1.2000
Centre Point					
27	2.0000	20.0000	0.0000	12.5000	0.8500

Replications

	# Points	# Replica per point	# Replica in Total
Cube Pts.	16	1	16
Star Pts.	10	1	10
Centre Pt.	1	1	1
Total	27		27

The expectation $E(y_j)$ of y_j in (5.50a) is called the expected quadratic *response surface*. Equation (5.50a) may be written in an alternative matrix version as

$$E(y_j) = \beta_0 + x_j^T A x_j + B^T x_j \ (j = 1, 2, ..., n),$$

(5.50b)

where $x_j = (x_{1j}, x_{2j}, ..., x_{kj})^T$ is a vector of the k factor-variables for the j-th observation; A is the $k \times k$ matrix of non-linear regression-parameters:

$$A = \begin{pmatrix} \beta_{11} & \cdots & \frac{1}{2}\beta_{1k} \\ \vdots & & \vdots \\ \frac{1}{2}\beta_{k1} & \cdots & \beta_{kk} \end{pmatrix} \text{ and } B = (\beta_1, \beta_2, ..., \beta_k)^T.$$

The parameters in (5.50a) or (5.50b) are estimated using the method of least squares. The estimates of the parameters are $\hat{A}$, $\hat{B}$ and $\hat{E}(y)$. We can use the expression for $\hat{E}(y)$ to find the optimum as a function of the independent variables $x_1, x_2, ..., x_k$.

Example 5.12

In a laboratory experiment to investigate the time t (in minutes) and temperature T (in °C) of a chemical process, we wish to get the maximum output. The response y is the chemical output in grams. We shall use the standardised notation, and the transformed quantitative variables are $x_1 = (t - 90 \text{ min.})/(10 \text{ min.})$ and $x_2 = (T - 145°C)/(5°C)$.

First a 2^2 experiment with factors x_1 and x_2 at the levels -1 and +1 is done. Then $n_c = 4$ observations are done at the centre point $(x_1, x_2) = (0, 0)$. Further observations are done once at each of the 4 star points $(x_1, x_2) : (-\sqrt{2}, 0), (+\sqrt{2}, 0), (0, -\sqrt{2})$ and $(0, +\sqrt{2})$. The experimental region is therefore

$(-\sqrt{2} \cdot 10 + 90; \sqrt{2} \cdot 10 + 90) = (75.86; 104.14)$ and

$(-\sqrt{2} \cdot 5 + 145; \sqrt{2} \cdot 5 + 145) = (137.93; 152.07)$.

The experiment is done in a randomised order. Note that the design is rotatable. The total number of experimental units is $2^2 + 2 \cdot 2 + 4 = n = 12$. Because $n_c = 4$, the design is not orthogonal; for orthogonality we need

$n_c^* = 4 \cdot \sqrt{1 \cdot 1 \cdot 2^2} + 2 \cdot 1 \cdot 0 = 8$ replications is the centre.

The observations are:

j	x_{1j}	x_{2j}	y_j
1	-1	-1	78.8
2	-1	1	91.2
3	1	-1	84.5
4	1	1	77.4
5	0	0	89.7
6	0	0	86.8
7	-1.4142	0	83.3
8	0	-1.4142	81.2
9	0	1.4142	79.5
10	1.4142	0	81.2
11	0	0	87.0
12	0	0	86.0

From this (for instance by SPSS as shown in Example 5.9) we obtain the estimated regression coefficients in (5.50): $b_0 = 87.37$, $b_1 = -1.38$, $b_2 = 0.36$, $b_{11} = -2.14$, $b_{22} = -3.09$, $b_{12} = -4.88$ and the estimated regression function

$$\hat{E}(y) = 87.37 - 1.38x_1 + 0.36x_2 - 2.14\,x_1^2 - 3.09\,x_2^2 - 4.88x_1x_2$$

and $SS(\text{Error}) = 24.0884$ with $12 - 6 = 6$ degrees of freedom. The estimate of σ^2 is (section 5.5) $s^2 = \dfrac{24.0884}{6} = 4.0144$.

From the estimated regression coefficients we find $\hat{A} = \begin{pmatrix} -2.14 & -\dfrac{1}{2} \cdot 4.88 \\ -\dfrac{1}{2} \cdot 4.88 & -3.09 \end{pmatrix}$

and $\hat{B}^T = (-1.38 \quad 0.36)$.

The maximum of the 2nd degree polynomial is found as $(x_1; x_2) = (-3.90; 3.14)$. Because this point lies outside the experimental range, a new experiment is recommended with as new centre point $(x_1, x_2) = (-3.9; 3.14)$ or in the experimental region at the point $(-3.9 \cdot 10 + 90; 3 \cdot 14 + 145) = (51; 160.7)$.

If we wish to find the optimum using SPSS, the program must be altered to SPSS-Program 3 using the Paste facility:

SPSS-Program 3

```
MATRIX.
COMPUTE A = {-2.14,-2.44;-2.44,-3.09}.
COMPUTE B={-1.38;0.36}.
COMPUTE XOPT=-0.5*INV(A)*B.
PRINT XOPT.
COMPUTE EIGVAL=EVAL(A).
PRINT EIGVAL.
END MATRIX.
```

Since the two eigenvalues -0.129195 and -5.100805 are negative, we have a maximum. If both the eigenvalues are positive we have a minimum, and if they have opposite signs, there is a saddle point.

5.8 Intrinsically Non-linear Regression

As well as polynomials there are also non-linear functions which are non-linear not only in the regressor variables but also non-linear in the parameters. We shall call such functions *intrinsically non-linear*, because they cannot be handled by the methods of multiple linear regression. In this topic we will restrict ourselves to some examples. The following functions play a special role in the theory of growth curves.

- the exponential function $f_E = \alpha + \beta e^{\gamma x}$
- the logistic function $f_L = \alpha/[1 + \beta e^{\gamma x}]$
- the Gompertz function $f_G = \alpha \exp(\beta e^{\gamma x})$.

In particular

- the Michaelis-Menten function $f_M = \alpha x / [1 + \beta x]$

is often used in biochemical applications.

These and further intrinsically non-linear functions are described in VB 4/35/0000 – 4/35/3003.

Example 5.10 -continued

We will estimate the parameters for the three above mentioned growth curve functions using the data in Example 5.10, and we will also construct optimal plans. We begin with the parameter estimation, and at the same time we obtain the residual variance in order to establish which model fits the data best. In this comparison we include the quadratic and cubic functions from section 5.6. The fitted functions have the following form

- the exponential function $\hat{y}_E = 132.96 - 56.42e^{-0.0677x}$

- the logistic function $\hat{y}_L = \dfrac{131.62}{1 + 0.7012e^{-0.0939x}}$

- the Gompertz function $\hat{y}_G = 132.19 \cdot e^{-0.5414e^{-0.0808x}}$

The estimated residual variances are:

Model	s^2
Quadratic	6.6816
Cubic	0.06258
Exponential	0.7606
Gompertz	0.2886
Logistic	0.1529

Therefore the cubic regression fits the data best, followed by the logistic function.

Often polynomials give a better fit than growth models. But polynomials are poor if the function has to be extrapolated outside the experimental region. This can be shown in our example. Figure 5.23 shows the fitted logistic function extrapolated up to an age of 80 months. Figure 5.24 shows the fitted cubic function extrapolated in the same region. It is clear that the growth of cattle between 60 and 80 months of age does not behave as the cubic regression suggests.

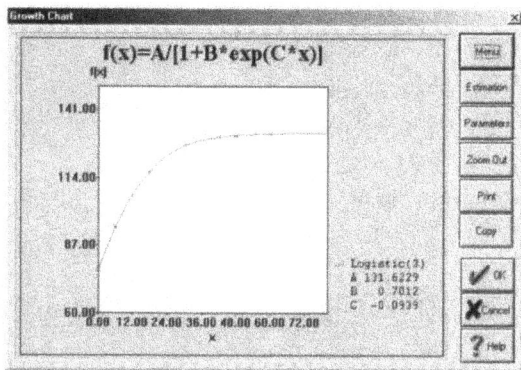

Figure 5.23 *Extrapolated logistic function for Example 5.10*

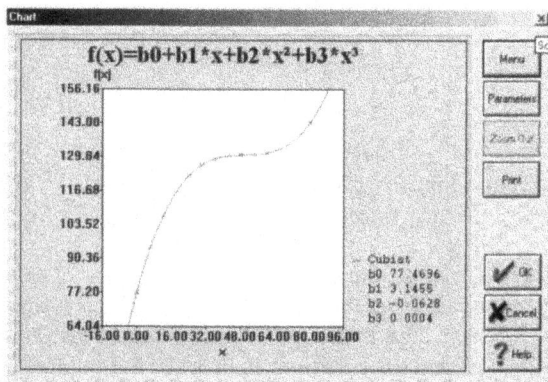

Figure 5.24 *Extrapolated cubic function for Example 5.10*

Table 5.11 shows how dangerous it may be if we extrapolate relations which have been reached by fitting data by polynomials outside the experimental region. We know that cattle are mature at about 5 years and will not grow very much after this age. Therefore the extrapolation with the intrinsically non-linear functions is reasonable.

Table 5.11 *Extrapolation of the non-linear functions fitted to the data of Example 5.10.*

Function	80 weeks	100 weeks
quadratic	104.01	60.18
cubic	143.88	188.05
exponential	132.71	132.90
Gompertz	132.08	132.17
logistic	131.57	131.62

Finally we give the *D*-optimal designs for 12 measurements in a future experiment in the interval [0; 60]. They are calculated from Table 5.9 (for the polynomials) and by the CADEMO-Module GROWTH.

Type of Function:	D-optimal Design

Quadratic
$$\begin{pmatrix} 0 & 30 & 60 \\ 4 & 4 & 4 \end{pmatrix}$$

Cubic
$$\begin{pmatrix} 0 & 16.6 & 43.4 & 60 \\ 3 & 3 & 3 & 3 \end{pmatrix}$$

Exponential
$$\begin{pmatrix} 0 & 13.7 & 60 \\ 4 & 4 & 4 \end{pmatrix}$$

Gompertz
$$\begin{pmatrix} 0 & 14.2 & 60 \\ 4 & 4 & 4 \end{pmatrix}$$

Logistic
$$\begin{pmatrix} 0 & 14.7 & 60 \\ 4 & 4 & 4 \end{pmatrix}$$

In the sequel we construct optimal designs (without restrictions) and optimal designs if at each design point we can measure only once – so – called replication – free designs (BOER et al. (2000)).

In the following example we show how to use SPSS to estimate the parameters of an intrinsically non-linear function. After entering the data we follow the menu sequence: Analyze – Regression – Nonlinear, and then enter the appropriate function into a dialog box such as Figure 5.25. We enter the starting values for the parameters as in Figure 5.26.

Example 5.13

Table 5.12 below contains the data from Table I from experiment 5 described in MICHAELIS und MENTEN (1913), in which the kinetics of the inversion effect were investigated (the dependent and independent variables are the rotation in degrees and the time in minutes respectively).

Table 5.12   Observations from a study by Michaelis and Menten (upper row time in minutes, lower row rotation in degrees).

Time (min)	0; 1	; 6	; 17	; 27	; 38	; 62	; 95	; 1372	; 1440
Rotation (deg)	0; 0.025;	0.117;	0.394;	0.537;	0.727;	0.877;	1.023	; 1.136;	1.178

We enter the data into the SPSS Data Editor and then as above select the Non-linear Regression procedure. We get Figure 5.25.

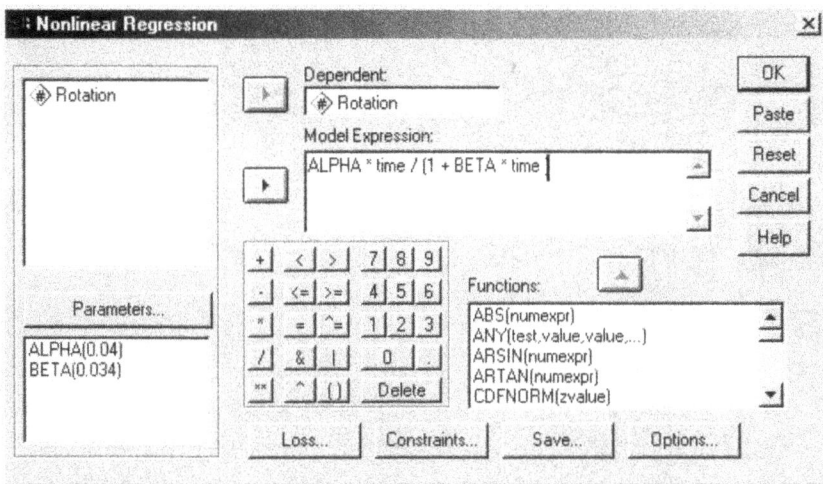

Figure 5.25 *SPSS-Dialog box for Non-linear Regression*

Next we click the Parameter button, which leads to Figure 5.26.

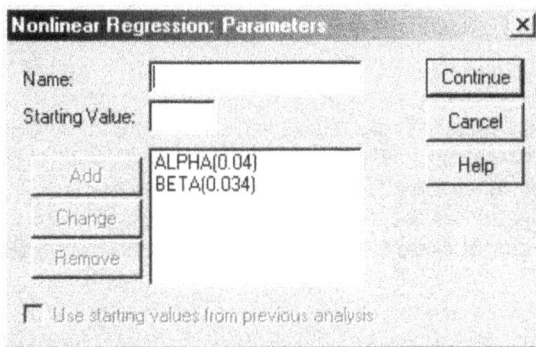

Figure 5.26 *SPSS-menu for parameter input*

Following BOER et al. (1999), we enter 0.04 and 0.034 as the starting values for the parameters alpha and beta respectively. We obtain the estimates 0.04135 and 0.03392. The values of Table 5.13 and the corresponding regression curve can be found in Figure 5.27.

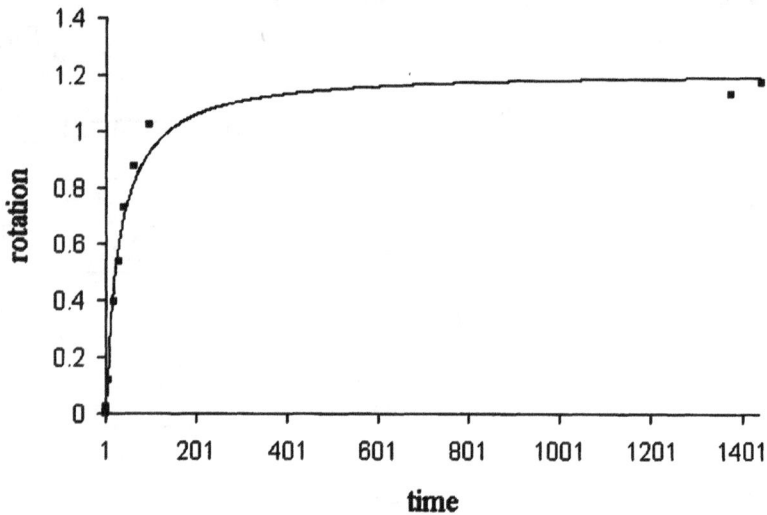

Figure 5.27 *Scatter-plot of the observations from Table 5.12 and the fitted function*

The locally optimal plans using a total of 10 measurements were obtained by BOER et al. (2000). The experimental region was (0;1440) for the unrestricted designs, and for the unreplicated locally optimal designs, the candidate set of possible experimental points was chosen as {5(1)35; 50;500; 800; 1000; 1200; 1300; 1435(1)1440}, where $a(1)b$ denotes the set of integers from a to b inclusive. For their optimality criteria the authors chose the D-optimal criterion and also the C-optimal criteria for estimation of both parameters. These led to the following designs:

Criterion	Optimal Design	Optimal replication-free Design
D	$\begin{pmatrix} 28.32 & 1440 \\ 5 & 5 \end{pmatrix}$	26,27,28,29,30,1436,1437,1438,1439,1440
C_1	$\begin{pmatrix} 21.55 & 1440 \\ 8 & 2 \end{pmatrix}$	18,19,20,21,22,23,24,25,26,1439,1440
C_2	$\begin{pmatrix} 20.29 & 1440 \\ 7 & 3 \end{pmatrix}$	18,19,20,21,22,23,24,1438,1439,1440

6 Theoretical Assumptions and their Practical Importance – the Robustness of Procedures

From time to time one sees concepts such as "theoretical" (or "mathematical"), and applied statistics. In the theory, it concerns the derivation of new theorems or procedures, such as for example statistical tests. For their exact validity, assumptions about the distribution of the random variables are necessary. We find these assumptions also in applied texts such as the present one, but do we for practical applications really need them?

As an example, we consider the comparison of two expectations. The two-sample t-test is based on a test statistic, which has a t-distribution with a non-centrality parameter (which is zero if the expectations are equal), provided that the random variables in the two populations are independent of each other and are normally distributed with equal variances.

Before using this test, should we test the normality of the distributions and the equality of variances using so-called pre-tests? There are two theoretical arguments against this. Furthermore we shall see below that there is an empirical third argument based on simulation.

Counter-argument 1

Pre-tests are mostly carried out on the same material as that used for the comparison of means. Thus the pre- and main tests are not independent; the overall risks (of the first and second kind) cannot be exactly calculated. We shall now demonstrate the problems that arise when two tests follow each other. Test 1 is the pre-test, Test 2 the main test. Consider Figure 6.1

Test 1 $H_0^!$ against $H_A^!$

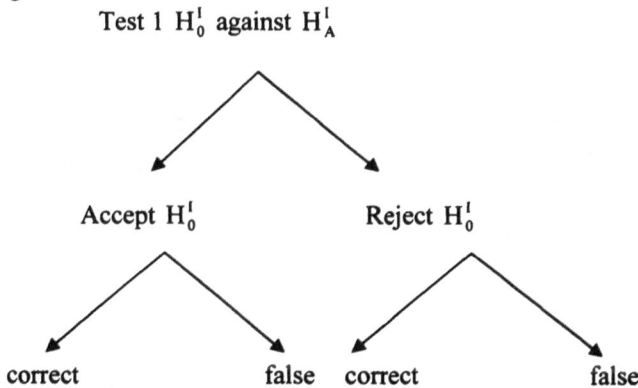

Accept $H_0^!$ Reject $H_0^!$

correct   false   correct   false

Figure 6.1 *Schema for the outcomes of a pre-test*

If $H_0^!$ is accepted, Test 2 is carried out, otherwise not. The risks of the first and second kind in Test 2 are connected, in a manner not clear to the user, with the risk of the second kind in Test 1. Therefore these risks are unknown. Conclusion: pre-tests on the same material lead to indeterminable risks in the main test.

Counter-argument 2

The spirit of the pre-test is to carry out the main test only whenever the first null hypothesis (that we have normal distributions and/or we have equal variances) of the pre-test(s) is accepted. In order to keep the risk of the 2nd kind sufficiently low, we have to plan the size of the experiment appropriately. Aside from the theoretical difficulties (which, in the case of tests about distributions for example, arise because of the difficulties of determining a "distance" from the null hypothesis), because of the lack of power of the tests available for the pre-test, we would end up with a far greater size of experiment than would be necessary for the actual (main) test. How many experimenters are going to accept that?

And what happens to the observations, when the pre-test leads to the rejection of the assumptions? Often a non-parametric test such as the Wilcoxon-Mann-Whitney test is recommended. This is sensitive not only to differences between the means, but also to those in all higher moments (which include the variances). It has been shown (see RASCH et al. (2007)) that when the variances are unequal, the Wilcoxon test gives significant differences too often. Thus the desired risk of the first kind, which we call the nominal α_{nom}, is not maintained.

Counter-argument 3 - robustness of statistical procedures when the assumptions are not fulfilled

As we have seen, when we use pre-tests we cannot achieve the desired values of the prerequisite error probabilities. Therefore in applications we can give up at the outset any exact specification of these risks, and as RASCH and GUIARD (2004) and RASCH et al. (2007) describe, make use of the following definition.

Definition 6.1
Given a confidence estimate d_α based on an experimental design V_n of size n for a Parameter θ from a class G of distributions with nominal confidence coefficient $1-\alpha_{nom}$ $(0 < \alpha_{nom} < 1)$ in G. For an element $h \in H \supset G$ from a class H of distributions which includes G, let $1-\alpha(V, h)$ be the actual confidence coefficient for d_α. Then we say d_α is ε-robust in H when

$$\underset{h \in H}{\text{Max}} \left| \alpha - \alpha(V,h) \right| \leq \varepsilon \tag{6.1}$$

Similarly we can define ε-robustness for tests or selection procedures. Since we can test a null hypothesis $H_0 : \theta = \theta_0$ so that we accept H_0 when θ_0 lies in a confidence interval constructed with confidence coefficient $1 - \alpha_{nom}$ corresponding to the risk of the first kind, and otherwise reject H_0, Definition 6.1 also covers the ε-robustness of tests as regards the risk of the 1st kind.

RASCH and GUIARD (2004) and RASCH et al. (2007) have summarised and evaluated the results, of a 10-year research programme carried out by a large group of researchers from several institutions. We refer to these articles and give here only a bare summary. We choose the class H as the class of distributions of continuous random variables, and G as the class of normal distributions, and it is sufficient if

$$\underset{h \in H}{\text{Max}} \left| \alpha_{nom} - \alpha(V,h) \right| \leq 0.2\alpha_{nom} \tag{6.2}$$

- a so-called 20%-robustness – holds. The numerous simulation studies described in RASCH and GUIARD (2004) and RASCH et al. (2007) (based on more than 10 000 samples) gave the following results: all t–tests (one-, two- and k-sample problems) and also the F-tests in the analysis of variance for the location parameter, are 20%-robust. This means that if $\alpha = 0.05$, then $0.04 \leq \alpha_{act} \leq 0.06$ holds. On the other hand the F-test for the equality of two variances is extremely sensitive to non-normality of the distributions. The Levene test, which as a result of this is now used in SPSS in place of the original F-test, has been shown to be 20%-robust. Analogous results on the importance of the heterogeneity of variances can be found in the above-mentioned articles, and also advice on when to use the Welch test instead of the t-test. In RASCH et al. (2007) it was shown that the t-test works quite well even for ordinal categorical variables.

Appendix A   Symbols

$Y_{i.} = y_{i.} = \sum\limits_{j=1}^{n_i} y_{ij}$ A point in the place of a suffix indicates summation over that suffix. In addition the letter may be capitalised

p Probability of a single event, general probability, proportion, the parameter of a binomial distribution

f, df Degrees of freedom

x, y, χ^2, F, s^2, r Random variables are printed bold; their realisations are indicated by the same letters printed normally

$u = \dfrac{y - \mu}{\sigma}$ Standardised random variable

e Random error, error component in a model

n Sample size, experiment size

N Size of a finite population, total size of several samples

$\ln$ Natural logarithm

$f(y)$ Density function of a continuous random variable y

$\Phi(u)$ Distribution function of the Standard Normal distribution

$\phi(u)$ Density function of the Standard Normal distribution

$N(\mu; \sigma^2)$ Abbreviation for a Normal distribution with expectation (mean) μ and variance σ^2

$N(0; 1)$ Abbreviation for the Standard Normal distribution $(\mu = 0, \sigma^2 = 1)$

$u(P), z(P)$ P-quantile of the $N(0; 1)$ distribution

$t(f; P)$ P-quantile of the t distribution with f degrees of freedom

$\chi^2(f; P)$ P-quantile of the χ^2 distribution with f degrees of freedom

$F(f_1; f_2; P)$ P-quantile of the F distribution with f_1 and f_2 degrees of freedom

Ω Parameter space

θ Notation for an undetermined parameter. The intra-class correlation coefficient

$\hat{\boldsymbol\theta}$ Estimating function for (estimator for) θ

$\hat\theta$ Estimate of θ (realization of $\hat{\boldsymbol\theta}$)

$E(y) = \mu_y = \mu$ Expectation (mean) of the random variable y

$\text{var}(y) = \sigma_y^2 = \sigma^2$ Variance of the random variable y

$$\bar{y}_. = \bar{y} = \frac{1}{n} \sum_{i=1}^{n} y_i$$ Arithmetic mean of the sample values

$$\bar{y}_. = \frac{1}{n} \sum_{i=1}^{n} y_i$$ Arithmetic mean of the random variables y_i, estimator for μ

$s = \sqrt{s^2}$ Estimate of $\sigma = \sqrt{\sigma^2}$

$\sigma_y = \sigma$ Standard deviation of the random variable y

$s_y = s$ Estimator for σ_y

$\mu_r = E[(y-\mu)^r]$ r-th central moment of a one dimensional random variable

$$m_r = \frac{1}{n} \sum_{i=1}^{n} (y_i - \bar{y}_.)^r$$ r-th central sample moment, estimator for μ_r

$$\gamma_1 = \frac{\mu_3}{\mu_2^{3/2}}$$ Skewness

$$g_1 = \frac{m_3}{m_2^{3/2}}$$ Sample skewness, estimator for γ_1 (in SPSS see page 34)

$$\gamma_2 = \frac{\mu_4}{\mu_2^2} - 3$$ Kurtosis

$$g_2 = \frac{m_4}{m_2^2} - 3$$ Sample kurtosis, estimator for γ_2 (in SPSS see page 35)

$\text{cov}(x,y) = \sigma_{xy}$ Covariance between two random variables x and y

$s_{xy} = \hat{\text{cov}}(x, y)$ Sample covariance, estimator for σ_{xy}

ρ Simple (product-moment) correlation coefficient

r Simple sample correlation coefficient, estimator for ρ

σ_a^2 Variance component of the factor A

$s_a^2, \hat{\sigma}_a^2$ Estimator for the variance component of the factor A

MSE   Mean square error $E[(\hat{\theta} - \theta)^2]$

β_i Regression coefficient

$b_i, \hat{\beta}_i$ Sample regression coefficient, estimator for β_i

H_0	Null hypothesis
H_A	Alternative hypothesis
α	Risk of the first kind in a statistical test (Type I error probability)
$1-\alpha$	Confidence coefficient
β, β'	Risk of the second kind (Type II error probability); risk in selection problems.
β'	Predetermined upper bound for β
$1-\beta$	Power of a test, probability of the correct choice in a selection problem
d	Least difference of practical interest in tests for a location parameter, expected half length in confidence intervals for a location
$(a;b)$	Confidence interval with limits a and b
$(a;b)$	Realisation of the confidence interval $(a;b)$
$A \succ B, B \prec A$	The factor B is nested within factor A
$A \times B$	The factors A and B are cross-classified
SS_x, SS	Sum of squares of the deviations from the mean (corrected sum of squares) for the variable x
MS	Mean square (of deviations from the mean)
$E(MS)$	Expectation of the MS
BIB	Balanced incomplete block design
PBIB	Partially balanced incomplete block design
$CEIL(x)$	Ceiling operator, equals x, if x is an integer, otherwise it is the integer part of $x + 1$

Appendix B Fundamentals in Statistics – Overview

The mathematics of stochastics was developed to handle random phenomena. It consists of two parts: probability theory and mathematical statistics.

B.1 Descriptive Statistics

Descriptive statistics deals with the description of data (independently of whether they stem from populations or samples). It thus forms the basis of inferential statistics. Data description includes both numerical and graphical methods.

B.1.1 Population

A population (or universe) is a set of elements in a well-defined environment at a given time. There must be a so-called operational definition of the population, so that it is possible to decide whether any element belongs to it or not. We can measure certain characteristics of the elements of the population; the result of such a measurement is called an observed value, or observation for short. Interest in statistics often lies in the set of measurements taken from the elements of the population, and this set of observations will often also be called the population (strictly it is the population of observations). The number of elements in the population is usually denoted by N and is called the population size. In practice populations are finite. In statistical theory populations are often assumed to be infinite. This is a good model, if N is large.

B.1.2 Population Mean and Variance

One of the first objectives of statistics is to summarise a population of N observations, $\{Y_1, Y_2, ..., Y_N\}$.
A measure of the location of the distribution of these observations is the *population mean*, also called the *expectation* or *expected value*. This is calculated as the arithmetic mean of the observations and is denoted by the symbol μ:

$$\mu = \sum_{i=1}^{N} Y_i / N .\tag{B.1}$$

A generalisation for general populations (distributions) can be found in section B.2.4.
A measure of how the distribution of observations is spread is called the *variance* of the population, or more strictly the *population variance*. This is calculated as the arithmetic mean of the squared deviations of the observations from the population mean. The variance is denoted by the symbol σ^2:

$$\sigma^2 = \sum_{i=1}^{N} (Y_i - \mu)^2 / N = \left[\sum_{i=1}^{N} Y_i^2 - \left(\sum_{i=1}^{N} Y_i \right)^2 / N \right] / N \tag{B.2}$$

The dimension of the variance is the square of the dimension of the measurements. Therefore the square root of the variance, called the *standard deviation* is often used. The standard deviation is denoted by σ.

Usually the two measures population mean and population variance are not sufficient to describe the population completely. Two further measures which are used are firstly the *skewness*, which gives one way of measuring how lop-sided the distribution is (more precisely it measures to what extent the distribution is asymmetrical about the mean). Secondly the *kurtosis* measures how "peaked" the distribution is in comparison with the normal or Gaussian distribution.) These two measures are introduced and handled in detail in chapter 3, section 3.1.

Example B.1

The population consists of {3,4,4,5,5,5,5,6,6,7}, so that $N = 10$. We can summarise these observations in a *frequency table*. To do this we first look at how many different values there are in the population. In this example we have five different values namely 3,4,5,6 and 7. The number of different values of the population is denoted by M. Here $M = 5$.

Table B.1   Frequency Table for Example B.1.

Y_i	f_i	f_i/N
3	1	0.1
4	2	0.2
5	4	0.4
6	2	0.2
7	1	0.1
Σ	10	1

f_i is called *frequency* and counts the number of times a certain observation Y_i occurs; f_i/N is called the *relative frequency*.

We find $\mu = 5$ and $\sigma^2 = 1.2$ for this distribution because

$$\sum_{i=1}^{10} Y_i = 50, \quad \sum_{i=1}^{10} Y_i^2 = 262, \text{ hence } \mu = 50/10 = 5.$$

$$\sigma^2 = (262-50^2/10)/10 = (262-250)/10 = 12/10 = 1.2.$$

If we have the frequency table available, the calculation of μ and σ^2 is easier using the following formulae:

$$\mu = \sum_{i=1}^{M} f_i Y_i / N \qquad\qquad (B.3)$$

$$\sigma^2 = (\sum_{i=1}^{M} f_i Y_i^2 - (\sum_{i=1}^{M} f_i Y_i)^2 / N)/ N \qquad\qquad (B.4)$$

where $N = \sum_{i=1}^{M} f_i$.

B.1.3 Graphical Description

The graphical procedures described in this section can be used equally for the values of a finite population and for the values of a sample.

A graph of the distribution can be a **bar graph** where the height of a bar represents the frequency (or relative frequency) of the corresponding value. A bar graph for the data of Example B.1 is shown in Figure B.1.

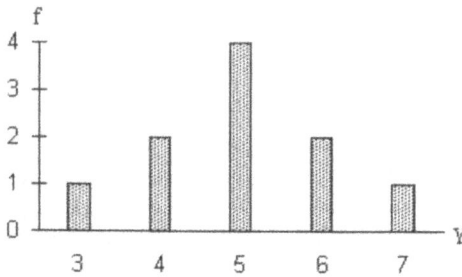

Figure B.1   *Bar graph for Example B.1*

Another quick and easy way to picture the shape of a distribution is offered by *stem-plots* (also called *stem-and-leaf* plots). The actual numerical values of the population (or the sample) are included in the graph. A stem-plot is mainly used for small numbers of observations that are all greater than zero. To construct a stem-plot each observation has to be split into a *stem* (often the first digits) and a *leaf* (the last digit). Then the stems are listed vertically in increasing order from top to bottom and a vertical line is drawn to the right of them. After this each leaf is added to the right of its stem. Usually the leaves are also arranged in increasing order from left to right within each stem.

Let us consider an example.

Example B.2

In Table B.2 we find withers height in cm of 30 calves. Let us define the metres and decimetres to be the stems, and the last digit (centimetres) as the leaves. Then we have the following stems:

9
10
11
12

Table B.2   *Withers height (in cm) of 30 Holstein-Friesian calves.*

108	103	103
112	106	113
111	114	102
112	123	115
100	105	92
104	97	105
106	105	97
109	108	94
119	102	102
102	110	100

There are four observations between 90 and 100 cm starting with the digit nine. They are 97, 92, 97 and 94. Thus the four leaves are 7, 2, 7 and 4, or, when ordered 2, 4, 7 and 7. These four digits are now written to the right of the vertical line, next to the nine.

The first row of the stem-plot is therefore 9 | 2477.

We proceed in the same way with the three other rows and obtain Figure B.2.

```
 9 | 2477
10 | 00222233455566889
11 | 01223459
12 | 3
```

Figure B.2   *Stem and leaf plot for Example B.2*

We can use a stem-plot to find the centre of the distribution; we can examine its shape, especially the number of peaks (modes) and whether the distribution is approximately symmetric.

Let us now assume that we learn that the first 15 entries of Table B.2 (i.e. the first column and the first 5 entries of the second column) are observations from male calves and the remaining ones from female calves. Then we can arrange the leaves of the male calves on the left hand side and the leaves of the female calves on the right hand side of the stems (we only have to draw a second vertical line left of the stems). This gives us more information and is shown in Figure B.3 (male leaves ordered from right to left)

```
male leaves   stem    female leaves

            |  9 | 2477
  986654320 | 10 | 02223558
      94221 | 11 | 035
          3 | 12 |
```

Figure B.3 *Stem-plot for Example B.2 for male and female calves separately*

It seems that the male calves are a little larger than female ones, the distribution of the females is symmetric, but the distribution of the males is skew.

B.1.4   A Rule of Thumb

The importance of the mean μ and standard deviation σ is shown by the following statement (*Tschebyscheff's inequality*).
For every (frequency) distribution the proportion of observations lying in the interval
$I = [\mu - 2\sigma, \mu + 2\sigma]$ or $I = \{\mu - 2\sigma \leq Y \leq \mu + 2\sigma\}$ is at least 0.75.
This is equivalent to saying that the proportion of observations of Y lying outside this interval I is at most 0.25, or the proportion of observations in the intervals $\{Y < \mu - 2\sigma$ or $Y > \mu + 2\sigma\}$ is at most 0.25.
This statement is in fact rather weak and is only useful for theoretical purposes; in practice we use the following rule of thumb:
About 5% of the observations lie outside the interval $I = \{\mu - 2\sigma \leq Y \leq \mu + 2\sigma\}$ or the relative frequency of observations $\{Y < \mu - 2\sigma$ or $Y > \mu + 2\sigma\}$ is about 0.05.

Example B.2 - continued

In Example B.2 we find $\mu = 105.97$ and $\sigma = 6.94$; thus $\mu + 2\sigma = 119.85$ and $\mu - 2\sigma = 92.09$. In table B2 one value is less than 92.09 and one is greater than 119.85. Thus the proportion lying outside the interval $I = \{\mu - 2\sigma \leq Y \leq \mu + 2\sigma\}$ is $2/30 = 0.067$ i.e. about 5%.

B.2   Frequencies and Probabilities

B.2.1   Introduction

If we take an element of a population *at random*, we use a procedure in which each element has the same probability (or chance) of being chosen. But what is this concept of probability? If we consider N elements and determine how often certain events A_i occur, then we call the number of elements with the event A_i the *absolute frequency* f_i of A_i. In many practical situations the *relative frequencies* $\dfrac{f_i}{N}$ have the property that with increasing N their values vary less and become nearly constant. The constant value to which the relative frequency of an event approaches is called the *probability* of that event. Probability theory has its roots in the mathematical analysis of gambling in the 17th and 18th centuries.

We think of the probability of a certain event as a mathematical abstraction of the relative frequency (r.f.) of this event. The r.f. is associated with events which are neither certain nor impossible, so-called random events (the r.f. of a certain event equals 1 and that of an impossible event equals 0).

Example B.3

We consider two such random events:

Event A: The yield of winter wheat (per ha) is larger than 33 dt.
Event B: The average height of winter wheat plants per plot is larger than 120 cm.

Table B.4 contains some possible results from a survey.

Table B.4   Distribution of yield and height of 1000 plot yields of winter wheat.

Height (cm)	Yield (dt/ha)		
	$\overline{A}: \leq 33$	$A: > 33$	Total
$\overline{B}: \leq 120$	700	100	800
$B: > 120$	150	50	200
Total	850	150	1000

$\overline{A}$ and $\overline{B}$ are called the complementary events of A and B respectively ($\overline{A}$ means: "not A").

We denote the r.f. of an event E by $f(E)$.

B.2.2   Combining Frequencies and Probabilities

We will develop the rules for combining relative frequencies and then transfer these to probabilities.

B.2.2.1   Properties of Relative Frequencies

<u>Property 1</u>   The r.f. of an event E is a real number between 0 and 1

$$0 \leq f(E) \leq 1 \tag{B.5}$$

In Example B.3 we have

$$f(A) = \frac{150}{1000} = 0.15,$$

$$f(B) = \frac{200}{1000} = 0.20.$$

<u>Property 2</u>   The r.f. $f(\overline{E})$ of the complementary event $\overline{E}$ of E is

$$f(\overline{E}) = 1 - f(E) \tag{B.6}$$

Again in Example B.3 we have

$$f(\overline{A}) = \frac{850}{1000} = 0.85 = 1 - f(A),$$

$$f(\overline{B}) = \frac{800}{1000} = 0.8 = 1 - f(B).$$

We now describe some operations on events.

The *union* (or sum) of two events A and B is denoted by $A \cup B$ and is the event that either A or B (or both) occurs.

The *intersection* (or product) of two events A and B is denoted by $A \cap B$ and is the event that A and B occur together.

We denote an event that will never occur (Impossible event) by I and an event that always occurs (Certain event) by C. Then the following are true:

$$A \cup \bar{A} = C \qquad A \cap \bar{A} = I$$

(Either A occurs or it does not, and it is impossible for A to occur and not occur at the same time, see Figure B.4).

Also $\bar{C} = I$ and $\bar{I} = C$.

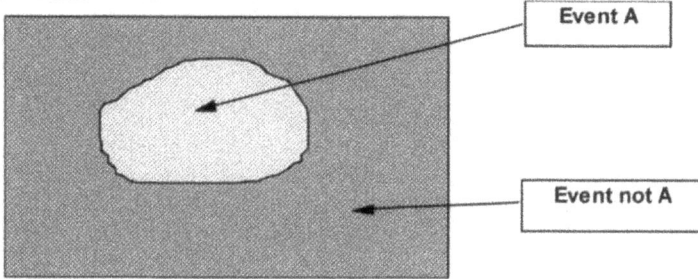

Figure B.4 *Events A and $\bar{A}$*

We see that

$$f(C) = 1$$

and therefore by (B.6)

$$f(I) = 1 - f(C) = 0.$$

Property 3

$$f(A \cup B) = f(A) + f(B) - f(A \cap B) \tag{B.7}$$

If two events A and B cannot occur together $((A \cap B) = I)$ then A and B are said to be *exclusive* (or mutually exclusive or *disjoint*). If A and B are exclusive then (B.7) reduces to:

$$f(A \cup B) = f(A) + f(B) \tag{B.7a}$$

In example B.3 $A \cup B$ is the event that either the yield is larger than 33 or the height is larger than 120. The r.f. of plots with $A \cap B$ (yield > 33 as well as height > 120) is found in Example B.3 to be

$$f(A \cap B) = \frac{50}{1000} = 0.05.$$

215

Therefore we get

$$f(A \cup B) = 0.15 + 0.20 - 0.05 = 0.30.$$

If we know that a plot has a yield > 33 what is the r.f. of B?
We have 150 plots with yield > 33, and 50 of them have a height > 120.
Therefore the r.f. of B given A (this event is denoted by $B|A$) is

$$f(B|A) \; = \; \frac{50}{150} \; = \; 0.333. \tag{B.8}$$

The events $A|B$ and $B|A$ are called conditional events, $f(B|A)$ and $f(A|B)$ are called conditional relative frequencies.

Property 4

If $f(B) > 0$ we have

$$f(A|B) \; = \; \frac{f(A \cap B)}{f(B)} \tag{B.9}$$

and if $f(A) > 0$ analogously

$$f(B|A) \; = \; \frac{f(A \cap B)}{f(A)} \tag{B.10}$$

Thus we can express $f(A \cap B)$ as

$$f(A \cap B) = f(A|B) \cdot f(B) = f(B|A) \cdot f(A) \tag{B.11}$$

Two events A and B are called *independent*, if $f(B|A) = f(B)$ and $f(A|B) = f(A)$ and this implies

$$f(A \cap B) = f(A) \cdot f(B) \tag{B.12}$$

In Example B.3 we have

$$f(A \cap B) \; = \; \frac{50}{1000} \; = \; 0.05$$

and therefore A and B are dependent because

$$0.05 = f(A \cap B) \neq f(A) \cdot f(B) = 0.15 \cdot 0.2 = 0.03,$$

so we can say that height and yield are not independent.

B.2.2.2 Probabilities

The "generalised relative frequency" or *probability* $P(A)$ of any event A is a real number having the properties 1 to 4 (strictly (B.7a) must be generalised to a countably infinite number of exclusive events).

Example B.4

Consider a gene locus in a population of people, animals or plants. At this locus two alleles A and a may occur at the same time, we call this diploid. We consider A to be the event that A occurs and a as the event that a occurs. The pair of alleles that occupy the two places at the locus are called the genotype. Since there are only two alleles $a = \overline{A}$ and $A = \overline{a}$.

In populations with random mating we only need to know the long run relative frequency i.e. probability $P(A)$ of the occurrence of the allele A to be able to compute the genotype probabilities using the four rules for combining probabilities. We assume $P(A) = 0.7$. If we have random mating and no inbreeding the events that a particular allele comes from the father or from the mother are independent. Let A_F, a_F denote the alleles A and a stemming from the father and A_M, a_M the alleles stemming from the mother. An offspring gets one allele from the mother and one allele from the father.

The genotype AA is $A_F \cap A_M$ and therefore if $P(A_F) = P(A_M) = P(A) = 0.7$ we have from (B.12) (independence)

$$P(AA) = P(A_F \cap A_M) = 0.7 \cdot 0.7 = 0.49.$$

The genotype Aa is

$$Aa = (A_F \cap a_M) \cup (A_M \cap a_F)$$

$P(a) = 1 - P(A) = 0.3$ from (B.6), and, because the two intersections are exclusive:

$$P(Aa) = P(A_F \cap a_M) + P(A_M \cap a_F) = 0.7 \cdot 0.3 + 0.7 \cdot 0.3 = 0.42 \text{ from (B.7a)}.$$

The genotype aa is

$$aa = a_F \cap a_M$$

and so

$$P(aa) = P(a_F \cap a_M) = 0.3 \cdot 0.3 = 0.09$$

Because $AA \cup Aa \cup aa = C$ we may check

$$1 = P(C) = P(AA) + P(Aa) + P(aa) = 0.49 + 0.42 + 0.09$$

The principle of independent segregation in genetics states that the parent transmits one of its two alleles randomly to its offspring. Thus in the mating $Aa \cdot Aa$ the probability that the father transmits A to the offspring is $1/2$ and the probability that the mother transmits A is 1/2, so that the probability that the offspring is AA is:

$$P \text{ (offspring is } AA) = P \text{ (father transmits } A) \cdot P \text{ (mother transmits } A)$$
$$= 1/2 \cdot 1/2 = 1/4.$$

Suppose we have a population with the following distribution of genotypes:

genotypes	AA	Aa	aa
probability	p	$2q$	r

We pick two individuals at random and cross them. What is the probability of the compound event that the mating is $Aa \cdot Aa$ and the offspring is AA? The event that the mating is $Aa \cdot Aa$ will be denoted by E, and the event that the offspring is AA as event F. Then $P(E \cap F) = P(E) \cap P(F \mid E)$.
But: $P(E) = P(Aa \cap Aa) = P(Aa) \cdot P(Aa) = 2q \cdot 2q = 4q^2$.
We know that the probability that the mating $Aa \cdot Aa$ produces offspring AA is 1/4; in other words $P(F \mid E) = 1/4$.
So we have $P(E \cap F) = P$ (mating is $Aa \cdot Aa$ and offspring is AA) $= 4q^2 \cdot 1/4 = q^2$.

B.2.3 Probability Distributions

B.2.3.1 Definitions

In this section we describe the relationship between random events and random variables.

Example B.4 continued

An individual is the offspring of parents, both of whom have genotype Aa. The possible events are:

$E = $ (offspring is AA or has $x = 2$ A alleles)
$F = $ (offspring is Aa or has $x = 1$ A allele)
$G = $ (offspring is aa or has $x = 0$ A allele).

The probabilities are $P(E) = 1/2 \cdot 1/2 = 1/4$; $P(F) = 2 \cdot 1/2 \cdot 1/2 = 1/2$ and $P(G) = 1/2 \cdot 1/2 = 1/4$, which can be represented graphically as in Figure B.5:

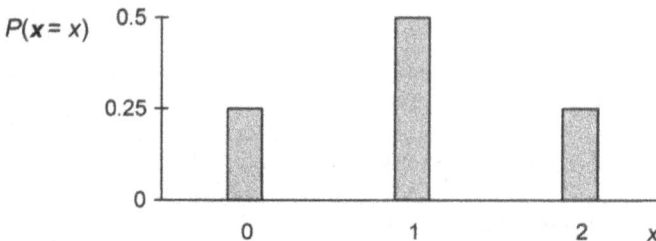

Figure B.5 *Probabilities of the distribution of the number of A-alleles*

Here we have expressed these events in terms of the number of A alleles present. This is a numerical description rather than a verbal one.

We call such a numeric function of the outcomes of an experiment of chance a *random variable* and denote it by using bold type for the letter which represents it. In this example the random variable is x, the number of A alleles and the possible outcomes of x are: $x = 0$, $x = 1$ or $x = 2$. (If the random variable x has an outcome, this is denoted by the letter x without being bold).

If the number of possible values of a random variable is (countably) finite, this random variable is called a discrete (random) variable.

In Figure B.5 the graph of the *probability function* of x is given, $P(x = x)$ for all possible values of x; thus $P(x = 0) = 1/4$, $P(x = 1) = 1/2$, $P(x = 2) = 1/4$.

For a random variable x we define the *distribution function* $F(x)$ by $F(x) = P(x \leq x)$. In Example B.4 the *discrete* variable x has the following distribution function:

$F(0) = P(x \leq 0) = P(x = 0) = 1/4$;

$F(1) = P(x \leq 1) = P(x = 0) + P(x = 1) = 3/4$ and

$F(2) = P(x \leq 2) = P(x = 0) + P(x = 1) + P(x = 2) = 1$.

The distribution function $F(x)$ can be used, e.g., to find the probability that a random variable lies between two values: $P(a < x \leq b) = P(x \leq b) - P(x \leq a) = F(b) - F(a)$.

A well-known variable arises in the following situation: consider n identical, independent trials of an experiment and let p denote the probability that a certain event E occurs as the outcome of a trial; the event E is usually called "success". The number of successes in the n trials is a random variable x with possible values $0, 1, ..., n$, and the probability function is defined by:

$$P(k \text{ successes in } n \text{ trials})$$

$$= P(x = k) = \binom{n}{k} p^k (1 - p)^{n-k}, \quad \text{for } k = 0, 1, 2, ..., n \qquad (B.13)$$

where

$$\binom{n}{k} = \frac{n \cdot (n-1)...(n-(k-1))}{k \cdot (k-1)...1} = \frac{n!}{(n-k)! k!}$$

and $k! = k \cdot (k-1) \cdot (k-2) ... 1$ and $0!$ is defined as 1.

To see this we consider all possible sequences of E's and not-E's. The probability assigned to any sequence having exactly k E's is $p^k(1-p)^{n-k}$. All of the $\binom{n}{k}$ sequences having exactly k E's would assign the value k to the random variable x, and the probability of that value k is the sum of these $\binom{n}{k}$ terms $p^k(1-p)^{n-k}$ corresponding to those sequences.

A variable x with probability function $P(x = k) = \binom{n}{k} p^k (1 - p)^{n-k}$, for $k = 0,1,2, ..., n$, $0 < p < 1$ is called a *binomial variable* with *parameters n and p*, or equivalently x is said to have a *binomial distribution*.

Example B.5

Suppose we randomly select 6 cards (with replacement) from an ordinary pack of playing cards. The probability of drawing a heart at any stage is 1/4. The number

k of hearts drawn in the six trials is a binomial variable with the parameters $n = 6$ and $p = 1/4$;

$$P(k = 0) = \binom{6}{0}\left(\frac{1}{4}\right)^0\left(\frac{3}{4}\right)^6 = \left(\frac{3}{4}\right)^6 = \frac{729}{4096} = 0.1780$$

$$P(k = 1) = \binom{6}{1}\left(\frac{1}{4}\right)^1\left(\frac{3}{4}\right)^5 = 6\left(\frac{1}{4}\right)\left(\frac{3}{4}\right)^5 = \frac{1458}{4096} = 0.3560$$

$$P(k = 2) = \binom{6}{2}\left(\frac{1}{4}\right)^2\left(\frac{3}{4}\right)^4 = 15\left(\frac{1}{4}\right)^2\left(\frac{3}{4}\right)^4 = \frac{1215}{4096} = 0.2966$$

$$P(k = 3) = \binom{6}{3}\left(\frac{1}{4}\right)^3\left(\frac{3}{4}\right)^3 = 20\left(\frac{1}{4}\right)^3\left(\frac{3}{4}\right)^3 = \frac{540}{4096} = 0.1318$$

$$P(k = 4) = \binom{6}{4}\left(\frac{1}{4}\right)^4\left(\frac{3}{4}\right)^2 = 15\left(\frac{1}{4}\right)^4\left(\frac{3}{4}\right)^2 = \frac{135}{4096} = 0.0330$$

$$P(k = 5) = \binom{6}{5}\left(\frac{1}{4}\right)^5\left(\frac{3}{4}\right)^1 = 6\left(\frac{1}{4}\right)^5\left(\frac{3}{4}\right) = \frac{18}{4096} = 0.0044$$

$$P(k = 6) = \binom{6}{6}\left(\frac{1}{4}\right)^6\left(\frac{3}{4}\right)^0 = \left(\frac{1}{4}\right)^6 = \frac{1}{4096} = 0.0002$$

Total   1.0000

We see that $k = 1$ is the most probable number of hearts drawn, because $P(k = 1)$ is the largest probability. The most probable number is called the *mode* of the distribution.

In a more general situation, suppose that we make n independent trials and that there are t possible exclusive results, say $E_1, E_2, ..., E_t$ with probabilities $p_1, p_2, ..., p_t$ and $\sum_{j=1}^{t} p_j = 1$. The probability that we shall get n_1 times E_1, n_2 times E_2, etc. is given by:

$$\frac{n!}{n_1! n_2! ... n_t!} p_1^{n_1} p_2^{n_2} ... p_t^{n_t} , \quad n_1 + n_2 + ... + n_t = n.$$

This reduces to (B.13) for $t = 2$, $n_1 = k$, $n_2 = n-k$, $p_1 = p$, $p_2 = 1-p$.

The binomial distribution is a discrete distribution and it can only take a finite number of values (0, 1, 2, ..., n). There also exist discrete distributions which can take a countably infinite number of values. The most well known is the Poisson distribution with parameter λ and probability function

$$P(x = k) = \frac{\lambda^k \cdot e^{-\lambda}}{k!} \quad (\lambda > 0, k = 0, 1, 2, ...)$$

A binomial distribution with large n and small p can be approximated by a Poisson distribution with $\lambda = np$.

Not all variables have integer values. The weight of a stone, the rainfall per square meter during a shower, the specific gravity of a certain material, etc., are all *continuous variables*. The number of possible values they can have is infinite, though it may be limited in practice by the precision of our measurement. The probability of any single one of the infinite number of possible values is in fact zero. However, the cumulative probability up to a certain value can be defined as for discrete variables by $F(x) = P(x \le x)$.

A distribution function $F(x)$ for a continuous variable is itself continuous and illustrated below.

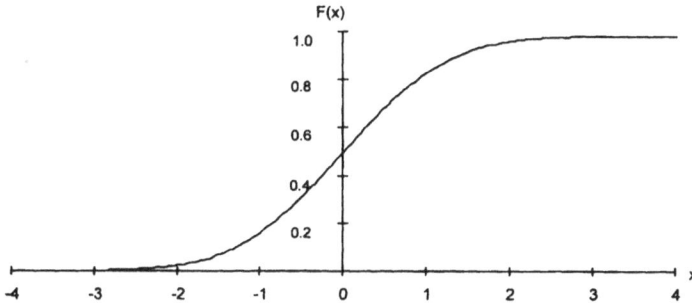

Figure B.6 *Graph of a distribution function*

Provided $F(x)$ is continuous and has a derivative at all points, the function $f(x) = \dfrac{dF(x)}{dx}$ is the (probability) *density function* of x. Conversely the distribution function $F(x)$ can be obtained from the density function $f(x)$ by integration. The density function $f(x)$ corresponding to the (cumulative) distribution function $F(x)$ is shown in Figure B.7:

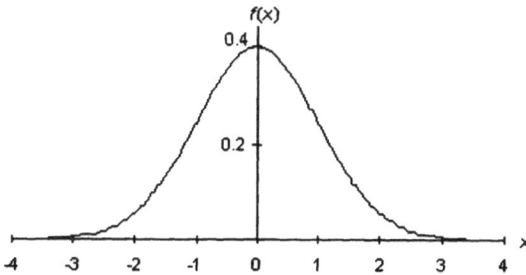

Figure B.7 *Graph of a density function*

A density function can be used to define a probability distribution in the range of values of a continuous random variable. This can be any continuous function $f(x)$ that is non-negative ($f(x) \ge 0$) and has the property that the area between its graph and the x-axis is 1:

$$\int_{-\infty}^{+\infty} f(x)dx = 1.$$

In terms of a specified density function, probability is assigned to events which are intervals in the continuum of the random variable x by the relation $P(E) = P(x$ takes a value in the interval $E) =$ Area under the graph of $f(x)$ above E.

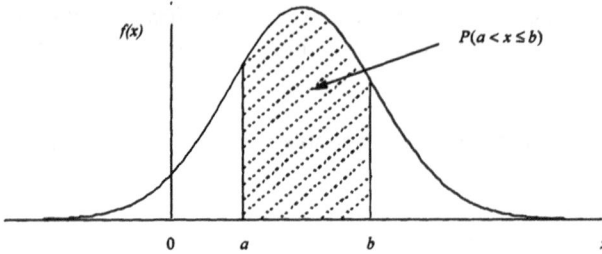

Figure B.8 *The graphical representation of the probability of event $a < x \leq b$*

The following properties are evident intuitively and will be assumed:

1. $0 \leq P(E) \leq 1$, for any event E;
2. P (E is contained in the whole space) $= 1$;
3. $P(E \cup F) = P(E) + P(F)$ for disjoint E, F;
4. $P(x = a) = 0$ for any number a, if x is continuous.

Property 1 reflects the fact that the area between $f(x)$ and the x-axis cannot be greater than 1, and property 2 states that the area over the whole region is exactly 1. Property 3 says that the area over a region consisting of two non-overlapping parts is the sum of the areas of those parts. It can be extended to *property 3*:
$P(E_1$ or E_2 or ...$) = P(E_1) + P(E_2) + ...$, if all E's are disjoint. Property 4 says that the area of a region of zero thickness is zero.

The most well-known continuous distribution is the *normal* or *Gaussian* distribution. Its density function is given by:

$$f(y) = \frac{1}{\sigma\sqrt{2\pi}} \exp\{-\frac{1}{2\sigma^2}(y - \mu)^2\}, \quad (\sigma > 0) \tag{B.14}$$

and its graph is given in Figure B.9 (e is the base of natural logarithms, $e = 2.7183$; $\exp(y) = e^y$).

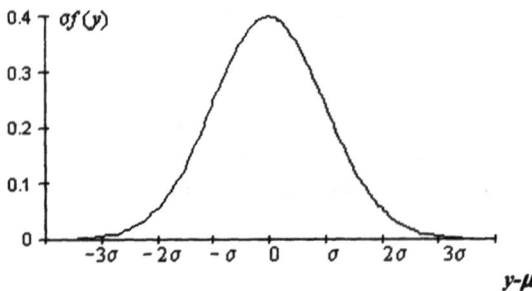

Figure B.9 *The graph of the density function of a normal distribution*

The density function of the standard normal variable x ($\mu = 0$, $\sigma = 1$) is:

$$\phi(x) = \frac{1}{\sqrt{2\pi}} \exp(-x^2/2).$$

The distribution function of the standard normal variable is:

$$\Phi(z) = \int_{-\infty}^{z} \frac{1}{\sqrt{2\pi}} \exp(-x^2/2)dx = P(x \leq z).$$

It can be shown that if x is a standard normal variable and $y = \mu + \sigma x$, y has a density function $f(y) = \frac{1}{\sigma\sqrt{2\pi}} \exp(-\frac{1}{2\sigma^2}(y - \mu)^2)$. We say x is distributed as $N(0;1)$; y as $N(\mu; \sigma^2)$.

The normal distribution is important for at least 3 reasons:

1. Many populations in the real world appear to have characteristics whose distributions are closely approximated by normal distributions.

2. The limiting distributions (in the mathematical sense) of many distributions are normal distributions. For example the t distribution tends to the normal distribution as the degrees of freedom increase. Similarly the chi-square distribution approaches a normal form with increasing degrees of freedom. Many discrete distributions also have this property. When n is large, the probability that a binomial variable k with parameters n and p is less or equal to a number k, is approximately equal to the probability that a standard normal variable x is less than $(k - np)/\sqrt{(np(1-p))}$, i.e.
    $$P(k \leq k) = P(x \leq (k - np)/\sqrt{(np(1-p))}).$$

3. It can be shown that, if the quantity y is the sum of a large number of independent small quantities with reasonable properties, y tends to be normally distributed. In other words, even if the distribution of the original population is far from normal, the distribution of the sample sum (and thus also the sample mean) tends to become normal, under a wide variety of conditions, as the size of the sample increases (this is the so-called *"central limit" theorem*).

Further continuous distributions which occur frequently in hypothesis tests and the construction of confidence intervals are:
    central (and non-central) t-distribution with f degrees of freedom as parameter;
    central (and non-central) χ^2-distribution with f degrees of freedom as parameter;
    central (and non-central) F-distribution with f_1 und f_2 degrees of freedom as parameters.
The non-central versions of these distributions all have a non-centrality parameter in addition to the above. Density functions, moments and more for these 3 distributions can be found in VB 1/41/0020, 1/41/0030 and 1/41/0040 respectively.

The *P*-quantile $(0 < P < 1)$ x_p of a continuous distribution with distribution function $F(x)$ is that *x*-value for which *F* is exactly equal to *P*.
This means the *P*-quantile is defined by

$$F(x_p) = P.$$

Figure B.10 illustrates this

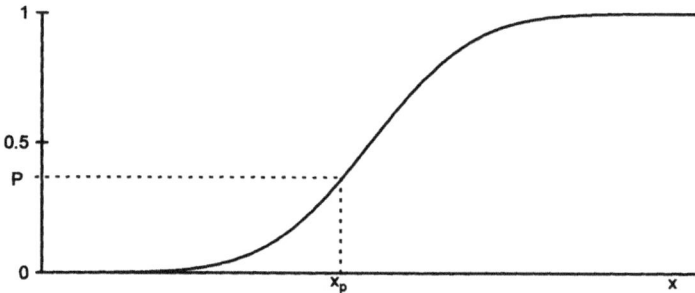

Figure B.10 *The P-quantiles x_p of a continuous distribution with distribution-function F(x)*

If we consider the density function $f(x)$ of the same distribution, the *P*-quantile is that value x_p for that the area under the graph of $f(x)$ to the left of x_p equals *P* or in mathematical notation:

$$\int_{-\infty}^{x_p} f(x)dx = F(x_p) = P$$

as shown in Figure B.11.

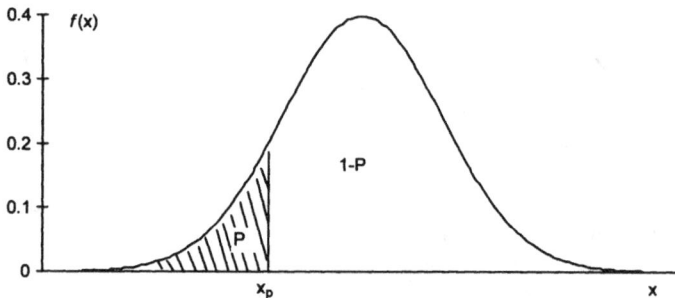

Figure B.11 *The P-quantile x_p and the density function f(x)*

Instead of saying that the area under $f(x)$ to the left of x_p equals *P* we can also say that the area to the right of x_p equals 1-*P*. This is because

$$1 - F(x_p) = 1 - P.$$

In this book we need the quantiles of several distributions:

Normal quantiles *u(P)=z(P)*

Since the normal distribution is symmetric about μ, μ is the 0.5 quantile. Therefore for the standard normal distribution:

$\Phi(0) = 0.5.$

The *P*-quantile *u(P)=z(P)* of a standard normal distribution is usually defined by:

$\Phi(u(P)) = P.$

For small α-values we need $u(\alpha)$ and $u(1-\alpha)$ or $u\left(\dfrac{\alpha}{2}\right)$ and $u\left(1-\dfrac{\alpha}{2}\right)$.

For $\alpha = 0.05$, $\Phi(u(0.05)) = 0.05$.

How can we use Table A1 to find $u(0.05)$?

Because of the symmetry of the normal distribution, we have

$\Phi(u) = 1 - \Phi(-u),$

so that $u(0.05)$ is certainly negative. [$\Phi(0) = 0.5!$]

from $\Phi(u(0.05)) = 0.05$ it follows
    $1 - \Phi(-u(0.05)) = 0.05$ or, after subtracting 1
    $-\Phi(-u(0.05)) = -0.95$ or
    $\Phi(-u(0.05)) = 0.95 = \Phi(u(0.95))$

so that

$-u(0.05) = u(0.95).$

But $u(0.95)$ can be found in the last row of Table A1 (infinite degrees of freedom):

$u(0.95) = 1.6449;$

therefore $u(0.05) = -1.6449.$

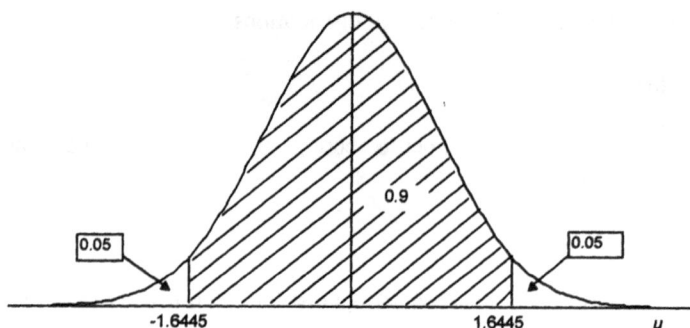

Figure B.12 *Areas under the standard normal density function*

In exactly the same way we find $u(0.975) = 1.96$ and therefore $u(0.025) = -1.96$.

t-quantiles *t(f;P)*

The t distribution (Student distribution) is symmetrical (about 0) and depends on a parameter f, called the degrees of freedom. The t-distribution with f degrees of freedom, $t(f)$, is defined as the quotient u/Z of independent random variables u and Z, where u is distributed as $N(0; 1)$ and Z is the square root of $\chi^2(f)/f$, where $\chi^2(f)$ has a chi-square distribution with f degrees of freedom.

From Table A1 we wish to find $t(3; 0.05)$, $t(10; 0.95)$ and $t(75; 0.95)$.

In row 3 and the 0.95 column we find
$t(3; 0.95) = 2.3534$ so that $t(3; 0.05) = -2.3534$
Similarly in row 10 we find $t(10; 0.95) = 1.8125$.
There is no row for $f = 75$ but we interpolate between row 70 and row 80

$$t(75; 0.95) = t(80; 0.95) + \frac{t(70; 0.95) - t(80; 0.95)}{2} = 1.6641 + \frac{1.6669 - 1.6641}{2}$$

$$= 1.6655, \text{ so that} \quad t(75; 0.05) = 1.6655$$

As f tends to infinity (∞), $t(f; P)$ tends to $u(P)$.

Chi-square-quantiles $\chi^2(f; P)$

These quantiles $\chi^2(f; P)$ are given in Table A2. The values of this distribution are all positive and there is no symmetry. The chi-square distribution with f degrees of freedom, $\chi^2(f)$, is defined as the sum $u_1^2 + u_2^2 + \dots + u_f^2$ of f independent $N(0; 1)$ random variables u_i ($i = 1, \dots, f$).

In row 10 we find for example in the column for 0.05 the value $\chi^2(10; 0.05) = 3.94$, and in column for 0.95 in the same row we find $\chi^2(10; 0.95) = 18.21$.

F-quantiles $F(f_1; f_2; P)$

The F-distribution with f_1 and f_2 degrees of freedom, $F(f_1; f_2)$, is defined as the quotient $(V/f_1) / (W/f_2)$, where V and W are independent random variables having $\chi^2(f_1)$ and $\chi^2(f_2)$ distributions respectively.

The F-quantiles depend on two parameters, the degrees of freedom f_1 and f_2. There is a relationship between the 0.05-quantiles and the 0.95-quantiles:

$$F(f_1; f_2; 0.05) = \frac{1}{F(f_2; f_1; 0.95)} \tag{B.15}$$

The P-quantiles for $P = 0.95$ are given in Table A3.
In Table A3 the first entry in $F(a; b; P)$ is always $a = f_1$, the second $b = f_2$.
we shall find $F(5; 20; 0.05)$.
First we find $F(20; 5; 0.95)$ in column 20 ($= f_1$ **not** f_2!) and row 5 ($= f_2$).

This gives 4.56. Then we find the required value from

$$F(5;20;0.05) = \frac{1}{4.56} = 0.219$$

Between F-quantiles with $f_1 = 1$ and t-quantiles the relation

$$F(1; f_2; 1-\alpha) = t^2(f_2; 1-\frac{\alpha}{2}) \tag{B.16}$$

holds. As an example we have $F(1; 2; 0.95) = 18.51$, and $t(2; 0.975) = 4.3027$ with $4.3027^2 = 18.51$.

B.2.4 Expectation

Let x be a discrete random variable with values $x_1, x_2, \ldots$ and corresponding probabilities $p_1, p_2, \ldots$ (thus $P(x = x_i) = p_i$).
The *expected value* of x or the *expectation* of x is defined to be the following weighted sum of its values:

$$E(x) = x_1 p_1 + x_2 p_2 + \ldots = \sum_j x_j p_j.$$

This is also called the *(population) mean* of x. Because it is determined by the probability distribution of x, it also is referred to as the mean of the distribution of x. The expectation $E(x)$ is usually denoted by μ. The expectation $E(x)$ characterises the location of the centre of the distribution of x.

Example B.6
The probability distribution of y of Example B.1 is:

$$P(y = 3) = 0.1 \qquad 3 \cdot 0.1 = 0.3$$
$$P(y = 4) = 0.2 \qquad 4 \cdot 0.2 = 0.8$$
$$P(y = 5) = 0.4 \qquad 5 \cdot 0.4 = 2.0$$
$$P(y = 6) = 0.2 \qquad 6 \cdot 0.2 = 1.2$$

$$P(y = 7) = 0.1 \qquad\qquad 7 \cdot 0.1 = 0.7$$

$$\text{Total} \quad 1.0 \qquad\qquad \text{Total} \quad 5.0$$

The mean $E(y) = 3 \cdot 0.1 + 4 \cdot 0.2 + 5 \cdot 0.4 + 6 \cdot 0.2 + 7 \cdot 0.1 = 5.0$.

Example B.7

In Example B.5 we will find the expected number of heart cards $E(k)$ in six random drawings (with replacement).

$$E(k) = 0 \cdot \frac{729}{4096} + 1 \cdot \frac{1458}{4096} + 2 \cdot \frac{1215}{4096} + 3 \cdot \frac{540}{4096} + 4 \cdot \frac{135}{4096} +$$

$$5 \cdot \frac{18}{4096} + 6 \cdot \frac{1}{4096} = \frac{6144}{4096} = 1.5.$$

We can find the expectation of this binomial variable k with $n = 6$ and $p = \dfrac{1}{4}$ also

as

$$E(k) = 6 \cdot \frac{1}{4} = 1.5.$$

In general the expectation of a binomial variable k with parameters n and p is:

$$E(k) = \sum_{j=0}^{n} jP(k = j) = \sum_{j=0}^{n} j \binom{n}{j} p^j (1 - p)^{n-j} = np.$$

For a continuous random variable x the expectation $E(x)$ is defined as

$$E(x) = \int_{-\infty}^{+\infty} xf(x)dx.$$

Example B.8

For the standard normal variable x the expectation is:

$$E(x) = \int_{-\infty}^{+\infty} x \, \frac{1}{\sqrt{2\pi}} \exp(-x^2/2)dx = 0.$$

For the normal variable $y = \mu + \sigma x$ the expectation is:

$$E(y) = \int_{-\infty}^{+\infty} y \, \frac{1}{\sigma\sqrt{2\pi}} \exp(-(y - \mu)^2/2\sigma^2)dy = \mu.$$

Expectation can be generalised to cope with a function $g(x)$ of a random variable x. In the discrete case we have $E[g(x)] = \sum_j g(x_j)p_j$ and in the continuous case

$$E[g(x)] = \int_{-\infty}^{+\infty} g(x)f(x)dx.$$

When dealing with the expectation of functions of a random variable, E can be treated as an operator, which obeys certain rules:

E1. $E(x + b) = E(x) + b$ where b is a constant

If we put $b = -\mu$, we obtain $E(x - \mu) = 0$.

E2. $E(ax) = aE(x)$ where a is a constant

Rule E1. and E2. together give

$$E(ax + b) = aE(x) + b.$$

E3.   If $g(x)$ and $h(x)$ are any two functions of a random variable x, $E[g(x) + h(x)] = E[g(x)] + E[h(x)]$.

Example B.9

For the probability distribution of y in Example B.6, we found $E(y) = 5$. If we want to know the expectation of $y + 3$, we can calculate it directly as

$$E(y + 3) = \sum_i 1(y_i + 3)p_i = (3 + 3) \cdot 0.1 + (4 + 3) \cdot 0.2 + (5 + 3) \cdot 0.4 + (6 + 3) \cdot 0.2$$

$+ (7 + 3) \cdot 0.1 = 0.6 + 1.4 + 3.2 + 1.8 + 1.0 = 8.$
Or using rule E1.: $E(y + 3) = E(y) + 3 = 5 + 3 = 8.$
If we want to know the expectation of $2y$, we can calculate it directly:

$$E(2y) = \sum_i (2 y_i)p_i = (2 \cdot 3) \cdot 0.1 + (2 \cdot 4) \cdot 0.2 + (2 \cdot 5) \cdot 0.4 +$$

$(2 \cdot 6) \cdot 0.2 + (2 \cdot 7) \cdot 0.1 = 0.6 + 1.6 + 4.0 + 2.4 + 1.4 = 10.$

Using rule E2.: $E(2y) = 2E(y) = 2 \cdot 5 = 10.$
If we want to know the expectation of y^2 we must calculate this directly as:

$$E(y^2) = \sum_i 2y_i^2 p_i = 3^2 \cdot 0.1 + 4^2 \cdot 0.2 + 5^2 \cdot 0.4 + 6^2 \cdot 0.2 + 7^2 \cdot 0.1 =$$

$= 0.9 + 3.2 + 10 + 7.2 + 4.9 = 26.2.$

Note that $E(y^2) = 26.2$ is not equal to $(E(y))^2 = 5^2 = 25$.

B.2.5 Variance

A very commonly used measure of the spread or variability of the distribution of x around its expectation $E(x)$ is the *variance* which is defined as $\text{var}(x) = E(x - \mu)^2$, with $\mu = E(x)$. The variance of a random variable is thus the averaged squared deviation of x

from its mean; it is denoted by σ^2. A useful relation is $\sigma^2 = E(x - \mu)^2 = E(x^2) - \mu^2$. The *standard deviation* of x is defined as $\sqrt{var(x)}$ and is denoted by σ. This is measured in the same units as the random variable and thus has a more direct interpretation than the variance. However the variance is fundamental to mathematical statistics.

Because $E(x - \mu) = 0$, we cannot simply average the deviations; we must first square them and average these squared values. Finally we take the square root to restore the dimension to that of the random variable.

Some rules for the variances of simple functions of x are:

V1. $var(x + b) = var(x)$ b is a constant
V2. $var(ax) = a^2 \, var(x)$ a is a constant

Rules V1. and V2. together give

$$var(ax + b) = a^2 \, var(x) = a^2 \sigma^2.$$

Example B.10

Returning to the probability distribution of y of Example B.6: the variance of y is $E(y - 5)^2$, because $E(y) = 5$.
Using the direct approach we find:

$$E(y - 5)^2 = \sum_i 3(y_i - 5)^2 \, p_i = (3 - 5)^2 \cdot 0.1 + (4 - 5)^2 \cdot 0.2 + (5 - 5)^2 \cdot 0.4 +$$

$$(6 - 5)^2 \cdot 0.2 + (7 - 5)^2 \cdot 0.1 = 0.4 + 0.2 + 0 + 0.2 + 0.4 = 1.2.$$

Alternatively we evaluate var(y) as $E(y^2) - (E(y))^2 = E(y^2) - 5^2 = 26.2 - 25 = 1.2$ (in Example B.9 we obtained $E(y^2) = 26.2$).

Theorem B.1

For a binomially distributed variable k with parameters n and p we have:

$E(k) = np$, and

$$var(k) = E(k - np)^2 = \sum_{j=0}^{n} (j - np)^2 \binom{n}{j} p^j (1 - p)^{n-j} = np(1 - p).$$

Example B.11

In Example B.5 we want to know the variance of k. Using $E(k) = 1.5$;
$var(k) = E(k - 1.5)^2$.

$$var(k) = (0 - 1.5)^2 \cdot \frac{729}{4096} + (1 - 1.5)^2 \cdot \frac{1458}{4096} + (2 - 1.5)^2 \cdot \frac{1215}{4096}$$

$$+ (3 - 1.5)^2 \cdot \frac{540}{4096} + (4 - 1.5)^2 \cdot \frac{135}{4096} + (5 - 1.5)^2 \cdot \frac{18}{4096}$$

$$+ (6 - 1.5)^2 \cdot \frac{1}{4096} = \frac{4608}{4096} = 1.125.$$

Using Theorem B.1 we can also find the variance of k with $n = 6$ and $p = \frac{1}{4}$ as

$$var(k) = 6 \cdot \frac{1}{4} \cdot \frac{3}{4} = \frac{18}{16} 4 = 1.125$$

Theorem B.2
A standard normal variable x has expectation $E(x) = 0$ and variance

$$var(x) = E(x - 0)^2 = \int_{-\infty}^{\infty} x^2 \frac{1}{\sqrt{2\pi}} \exp(-\frac{x^2}{2}) dx = 1.$$

Therefore using the rules E1. and E2., the normally distributed variable $y = \mu + \alpha x$ has expectation $E(y) = \mu$, and using rules V1. and V2., variance

$$var(y) = E(y - \mu)^2 = \sigma^2$$

B.2.6 Covariance

So far we have only considered one random variable at a time. When we measure several characteristics of each of the objects in a sample, we model these by several random variables. For example we could measure the height (x) and shoe size (y) of students.

The values of a pair of discrete random variables (x, y) are pairs of numbers (often integers) and the probability distribution in the set of possible pairs is described by a probability function of two arguments: $p(x,y) = P(x = x$ and $y = y)$.

The tabulation of such a function is often set out conveniently as a two-way table, with the possible values of x being the rows, and the possible values of y forming the columns.

	y_1	y_2	
x_1	$p(x_1, y_1)$	$p(x_1, y_2)$	...
x_2	$p(x_2, y_1)$	$p(x_2, y_2)$	...
.	.	.	
.	.	.	
.	.	.	

Simple functions $g(x, y)$ of the two random variables are $g(x, y) = x + y$ or $g(x, y) = x \cdot y$. The expectation of such a function is defined as:

$$E\{g(x,y)\} = \sum_{xy} \sum g(x,y) p(x,y).$$

For a pair of continuous variables (x, y) we work with the joint density function $f(x,y)$. The expectation of a function $g(x, y)$ is then defined as:

$$E\{g(x,y)\} = \int_{-\infty}^{+\infty} \int_{-\infty}^{+\infty} g(x,y) f(x,y) dx dy.$$

Two rules which follow directly from the definitions are:
$E(x + y) = E(x) + E(y)$ and
$E(ax+by) = aE(x) + bE(y)$
for arbitrary constants a and b.
If we want to find the variance of $x + y$, we use:

$$
\begin{aligned}
\text{var}(x+y) \quad &= \quad E\{(x+y) - E(x+y)\}^2 = E\{(x+y) - (E(x) + E(y))\}^2 \\
&= \quad E\{(x - E(x)) + (y - E(y))\}^2 = E\{(x - E(x))^2 + \\
& \qquad 2(x - E(x))(y - E(y)) + (y - E(y))^2\} \\
&= \quad E\{(x - E(x))^2\} + 2E\{(x - E(x))(y - E(y))\} + E\{(y - E(y))^2\} \\
&= \quad \text{var}(x) + 2\text{cov}(x, y) + \text{var}(y).
\end{aligned}
$$

Here we have defined the quantity $\text{cov}(x, y) = E\{(x - E(x))(y - E(y))\}$, and this is called the *covariance* of x and y. A useful relation is $\text{cov}(x, y) = E(x \cdot y) - E(x)E(y)$. The covariance of x and y is the mean of the products of the deviations of x and y from their respective means   If the two random variables are positively (negatively) related then large values of x will tend to be associated with large (small) values of y. The covariance is then positive (negative). If the random variables are statistically independent, we have $P(x = x \cap y = y) = P(x = x)P(y = y)$. We then find that $E(x \cdot y) = E(x) \cdot E(y)$, so that the covariance $\text{cov}(x, y) = E(x \cdot y) - E(x)E(y) = 0$.
Be aware that for two random variables the covariance may sometimes be zero, but this does not always imply that they are independent. On the other hand, if two variables are independent, their covariance is always equal to zero. If $\text{cov}(x, y) = 0$, the random variables x and y are called *uncorrelated*. Often the strength of the (linear) relation between two random variables is measured by the (population) correlation coefficient:

$$
\rho_{xy} \; = \; \rho(x,y) \; = \; \frac{\text{cov}(x,y)}{\sqrt{\text{var}(x)\,\text{var}(y)}} \;, \quad \text{where } -1 \le \rho(x,y) \le 1 \tag{B.19}
$$

The rules for operating with variances and covariances are as follows:

C1. $\text{var}(x+y) = \text{var}(x) + \text{var}(y) + 2\text{cov}(x, y)$
C2. $\text{var}(x-y) = \text{var}(x) + \text{var}(y) - 2\text{cov}(x, y)$
C3. $\text{cov}(x, y) = \text{cov}(y, x)$
C4. $\text{cov}(ax, y) = a\,\text{cov}(x, y); \; \text{cov}(x+b, y) = \text{cov}(x, y)$
C5. $\text{cov}(x, x) = \text{var}(x)$
C6. If x and y are independent, then $\text{var}(x+y) = \text{var}(x) + \text{var}(y)$ and $\text{var}(x-y) = \text{var}(x) + \text{var}(y)$
C7. If $x_1, x_2, ..., x_n$ are independent, then $\text{var}(x_1 + x_2 + ... + x_n) = \text{var}(\Sigma x_i) = \text{var}(x_1) + \text{var}(x_2) + ... + \text{var}(x_n) = \Sigma\,\text{var}(x_i)$.

Example B.13
We have n independent trials of an experiment which give values $x_1, x_2, ..., x_n$. All the x_i have expectation $E(x_i) = \mu$ and variance $\text{var}(x_i) = \sigma^2$. The arithmetic mean $\bar{x} = \dfrac{x_1 + x_2 + ... + x_n}{n}$ of these random variables is itself a random variable. Its expectation is:

$$E(\bar{x}) = E[(x_1 + x_2 + \ldots + x_n)/n] = \frac{1}{n}\{E(x_1 + x_2 + \ldots + x_n)\} =$$

$$\frac{1}{n}\{E(x_1) + E(x_2) + \ldots + E(x_n)\} = \frac{1}{n}(\mu + \mu + \ldots + \mu) = \frac{1}{n}(n\mu) = \mu.$$

The variance of $\bar{x}$ is (using C6. and C7.)

$$\mathrm{var}(\bar{x}) = \mathrm{var}(\frac{x_1 + x_2 + \ldots + x_n}{n}) = \frac{1}{n^2}\mathrm{var}(x_1 + x_2 + \ldots + x_n)$$

$$= \frac{1}{n^2}(\mathrm{var}(x_1) + \mathrm{var}(x_2) + \ldots + \mathrm{var}(x_n))$$

$$= \frac{1}{n^2}(\sigma^2 + \sigma^2 + \ldots + \sigma^2) = \frac{1}{n^2}(n\sigma^2) = \frac{\sigma^2}{n}.$$

B.3 Sampling Distributions

B.3.1 Sample Mean $\bar{x}$

Often a population cannot be measured completely, in which case a random sample of n elements is taken. It is assumed that the population is very large (more than 1000 elements) or that sampling is done with replacement. The average of the observations in the sample can be calculated. We will now use an example to investigate the distribution of this calculated random variable:

Example B.14

Consider a population consisting of the 5 elements 1,2,3,4,5. From this population 2 elements are taken at random with replacement. We shall calculate the sample means of all possible different samples. Let x_1 represent the first number chosen and x_2 the second number. $\bar{x}$ denotes the sample mean. The probability function of x, a randomly chosen element of this population, is defined by:

$$P(x=1) = P(x=2) = P(x=3) = P(x=4) = P(x=5) = 1/5 = 0.2.$$

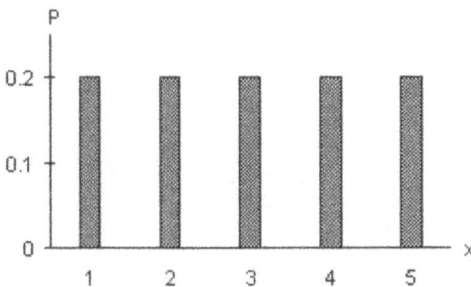

Figure B.13 *Bar Graph for Example B.14*

233

For x we find

$$E(x) = 1 \cdot 0.2 + 2 \cdot 0.2 + 3 \cdot 0.2 + 4 \cdot 0.2 + 5 \cdot 0.2 = 3$$
$$E(x^2) = 1^2 \cdot 0.2 + 2^2 \cdot 0.2 + 3^2 \cdot 0.2 + 4^2 \cdot 0.2 + 5^2 \cdot 0.2 = 11$$
$$var(x) = E(x^2) - (E(x))^2 = 11 - 3^2 = 2.$$

The possible outcomes of (x_1, x_2) and $\bar{x}$ are:

(x_1, x_2)	$\bar{x}$	(x_1, x_2)	$\bar{x}$
(1,1)	1	(3,4)	3.5
(1,2)	1.5	(3,5)	4.0
(1,3)	2.0	(4,1)	2.5
(1,4)	2.5	(4,2)	3.0
(1,5)	3.0	(4,3)	3.5
(2,1)	1.5	(4,4)	4.0
(2,2)	2.0	(4,5)	4.5
(2,3)	2.5	(5,1)	3.0
(2,4)	3.0	(5,2)	3.5
(2,5)	3.5	(5,3)	4.0
(3,1)	2.0	(5,4)	4.5
(3,2)	2.5	(5,5)	5.0
(3,3)	3.0		

$P(x_1 = i, x_2 = j) = P(x_1 = i) \cdot P(x_2 = j) = 1/5 \cdot 1/5 = 1/25$, because x_1 and x_2 are statistically independent, which follows from the random sampling with replacement.
The probability distribution of $\bar{x}$, the so-called *sampling distribution* of $\bar{x}$ is thus:

$\bar{x}$	$P(\bar{x} = \bar{x})$		
1	1/25	=	0.04
1.5	2/25	=	0.08
2.0	3/25	=	0.12
2.5	4/25	=	0.16
3.0	5/25	=	0.20
3.5	4/25	=	0.16
4.0	3/25	=	0.12
4.5	2/25	=	0.08
5.0	1/25	=	0.04

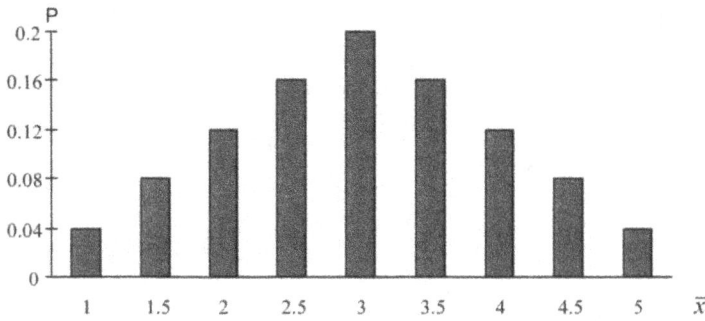

Figure B.14 *Graph of the distribution of $\bar{x}$*

We get for
$E(\bar{x}) = 1 \cdot 0.04 + 1.5 \cdot 0.08 + 2.0 \cdot 0.12 + 2.5 \cdot 0.16 + 3.0 \cdot 0.20 + 3.5 \cdot 0.16 + 4.0 \cdot 0.12 + 4.5 \cdot 0.08$
$+ 5.0 \cdot 0.04 = 3$
$E(\bar{x}^2) = 1^2 \cdot 0.04 + 1.5^2 \cdot 0.08 + 2.0^2 \cdot 0.12 + 2.5^2 \cdot 0.16 + 3.0^2 \cdot 0.20 + 3.5^2 \cdot 0.16 +$
$+ 4.0^2 \cdot 0.12 + 4.5^2 \cdot 0.08 + 5.0^2 \cdot 0.04 = 10$
$\text{var}(\bar{x}) = E(\bar{x}^2) - (E(\bar{x}))^2 = 10 - 3^2 = 1.$

We now see that this result is in agreement with the result of Example B.13. There it was demonstrated that if we have n independent trials of an experiment having outcomes: x_1, $x_2,...,x_n$, which all have expectation $E(x_i) = \mu$ and variance var $(x_i) = \sigma^2$ the sample mean has expectation $E(\bar{x}) = \mu$ and variance $\text{var}(\bar{x}) = \sigma^2/n$.
In our example the independent trials are the random drawings with replacement which give rise to the $n = 2$ independent measurements x_1 and x_2 with $E(x_i) = \mu = 3$ and $\sigma^2 = 2$. Hence $E(\bar{x}) = 3$ and $\text{var}(\bar{x}) = \sigma^2/2 = 2/2 = 1$.
Another useful property is that the sampling distribution of $\bar{x}$ tends to become symmetric very soon and with increasing n it looks more and more like a normal distribution with mean μ and variance σ^2/n. This is also true for the sample sum $n\bar{x}$, which with increasing n behaves as a normal variable with mean $n\mu$ and variance $n\sigma^2$. This is already stated in the so-called 'central limit' theorem, see the last paragraph of section B.2.3.1. This result does not require the original measurements to be normally distributed, only that they are independent and have the same distribution.

Measurements such as height and weight are often themselves a combination of many variable components. Even when these components are not normally distributed, we find that these sorts of measurements can often be satisfactorily modelled by normal distributions.
If the original distribution of x_i is normal, the sample mean $\bar{x}$ of n independent x_i's is again normal with mean μ and variance σ^2/n. In general any linear combination
$\sum\limits_{i=1}^{n} a_i x_i$ of independent *normal* random variables $x_1, x_2, ..., x_n$ is also a normal variable
with mean $\sum\limits_{i=1}^{n} a_i \mu_i$, and variance $\sum\limits_{i=1}^{n} a_i^2 \sigma_i^2$, where $E(x_i) = \mu_i$ and $\text{var}(x_i) = \sigma_i^2$.

235

B.3.2 Sample variance s^2

Another sampling distribution can be constructed for the *sample variance*

$$s^2 = \frac{\sum\limits_{i=1}^{n}(x_i - \bar{x})^2}{n-1} = \frac{\sum\limits_{i=1}^{n} x_i^2 - (\sum\limits_{1}^{n} x_i)^2 / n}{n-1} \qquad (B.20)$$

Remark

For $n = 2$

$$s^2 = \sum_{i=1}^{2}(x_i - \bar{x})^2 / (2-1) = \sum_{i=1}^{2}\left(x_i - \frac{x_1 + x_2}{2}\right)^2 = \left(\frac{x_1 - x_2}{2}\right)^2 + \left(\frac{x_2 - x_1}{2}\right)^2 = (x_1 - x_2)^2 / 2$$

Example B.14 continued

For the distribution as given in Example B.14 we calculate the sampling distribution of s^2 for $n = 2$ random drawings with replacement from the population. The possible outcomes of (x_1, x_2) and s^2 are:

(x_1,x_2)	s^2	(x_1,x_2)	s^2
(1,1)	0.0	(3,4)	0.5
(1,2)	0.5	(3,5)	2.0
(1,3)	2.0	(4,1)	4.5
(1,4)	4.5	(4,2)	2.0
(1,5)	8.0	(4,3)	0.5
(2,1)	0.5	(4,4)	0.0
(2,2)	0.0	(4,5)	0.5
(2,3)	0.5	(5,1)	8.0
(2,4)	2.0	(5,2)	4.5
(2,5)	4.5	(5,3)	2.0
(3,1)	2.0	(5,4)	0.5
(3,2)	0.5	(5,5)	0.0
(3,3)	0.0		

The probability distribution of s^2, the sampling distribution of s^2 is thus:

s^2	$P(s^2 = s^2)$
0.0	$\dfrac{5}{25} = 0.2$
0.5	$\dfrac{8}{25} = 0.32$
2.0	$\dfrac{6}{25} = 0.24$
4.5	$\dfrac{4}{25} = 0.16$
8.0	$\dfrac{2}{25} = 0.08$

The expected value of s^2 is

$$E(s^2) = 0.0 \cdot 0.20 + 0.5 \cdot 0.32 + 2.0 \cdot 0.24 + 4.5 \cdot 0.16 + 8.0 \cdot 0.08 = 2 = \text{var}(x) = \sigma^2.$$

The expectation of s^2 is always equal to the variance $\text{var}(x)$, that is to say

$$E(s^2) = \sigma^2. \tag{B.21}$$

Appendix C   Matrices

A matrix is a rectangular scheme (array) of elements If the matrix has $a \geq 1$ rows and $b \geq 1$ columns, it is called an $(a \times b)$-matrix. If $a = b$ the matrix is a square matrix of order a. If $b = 1$ the matrix is called a (column) vector. If $a = b = 1$ the matrix reduces to a real number (also called a scalar). Matrices are usually denoted by capital letters such as A, B, X and their elements by the corresponding indexed small letters like a_{ij}, b_{ij} or x_{ij}. We also use the notations $X = (x_{ij})$; $i = 1, ..., a$, $j = 1, ..., b$ and

$$X = \begin{pmatrix} x_{11} & \cdots & x_{1b} \\ x_{21} & \cdots & x_{2b} \\ \vdots & \vdots & \vdots \\ x_{a1} & \cdots & x_{ab} \end{pmatrix}.$$

Here x_{ij} is the element in the i-th row and the j-th column of X. If $b = 1$ then we obtain a column vector and change the notation. The capital letter becomes a small letter and the column suffix is dropped

$$X = x = \begin{pmatrix} x_{11} \\ x_{21} \\ \vdots \\ x_{a1} \end{pmatrix} = \begin{pmatrix} x_1 \\ x_2 \\ \vdots \\ x_a \end{pmatrix}.$$

We say that a matrix X is transposed and thus becomes X^T (the transpose of X) if rows and columns are interchanged. This means

$$X^T = \begin{pmatrix} x_{11} & \cdots & x_{a1} \\ x_{12} & \cdots & x_{a2} \\ \vdots & \vdots & \vdots \\ x_{1b} & \cdots & x_{ab} \end{pmatrix}.$$

If we transpose a column vector

$$x = \begin{pmatrix} x_1 \\ \vdots \\ x_a \end{pmatrix}$$

the result $x^T = (x_1, ..., x_a)$ is called a row vector.
If the transposed matrix A^T of a square matrix A equals A ($A^T = A$), A is called a symmetric matrix.

Before we can proceed, we have to define the basic operations on matrices.
(In what follows we shall consider all elements to be real numbers, although wider definitions are possible).

<u>Addition:</u>   Two matrices A and B can be added if they have the same number of rows and the same number of columns. The sum $A+B$ is then obtained by adding the entries of A and B elementwise.
We have

$$A + B = B + A$$

<u>Multiplication by a real number</u>:
A matrix A is multiplied by a real number c when each element of A is multiplied by c.
Thus

$$cA = (ca_{ij})$$

<u>Subtracting Matrices</u>:
A matrix B is subtracted from a matrix A by the rule
$A-B = (a_{ij}-b_{ij})$
Note that if we define $-B$ as B multiplied by the real number -1, we get
$A-B = A + (-B)$.

<u>Multiplying Matrices</u>:
An $(a \times b)$ matrix A can be multiplied by a $(c \times d)$-matrix B ($A \cdot B$), if (and only if) the number b of columns of A equals the number c of rows of B ($b = c$). The product is an $(a \times d)$-matrix C with elements

$$c_{ij} = \sum_{k=1}^{b} a_{ik} b_{kj} \quad i = 1,...,a, \ j = 1,...,d$$

As an example let us consider the matrices

$$A = \begin{pmatrix} 3 & 2 & 1 \\ 1 & 4 & 5 \end{pmatrix} \text{ and } B = \begin{pmatrix} 1 & 0 & 1 & 0 \\ 3 & 1 & 0 & 0 \\ 1 & 2 & 0 & 1 \end{pmatrix}$$

A is a (2×3)-matrix and B a (3×4)-matrix. The product $A \cdot B$ is therefore a (2×4)-matrix.

$$AB = A \cdot B = \begin{pmatrix} 10 & 4 & 3 & 1 \\ 18 & 14 & 1 & 5 \end{pmatrix}$$

The calculation of the first entry of $AB = A \cdot B$ proceeds as follows. The first row of A has to be multiplied elementwise by the first column of B and the products summed. . Therefore we obtain

$$3 \cdot 1 + 2 \cdot 3 + 1 \cdot 1 = 10$$

In this example the product $B \cdot A$ can not be calculated; it is not defined because B has 4 columns and A has 2 rows.

If we now reduce the matrix B by dropping columns 3 and 4, we get a situation where both products exist. First we multiply

$$A = \begin{pmatrix} 3 & 2 & 1 \\ 1 & 4 & 5 \end{pmatrix} \text{ by } B = \begin{pmatrix} 1 & 0 \\ 3 & 1 \\ 1 & 2 \end{pmatrix}.$$

The product

$$AB = \begin{pmatrix} 10 & 4 \\ 18 & 14 \end{pmatrix}$$

is a (2×2)-matrix.

This time we can also calculate

$$B \cdot A = \begin{pmatrix} 3 & 2 & 1 \\ 10 & 10 & 8 \\ 5 & 10 & 11 \end{pmatrix}$$

which is a (3×3)-matrix.

Warning: never confuse AB with BA; the result is usually different, and as we have seen sometimes only one of the products is defined.

Determinants:

The determinant $|A|$ of a square matrix A (only square matrices have determinants) is a real number. If the order of the square matrix A is 2 the determinant $|A|$ of

$$A = \begin{pmatrix} a_{11} & a_{12} \\ a_{21} & a_{22} \end{pmatrix}$$

is

$$|A| = a_{11} \cdot a_{22} - a_{12} \cdot a_{21}.$$

Using the matrix $AB = \begin{pmatrix} 10 & 4 \\ 18 & 14 \end{pmatrix}$ above, we obtain

$$|AB| = 10 \cdot 14 - 4 \cdot 18 = 68.$$

If the order of a square matrix A is 3 we obtain the determinant $|A|$ of

$$A = \begin{pmatrix} a_{11} & a_{12} & a_{13} \\ a_{21} & a_{22} & a_{23} \\ a_{31} & a_{32} & a_{33} \end{pmatrix}$$

as follows. Select any row or column and fix it for the remainder of the calculation. We will take the first row. We obtain $|A|$ in two stages. First we multiply each element of our chosen row by the determinant of the matrix of order 2 which remains when the row and the column through that element are both deleted.
Thus we evaluate

$$P_1 = a_{11} \begin{vmatrix} a_{22} & a_{23} \\ a_{32} & a_{33} \end{vmatrix}$$

$$P_2 = a_{12} \begin{vmatrix} a_{21} & a_{23} \\ a_{31} & a_{33} \end{vmatrix}$$

and

$$P_3 = a_{13} \begin{vmatrix} a_{21} & a_{22} \\ a_{31} & a_{32} \end{vmatrix} .$$

These products P_1, P_2, P_3 are combined linearly with alternating signs:

$$(-1)^{1+1}P_1 + (-1)^{1+2}P_2 + (-1)^{1+3}P_3 = P_1 - P_2 + P_3 = |A| .$$

The exponents of (-1) in the expression above are the sums of the suffixes of the multiplier a_{ij} in P_j.

In the example above BA is a square matrix of order 3 and

$$P_1 = 3 \cdot \begin{vmatrix} 10 & 8 \\ 10 & 11 \end{vmatrix}, \ P_2 = 2 \cdot \begin{vmatrix} 10 & 8 \\ 5 & 11 \end{vmatrix}, \ P_3 = 1 \cdot \begin{vmatrix} 10 & 10 \\ 5 & 10 \end{vmatrix}$$

and therefore

$$|BA| = 3 \cdot (110\text{-}80) - 2 \cdot (110\text{-}40) + 1 \cdot (100\text{-}50) = 3 \cdot 30 - 2 \cdot 70 + 50 = 0.$$

Thus $|AB| = 68$, but $|BA| = 0$ in this example. A matrix whose determinant equals zero is called singular.
This principle can be extended to higher order square matrices but this will not be done here.

The Inverse A^{-1} of A:
"Division" by a Matrix A is accomplished by multiplying by its inverse A^{-1}, which is defined for any square matrix whose determinant is not zero.

First we define the identity matrix I_a of order a as a square matrix of order a of the form

$$I_a = \begin{pmatrix} 1 & 0 & \cdots & 0 \\ 0 & 1 & & 0 \\ \vdots & & \ddots & \vdots \\ 0 & \cdots & \cdots & 1 \end{pmatrix}$$

That is to say any element whose row suffix equals its column suffix (these elements constitute the leading diagonal of the matrix) equals 1 and all other elements equal zero.

It can be seen that for square matrices A and I_a of the same order, with I_a defined as above, then $A I_a = I_a A = A$.

The inverse A^{-1} of a square matrix A of order a is the (uniquely defined) square matrix of order a which satisfies

$$AA^{-1} = A^{-1}A = I_a.$$

The calculation of A^{-1} can be carried out using techniques involving determinants. We do not need to pursue these in detail, since programs for the purpose are readily available. If the determinant of A is zero, the inverse of A does not exist.

If A is a square matrix of order $a>1$, then every solution λ of the equation $|A - \lambda I_a| = 0$ (which is a polynomial equation of order a) is called an *eigenvalue* of A. If A is symmetric, then all the eigenvalues of A are real. The *trace* of a square matrix A is the sum of the eigenvalues, and the determinant of A is their product.

Tables

Table A1   *P-quantiles of the t- distribution with f degrees of freedom (for f = ∞, P-quantiles of the standard normal distribution).*

f	P								
	0.60	0.70	0.80	0.85	0.90	0.95	0.975	0.99	0.995
1	0.3249	0.7265	1.3764	1.9626	3.0777	6.3138	12.7062	31.8205	63.6567
2	0.2887	0.6172	1.0607	1.3862	1.8856	2.9200	4.3027	6.9646	9.9248
3	0.2767	0.5844	0.9785	1.2498	1.6377	2.3534	3.1824	4.5407	5.8409
4	0.2707	0.5686	0.9410	1.1896	1.5332	2.1318	2.7764	3.7469	4.6041
5	0.2672	0.5594	0.9195	1.1558	1.4759	2.0150	2.5706	3.3649	4.0321
6	0.2648	0.5534	0.9057	1.1342	1.4398	1.9432	2.4469	3.1427	3.7074
7	0.2632	0.5491	0.8960	1.1192	1.4149	1.8946	2.3646	2.9980	3.4995
8	0.2619	0.5459	0.8889	1.1081	1.3968	1.8595	2.3060	2.8965	3.3554
9	0.2610	0.5435	0.8834	1.0997	1.3830	1.8331	2.2622	2.8214	3.2498
10	0.2602	0.5415	0.8791	1.0931	1.3722	1.8125	2.2281	2.7638	3.1693
11	0.2596	0.5399	0.8755	1.0877	1.3634	1.7959	2.2010	2.7181	3.1058
12	0.2590	0.5386	0.8726	1.0832	1.3562	1.7823	2.1788	2.6810	3.0545
13	0.2586	0.5375	0.8702	1.0795	1.3502	1.7709	2.1604	2.6503	3.0123
14	0.2582	0.5366	0.8681	1.0763	1.3450	1.7613	2.1448	2.6245	2.9768
15	0.2579	0.5357	0.8662	1.0735	1.3406	1.7531	2.1314	2.6025	2.9467
16	0.2576	0.5350	0.8647	1.0711	1.3368	1.7459	2.1199	2.5835	2.9208
17	0.2573	0.5344	0.8633	1.0690	1.3334	1.7396	2.1098	2.5669	2.8982
18	0.2571	0.5338	0.8620	1.0672	1.3304	1.7341	2.1009	2.5524	2.8784
19	0.2569	0.5333	0.8610	1.0655	1.3277	1.7291	2.0930	2.5395	2.8609
20	0.2567	0.5329	0.8600	1.0640	1.3253	1.7247	2.0860	2.5280	2.8453
21	0.2566	0.5325	0.8591	1.0627	1.3232	1.7207	2.0796	2.5176	2.8314
22	0.2564	0.5321	0.8583	1.0614	1.3212	1.7171	2.0739	2.5083	2.8188
23	0.2563	0.5317	0.8575	1.0603	1.3195	1.7139	2.0687	2.4999	2.8073
24	0.2562	0.5314	0.8569	1.0593	1.3178	1.7109	2.0639	2.4922	2.7969
25	0.2561	0.5312	0.8562	1.0584	1.3163	1.7081	2.0595	2.4851	2.7874
26	0.2560	0.5309	0.8557	1.0575	1.3150	1.7056	2.0555	2.4786	2.7787
27	0.2559	0.5306	0.8551	1.0567	1.3137	1.7033	2.0518	2.4727	2.7707
28	0.2558	0.5304	0.8546	1.0560	1.3125	1.7011	2.0484	2.4671	2.7633
29	0.2557	0.5302	0.8542	1.0553	1.3114	1.6991	2.0452	2.4620	2.7564
30	0.2556	0.5300	0.8538	1.0547	1.3104	1.6973	2.0423	2.4573	2.7500
40	0.2550	0.5286	0.8507	1.0500	1.3031	1.6839	2.0211	2.4233	2.7045
50	0.2547	0.5278	0.8489	1.0473	1.2987	1.6759	2.0086	2.4033	2.6778
60	0.2545	0.5272	0.8477	1.0455	1.2958	1.6706	2.0003	2.3901	2.6603
70	0.2543	0.5268	0.8468	1.0442	1.2938	1.6669	1.9944	2.3808	2.6479
80	0.2542	0.5265	0.8461	1.0432	1.2922	1.6641	1.9901	2.3739	2.6387
90	0.2541	0.5263	0.8456	1.0424	1.2910	1.6620	1.9867	2.3685	2.6316
100	0.2540	0.5261	0.8452	1.0418	1.2901	1.6602	1.9840	2.3642	2.6259
300	0.2536	0.5250	0.8428	1.0382	1.2844	1.6499	1.9679	2.3451	2.5923
500	0.2535	0.5247	0.8423	1.0375	1.2832	1.6479	1.9647	2.3338	2.5857
∞	0.2533	0.5244	0.8416	1.0364	1.2816	1.6449	1.9600	2.3263	2.5758

Table A2   *P-quantiles $\chi^2(f;p)$ of the χ^2-distribution (critical values of the chi-square test) with f degrees of freedom.*

f	0.005	0.010	0.025	0.050	0.100	0.250	0.500	0.750	0.900	0.950	0.975	0.990	0.995
1	$3927 \cdot 10^{-8}$	$1571 \cdot 10^{-7}$	$9821 \cdot 10^{-7}$	$3932 \cdot 10^{-6}$	0.01579	0.1015	0.4549	1.323	2.706	3.841	5.024	6.635	7.879
2	0.01003	0.02010	0.05064	0.1026	0.2107	0.5754	1.386	2.773	4.605	5.991	7.378	9.210	10.60
3	0.07172	0.1148	0.2158	0.3518	0.5844	1.213	2.366	4.108	6.251	7.815	9.348	11.34	12.84
4	0.2070	0.2971	0.4844	0.7107	1.064	1.923	3.357	5.385	7.779	9.488	11.14	13.28	14.86
5	0.4117	0.5543	0.8312	1.145	1.610	2.675	4.351	6.626	9.236	11.07	12.83	15.09	16.75
6	0.6757	0.8721	1.237	1.635	2.204	3.455	5.348	7.841	10.64	12.59	14.45	16.81	18.55
7	0.9893	1.239	1.690	2.167	2.833	4.255	6.346	9.037	12.02	14.07	16.01	18.48	20.28
8	1.344	1.646	2.180	2.733	3.490	5.071	7.344	10.22	13.36	15.51	17.53	20.09	21.96
9	1.735	2.088	2.700	3.325	4.168	5.899	8.343	11.39	14.68	16.92	19.02	21.67	23.59
10	2.156	2.558	3.247	3.940	4.865	6.737	9.342	12.55	15.99	18.21	20.48	23.21	25.19
11	2.603	3.053	3.816	4.575	5.578	7.584	10.34	13.70	17.28	19.68	21.92	24.72	26.76
12	3.074	3.571	4.404	5.226	6.304	8.438	11.34	14.85	18.55	21.03	23.34	26.22	28.30
13	3.565	4.107	5.009	5.892	7.042	9.299	12.34	15.98	19.81	22.36	24.74	27.69	29.82
14	4.075	4.660	5.629	6.571	7.790	10.17	13.34	17.12	21.06	23.68	26.12	29.14	31.32
15	4.601	5.229	6.262	7.261	8.547	11.04	14.34	18.25	22.31	25.00	27.49	30.58	32.80
16	5.142	5.812	6.908	7.962	9.312	11.91	15.34	19.37	23.54	26.30	28.85	32.00	34.27
17	5.697	6.408	7.564	8.672	10.09	12.79	16.34	20.49	24.77	27.59	30.19	33.41	35.72
18	6.265	7.015	8.231	9.390	10.86	13.68	17.34	21.60	25.99	28.87	31.53	34.81	37.16
19	6.844	7.633	8.907	10.12	11.65	14.56	18.34	22.72	27.20	30.14	32.85	36.19	38.58
20	7.434	8.260	9.591	10.85	12.44	15.45	19.34	23.83	28.41	31.41	34.17	37.57	40.00

P

Table A2   continued

f	0.005	0.010	0.025	0.050	0.100	0.250	0.500	0.750	0.900	0.950	0.975	0.990	0.995
							P						
21	8.034	8.897	10.28	11.59	13.24	16.34	20.34	24.93	29.62	32.67	35.48	38.93	41.40
22	8.643	9.542	10.98	12.34	14.04	17.24	21.34	26.04	80.81	33.92	36.78	40.29	42.80
23	9.260	10.20	11.69	13.09	14.85	18.14	22.34	27.14	32.01	35.17	38.08	41.64	44.18
24	9.886	10.86	12.40	13.85	15.66	19.04	23.34	28.24	33.20	36.42	39.36	42.98	45.56
25	10.52	11.52	13.12	14.61	16.47	19.94	24.34	29.34	34.38	37.65	40.65	44.31	46.93
26	11.16	12.20	1384	15.38	17.29	20.84	25.34	30.43	35.56	38.89	41.92	45.64	48.29
27	11.81	12.88	14.57	16.15	18.11	21.75	26.34	31.53	36.74	40.11	43.19	46.96	49.64
28	12.46	13.56	15.31	16.93	18.94	22.06	27.34	32.62	37.92	41.34	44.46	48.28	50.99
29	13.12	14.26	16.05	17.71	19.77	23.57	28.34	33.71	39.09	42.56	45.72	49.59	52.34
30	13.79	14.95	16.79	18.49	20.60	24.48	29.34	34.80	40.26	43.77	46.98	50.89	53.67
40	20.71	22.16	24.43	26.51	29.05	33.66	39.34	45.62	51.80	55.76	59.34	63.69	66.77
50	27.99	29.71	32.36	34.76	37.69	42.94	49.33	56.33	63.17	67.50	71.42	76.15	79.49
60	35.53	37.48	40.48	43.19	46.46	52.29	59.33	66.98	74.40	79.08	83.30	88.38	91.95
70	43.28	45.44	48.76	51.74	55.33	61.70	69.33	77.58	85.53	90.53	95.02	100.42	104.22
80	51.17	53.54	57.15	60.39	64.28	71.14	79.33	88.13	96.58	101.88	106.63	112.33	116.32
90	59.20	61.75	65.65	69.13	73.29	80.62	89.33	98.65	107.56	113.14	118.14	124.12	128.30
100	67.33	70.06	74.22	77.93	82.36	90.13	99.33	109.14	118.50	124.34	129.56	135.81	140.17

Table A3   *95%-quantiles of the F distribution with f_1 and f_2 degrees of freedom.*

f_1 / f_2	1	2	3	4	5	6	7	8	9
1	161.4	199.5	215.7	224.6	230.2	234.0	236.8	238.9	240.5
2	18.51	19.00	19.16	19.25	19.30	19.33	19.35	19.37	19.38
3	10.13	9.55	9.28	9.12	9.01	8.94	8.89	8.85	8.81
4	7.71	6.94	6.59	6.39	6.26	6.16	6.09	6.04	6.00
5	6.61	5.79	5.41	5.19	5.05	4.95	4.88	4.82	4.77
6	5.99	5.14	4.76	4.53	4.39	4.28	4.21	4.15	4.10
7	5.59	4.74	4.35	4.12	3.97	3.87	3.79	3.73	3.68
8	5.32	4.46	4.07	3.84	3.69	3.58	3.50	3.44	3.39
9	5.12	4.26	3.86	3.63	3.48	3.37	3.29	3.23	3.18
10	4.96	4.10	3.71	3.48	3.33	3.22	3.14	3.07	3.02
11	4.84	3.98	3.59	3.36	3.20	3.09	3.01	2.95	2.90
12	4.75	3.89	3.49	3.27	3.11	3.00	2.91	2.85	2.80
13	4.67	3.81	3.41	3.18	3.03	2.92	2.83	2.77	2.71
14	4.60	3.74	3.34	3.11	2.96	2.85	2.76	2.70	2.65
15	4.54	3.68	3.29	3.06	2.90	2.79	2.71	2.64	2.59
16	4.49	3.63	3.24	3.01	2.85	2.74	2.66	2.59	2.54
17	4.45	3.59	3.20	2.96	2.81	2.70	2.61	2.55	2.49
18	4.41	3.55	3.16	2.93	2.77	2.66	2.58	2.51	2.46
19	4.38	3.52	3.13	2.90	2.74	2.63	2.54	2.48	2.42
20	4.35	3.49	3.10	2.87	2.71	2.60	2.51	2.45	2.39
21	4.32	3.47	3.07	2.84	2.68	2.57	2.49	2.42	2.37
22	4.30	3.44	3.05	2.82	2.66	2.55	2.46	2.40	2.34
23	4.28	3.42	3.03	2.80	2.64	2.53	2.44	2.37	2.32
24	4.26	3.40	3.01	2.78	2.62	2.51	2.42	2.36	2.30
25	4.24	3.39	2.99	2.76	2.60	2.49	2.40	2.34	2.28
26	4.23	3.37	2.98	2.74	2.59	2.47	2.39	2.32	2.27
27	4.21	3.35	2.96	2.73	2.57	2.46	2.37	2.31	2.25
28	4.20	3.34	2.95	2.71	2.56	2.45	2.36	2.29	2.24
29	4.18	3.33	2.93	2.70	2.55	2.43	2.35	2.28	2.22
30	4.17	3.32	2.92	2.69	2.53	2.42	2.33	2.27	2.21
40	4.08	3.23	2.84	2.61	2.45	2.34	2.25	2.18	2.12
60	4.00	3.15	2.76	2.53	2.37	2.25	2.17	2.10	2.04
120	3.92	3.07	2.68	2.45	2.29	2.17	2.09	2.02	1.96
∞	3.84	3.00	2.60	2.37	2.21	2.10	2.01	1.94	1.88

Table A3   *continued*

f_1 / f_2	10	12	15	20	24	30	40	60	120	∞
1	241.9	243.9	245.9	248.0	249.1	250.1	251.1	252.2	253.3	254.3
2	19.40	19.41	19.43	19.45	19.45	19.46	19.47	19.48	19.49	19.50
3	8.79	8.74	8.70	8.66	8.64	8.62	8.59	8.57	8.55	8.53
4	5.96	5.91	5.86	5.80	5.77	5.75	5.72	5.69	5.66	5.63
5	4.74	4.68	4.62	4.56	4.53	4.50	4.46	4.43	4.40	4.36
6	4.06	4.00	3.94	3.87	3.84	3.81	3.77	3.74	3.70	3.67
7	3.64	3.57	3.51	3.44	3.41	3.38	3.34	3.30	3.27	3.23
8	3.35	3.28	3.22	3.15	3.12	3.08	3.04	3.01	2.97	2.93
9	3.14	3.07	3.01	2.94	2.90	2.86	2.83	2.79	2.75	2.71
10	2.98	2.91	2.85	2.77	2.74	2.70	2.66	2.62	2.58	2.54
11	2.85	2.79	2.72	2.65	2.61	2.57	2.53	2.49	2.45	2.40
12	2.75	2.69	2.62	2.54	2.51	2.47	2.43	2.38	2.34	2.30
13	2.67	2.60	2.53	2.46	2.42	2.38	2.34	2.30	2.25	2.21
14	2.60	2.53	2.46	2.39	2.35	2.31	2.27	2.22	2.18	2.13
15	2.54	2.48	2.40	2.33	2.29	2.25	2.20	2.16	2.11	2.07
16	2.49	2.42	2.35	2.28	2.24	2.19	2.15	2.11	2.06	2.01
17	2.45	2.38	2.31	2.23	2.19	2.15	2.10	2.06	2.01	1.96
18	2.41	2.34	2.27	2.19	2.15	2.11	2.06	2.02	1.97	1.92
19	2.38	2.31	2.23	2.16	2.11	2.07	2.03	1.98	1.93	1.88
20	2.35	2.28	2.20	2.12	2.08	2.04	1.99	1.95	1.90	1.84
21	2.32	2.25	2.18	2.10	2.05	2.01	1.96	1.92	1.87	1.81
22	2.30	2.23	2.15	2.07	2.03	1.98	1.94	1.89	1.84	1.78
23	2.27	2.20	2.13	2.05	2.01	1.96	1.91	1.86	1.81	1.76
24	2.25	2.18	2.11	2.03	1.98	1.94	1.89	1.84	1.79	1.73
25	2.24	2.16	2.09	2.01	1.96	1.92	1.87	1.82	1.77	1.71
26	2.22	2.15	2.07	1.99	1.95	1.90	1.85	1.80	1.75	1.69
27	2.20	2.13	2.06	1.97	1.93	1.88	1.84	1.79	1.73	1.67
28	2.19	2.12	2.04	1.96	1.91	1.87	1.82	1.77	1.71	1.65
29	2.18	2.10	2.03	1.94	1.90	1.85	1.81	1.75	1.70	1.64
30	2.16	2.09	2.01	1.93	1.89	1.84	1.79	1.74	1.68	1.62
40	2.08	2.00	1.92	1.84	1.79	1.74	1.69	1.64	1.58	1.51
60	1.99	1.92	1.84	1.75	1.70	1.65	1.59	1.53	1.47	1.39
120	1.91	1.83	1.75	1.66	1.61	1.55	1.50	1.43	1.35	1.25
∞	1.83	1.75	1.67	1.57	1.52	1.46	1.39	1.32	1.22	1.00

Table A4   95%-quantiles of the studentised range distribution depending on a (number of populations) and f (degrees of freedom).

a \ f	2	3	4	5	6	7	8	9	10
1	17.97	26.98	32.82	37.08	40.41	43.12	45.40	47.36	49.07
2	6.085	8.331	9.798	10.88	11.74	12.44	13.03	13.54	13.99
3	4.501	5.910	6.825	7.502	8.037	8.478	8.853	9.177	9.462
4	3.927	5.040	5.757	6.287	6.707	7.053	7.347	7.602	7.826
5	3.635	4.602	5.218	5.673	6.033	6.330	6.582	6.802	6.995
6	3.461	4.339	4.896	5.305	5.628	5.895	6.122	6.319	6.493
7	3.344	4.165	4.681	5.060	5.359	5.606	5.815	5.998	6.158
8	3.261	4.041	4.529	4.886	5.167	5.399	5.597	5.767	5.918
9	3.199	3.949	4.415	4.756	5.024	5.244	5.432	5.595	5.739
10	3.151	3.877	4.327	4.654	4.912	5.124	5.305	5.461	5.599
11	3.113	3.820	4.256	4.574	4.823	5.028	5.202	5.353	5.487
12	3.082	3.773	4.199	4.508	4.751	4.950	5.119	5.265	5.395
13	3.055	3.735	4.151	4.453	4.690	4.885	5.049	5.192	5.318
14	3.033	3.702	4.111	4.407	4.639	4.829	4.990	5.131	5.254
15	3.014	3.674	4.076	4.367	4.595	4.782	4.940	5.077	5.198
16	2.998	3.649	4.046	4.333	4.557	4.741	4.897	5.031	5.150
17	2.984	3.628	4.020	4.303	4.524	4.705	4.858	4.991	5.108
18	2.971	3.609	3.997	4.277	4.495	4.673	4.824	4.956	5.071
19	2.960	3.593	3.977	4.253	4.469	4.645	4.794	4.924	5.038
20	2.950	3.578	3.958	4.232	4.445	4.620	4.768	4.896	5.008
24	2.919	3.532	3.901	4.166	4.373	4.541	4.684	4.807	4.915
30	2.888	3.486	3.845	4.102	4.302	4.464	4.602	4.720	4.824
40	2.858	3.442	3.791	4.039	4.232	4.389	4.521	4.635	4.735
60	2.829	3.399	3.737	3.977	4.163	4.314	4.441	4.550	4.646
120	2.800	3.356	3.685	3.917	4.096	4.241	4.363	4.468	4.560
∞	2.772	3.314	3.633	3.858	4.030	4.170	4.286	4.387	4.474

Table A4   *continued*

a ╲ f	11	12	13	14	15	16	17	18	19
1	50.59	51.96	53.20	54.33	55.36	56.32	57.22	58.04	58.83
2	14.39	14.75	15.08	15.38	15.65	15.91	16.14	16.37	16.57
3	9.717	9.946	10.15	10.35	10.53	10.69	10.84	10.98	11.11
4	8.027	8.208	8.373	8.525	8.664	8.794	8.914	9.028	9.134
5	7.168	7.324	7.466	7.596	7.717	7.828	7.932	8.030	8.122
6	6.649	6.789	6.917	7.034	7.143	7.244	7.338	7.426	7.508
7	6.302	6.431	6.550	6.658	6.759	6.852	6.939	7.020	7.097
8	6.054	6.175	6.287	6.389	6.483	6.571	6.653	6.729	6.802
9	5.867	5.983	6.089	6.186	6.276	6.359	6.437	6.510	6.579
10	5.722	5.833	5.935	6.028	6.114	6.194	6.269	6.339	6.405
11	5.605	5.713	5.811	5.901	5.984	6.062	6.134	6.202	6.265
12	5.511	5.615	5.710	5.789	5.878	5.953	6.023	6.089	6.151
13	5.431	5.533	6.625	5.711	5.789	5.862	5.931	5.995	6.055
14	5.364	5.463	5.554	5.637	5.714	5.786	5.852	5.915	5.974
15	5.306	5.404	5.493	5.574	5.649	5.720	5.785	5.846	5.904
16	5.256	5.352	5.439	5.520	5.593	5.662	5.727	5.786	5.843
17	5.212	5.307	5.392	5.471	5.544	5.612	5.675	5.734	5.790
18	5.174	5.267	5.352	5.429	5.501	5.568	5.630	5.688	5.743
19	5.140	5.231	5.315	5.391	5.462	5.528	5.589	5.647	5.701
20	5.108	5.199	5.282	5.357	5.427	5.493	5.553	5.610	5.663
24	5.012	5.099	5.179	5.251	5.319	5.381	5.439	5.494	5.545
30	4.917	5.001	5.077	5.147	5.211	5.271	5.327	5.379	5.429
40	4.824	4.904	4.977	5.044	5.106	5.163	5.216	5.266	5.313
60	4.732	4.808	4.878	4.942	5.001	5.056	5.107	5.154	5.199
120	4.641	4.714	4.781	4.842	4.898	4.950	4.998	5.044	5.086
∞	4.552	4.622	4.685	4.743	4.796	4.845	4.891	4.934	4.974

Table A5   Quantiles $d[p; f; 1-\alpha_e]$ with $\alpha_e = 0.05$ for the two-sided Dunnett test for comparing p treatments with a control in an optimal design with $n_i = n$ for $i = 1, ..., k\text{-}1 = p$ and $n_k \approx n \sqrt{p}$.

f	p=2	3	4	5	6	7	8	9	10	11	12	14	16	18	20
2	5.47	6.19	6.72	7.13	7.46	7.74	7.98	8.20	8.38	8.55	8.71	8.98	9.21	9.42	9.60
3	3.90	4.34	4.66	4.92	5.12	5.30	5.45	5.58	5.70	5.80	5.90	6.07	6.22	6.35	6.46
4	3.33	3.68	3.93	4.12	4.28	4.42	4.53	4.64	4.73	4.81	4.89	5.02	5.14	5.24	5.33
5	3.05	3.34	3.56	3.72	3.86	3.97	4.07	4.16	4.24	4.31	4.38	4.49	4.59	4.68	4.75
6	2.88	3.14	3.33	3.48	3.60	3.71	3.80	3.88	3.95	4.01	4.07	4.17	4.26	4.34	4.40
7	2.77	3.01	3.19	3.32	3.43	3.53	3.61	3.68	3.75	3.81	3.86	3.96	4.04	4.11	4.17
8	2.69	2.92	3.08	3.21	3.31	3.40	3.48	3.55	3.61	3.66	3.71	3.80	3.88	3.95	4.01
9	2.63	2.85	3.00	3.13	3.23	3.31	3.38	3.45	3.50	3.56	3.60	3.69	3.76	3.82	3.88
10	2.58	2.79	2.94	3.06	3.16	3.24	3.31	3.37	3.42	3.47	3.52	3.60	3.67	3.73	3.78
11	2.55	2.75	2.89	3.01	3.10	3.18	3.25	3.31	3.36	3.41	3.45	3.53	3.59	3.65	3.70
12	2.52	2.71	2.86	2.97	3.05	3.13	3.20	3.25	3.31	3.35	3.39	3.47	3.53	3.59	3.64
13	2.49	2.68	2.82	2.93	3.02	3.09	3.15	3.21	3.26	3.31	3.35	3.42	3.48	3.54	3.59
14	2.47	2.66	2.80	2.90	2.99	3.06	3.12	3.18	3.22	3.27	3.31	3.38	3.44	3.49	3.54
15	2.45	2.64	2.77	2.87	2.96	3.03	3.09	3.14	3.19	3.24	3.27	3.34	3.40	3.46	3.50
16	2.44	2.62	2.75	2.85	2.94	3.00	3.06	3.12	3.16	3.21	3.25	3.31	3.37	3.42	3.47
17	2.42	2.60	2.73	2.83	2.91	2.98	3.04	3.09	3.14	3.18	3.22	3.29	3.35	3.40	3.44
18	2.41	2.59	2.72	2.82	2.90	2.96	3.02	3.07	3.12	3.16	3.20	3.26	3.32	3.37	3.42
19	2.40	2.58	2.70	2.80	2.88	2.95	3.00	3.06	3.10	3.14	3.18	3.24	3.30	3.35	3.39
20	2.39	2.57	2.69	2.79	2.87	2.93	2.99	3.04	3.08	3.12	3.16	3.22	3.28	3.33	3.37
21	2.38	2.56	2.68	2.78	2.85	2.92	2.97	3.02	3.07	3.11	3.14	3.21	3.26	3.31	3.35
22	2.37	2.55	2.67	2.76	2.84	2.91	2.96	3.01	3.05	3.09	3.13	3.19	3.25	3.29	3.34
23	2.37	2.54	2.66	2.75	2.83	2.90	2.95	3.00	3.04	3.08	3.12	3.18	3.23	3.28	3.32
24	2.36	2.53	2.65	2.75	2.82	2.88	2.94	2.99	3.03	3.07	3.10	3.17	3.22	3.27	3.31
25	2.35	2.52	2.64	2.74	2.81	2.88	2.93	2.98	3.02	3.06	3.09	3.15	3.21	3.25	3.30
26	2.35	2.52	2.64	2.73	2.80	2.87	2.92	2.97	3.01	3.05	3.08	3.14	3.20	3.24	3.28
27	2.34	2.51	2.63	2.72	2.80	2.86	2.91	2.96	3.00	3.04	3.07	3.13	3.19	3.23	3.27
28	2.34	2.51	2.63	2.72	2.79	2.85	2.91	2.95	2.99	3.03	3.07	3.13	3.18	3.22	3.26

Table A5 continued

f	p=2	3	4	5	6	7	8	9	10	11	12	14	16	18	20
29	2.33	2.50	2.62	2.71	2.78	2.85	2.90	2.94	2.99	3.02	3.06	3.12	3.17	3.21	3.25
30	2.33	2.50	2.61	2.70	2.78	2.84	2.89	2.94	2.98	3.02	3.05	3.11	3.16	3.20	3.24
35	2.31	2.48	2.59	2.68	2.75	2.81	2.86	2.91	2.95	2.99	3.02	3.08	3.13	3.17	3.21
40	2.30	2.46	2.58	2.66	2.73	2.79	2.84	2.89	2.93	2.96	3.00	3.05	3.10	3.14	3.18
45	2.29	2.45	2.57	2.65	2.72	2.78	2.83	2.87	2.91	2.95	2.98	3.03	3.08	3.12	3.16
50	2.29	2.44	2.56	2.64	2.71	2.77	2.82	2.86	2.90	2.93	2.96	3.02	3.07	3.11	3.15
60	2.27	2.43	2.54	2.63	2.69	2.75	2.80	2.84	2.88	2.91	2.94	3.00	3.04	3.09	3.12
80	2.26	2.42	2.52	2.61	2.67	2.73	2.78	2.82	2.85	2.89	2.92	2.97	3.02	3.06	3.09
100	2.25	2.41	2.51	2.59	2.66	2.71	2.76	2.80	2.84	2.87	2.90	2.95	3.00	3.04	3.07
120	2.25	2.40	2.51	2.59	2.65	2.71	2.75	2.79	2.83	2.86	2.89	2.94	2.99	3.03	3.06
200	2.24	2.39	2.49	2.57	2.64	2.69	2.74	2.78	2.81	2.84	2.87	2.92	2.97	3.00	3.04
∞	2.22	2.37	2.47	2.55	2.61	2.66	2.71	2.75	2.78	2.81	2.84	2.89	2.93	2.97	3.00

Table A6   Quantiles $d[p; f; 1-\alpha_e]$ with $\alpha_e = 0.05$ for the two-sided Dunnett test for comparing p treatments with a control in a balanced design with $n_i = n$ for $i = 1, ..., k = p + 1$.

f	p=2	3	4	5	6	7	8	9	10	11	12	14	16	18	20
2	5.42	6.06	6.52	6.85	7.12	7.35	7.54	7.71	7.85	7.98	8.10	8.31	8.49	8.64	8.77
3	3.87	4.26	4.54	4.75	4.92	5.06	5.18	5.28	5.37	5.45	5.53	5.66	5.77	5.87	5.95
4	3.31	3.62	3.83	3.99	4.13	4.23	4.33	4.41	4.48	4.55	4.60	4.71	4.79	4.87	4.94
5	3.03	3.29	3.48	3.62	3.73	3.82	3.90	3.97	4.03	4.09	4.14	4.23	4.30	4.37	4.42
6	2.86	3.10	3.26	3.39	3.49	3.57	3.64	3.71	3.76	3.81	3.86	3.94	4.00	4.06	4.11
7	2.75	2.97	3.12	3.24	3.33	3.41	3.47	3.53	3.58	3.63	3.67	3.74	3.81	3.86	3.91
8	2.67	2.88	3.02	3.13	3.22	3.29	3.35	3.41	3.46	3.50	3.54	3.61	3.67	3.72	3.76
9	2.61	2.81	2.95	3.05	3.14	3.20	3.26	3.32	3.36	3.40	3.44	3.51	3.56	3.61	3.65
10	2.57	2.76	2.89	2.99	3.07	3.14	3.19	3.24	3.29	3.33	3.36	3.43	3.48	3.53	3.57
11	2.53	2.72	2.84	2.94	3.02	3.08	3.14	3.19	3.23	3.27	3.30	3.36	3.42	3.46	3.50
12	2.50	2.68	2.81	2.90	2.98	3.04	3.09	3.14	3.18	3.22	3.25	3.31	3.36	3.41	3.45
13	2.48	2.65	2.78	2.87	2.94	3.00	3.06	3.10	3.14	3.18	3.21	3.27	3.32	3.36	3.40
14	2.46	2.63	2.75	2.84	2.91	2.97	3.02	3.07	3.11	3.14	3.18	3.23	3.28	3.32	3.36
15	2.44	2.61	2.73	2.82	2.89	2.95	3.00	3.04	3.08	3.12	3.15	3.20	3.25	3.29	3.33
16	2.42	2.59	2.71	2.80	2.87	2.92	2.97	3.02	3.06	3.09	3.12	3.18	3.22	3.26	3.30
17	2.41	2.58	2.69	2.78	2.85	2.90	2.95	3.00	3.03	3.07	3.10	3.15	3.20	3.24	3.27
18	2.40	2.56	2.68	2.76	2.83	2.89	2.94	2.98	3.01	3.05	3.08	3.13	3.18	3.22	3.25
19	2.39	2.55	2.66	2.75	2.81	2.87	2.92	2.96	3.00	3.03	3.06	3.11	3.16	3.20	3.23
20	2.38	2.54	2.65	2.73	2.80	2.86	2.90	2.95	2.98	3.02	3.05	3.10	3.14	3.18	3.22
21	2.37	2.53	2.64	2.72	2.79	2.84	2.89	2.93	2.97	3.00	3.03	3.08	3.13	3.17	3.20
22	2.36	2.52	2.63	2.71	2.78	2.83	2.88	2.92	2.96	2.99	3.02	3.07	3.11	3.15	3.19
23	2.36	2.51	2.62	2.70	2.77	2.82	2.87	2.91	2.95	2.98	3.01	3.06	3.10	3.14	3.17
24	2.35	2.51	2.61	2.70	2.76	2.81	2.86	2.90	2.94	2.97	3.00	3.05	3.09	3.13	3.16
25	2.34	2.50	2.61	2.69	2.75	2.81	2.85	2.89	2.93	2.96	2.99	3.04	3.08	3.12	3.15
26	2.34	2.49	2.60	2.68	2.74	2.80	2.84	2.88	2.92	2.95	2.98	3.03	3.07	3.11	3.14
27	2.33	2.49	2.59	2.67	2.74	2.79	2.84	2.88	2.91	2.94	2.97	3.02	3.06	3.10	3.13
28	2.33	2.48	2.59	2.67	2.73	2.78	2.83	2.87	2.90	2.93	2.96	3.01	3.05	3.09	3.13

Table A6   *continued*

f	$p=2$	3	4	5	6	7	8	9	10	11	12	14	16	18	20
29	2.32	2.48	2.58	2.66	2.73	2.78	2.82	2.86	2.90	2.93	2.96	3.00	3.05	3.08	3.11
30	2.32	2.47	2.58	2.66	2.72	2.77	2.82	2.86	2.89	2.92	2.95	3.00	3.04	3.08	3.11
35	2.30	2.46	2.56	2.64	2.70	2.75	2.79	2.83	2.86	2.89	2.92	2.97	3.01	3.05	3.08
40	2.29	2.44	2.54	2.62	2.68	2.73	2.77	2.81	2.84	2.87	2.90	2.95	2.99	3.02	3.05
45	2.28	2.43	2.53	2.61	2.67	2.72	2.76	2.80	2.83	2.86	2.89	2.93	2.97	3.01	3.04
50	2.28	2.42	2.52	2.60	2.66	2.71	2.75	2.79	2.82	2.85	2.87	2.92	2.96	2.99	3.02
60	2.27	2.41	2.51	2.58	2.64	2.69	2.73	2.77	2.80	2.83	2.86	2.90	2.94	2.97	3.00
80	2.25	2.39	2.49	2.56	2.62	2.67	2.71	2.75	2.78	2.81	2.83	2.88	2.92	2.95	2.98
100	2.24	2.39	2.48	2.55	2.61	2.66	2.70	2.74	2.77	2.79	2.82	2.86	2.90	2.93	2.96
120	2.24	2.38	2.47	2.55	2.60	2.65	2.69	2.73	2.76	2.79	2.81	2.86	2.89	2.93	2.95
200	2.23	2.37	2.46	2.53	2.59	2.64	2.68	2.71	2.74	2.77	2.79	2.84	2.87	2.91	2.93
∞	2.21	2.35	2.44	2.51	2.57	2.61	2.65	2.69	2.72	2.74	2.77	2.81	2.85	2.88	2.91

References

Bechhofer, R. E. (1954) A Single Sample Multiple Decision Procedure for Ranking Means of Normal Populations with Known Variances. Ann. Math. Statist., 25, 16-39.

Bechhofer, R. E., Dunnett, C. W. (1988) Percentage points of multivariate t distribution. Selected Tables in Mathematical Statistics, Vol. II, American Mathematical Society, Providence, Rhode Island.

Bock, J. (1998) Bestimmung des Stichprobenumfanges für biologische Experimente und kontrollierte klinische Studien. R. Oldenbourg Verlag, München Wien.

Boer, E.P.J, Rasch, D.A.M.K,. Hendrix, E.M.T. (2000) Locally optimal Designs in Non-linear Regression: A Case Study of the Michaelis-Menten Function. In: Balakrishnan, N., Ermakov, S.M., and Melas, V.B. (eds.) "Advances in Stochastic Simulation Methods". Birkhäuser, Boston.

Casagrande, J.T, Pike, M.C., Smith, P.G. (1978) An Improved Approximate Formula for Calculating Sample Sizes for Comparing Two Binomial Distributions. Biometrics, 34, 483-486.

Cochran, W. G, Cox, G. M. (1957) Experimental Designs. 2nd ed., Wiley, New York.

Fleiss, J.L. (1981) Statistical Methods for Rates and Proportions. 2nd ed.. Wiley, New York.

Freund, J. E. (1992) Mathematical Statistics. 5th ed. Prentice-Hall International, Englewood Cliffs

Guiard, V. (1996) Different definitions of Δ-correct Selection for the indifference zone formulation. In Miescke, K. and Rasch, D. (Eds.) Special issue on 40 years of Statistical Selection Theory. J. Statist. Planning and Inference, 54, Part I, 175-199.

Gupta, S. S., Panchapakesan, S. (1972) On multiple decision procedures. J. Math. Phys. Sciences, 6, 1-72.

Gupta, S. S, Panchapakesan, S. (1979) Multiple Decision Procedures: Theory and Methodology of Selecting and Ranking Populations. Wiley, New York.

Herrendörfer, G., Schmidt, J. (1978) Estimation and Test for the Mean in a Model II of Analysis of Variance. Biom. J., 20, 355-361.

Hinkelmann, K., Kempthorne, O. (1994) Design and Analysis of Experiments Vol I. Wiley , New York.

Hinkelmann, K., Kempthorne, O. (2005): Design and Analysis of Experiments. Vol. II. Advanced Experimental Design. Wiley, New York

Hochberg, Y., Tamhane, A. C. (1987) Multiple Comparison Procedures. Wiley, New York

Kubinger, K-D.; Rasch, D., Šimečková, M (2007) Better to use H$_0$ $\rho \leq \lambda$ than H$_0$ $\rho = 0$ when testing a correlation coefficient's significance. Psychology Science, in print.

Linder, A. (1959) Planen und Auswerten von Versuchen. 2. Auflage , Birkhäuser, Basel

Lindman, H. R. (1991) Analysis of Variance in Experimental Design. Springer, New York.

Melas, V.B. (2006) Functional Approach to Optimal Experimental Design. Springer, Heidelberg

Khuri, A. I., Cornell, J. A. (1987) Response Surfaces: Design and Analysis. Marcel Dekker, Inc., New York

Michaelis, L., Menten, M.L. (1913) Die Kinetik der Inverteinwirkung. Biochem. Z., 49, 333 – 369.

Miescke, K., Rasch, D. (Eds.) (1996) Special Issue on 40 years of Statistical Selection Theory. Journal of Statist. Planning and Inference, vol. 54, no 2, 3.

Myers, R.H. (1976) Response Surface Methodology. Edwards Brothers (distributors), Ann Arbor.

Pukelsheim, F. (1993) Optimal Design of Experiments Wiley, New York.

Pukelsheim, F. (2006) Optimal Design of Experiments. Classics in Applied Mathematics, Volume 50,. Society for Industrial and Applied Mathematics: Philadelphia, PA.

Raghavarao, D. (1971) Construction and combinatorial problems in design of experiments. Wiley, New York.

Raghavarao, D. (2005) Block Designs: analysis, combinatorics and application. World Scientific, New Jersey.

Rasch, D., Herrendörfer, G. (1985) Experimental Designs -Sample Size Determination and Block Designs. Reidel Publ. Co., Dordrecht.

Rasch, D, Tiku, M. L., Sumpf, D. (Eds.) (1994) Elsevier's Dictionary of Biometry. Elsevier Science. B.V., Amsterdam.

Rasch, D. (1995) Einführung in die Mathematische Statistik. Johann Ambrosius Barth, Heidelberg.

Rasch, D. (1996) Software for Selection Procedures. In Miescke, K. and Rasch, D. (Eds.), Special Issue on 40 Years of Statistical Selection Theory. J. Statist. Planning and Inference., vol. 54, Part II, 345-358.

Rasch, D, Verdooren L.R., Gowers, J.I. (1999) Fundamentals in the Design and Analysis of Experiments and Surveys - Grundlagen der Planung und Auswertung von Versuchen und Erhebungen. R. Oldenbourg Verlag, München Wien.

Rasch, D., Guiard, V. (2004) The Robustness of Parametric Statistical Methods. Psychology Science, 46; 175-208.

Rasch, D., Kubinger, K.D. (2006) Statistik für das Psychologiestudium – Mit Softwareunterstützung zur Planung und Auswertung von Untersuchungen sowie zu sequentiellen Verfahren. Spektrum Akademischer Verlag Elsevier GmbH München.

Rasch, D., Mašata, O. (2006) Methods of Variance Component Estimation. Czech J. of Animal Science, 51, 227-235.

Rasch, D, Herrendörfer, G, Bock, J, Victor, N, & Guiard, V. (2007) Verfahrensbibliothek Versuchsplanung und - auswertung, 2. verbesserte Auflage in einem Band mit CD. R. Oldenbourg Verlag München Wien.

Rasch, D, Teuscher, F., Guiard, V. (2007) How robust are tests for two independent samples? J. Statist. Plann, Inference. in print.

Rasch, D and Šimečková, M (2007) Determining the size of experiments for the one-way ANOVA model I for ordered categorical data. In: Lopez-Fidalgo.J.; Rodriguez, Diaz J.M.; Torsney B. (eds.) MODA 8 - Advances in Model-Oriented Design and Analysis. Springer, Heidelberg, 175 – 182.

Sarhai, H. and Kurschid, A. (1996) Formulae and Tables for the Determination of Sample Sizes and Power in Clinical Trials for Testing Differences in Proportions for the Two-Sample Design: a Review. Statistics in Medicine, 15, 1-21.

Sarhai, H., Ojeda, M.M. (2004) Analysis of Variance for Random Models, Balanced Data. Birkhäuser Boston.

Sarhai, H., Ojeda, M.M. (2006) Analysis of Variance for Random Models, Unbalanced Data. Birkhäuser Boston.

Scheffé, H. (1959) The Analysis of Variance. Wiley, New York.

Schneider, B. (1992) An interactive computer program for design and monitoring of sequential clinical trials. In Proceedings of the XVIth International Biometric Conference (S. 237–250). Hamilton, New Zealand.

Steger, H., Püschel, F. (1960) Der Einfluß der Feuchtigkeit auf die Haltbarkeit des Carotins in künstlich getrocknetem Grünfutter. Die Deutsche Landwirtschaft, 11, 301-303.

Stein, Ch. (1945) A Two Sample Test for a Linear Hypothesis whose Power is Independent of the Variance. Ann. Math. Statist., 16, 243-258.

Thomas, E. (2006) Feldversuchswesen. Verlag Eugen Ulmer, Stuttgart.

VB   = *Rasch et al.*(2007).

Wald, A. (1947) Sequential analysis. Wiley, New York

Welch, B. L. (1947) The Generalisation of "Student's" Problem when Several Different Population Variances are involved. Biometrika , 34, 28-35.

Wellek, St. (2003) Testing Statistical Hypotheses of Equivalence. Chapman & Hall, London.

Whitehead, J. (1992) The Design and analysis of Sequential Clinical Trials, 2nd ed.. Wiley, New York.

Wu, J, Hamada, M. (2000) Experiments: Planning, Analysis, and Parameter Design Optimization. Wiley, New York.

Subject Index

(a-1)-dimensional normal distribution 69

A priori information 15, 48, 74, 82

Absolute frequency 210

Abstract random sample 10, 35

Algorithm A 47

Algorithm B 47

Allocation of treatments 16

Alternative hypothesis 72ff, 75ff, 80ff

Analysis of variance 99ff
- Cross-classification 108ff
- Nested classification 126ff
- Mixed model 118ff, 132ff
- Model I 99ff, 110ff, 128ff
- Model II 99, 106ff, 114ff
- One-way 100ff
- Two-way 108ff

ANOVA tables 101ff

Balanced incomplete block design 18, 27, 28

Bar graph 233ff

Behrens-Fisher problem 82

Bias of an estimator 35ff

BIB 18, 27ff
- existence of 27

Binomial distribution 39, 219

Block, Blocking 15ff

Block design 16ff, 24, 108ff

Block factor 17

Block size 17

Bonferroni inequality 137

Bounding the variance of an estimator 38ff

C_1- optimality 166

C_2- optimality 166

CADEMO 1, 20

CEIL 38

Central limit theorem 223, 235

Certain event 215

Character 5, 6

Chi-square distribution 226

Chi-square quantile 226, 244

Coefficient of determination 174, 184

Combination of levels 30

Common variance 81ff

Comparison of two proportions 90ff

Comparisonwise risk see Per comprison risk 137

Complementary events 214

Complete block design 17ff

Complete factorial experiment 30

Completely balanced incomplete block design 27

Completely randomised design 23

Components of variance *see* Variance components

Conditional expectation 155

Confidence coefficient 45

Confidence interval 45ff
- for a difference in means 62ff
- independent samples 63
  - equal variances 63
  - unequal variances 64
- for a probability 57ff
- for a single mean 46ff
- for a variance 55ff
- for paired observations 61
- for regression coefficients 160ff

Confounding 30

Connected incomplete block design 26

Constant factor 14

Continuous character 6

Continuous (random) variable 221

Correlation coefficient 153ff, 173ff, 183ff, 232
- multiple 184
- partial 184ff

Cost function 8

Covariance 232

Covariance matrix 61, 123, 157, 180

Cross-classification 108ff

Degrees of freedom 47ff, 102ff, 226ff

Density function 221 ff

Design matrix 123, 180

Design factor 14

Design problem 2ff, 155, 186

Determination of sample sizes 38ff, 70, 76ff, 89

Difference of practical interest 75, 77, 80

Disconnected incomplete block design 26

Discrete character 6

Discrete variable 219

Distribution 218ff

Distribution function 219ff
- of the standard normal variable 223ff
D-optimality 166, 193, 202
Dunnett-test 145ff, 250ff

ε-robustness 204
Equireplicated 25
Equivalence test 95ff
Error of the first kind 72
Error of the second kind 72
Estimate 35
Estimated regression functions 158
Estimation function 35ff
Estimation of parameters 33ff, 35ff, 37
see also Least Squares Method and
Maximum-Likelihood-Method
Estimator 35ff
Event 213ff
Expectation 33, 227ff
- of a binomial disribution 228
Expected value - see Expectation
Expected half-width 47ff, 61, 63
Expected width see Expected half-
width and Confidence interval for
mean(s)
Experiment 5
Experiment size see Size of an
experiment
Experimental conditions 5
Experimental design 3ff, 15ff, 30,
200ff
Experimental region 186
Experimental result 5
Experimental unit 5, 17, 18
Experimentwise risk see Risk per
experiment

Factor 5, 14, 30, 100ff
Factor level combination 30
Factor levels 6, 14, 99ff
Factorial experiments 30ff
Family of distributions 34
Family of normal distributions 33
Fisher's inequality 27
Fixed effects model 99ff
Fourth moment 34
Fourth sample moment 34
F-quantile 227, 246
Fractional factorial designs 30

Frequency 210
- Absolute 210
- Relative 210
Frequency table 210

General regression model 176
Generalised least squares (GLS) 99,
123
G-optimality 166

Half expected width see Expected half
width
Hierarchical classification 108 and see
Nested classification
Hypothesis 71ff
- alternative 71ff
- null 71ff
Hypothesis tests see under Tests

Impossible event 215
Incidence matrix 24
Incomplete block design 17ff
Incorrect selection 69
Independent samples 80ff
Indifference zone 68ff
Interaction 29ff, 108ff
Intercept 158
Intersection of events 215
Interval estimation 45ff
Intraclass-correlation coefficient 52
Investigation 5

Kurtosis 34

Least squares estimate 37ff, 155ff,
177ff
Least squares estimator 38ff, 155ff,
179ff
Least squares method 37ff, 155ff
Level of a factor 29
Levene Test 89ff
Linear regression models 153ff
LSE = Least squares estimator

Maxi-min size 103, 112, 121ff, 128
Maximum likelihood method 37, 40
Mean 10, 33, 46ff, 54, 71ff, 227ff
Mean Square 100ff
Mean squared error 35
Measurement 5

Method of least squares 37, 155ff
Minimal difference of practical interest
  see Difference of practical interest
Minimal sample size 4, 16, 49, 64ff,
  76, 82, 88, 103ff, 147, 171
Mini-min size 103
Mixed model 118ff, 134ff
Mode 220
Model I analysis of variance 32, 100ff
Model I regression 152ff, 156ff, 166ff
Model II analysis of variance 52, 106ff
Model II regression 152, 156ff, 173ff
Model selection 8, 189, 190
Moments 34ff, 40
MSE-optimal 39
Multiple comparisons (of means) 137ff
  - with a standard 138ff
Multiple correlation coefficient 184
Multiple observations 10
Multiple regression 176ff, 191ff
Multiple *t*-test 139ff

Nested classification 126ff, 134ff
Noise factor 14
Nominal scale 6
Non-central *t*-distribution 76, 223
Non-centrality parameter 73, 75, 102,
  203, 223
Non-linear relationship 152, 186ff
Non-parametric methods 4, 204
Normal distribution 4, 34, 71ff, 223ff,
  243
  - density function 222
  - standard variable 223
Normal quantile 225, 243
Normal random variable 223
Null hypothesis 71ff

Observation 5
  - multiple 10
One-sided alternative hypothesis 75, 80
One-way analysis of variance 100ff
Optimal experimental design 16, 166ff,
  200ff
  - replication-free 200, 202
Optimality criterion 8, 16, 166, 200,
  202
Ordinal scale 6
Orthogonality 193

Paired observations *t*-test 79
Parameter 33ff, 39, 219, 223
Parameter space 33, 34
Parameter vector 33ff
Parametric methods 4
Partial correlation coefficient 184ff
Partially balanced incomplete block
  design 29
PBIB 29
Per comparison risk 137ff, 147
Point estimation 35ff, 40 *see also*
  Estimation of parameters
Pooled variance estimator 63, 81ff, 172
Population 4, 67, 209
Population mean 40ff, 209
Population size 209
Power function 73ff
Precision requirement 3, 35, 38
  - for confidence intervals 46ff
  - for point estimation 38ff
  - for tests 74ff
  - in ANOVA models 103, 128ff
  - in regression analysis 171
  - in selection procedures 69ff
Predictor variable 155, 176
Pre-test 203ff
Probabilities 213ff
  - estimation of 40
  - confidence interval for 57ff
  - comparison between two 90ff
Probability distribution 218ff
Probability function 219ff
Probability of an incorrect selection 69
Problem formulation 8
Product-moment correlation coefficient
  151
Proper design 25
Proportions *see* Probabilities

Quadratic regression 186
Qualitative character 6
Qualitative factor 14
Quantile 224ff
  - of the chi-square distribution 226,
    244
  - of the *F*-distribution 227, 246
  - of the normal distribution 225, 243
  - of the *t*-distribution 226, 243
Quantitative character 6
Quantitative factor 13, 14

Random effects model 199
Random sample 10ff, 14, 19, 33, 35
Random sampling procedure 19ff
Random variable 5, 219ff
Randomisation 6, 11, 13ff, 18ff,
- in experimental designs 23ff
- in block designs 24ff
Rank correlation coefficient 152
Realisation of a random variable 5, 7,
  32
Regression 149f
- intrinsically non-linear 197ff
- linear 152ff
- model I 152ff, 166, 176, 186
- model II 152ff, 173, 183
- multiple 176ff
  - linear 176ff
  - quadratic 189ff
- non-linear 151, 186, 197
- simple 160ff
  - linear 155, 160ff
  - polynomial 186ff
Regression function 152
- estimated 158
Regression model 152
Regressor variable 155
Relative frequency 210ff
Replication 10ff
- in block designs 10
Residual factor 14
Residual variance 52, 182, 198
Residuals 164
Response surface 196
Response variable 155
r.f see Relative frequency
Risk of the first kind 72ff, 77, 203ff
Risk of the second kind 72ff, 77, 171
Risk per experiment 137ff, 143
Robustness 204
Rotatability 193
Rotatable design 193

Sample 19
Sample coefficient of determination
  174
Sample kurtosis 35
Sample mean 34, 233ff
Sample moment 34
Sample regression coefficient 180
Sample size 10
Sample skewness 34

Sample survey 5
Sample variance 34, 236
Sampling 5, 14
- with replacement 41
- without replacement 41
Sampling distribution 233ff
Sampling unit 5
Scatter-plot 151ff, 162
Second order central composite designs
  191ff
Selection procedures 66ff
Sequential experiment 3,4,5
Sequential test 84, 94
Sequential triangle test 84, 94
Significance level 75,170
Simple linear regression see Regression
  – simple linear
Simple regression see Regression -
  simple
Simultaneous risk 137ff
Size of an experiment 30
Skewness 34
Smallest possible sample size see
  Minimal sample size
SPSS 1, 31
SPSS data file 31
Standard deviation 210, 230
Standard normal density 223
Standard normal distribution 223ff, 243
Standard normal variable 223, 228
Standardised moment 34
Statistical experiment 5, 16
Statistical experimental design 15
Statistical model 16
Statistical planning of an experiment 16
Statistical selection method 67ff
Statistical test 71ff
Stem-and-leaf plot (stem-plot) 211
Stratification 14, 22
Stratified sampling 22
Student distribution 226
Student's test statistic 75
Subset selection method 67
Sum of squares 37, 100ff

t-distribution 47, 75, 226
t-quantiles 226, 243
t-test
- for means 75
- multiple 139ff
- single samples 75

- two samples 80ff
  - independent samples 80ff
    - equal variances 81
    - unequal variances 82
  - paired observations 79
- for regression coefficients 169, 183
Test statistic 75ff
Tests of hypotheses 72ff
- for means *see* *t*-test *and* multiple comparisons
- for regression coefficients 169, 183
- for variances 87ff
- sequential 84ff, 94ff
Third moment 34
Third sample moment 34
t-quantile 226, 243
Treatment 14
Treatment factor 14, 30
Triangle test 84, 86ff, 95ff
Tschebyscheff's inequality 213
Tukey-test 143ff
Two-sided alternative hypothesis 75
Two-way analysis of variance 108ff

Two-way cross-classification 108ff
two-way nested (or hierarchical) classification 126ff
Type I risk 72ff
Type II risk 72ff

Unbiased estimator 35ff
Uncorrelated variables 232
Union of events 215
Universe 4
Unrestricted random sampling 19
Unrestricted randomisation 23

Variance 34, 209ff, 229ff
- of an estimator 35
Variance bound 35ff
Variance components 106ff
Variance covariance matrix 180
Variance matrix 180

wor *see* Sampling without replacement
wr *see* Sampling with replacement

International Management

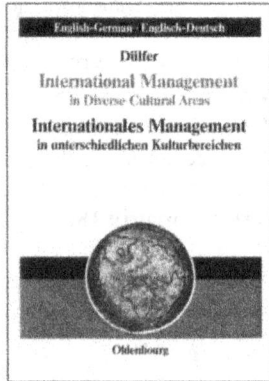

Eberhard Dülfer

International Management in Diverse Cultural Areas

Internationales Management in unterschiedlichen Kulturbereichen

1999 | 1.052 S. | 64 Abb. | gb.
€ 54,80 | ISBN 978-3-486-25205-7
Global Text

- Basics.
- Long-term Fields of Operation for International Management.
- The Process of Internationalization.
- Business Systems Used Abroad.
- How to Consider the Unfamiliar Environment: The Core Problem of international Management.
- Influences of the Global Environment on Management; Labor and Consumption Behavior in Host Countries.
- Particularities of the Interactional Relationship in Foreign Business from the Perspective of the Decision Maker (Manager).
- Challenges for the Manager Abroad.

- Grundlagen.
- Langfristig aktuelle Operationsfelder des Internationalen Managements.
- Die Internationalisierung der Unternehmung.
- Auslands- Geschäftssysteme.
- Berücksichtigung des fremden Umfeldes als Kernproblem des Internationalen Managements.
- Einflüsse der globalen Umwelt auf das Führungs-, Arbeits- und Konsumverhalten in Gastländern.
- Besonderheiten der Interaktionsbeziehungen im Auslandsgeschäft aus der Sicht des Entscheidungsträgers (Manager).
- Anforderungen an den Auslandsmanager.

Professor Dr. Dr. h.c. Eberhard Dülfer war von 1967 bis 1991 geschäftsführender Direktor des Instituts für Kooperation in Entwicklungsländern an der Universität Marburg.

Oldenbourg

www.ingramcontent.com/pod-product-compliance
Lightning Source LLC
Chambersburg PA
CBHW080357030426
42334CB00024B/2901